GOLDEN
JERUSALEM

GOLDEN JERUSALEM

Menashe Har-El

gefen
publishing house
JERUSALEM ◆ NEW YORK

Typesetting: Raphaël Freeman, Jerusalem Typesetting
Cover Design: Studio Paz

1   3   5   7   9   8   6   4   2

Gefen Publishing House
POB 36004, Jerusalem 91360, Israel
972-2-538-0247 • orders@gefenpublishing.com

Gefen Books
12 New Street Hewlett, NY 11557, USA
516-295-2805 • orders@gefenpublishing.com

www.israelbooks.com

Printed in Israel   *Send for our free catalogue*

ISBN 965-229-254-0

In memory of my parents, lovers of Zion, who brought me to Jerusalem in the year 5681 (1921), and to honor the soul of my brother Ya'akov Har-El, the glory of the family

CONTENTS

*Rabbi Akiva – illustration taken from
sixteenth-century Haggada*

R. Akiba was a shepherd of Ben Kalba Sabua. Ben Kalba Sabua's daughter saw that R. Akiba was a modest and noble man, and she asked him, 'If I were betrothed to you, would you go away to study at an academy?' 'Yes', he replied. She was then secretly betrothed to him and sent him away. When her father heard what she had done, he banished her from his house and vowed that she would never benefit from his estate.

In the cold, bitter winter, she married R. Akiba. They were terribly poor, and were forced to sleep on straw. In the morning, R. Akiba would pick the straw from his wife's hair. 'If only I could afford it,' he told her, 'I would give golden Jerusalem to you!'

Later, Elijah came to them in the guise of a mortal, and cried out at the door, 'Give me some straw, for my wife is in confinement and I have nothing for her to lie on.' 'See!' R. Akiba observed, 'there is a man who does not even possess straw, as we do.' So she told him, 'Go, and become a scholar.' And R. Akiba left her, and spent twelve years studying under R. Eliezer and R. Joshua.

(Babylonian Talmud *1 Ketubot* 60b; Nedarim 50)

AUTHOR'S PREFACE

This book discusses the interrelationship of man and landscape in greater Jerusalem, the interaction of geographical conditions of the capital, described in terms of its history, archaeological discoveries and material and spiritual-cultural achievements. Jerusalem, more than any other place in the world, is the result of the harmony between geography and Jewish cultural creativity. The sites of the city are examined in this light: Mount Moriah, Mount Zion, the mountain of the House of Zion, the mountain of God, the Temple Mount and the Mount of Olives; the Valley of Rephaim, the Valley of Kidron, the Valley of Cheesemakers and the Valley of Revelation are not only geographical place names, but are intrinsic components of the magnificent history of Jerusalem.

The yearning of the Jewish nation for Jerusalem and the Land of Zion has been expressed in four thousand years of Jewish literature, and even more – in the immigration of great numbers of Jews to the Holy Land and the Holy City. However, it is perhaps most illuminating to note the following paragraph from the book *City of the Great King*, written by the non-Jewish physician, Dr. James T. Barclay, who made valuable observations about the city (1857), and provided the following amazing vision of its future: "This city of cities will cover an area of more than a hundred square miles; and will number its inhabitants by millions. It can be rendered very accessible by a short railway from El-Arish, Askalon or perhaps still better – Gaza – reputed the very best seaport on all the coast of Syria… Such a city, in such a climate, in a position so advantageous in a civil, commercial and geographical point of view, might well claim to be the mistress of the world, when Judea shall have again become inhabited by its rightful owners."

Jerusalem was unique in that her defense and economy were self-sustaining, as opposed to other ancient Near Eastern cities. Jerusalem was the only city in the region in which the inhabitants, the Israelites, exploited and developed the natural sources of water to the extent that five types of water sources were available: the Gihon Spring and its long underground tunnel extending to a length of 533 meters; Ein-Rogel, reaching to a depth of 38 meters, cisterns hewn from rock in every home and edifice; fifteen pools in Jerusalem's numerous valleys; and finally; the longest – 68 km – and most sophisticated aqueduct found in the Middle East.

The Israelites probably devised the terrace system of agriculture in order to cultivate as much of the hilly ground as possible for grain fields, vineyards and olive groves. Thus, it is not surprising that the Judean Hills constitute a cultivated rather than a natural landscape.

The fortification of Jerusalem, including city walls, towers, and fortresses, attained a level of architectural sophistication hitherto unknown in the area. For example, at the Western Wall a single stone, which was unearthed, weighed 550 tons, was 14 meters high and 3 meters wide. In addition, the southern wall of the Temple Mount reached a height of 50 meters.

Along with the history of the city, from the Canaanite period to modern times – and the strong, unbroken connection of the Jewish people to the city throughout – the book presents aspects of the changes since the 1967 war, under Israeli government, including the planning and projected role of the reunited city, and the archaeological excavations in progress at various sites, among them the southern wall of the Temple Mount.

Chapter I presents the geography of the Judean Mountains and the history of Jerusalem over the centuries, bringing into focus the choice of the city as the capital in preference to the other cities of Samaria and Judea. Special emphasis is placed on the available sources of livelihood in the city and its vicinity, sufficient to support a population of 200,000 at the end of the Second Temple period, despite the difficult terrain and climate problems.

Chapter II describes the Second Temple in Jerusalem, on the basis of the model at the Holyland Hotel in Jerusalem. The function of each site on the model is discussed, as are the phases of the Zealot rebellions against foreign rule, up to the final destruction. This chapter is a comprehensive prerequisite for a visit to the Old City of today.

Chapter III describes the specific functions of various sites outside the

Old City, in the light of modern historical, archaeological and geographical science.

Chapters IV and V deal with Jerusalem during the First and Second Temple periods, and consider the problems of identifying various sites, such as the Lower City, Mount Zion, the Citadel of Zion, the City of David, the Tombs of the House of David and the synagogues, as well as the city walls and gates.

Chapter VI surveys the present city walls, gates and quarters in the light of archaeological finds. The discussion of the city gates includes the possible interpretation of their names and functions, as related to their locations, dating them over six major periods of construction, and describing the roads leading away from the city. Quarters and sites along the main roads are presented, and points mentioned in earlier chapters may be referred to again for the convenience of the visitor.

Chapter VII describes the Jewish Quarter of the Old City from its foundation during the time of the Ramban until the present, and discusses the archaeological investigations conducted there.

Chapter VIII discusses the sites holy to Christianity in Jerusalem and on the Mount of Olives and describes the Christian Quarter of the Old City.

Chapter IX surveys Jerusalem and the Temple Mount during the Moslem era and deals with Moslem structures found on and around the Temple Mount.

The book is intended to enrich and illuminate all those who roam through the city, to facilitate understanding and identification of various sites and structures while providing a proper perspective for the historical view, which is indispensable in Jerusalem. It deals with details as well as with general phenomena, and is thus suitable for teachers and students alike, and for those who strive to know the city in all its aspects.

I should like to thank the late Prof. B. Mazar, archaeologist and historian of Jerusalem, who revealed the walls and gates of the Temple Mount; the late Prof. N. Avigad, expert on the necropolis of Jerusalem and the excavations of "Mount Zion"; the late Prof. M. Avi-Yonah who made it possible to present the Second Temple period in such wide scope. the late Prof. Y. Prawer's studies of the Crusader period were essential, as were Prof. E. Sivan's observations on the history of the Moslems in Jerusalem, and Prof. D. Shapira's comments on Christianity. Thanks are also due to my friend Prof. I. Kolat for his important comments on the history of the modern city and Prof. Miriam Rosen-Ayalon, who devoted much time to an elucidation of the architecture and art of the gates and walls of the city during the Moslem period.

I am grateful to the former President of Israel, the late Yitzhak Ben-Zvi, the late Prof. S.D. Goitein, the late Prof. Y. Ashtor, the late Prof. Sh. Safrai, Prof. Z. Vilnai, the late Prof. K.M. Kenyon, Prof. D. Ussishkin, and Prof. Ruth Amiram, whose monographs and books I have used. Special thanks to the archaeologist of the Western wall, Mr. M. Ben-Dov, who elucidated many points about the archaeology of this area and provided me with up-to-date information and material. In addition, I would like to thank Prof. Dani Bahat for reading throughout the manuscript and contributing his knowledgeable comments.

Finally, I should like to acknowledge my debt to the Israel Exploration Society, Israel Museum, Department of Antiquities, Mossad Bialik and Dvir, and especially to Carta House; my friends Prof. A. Flexer and Prof. E. Efrat, Prof. Yigal Shilo and Prof. G. Barkai, who permitted me to publish their excellent maps. Many thanks to Mr. Peter Grossman who sketched my maps.

Last but not least, I should like to thank the late Major-General R. Zeevy, who edited this book with much devotion and love of Jerusalem.

Jerusalem, 2003
Menashe Har-El

CHAPTER I

JERUSALEM, THE CITY THAT IS COMPACT TOGETHER

Simon replied: "We have neither taken any other man's land,
nor do we hold dominion over other people's territory,
but only over the inheritance of our fathers.
On the contrary, for a certain time it was unjustly held by our enemies;
but we, seizing the opportunity, hold fast the inheritance of our father."
Maccabees I XV, 33–34

Why did the ancient Israelites take possession of the Judean Mountains and convert the area into the greatest center of settlement in the country?

The Judean Mountains are barren in comparison with the mountains in the north of the country; for the most part they are desert, as well as being more rugged than the mountains of Samaria and Galilee. The soil in the area is not only poorer than anywhere else in the mountain region, but poorer also than that of any of the country's regions of Mediterranean climate. Natural water resources in the Judean Mountains are the fewest and the least abundant of the whole northern part of the country. In addition, because of the steeply rising mountainsides, approach roads are irregular and inconvenient. Nevertheless, for more than one thousand years, the political, religious and administrative center of the country was in that locality, rather than in the more fertile mountains of Samaria and Galilee. Moreover, at the end of the Second Temple period, Jerusalem, the capital city of Judea, had a population of some 100,000; it was thus one of the largest cities in the mountain regions of the ancient East.

How did the inhabitants of this mountainous region earn their livelihood?

How were the multitudes of pilgrims (totaling, in the three annual pilgrim-ages, one million souls) supplied with the necessities of life? What was the relationship between Jerusalem and the fortified cities of the foothills, on the one hand, and the forts in the Judean Desert, on the other? And what was the relationship between the people of Israel and their capital compared to the connections of other nations with Jerusalem?

Let us begin by studying the special structure of the Judean Mountains, the roads crossing them, and the efforts made by the Jewish settlers to ensure their own livelihood and safety.

The Structure of the Judean Mountains

…and upon the high mountains of Israel shall their fold be.

Ezekiel XXXIV, 14

The Judean Mountains are high and appear as one solid mass, unbreached by valleys. The length of the range Mount Baal-Hatzor in the north to the Beer-sheba valley in the south, is almost 100 km, and its width is 40–50 km. The spine of the Judean Mountains is the watershed, unique among the mountain-ous regions of the country. The transition to the Judean Mountains from the foothills in the west, on the one hand, and from the desert in the east, on the other, is quite steep. The desert and foothills thus serve as access and egress to the mountains, and forts to guard the roads were built in both areas.

The Judean Mountains may be divided into three sections:

1. The Hebron Mountains: This is the longest part – about 50 km – and includes the following important settlements: Hebron, Beth-Zur, Beth-lehem, Tekoa and Gush-Etzion, as well as the major part of the Judean Desert, the large oasis of Ein Gedi and the great fort of Massada in the east. In the west, the forts of Devir, Lachish, Maresha, Makeda and Azeka were established at the mouths of riverbeds leading out of the mountains.
2. The Jerusalem Mountains: These are about 20 km long, and the area includes Jerusalem, the capital city, Gibeon, Givat-Shaul, Kiryat-Yearim; Beth-Horon, on the road to the valley of Ayalon and Latrun in the west; and Jericho, the largest oasis in the country, in the east. The forts of Beth-Shemesh, Zor'ah and Ayalon were erected as the western outlets of the valleys.
3. The Beth-El Mountains: Their length is over 20 km, and they include the

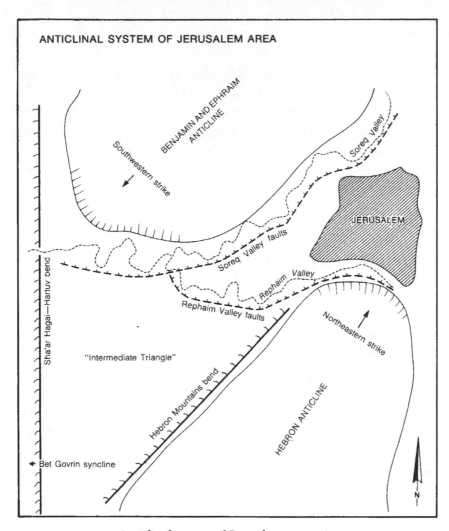

Anticlinal system of Jerusalem mountains

settlements of Beth-El, Ramah, Geva, Mizpah, Ophrah and Baal-Hatzor, in the environs of Shechem (Nablus); the oasis of Archelaus at the mount of the 'Auja Valley in the east, and the fort of Beer-Zayit, on the slope of the main ascent to the plateau, in the west.

The Hebron and Beth-El mountains are some 1000 m above sea level, and the Jerusalem Mountains about 800 m. The latter therefore appear as a saddle of the Judean Mountains. Farther north in the Judean Mountains, climatic conditions improve; the plateau widens progressively and the western foothills become more extensive. The Hebron mountains have no western foothills; instead, they slope steeply to the Shephelah in the west and down to the Dead Sea Valley in the east. The Jerusalem mountains have three ridges: that of Bethlehem, Betar, and the Elah Valley; Zova, Kiryat Yearim, and the Zor'ah–Eshtaol Valley; and that of Gibeon and the Ayalon Valley. These regions serve to this day as the economic hinterland of the mountain masses, and the transportation routes run along their heights or in their valleys. The ridges of the Beth-El mountains run west and are characterized by wider plateaux, such as those of Gibeon, Mizpah, Ramah, Beth-Horon, and Beth-El. The Ramah plateau is the site of the Jerusalem airfield, Atarot.

Roads

And I will make all My mountains a way,
and My highways shall be raised on high.

Isaiah XLIX, 11

Due to the continuity of the watershed zone, the Judean Mountains have a unique road system. No other mountainous region in the country can be similarly traversed throughout its length on what is more or less a plateau, as is the case with the Judean Mountains and the Road of the Patriarchs. This road, which passes along the hill ridges, runs from Beersheba, capital of the Negev, to Hebron, city of the Patriarchs; and thence to Beth-Zur, a fort in the times of Rehoboam and the Hasmoneans; Bethlehem; David's city, Jerusalem, the capital; Givat-Shaul, capital of Saul and of the tribe of Benjamin; Beth-El, the capital of the Kingdom of Israel and Jeroboam; the peak of Baal-Hatzor; and thus to Shechem, the center of Samaria. The route served either as an alternative to part of the Sea Road (Via Maris) and part of the King's Road, or constituted a continuation of these international routes.

Once the Patriarchs' Road had reached Shechem, access was easy to both the Sea Road, running along the Shechem Valley in the west, and to the King's Road leading from Egypt, through Eilat and the mountains of Trans-jordan – the mountains of Edom, Moab and Ammon. It was also possible to take a different road from Egypt: the Shur Road, through Kadesh-Barnea, Nitzana and Beersheba, where the Patriarch's Road would be followed up to Shechem, and thence to the King's Road north of the Yabbok river. This was the shorter route, which avoided the difficult and dangerous desert region in the southern stretch of the King's Road. The Road of the Patriarchs was thus an international highway as well. Several journeys along this road are described in the Bible: that of the Patriarchs from Mesopotamia to Canaan through the Yabbok Valley and Shechem; that of the Ishmaelite caravan that purchased Joseph en route from Gilead to Egypt; the journeys of enemies of Israel, from Samaria to Jerusalem; and the campaign of Shishak, king of Egypt, from Judea to Samaria and Sukkoth in the Yabbok Valley. The major towns of the Judean Mountains and the other mountain regions of Israel were thus located along the Road of the Patriarchs.

The Choice of the Judean Mountains

Their God is a God of the hills; therefore they were stronger than we.

1 Kings xx, 23

The Children of Israel took possession of the Judean Mountains and made them the country's greatest center of ancient settlement for the following reasons:

1. The Israelites, who were shepherds in Egypt, arrived in Canaan from the south. The Judean Mountains were closest to the deserts of Sinai and the Negev, and the Israelites were able to continue their cattle raising and sheep-herding there. The tribes of Caleb, the Kenites and the Jerachmeelites penetrated the south of Judea while the Israelites were in the desert.

2. Rugged mountains are difficult to colonize, and the Canaanites were thus reluctant to settle in the area. Relatively weaker and smaller nations and tribes set up outposts in the mountains; among these were the Hivites, the Horites, the Hittites, the Jebusites and the Perizites. During the Canaanite period there were very few permanent settlements in the Judean Mountains, and most of these were located beside springs. During the early period of the Israelite monarchy, however, there were many permanent settlements throughout the Judean Mountains as well as the desolate Judean desert.

3. The structure of the Judean Mountains afforded natural protection against the numerous enemies who harassed the kingdoms of Judah and Israel on all sides – Philistines and Canaanites in the west, Edomites and Amalekites in the south, Moab and Ammon in the east. The Judean Mountains were also far from the two international highways, the Sea Road in the west and the King's Road in the east, which were thoroughfares for the

invading forces marching from Mesopotamia to Egypt and back again. The Patriarch's Road could be fortified north and south of Jerusalem, and any invasion of Jerusalem could be forestalled from the Levonah ascent, Yeshanah, the Gofna ascent, Beth-El, Mizpah and Givat-Shaul in the north; and near Hebron, and at Beth-Zur, Beth-Zechariah and Bethlehem in the south.

The Choice of Jerusalem

O thou that tellest good tidings to Zion,
get thee up into the high mountain;
O thou that tellest good tidings to Jerusalem
lift up thy voice with strength

Isaiah XL, 9

The Israelites' choice of Jerusalem as a capital city, rather than Givat-Shaul (the capital of Saul's kingdom), or Gibeon (the chief and religious center in Solomon's day), Beth-El (the site of the temple built by Jeroboam, king of

Jerusalem – Judean Desert border

Israel), or Hebron (Where David reigned for seven and a half years), was governed by the following factors:

1. Jerusalem, located in the lowest part of the Jerusalem Mountains – which gave rise to the phrase "Jerusalem, surrounded by mountains" – is built on two ridges. It was naturally fortified by the steep Kidron Valley in the east, and the Valley (or the Cheesemongers' Valley) and the Ben-Hinnom Valley in the west and south. No other city has the same type of natural fortification. It is noteworthy that about 60% of the *tels* in the mountains of Judea and Samaria are on hill ridges and only 40% are on hill and mountaintops.

2. Jerusalem was located on the lengthwise Patriarchs' Road as well as on the breadthwise Jaffa–Jericho–Rabbat Ammon road connecting the Sea Road and the King's Road. The Jerusalem Mountains constitute a saddle of the Judean Mountains and lie 200 m below the remainder of the Judean Mountains. The only riverbed penetrating the core of the mountains on the west is the Sorek–Rephaim Valley, which affords easy

access to Jerusalem from the coast. This was probably the route taken by the Philistines on their way to fight David in the valley of Rephaim, at the head of this road (*II Samuel* v, 17–18). There were, in fact, three Israelite forts that guarded this passage: Hurvat Tura, near Bar-Giora, overlooking the Sorek Valley; Betar, commanding the Rephaim riverbed; and Manahat, similarly situated in relation to the Rephaim Valley. The only riverbed in the Judean desert, which possesses abundant sources of water throughout its length is the Qelt, which rises to the north of Jerusalem and empties into the Jordan near Jericho; it was therefore a route westward to Transjordan. Herod built Jericho and erected the fort of Kipros (visible from Mount Scopus in Jerusalem) at the eastern end of the Qelt Valley to protect this highway. Because of its location at the crossroads, Jerusalem became the commercial center, not only for the Judean Mountains, but also for the coast and for Ammon and Moab. In the *Letter of Aristeas* (114–115), a non-Jewish historian living in the early part of the third century B.C.E., reports that "Arabs brought to Jerusalem perfumes, precious stones and much gold, for the country was suitable for many crafts; it was well supplied with all important goods, since there were convenient ports at Ashkelon, Jaffa and Gaza, as well as at Talmaida (Acre) founded by the King, not far from the above-mentioned places."

3. The Temple Mount was located on the eastern ridge of Jerusalem, 740 m above sealevel, (in preference to the Upper City, 770 m high, on the western ridge) because of its proximity to the Gihon Spring, which gave the city its main water supply of approximately 50 cu m an hour. Other cities lacked water sources or were only poorly supplied.

4. The nearby desert provided safe refuge during times of emergency or war. The inhabitants of Jerusalem have traditionally relied on the forts of the Judean Desert. David hid there from Saul and traveled through the desert en route to Mahanaim, fleeing from Absalom; the desert was also the scene of Zedekiah's flight to Jericho, when the Chaldeans sought him after the destruction of the First Temple. Jonathan the Hasmonean retreated to the wilderness of Tekoa before the onslaught of Bachides, and returned through Michmas to take Jerusalem from the Hellenists. The Hasmonean kings and the Zealots were far-seeing enough to fortify the posts in the Judean Desert: Masada, Aristobleas, Herodion, Horkania and Alexandrion. Herod fled to the desert with his household, in

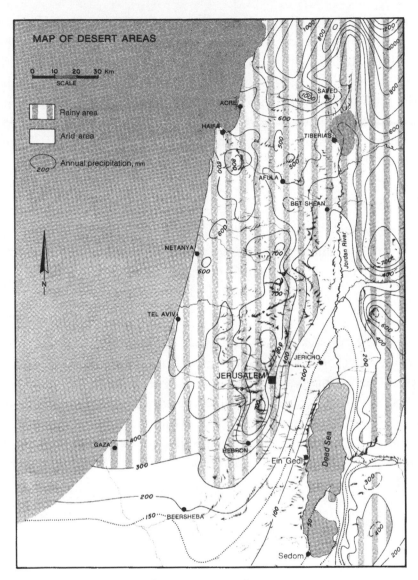

Map of precipitation in desert areas

fear of the Jews and the Parthians, and re-entered Jerusalem in triumph from Masada, having had himself crowned king over Israel. Bar-Giora who apparently had his stronghold at Ein Farah in the Qelt Valley, took Herodion and Tekoa, and thence reached Jerusalem. Masada, in the Judean Desert, was the refuge of the Zealots during the Roman Revolt, and served as the base for their sorties to aid Jerusalem, then under siege. The sects in the Judean Desert found peace and security for the practice of their religious belief. Bar-Kochba's rebels fled the desert for fear of Hadrian, and one of their chief bases was at Herodion. The Jewish inhabitants of Jerusalem and Christian refugees during the period of Persian rule, in the early seventh century C.E. found safety in Jericho and the Judean Desert. Archaeological research has proved that the Judean Desert was an area of Jewish settlement during the First and Second Temple periods, as well as in the time of the *Mishnah* and *Talmud*; no Canaanite sites have been discovered, except for Jericho.

Sources of Livelihood

> *For as the rain cometh down, and the snow from heaven,*
> *and returneth not thither, except it water the earth*
> *and make it bring forth and bud, and give seed*
> *to the sower and bread to the eater.*
>
> *Isaiah LV, 10*

What were the sources of livelihood that enabled Jerusalem to support a population of 100,000 at the end of the Second Temple period?

The ancient inhabitants lived by the cultivation of the "seven crops" and cattle raising. However, the seven crops were not all of the same nutritive value and were not cultivated in equal measure in the country. Neither do they have equal standing in the Bible. The three most important groups (and those most often mentioned) are grain (wheat and oats), wine and oil. For example:

> *That I will give the rain of your land in its season, the former*
> *rain and the latter rain, that thou mayest gather in thy corn,*
> *and thy wine, and thine oil.*
>
> *Deuteronomy XI, 14*

> *So God give thee of the dew of heaven and of the fat places of*
> *the earth, and plenty of corn and wine.*
>
> *Genesis XXVII, 28*

> *And wine that maketh glad the heart of man, making the face*
> *brighter than oil, and bread that stayeth man's heart.*
>
> *Psalms CIV, 15*

In the Talmud (*Baba Metziah*, 107a), Rabbi Johanan explains the verse

> *And blessed shalt thou be in the field:*
> *That thy estate shall be divided in three (equal) portions of*
> *cereals, olives and vines.*

These represented what are known today as the three basic nutritive elements: proteins, carbohydrates and fats. The yields of these crops were easily stored for long periods in the hot, dry climate, and kings laying in supplies at forts and strongholds for possible siege and war included these crops. Of Rehoboam, king of Judah, it was said:

> *And he fortified the strongholds, and put captains in them,*
> *and store of victual, and of oil and wine.*
>
> *II Chronicles XI, 11*

And of Hezekiah, king of Judah:

> *Storehouses also for the increase of corn, and wine, and oil:*
> *and stalls for all manner of beasts, and flocks in folds.*
>
> *II Chronicles XXXII, 28*

Archaeological excavations of fortified cities have in fact uncovered storehouses for grain and large clay pots for oil and wine.

Millstones for hand-grinding of crops

Terrace Agriculture

And the daughters of Jerusalem went forth to dance in the vineyards.
Tractate Ta'anith 4, 5

Grain is grown on plains, in valleys and on plateaux, which are virtually non-existent in the Judean Mountains. The natural habitat of the olive is the friable chalk rock, or deep soil, also rare in that area. The grapevine was the only plant that would grow throughout the mountainous regions, and even then not in the very rugged areas. How then could the ancients grow grain, wine and oil among these stony crags? The Judean Mountains not only posed the problem of bringing bread out of the earth, but also of creating soil out of the rock. The Jerusalem Mountains contain many valleys and ridges running west in the direction of the rains; these constituted the agricultural hinterland of the city. We know now that the Israelites were the first to develop mountain agriculture. Investigation has revealed that in approximately 30% of the Judean mountains terraces were artificially built, the highest percentage in

Israelite agricultural terracing in the Judean hills

Oil press with screw mechanism to arrest the oil flow

any Mediterranean country. How do we know that the Israelites were the first to evolve terrace agriculture?

The Israelites were agriculturists in Egypt for four hundred years and cultivated irrigated crops, along with sheep raising. During their forty years of desert wanderings in Sinai and the Negev they practiced flash-flood agriculture, based in turn on the terrace culture. They apparently introduced terrace agriculture in the Negev. Upon entering Canaan, and finding that they were constantly surrounded by enemies who hampered their efforts and denied them the plains and valleys, the Israelites realized that they would have to be economically self-sufficient and thereupon began to cultivate every scrap of suitable land with a diligence unmatched in the history of the Mediterranean countries. The mountains of Galilee and Samaria have far fewer terraces than the Judean Mountains. The plateaux of the Judean Mountains and their valleys, such as the watershed zone between the Kidron Valley (*Tosefta, Menahot 21*) and the Sorek Valley, served for the cultivation of grain. "And it shall be as when the harvestman gathereth the standing corn, and reapeth the ears with his arm; yea, it shall be as when one gleaneth ears in the valley of Rephaim" (*Isaiah* XVII, 5). Grapevines were cultivated on the steep slopes which served for olive groves, thanks to the thick layer of accumulated alluvium. Olives were also grown on the Mount of Olives, with its crumbly chalky rock; ancient oil-presses have been found there. In modern times grain is hardly ever grown in the Jerusalem Mountains; most of the terraces are neglected, since they are too narrow for the operation of agricultural machinery. Olives are cultivated today on chalk and clay rock and on the lower part of mountain slopes.

Sheep Raising

> *My sheep wandered through all the mountains,*
> *and upon every high hill.*
>
> Ezekiel XXXIV, 6

The serious dearth of agricultural areas made the Judean Desert a typical region for sheep raising, which was an important auxiliary occupation. Sheep were traditionally the property of nomads and farmers, and were commercially important. The needs of sheep were few, while their uses were many: "Ye did eat the fat, and you clothed you with the wool, ye killed the fatlings" (*Ezekiel* XXXIV, 3). The meat was widely eaten and used especially for sacrifices on holidays and feasts. The fat was used for cooking and frying, while the milk and its products served as food. The skins were made into clothing, footwear and harness. Wool was invaluable; there was no alternative for it in those days, especially as linen was unsuitable for the cool weather of the mountainous regions. Sheep's wool therefore was used for expensive woolen clothing, while goat's hair was used for outer garments and drugs. Commerce in mutton and wool was common in Jerusalem. Jewish sources mention "market of fattened animals" and "market of wools" (*Eruvin* 9, 10). Flavius Josephus noted that the new city had wool shops and a clothing market (*Wars* 5, 8). Thus, the industry of Jerusalem was supplied by sheep and goats from the Judean Desert.

The desert was of considerable economic importance, providing a basis for raising sheep and cattle. The dates, persimmon, balsam, myrrh and frankincense, which were cultivated along the shores of the Dead Sea, were

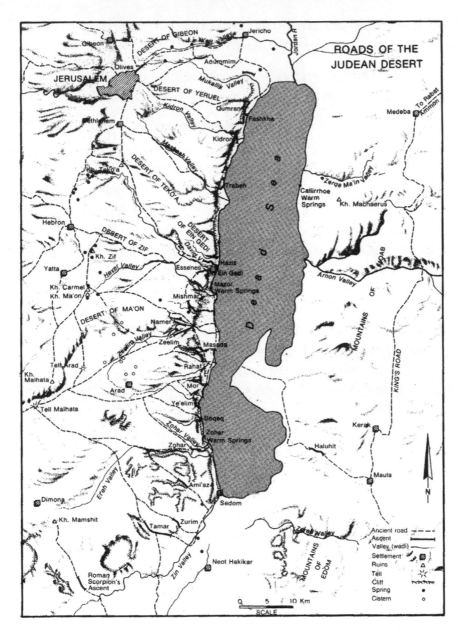

Ancient Roads of the Judean Desert

exported, as was the pitch found there, while the medicinal hot springs were
a popular attraction. The Judean Desert was divided into seven regions, from
north to south: Beth-Aven, Gibeon, Jeruel, Tekoa, Ein Gedi, Zif and Maon.
It contained no less than twenty-four highways and roads leading from the
Dead Sea to the Judean Mountains and Jerusalem.

Agriculture of the Judean Mountains
and the Samarian Mountains in Literature

But the land, whither ye go over to possess it, is a land of hills and valleys,
and drinketh water as the rain of heaven cometh down.

Deuteronomy XI, 11

Agriculture in the Judean and the Samarian mountains is alluded to several times in literature. The *Letter of Aristeas* (107, 112–116) mentions Israelite agriculture and sheep and goatraising in Samaria and Judea, describing the ancients as having built the city (Jerusalem) "with much wisdom; of just the right size, the land being great and good, with open country in the region of Samaria; other parts of the land, which border on Edom, are mountainous, and other parts lie in the heart of the country. The entire country required cultivating with constant care, and as this was done, there was plentiful supply of produce throughout the land. However, cities which are large and rich tend to disregard the rest of the country; the inhabitants grow numerous and follow the natural tendency of humanity toward pleasure. In truth," says Aristeas, "the inhabitants love agricultural work, and their country is rich in olive trees, grain crops and vegetables, and even vineyards and honey, although other types of fruits and dates cannot grow there. However, there is livestock of many kinds, and ample pasturage." Aristeas notes the good sense of the settlers, who realized that the land required many towns, and built up the city and the villages with great logic. He describes the country as being rich in all natural resources, with much water and natural cover (the hills), and the perennial river Jordan supplying water.

Josephus (*Against Apion* I, 12) stresses the Jewish penchant for agriculture:

We neither inhabit a maritime country, nor do we delight in merchandise;…
but the cities we dwell in are remote from the sea, and having a fruitful
country for our habitation, we take pains in cultivating that only.

Elsewhere (*Wars* III, 3) he says:

The country of Samaria… is exactly of the same nature
as Judea; for both countries are made up of hills and valleys, and
are moist enough for agriculture, and are very fruitful. They
have an abundance of trees, and are full of autumnal fruit, both

City of David: Zion (at left); Zion Citadel (center); at right – Mount Zion
Illustrator: Ronald Greenberg. (Courtesy of El-Ad Society, Visitors Center, City of David)

At the Western Wall near Robinson's Arch
Inscription reads: "And when you will see this, your heart will rejoice and
your bones will flourish like an herb." (Isaiah 66:14) (M. Har-El)

Rosh Emeth, Ayn Aruv in Jerusalem (M. Har-El)

Gihon Spring in the City of David

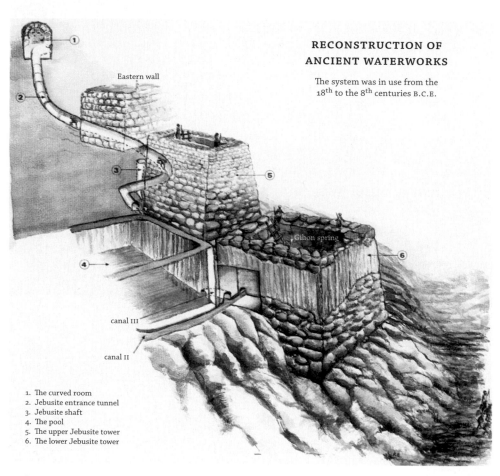

RECONSTRUCTION OF ANCIENT WATERWORKS

The system was in use from the 18th to the 8th centuries B.C.E.

Eastern wall

Gihon spring

canal III

canal II

1. The curved room
2. Jebusite entrance tunnel
3. Jebusite shaft
4. The pool
5. The upper Jebusite tower
6. The lower Jebusite tower

Reconstruction of ancient waterworks: Gihon Spring, its towers and the Jebusite wall
Courtesy of El Ad Society, Visitors Center, City of David

Nikra Spring in Jerusalem (M. Har-El)

Pool of the Towers near the Jaffa Gate (M. Har-El)

*Yemin Moshe neighborhood and the Ayn Aruv aqueduct in
Jerusalem (at the bottom step (M. Har-El)*

Upper "Solomon's Pool" (A. Erev)

*Water channel from Ein 'Arub (at left) on its way to the Temple
Mount (at right) and the Western Wall. (A Erev)*

1. Givati parking lot
2. Visitors' Center and the pit
3. Area G
4. Warren's Shaft
5. Area E
6. The Gihon spring and Hezekiah's Tunnel
7. Tombs of the House of David
8. Tunnel exit Shiloah pool

Scene of David's City and archeological excavation sites
(Courtesy of El Ad Society, Visitors Center, City of David)

that which grows wild, and that which is the result of the cultivation.
They are not naturally watered by many rivers, but derive
their chief moisture from rainwater, of which they have no
want; and for those rivers which they have, all their waters are
exceeding sweet: by reason also of the excellent grass they
have, their cattle yield more milk than those in other places;
and, what is the greatest sign of excellency and of abundance,
they each of them are very full of people.

Present-day settlers in the "corridor" engage in a substantially different type of agriculture, cultivating deciduous fruit orchards rather than olives and grape-vines, and practicing dairy farming, poultry-keeping and market gardening.

Sources of Water

Springs are more scarce in this region than anywhere else in the northern mountains. How, then, did the inhabitants of Jerusalem obtain their water? They had other sources of supply, which were:

Cisterns

Nevertheless a fountain or cistern,
wherein is a gathering of water, shall be clean.

Leviticus XI, 36

The Israelites, who settled in mountains poor in natural water sources, dug cisterns for their homes to provide water for the household all the year round. Roofs were provided with gutters, and courtyards were paved with stone, in order to trap every drop of water for the cisterns. "Eat ye every one of his vine, and every one of his figtree, and drink ye every one the waters of his own cistern" (*II Kings* XVIII, 31 and *Isaiah* XXXVI, 16). The eminent archaeologist, W.F. Albright, believes that waterproofing the cisterns with lime mortar was first devised by the Israelites to prevent the rainwater from seeping through the fissured mountain rocks. "They have forsaken Me, the fountain of living waters, and hewed them out cisterns, broken cisterns, that can hold no water" (*Jeremiah* II, 13). The cisterns in use were limed cisterns, retaining every drop of water, and were easily excavated out of the soft *melekeh* rock of the two ridges of Jerusalem. The collection of rainwater in cisterns and pools made it possible to build homes, not only close to springs, but in every site and topographical location. Ancient Jerusalem thus spread westwards, towards the Upper City, north to Bezetha, and many settlements were established in the Judean Mountains, once the Israelites had taken possession of them. Cisterns possessed numerous advantages. They could be built in any location; they collected rainwater from rooftops and courtyards; their waters were clear and potable; there was virtually no evaporation from the covered cisterns, and thanks to their tight covering they did not spread malaria. Cisterns were private property (*II Kings* XVIII, 31: *Bezah* 10, 5). During emergencies the cistern was the only reliable water source, and pilgrims also used cistern water. In addition to its normal purposes, the cistern served as a place of detention and imprisonment (*Genesis* XXXVII; *Proverbs* XXVIII, 17; *Jeremiah* XXXVIII, 6; *Isaiah* XXIV, 22; *Zechariah* IX, 11), as well as affording concealment and refuge (*I Samuel* XIII, 6; *Proverbs* XXVIII, 17). Many homes possessed two cisterns – one which gathered the rainwater from the rooftop, and served for drinking (the water being relatively pure) and another which collected the water from the courtyard and served for washing and laundering (*Eruvin*, 8, 6). The Arab historian, Yakut (1174–1229) noted that all houses in Jerusalem had one or two cisterns.

There were several methods of excavating cisterns. A cave might be walled up, its walls limed, and a small opening made at the top. This is the meaning of the passage in *Exodus* XXI, 33, "And if a man shall open a pit...", and is referred to in *Ta'anith* 3, 8: "rains that will fill cisterns, pits and caverns." Alternatively, a cistern might be built of stones, its floor paved and its walls limed (*Isaiah* XIV, 19); a pool might also be constructed over a cistern.

The courtyard of the Temple Mount had thirty-six cisterns, hewn out of the *mizi helu* and *melekeh* rock, which is relatively soft, with a total capacity of 16,000 cu m. One of the cisterns contained 12,000 cu m and was 19 m deep. These cisterns became filled with rainwater and were also supplied from distant sources through specially constructed aqueducts. In 1860 there were 992 cisterns in Jerusalem, 950 of these in the Old City. At the end of the Turkish period Jerusalem possessed 6,600 cisterns, with a capacity of 500,000 cu m. During the War of Liberation Jewish Jerusalem had 1053 cisterns, containing 1,000,000 cu m water, which saved its inhabitants from dying of thirst.

Pools

Cistern waters were sufficient only for domestic purposes, and the inhabitants of the capital began to collect the rainwater flowing throughout the city and its environs in pools for other activities needing much water. The pools were constructed mainly in the central vale (Cheesemongers' Valley) lying between the Upper and Lower City. These waters were used for laundering, (hence the name, "fuller's field" in *Isaiah* xxxvi, 2 and the "launderers' landmark" mentioned in Josephus' *Wars*); for watering animals; for irrigating gardens: "I made me gardens and parks, and I planted trees in them of all kinds of fruits; I made me pools of water, to water therefrom the wood springing up with trees" (*Ecclesiastes* ii, 5, 6); for textile and tanning industries; and for manufacturing milk products (*ii Samuel* xvii, 29), which was the reason for naming the valley the Cheesemongers' Valley (*Wars of the Jews* v, 4, 1) and to the gate (*Nehemiah* iii, 13) being known as the Cheese Gate.

The pool at the end of the valley was called the Pool of Shelah (= Siloam), which has two meanings: (1) irrigation channel, and (2) the pool where skins were tanned – and the gate at the south of the valley was also known as the Clay Gate, as cooking utensils and other items of pottery were produced there (*Jeremiah* xix, 2). The pool of Siloam is known in Arabic as Birket al-Hamra (hamra-clay) meaning the Clay Pool. Possibly the meaning of the name Kidron Valley may also be determined in this connection, since *kederah* means a cooking pot, which may have been made of the clay accumulated in the valley floor alluvium. The pools were also used in the making of soap from the "pit of potassium," mentioned by Professor S. Klein in his book *Eretz Yehuda*. The *Mishnah* also notes: "(He) that takes out [on the Sabbath] soda, soap, cimolian earth, or lion's-leaf enough to cleanse a garment small as a hairnet. R. Judah says, 'Enough to spread over a stain' " (*Sabbath* 9, 5 and *Niddah* 9, 6). No other city affords conditions so convenient for excavating pools and collecting water; there are numerous hills and valleys around Jerusalem, and the soft rock is easily hewn, lying as it does on a foundation of marl and clay suitable for holding water. This is well evidenced by the eleven pools within the ancient walls, and the four pools outside: the Dragon's (Sultan's) and Mamillah Pools in the west, and Sitt Miriam and Shimon Hatzadik Pools to the east of the city. The westerly expansion during the Israelite monarchy included the Cheesemongers' Valley, for its favorable water-collecting properties, among other reasons. The pools made the utilization of floodwaters possible. Some pools were built at weak spots in the city walls and were thus used as a shield, and sometimes the wall of the pool served also as the City Wall. The water added a decorative element to the city, and fountains could be operated in the royal palace.

Pools, however, had certain disadvantages: evaporation was heavy, especially in the heat of summer; sewage and other pollution rendered the water unfit to drink and led to epidemics of malaria; the pools gradually became silted up, and heavy floods would damage the holding walls. For this last reason no pools were constructed in the long, narrow Kidron Valley, but only in wide, low-lying valleys.

Aqueducts and Tunnels

The crowning achievement of all the water projects was the digging of tunnels almost every spring in the Judean and Jerusalem Mountains, in order to utilize every available vein of water in the heart of the rock, and to bring water from outlying sources into the walled city. Hezekiah, king of Judah, dug the tunnel from the Gihon Spring (Which yields about 50 cu m per hour) taking the water to the Pool of Siloam: "This same Hezekiah also stopped the upper spring of the waters of Gihon, and brought them straight down on the west side of the city of David. And Hezekiah prospered in all his works" (*II Chronicles* XXXII, 30). The amazing fact about this tunnel is that it was excavated over a length of 533 m, with a gradient of 2.18 m, i.e., a gradient of just over 4 to 1000. Another farsighted project was the aqueduct from the 'Arrub springs, south of the Etzion Bloc, at a height of 820 m above sea-level to Jerusalem (750 m), i.e., a slope of 70 m over a distance of 68 km, the gradient being about 1%. In this way the inhabitants of Jerusalem in the time of the Second Temple ingeniously solved the problem of water supply. Four tunnels were constructed, and stone piping (visible today south of Rachel's Tomb, near the road and east of it) was laid to bring the water by force of gravity to Jerusalem. In other water projects of the country the water was conveyed from abundant sources in the hills to the Coastal Plain or to the Jordan Valley. Examples are: the 16 km aqueduct leading from the Kabri springs to Acre; that bringing water over 7 km from the Shuni springs to Caesarea; and those leading to the Jordan Valley, such as the one from the Yavneel Valley to Tiberias, over 12 km, or from the Moda springs at the foot of Mount Gilboa to Beth-Shean, 7 km long, and from the Qelt Valley springs to Herod's Jericho over 12 km. The great 'Arrub–Jerusalem aqueduct faced difficulties of estimating virtually indistinguishable differences in height, and the 'Arrub springs themselves are relatively poor. A project of this kind, carried out in order to fill the pools and cisterns of the Temple Mount, could only have been possible for Jerusalem, which lies lower than the surrounding hills; it would have been impossible, for instance, for Givat-Shaul, Gibeon or Beth-El, which stand higher than the hill around them.

In each period, the ancients utilized a new type of water source and set up a new water project. During the Canaanite period permanent settlements were established mainly near springs; cisterns and pools were added in the Israelite period; in the Hasmonean and Roman periods aqueducts spanned great distances. Thus, by the end of the Second Temple period, Jerusalem made use of five sources of water supply: the Gihon spring, the Rogel well, ubiquitous cisterns, pools in the valleys, and aqueducts from the 'Arrub spring and from Wadi el-Biar, north-east of the Etzion Bloc. These phenomena are unparalleled in any other city in the Judean Mountains. The citizens of Jerusalem never succumbed to thirst, nor did they ever surrender as a result of lack of water. The food supply, however, was insufficient in times of siege (Josephus, *Wars v, 10, 3*). *The British Mandate government early established a pump at the Pools of Solomon to bring water to Jerusalem, and in 1936 the waters of Rosh Ha'Ayin began to flow to the city. Jerusalem is supplied today by the National Water Carrier.*

The Forts of the Shephelah (Low Land)

> *And the king of Assyria sent Rabshakeh from Lachish to*
> *Jerusalem unto king Hezekiah with a great army.*
> Isaiah xxxvi, 2

The defense of Jerusalem, the capital city, was also based on a line of fortified cities in the Shephelah, the foothills of the Judean Mountains, and in the valleys leading out of the mountains. These cities were Devir, Lachish, Maresha, Makeda, Azeka, Beth-Shemesh, Zor'ah, Ayalon and Lower Beth-Horon. Command of these cities ensured command of Jerusalem as well. The Amorites therefore fortified the Shephelah cities; and before taking possession of the mountains, Joshua and his successors conquered Jeremoth, near the Elah Valley in the north and Lachish and Eglon in the south. Rehoboam and other kings of Judah fortified these and other cities as a defense against enemies seeking to take Jerusalem, such as Shishal, king of Egypt (in the time of Rehoboam), Sennacherib, king of Assyria, who besieged the Shephelah forts in the time of Hezekiah, and Nebuchadnezzar, king of Babylon in the time of Zedekiah, king of Judah. The Hellenists went up through Maresha to Hebron and Beth-Zur before invading Jerusalem in the time of the Maccabees. The Romans, headed by Vespasian, Cerealis and Titus, also put siege to Jerusalem at the end of the

Second Temple period, once the fortified cities of the Shephelah had fallen. The Crusaders approached Jerusalem by way of Latrun and Nebi-Samwil. In the First World War, General Allenby reached the city through the passes in the Shephelah foothills. During the 1948 War of Independence, Jerusalem was truly freed only after the liberation of the Shephelah hills. The Jerusalem Corridor and the Shephelah were later intensively settled by Israel, ensuring a solid line of Jewish settlement from the mountains to the coast.

Jerusalem Over the Centuries

As has been noted, Jerusalem was, throughout history, the most important city of the Judean Mountains, and especially during periods of Jewish rule. This was due to its location on a ridge surrounded and protected by valleys. The city was at the crossroads of the mountain highways; it enjoyed a rich economic hinterland, located as it was between the cultivated regions of the west and the wilderness in the east, and ensured of an adequate water supply.

Jerusalem in the Canaanite Period (3000–1200 B.C.E.)

> Thine origin and thy nativity is of the land of the Canaanite;
> the Amorite was thy father and thy mother was a Hittite
>
> Ezekiel XVI, 3

Many investigators, among them Macalister (1925), Crowfoot (1927–28) and Kathleen Kenyon (1961–67), carried out archaeological excavations in Jerusalem, and discovered sherds from the early middle and late Canaanite periods, evidence of the existence of the city in the third millennium B.C.E., when its location was determined by the proximity to the Gihon spring. The Egyptian Execration Texts, from the nineteenth century B.C.E., mention the city as "*Rushlamem.*" Professor Kenyon discovered a wall, 2.5 m wide, dating to the same period, near the Gihon spring.

At the time of the Patriarch Abraham, the king of Jerusalem was Melchizedek the king of Shalem, who was a priest of God the Most High (*Genesis* XIV, 18). Thus, Jerusalem was important and holy even at that early date, and was identified with the site of Mount Moriah. Its sacred attributes may have been due to the Gihon spring, the richest of all the springs on the mountain plateau; it gushes forth erratically and was therefore magical in the eyes of the ancients. Several kings of Judah were crowned at the spring.

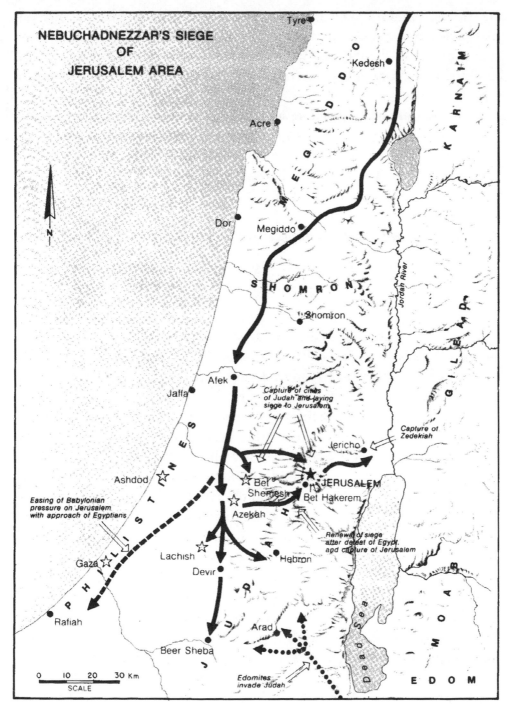

Nebuchadnezzar's siege of the Jerusalem area

Jerusalem was important in the late Canaanite period as well, and was mentioned in the El-Amarna letters (Egypt, fourteenth century, B.C.E.) as a central city in the Judean Mountains. The letter of Eved-Hibah, king of Jerusalem, to Pharaoh, was inscribed in the cuneiform Accadian, on a clay tablet.

At the time of the Israelite settlement, the king of Jerusalem was an Amorite, who headed a coalition of kings of the mountain and Shephelah cities; he was apparently an Egyptian vassal, as hinted in Joshua IV. According to Prof. N. Avigad, Jerusalem's territory during *586 B.C.E.,* the Jebusite period, was approximately 80 dunam (20 acres).

Jerusalem During the First Temple Period (1200–586 B.C.E.)

> *And I will make them one nation in the land,*
> *upon the mountains of Israel*
>
> Ezekiel XXXVII, 22

At the time of David, Jerusalem was a Jebusite city (*II Samuel* II, 5). David brought the Ark of the Covenant from Kiryat-Yearim to Jerusalem and bought the threshing ground of Araunah the Jebusite for the site of the Temple (*II Samuel* XXIV, 24). The city thus attained the status of a religious center for the tribes of Israel. The Temple was built in the time of Solomon, and since then the city has been hallowed by the people of Israel as their sole great religious and national center. Jerusalem is mentioned 656 times in Scriptures and is called by seventy different titles. Solomon concluded treaties with the kings of Egypt, Amon, Moab, Tyre and the Hittites, and raised Jerusalem to international status. Senacherib's failure to take Jerusalem raised its significance above that of the other cities which sought sanctity. The great number of powers that ruled in Jerusalem is further evidence of the city's importance at the junction of the main highways. However, it is noteworthy that all through its early period and throughout the Canaanite period Jerusalem was a provincial capital; only in the Israelite monarchy, beginning with David and Solomon, did the gentile city become the national and political capital of Israel, and its spiritual and religious center, symbolizing the unity of the tribes of Israel.

According to N. Avigad the city's territory during the time of Solomon measured 430 dunam and during the time of Hezekiah, 650 dunam.

Jerusalem During the Second Temple Period (536 B.C.E.–70 C.E.)

*He who has not seen the Temple in its full construction has never seen
a glorious building in his life.*

Sukkah 51b

The declaration of Cyrus that he permitted Jews to reconstruct Jerusalem and its Temple (*Ezra* I, 2–3) was made in 538 B.C.E., and in 445 B.C.E. the Persians appointed Nechemia governor of Jerusalem.

In the period of the Return to Zion, Jewish rule in Jerusalem and Judea became established, and it expanded during the Hasmonean period. Political autonomy was granted to the Jewish community. Nehemiah repaired the walls of Jerusalem in fifty-two days (*Nehemiah* VI, 15), and Hyrcanus the Hasmonean rebuilt the walls and towers of the city. Herod's Temple was built by 10,000 workmen and 1,000 priests, with 1,000 wagons conveying the construction materials. About eight years were required to build the Temple courtyard and the porticos, and a further 18 months for the Temple itself (*Antiquities* XV, 11, 5–6). It was therefore said that whoever had not seen Herod's building had never seen a beautiful building (*Baba Bathra* 4a). The city and its walls were under construction for about forty-six years (*St. John* 11, 20). The city's territory during King Herod's time was 1,800 dunam.

During the Second Temple period which lasted over 600 years, Jerusalem served as the religious and political center of the Jewish people in both the Land of Israel and the Diaspora; during the First Temple period, on the other hand, the city held this position for the Land of Israel only. The law was studied in public, schools were established, pilgrimages were made and synagogues built – all manifestations of the sanctity of the city. According to Talmudic legend, there were 408 synagogues in Jerusalem, each of which had its affiliated school (for study of the Bible) and house of study (for the *Mishnah*) (*Yerushalmi, Megillah* 84). This number of synagogues is no doubt an exaggeration, but there is a nucleus of historical truth in it. Synagogues were established for the sake of public religious experience, while the Temple was the focus of public life in the city. The Jerusalem Temple was the only central institution of the nation in the country and outside it. The Temple of Onias at Leontopolis, in Egypt, was also well known, but it was located in a distant settlement in Egypt and did not weaken the tie between Egyptian Jewry and the Jerusalem Temple. Philo of Alexandria notes that tens of thousands of

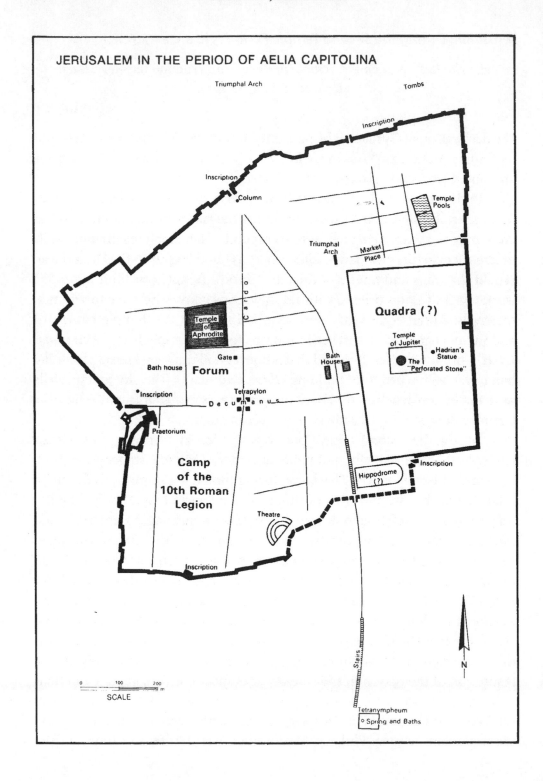

JERUSALEM IN THE PERIOD OF AELIA CAPITOLINA

Triumphal Arch

Tombs

Inscription

Inscription

Column

Temple
Pools

Triumphal
Arch

Market
Place

Cardo

Quadra (?)

Temple
of
Aphrodite

Temple
of Jupiter

Hadrian's
Statue

The
"Perforated Stone"

Gate

Bath
Houses

Bath house

Forum

Inscription

Tetrapylon

Decumanus

Praetorium

Camp
of the
10th Roman
Legion

Inscription

Hippodrome
(?)

Inscription

Theatre

Inscription

Stairs

N

0   100   200
                    m
SCALE

Tetranympheum
Spring and Baths

Jews from many cities at all points of the compass thronged to the Temple on each holiday (*On the Special Laws* I, 69). Jews were commanded not only to make pilgrimages to the country, but also to settle there, while Moslems and Christians were bound only to make pilgrimages. The Jews paid a tax of half a shekel per person to the central Temple, and 24 delegations of the people from 24 different areas of the country corresponding to the twenty-four priestly guards of the Sanctuary, used to go up to Jerusalem. The longing for and dedication of the Jews to the pilgrimage to Jerusalem was as strong after the destruction of the Second Temple as before, and the pilgrimages to the devastated city were continued. Jerusalem's significance as a religious and national center was considerably augmented after the army of the Greek-Hellenist empire failed in its total conquest, and it is doubtful whether the imperial Roman army would have overcome the city, had it not been for the tragic and unnecessary civil war during the final battle.

During the Second Temple period the city area expanded to 3,700 dunams – about about four sq km – the greatest up to that time. (Today's Old City measures 970 dunams.) The Temple Mount had an area of some 144 dunams, greater than the area of any of the famous pagan temples in Greece and Italy. It also exceeded all other temples in the Mediterranean countries in magnificence. At this period, the techniques of terrace agriculture were highly sophisticated, especially the collection of water and its conveyance over a distance; the water systems were technologically superior to many other great projects in ancient lands.

The Roman Revolt began with the cessation of sacrifices to the health of Caesar (*Wars of the Jews* II, 17, 2).

Jerusalem in the Roman Period (70–324 C.E.)

> *Rabbi (Akiba) used to expound: there shall step forth a star*
> *out of Jacob, this is the king Messiah.*
> *Lamentations Rabbah II, 2*

Jews continued to live in Jerusalem after its partial destruction, and worshiped God on the rubble of the Temple Mount. When Hadrian planned to erect a Roman city there, thus desecrating its sanctity, the Bar-Kochba Revolt erupted and the city was taken again by Jews (132–135 C.E.). However, the revolt failed and Jerusalem and Betar fell.

There were 75 Jewish settlements in Judea before the Bar-Kochba Revolt, all of which were destroyed after the fall of Betar. Jews, nevertheless, still remained in the Judean Mountains. The Galilee continued to be a Jewish stronghold, and the majority of its population was Jewish. Before the destruction of the Second Temple, there were 63 Jewish towns in Galilee, 56 of which remained after the destruction; i.e., Jews constituted three-quarters of the population of the coastal area and Transjordan (M. Avi-Yonah, *Biyemei Roma Ubizantiyon*, [*In the Time of Rome and Byzantium*] Jerusalem, 1961). After the fall of Betar, Jews were forbidden to live in Jerusalem under penalty of death, but mention is made, in the *Lament of the Cedars of Lebanon*, of Rabbi Hanina ben-Teradion gathering groups of people at the gates of Zion. The edict was thus apparently not fully enforced. Faith in redemption was strong even when the First Temple was destroyed; when Jeremiah purchased the field of his uncle at Anatot he said: "For thus saith the Lord of Hosts, the God of Israel, houses and fields and vineyards shall yet again be bought in this land… Men shall buy fields for money… in the land of Benjamin, and in the places about Jerusalem, and in the cities of Judah, in the cities of the hill-country, and in the cities of the lowland, and in the cities of the South; for I will cause their captivity to return, saith the Lord" (XXXIII, 15, 44).

The soil of the Land of Israel continued to be sacred to the Jews after the Bar-Kochba war. Rabbi Meir ruled: "None may hire houses to them (gentiles) in the Land of Israel, or, needless to say, fields" (*Avodah Zarah* I, 8).

Despite the edicts against the Jews, Jewish were built in the third century on Mount Zion in Jerusalem and in other parts of the country, especially Galilee.

Faith in redemption was constant in the hearts of the Jews of the country, and Rabbi Shimon Bar-Yochai hoped for the aid of the Persians against the

*On the left: Roman coin from the period after the Bar-Kochba Revolt: A Judean woman
sits leaning against a date tree, guarded by a Roman. Legend: Captive Judea.
On the right: From the period of Shimon the Maccabee – date tree, and
beneath it baskets with dates. Legend: To the redemption of Zion*

Romans, saying that a Persian horse tethered in the Land of Israel would be the precursor of the Messiah (*Lamentations Rabbah* 16, 31, 13). One legend tells of a Roman emperor who asked a Roman notable whether Israel could be destroyed and received the answer: "You cannot do away with all of them" (*Avodah Zarah*, 10, 2).

Jerusalem in the Byzantine Period (324–637 c.e.)

With the ascendance of Christianity, Jerusalem became holy to two competing religions. Constantine, following Helena, erected splendid churches in Jerusalem, among other reasons in order to hamper the return of Jews to Zion. At that time Jews were forbidden to live in Jerusalem; it was the only city in the country with a Christian majority. Hieronymus, a Church father in the fourth century, noted that Jews were allowed to enter Jerusalem only on the eve of the Ninth of Av, to lament the destruction of the Temple and the city. Pilgrimages of this type are described in *Lamentations Rabbah* I, 17–19, as going up in silence and coming down in silence, going up in tears and coming down in tears, going up in the dark of the night and coming down in the dark of the night. The words of Rabbi Yohanan are evidence of the pilgrimage to Jerusalem; he describes the earthly Jerusalem as being accessible to all.

Nonetheless, in 361 c.e. the Emperor Julian, conferring with delegates of the Jewish communities of Syria and Cilicia, made the following promise in connection with Jerusalem: "I shall proceed with all rapidity to reconstruct the temple to the all-highest God"; in the course of his campaign against the Persians, Julian sent the following proclamation to the Jews of Mesopotamia: "I am reconstructing with all rapidity the new temple to the all-highest God."

Jews hoped again for redemption during the reign of the empress Eudocia (443), who was Hellenistic in outlook and apparently favorably inclined toward the Jews. The Jews of Galilee sent the following letter to the community: "The time of our exile is past, and the ingathering of our tribes is at hand, since the kings of the Romans have decreed that our city Jerusalem be returned to us. Make haste to ascend to Jerusalem at the festival of Sukkoth, for our kingdom shall be renewed in Jerusalem" (*Sefer Hayishuv* I, p. 33). The Jews were then allowed to settle in Jerusalem (M. Avi-Yonah, *Biyemei Roma Ubizantiyon*).

During the later Byzantine period, despite harassment by the Christians, Jews erected many synagogues, such as the one at Beth-Alpha in the Jezreel Valley, at Husifa on the Carmel, at Hammath-Gader in the Yarmuk Valley, at Jericho and Na-aran north of the Dead Sea, and at Ashdod, Ashkelon and

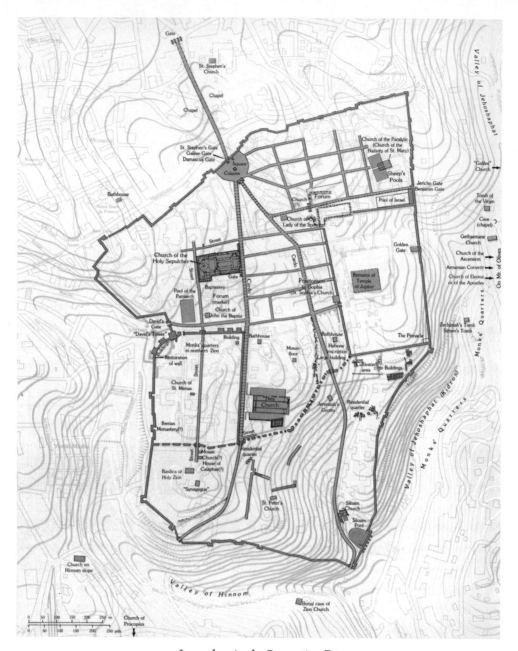

Jerusalem in the Byzantine Era

Gaza. During the role of Justinian, at the beginning of the sixth century, edicts against the Jews were promulgated, and they were prohibited from serving in any government posts. There were then 43 Jewish settlements in the country – 12 towns and 31 villages. (After the Bar-Kochba war there were 200 Jewish settlements.) The Karaite Sahl ben-Mazliah wrote that noone of Israel could

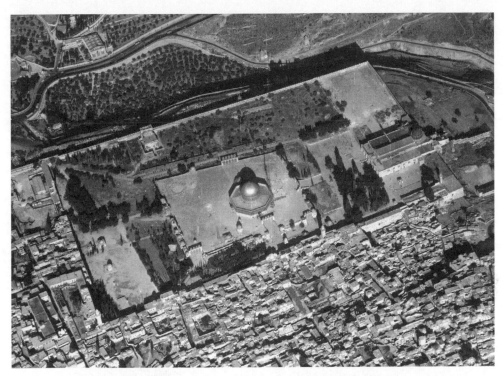

Temple Mount and the western wall in the Old City

come to Jerusalem; the Jews of the east prayed in Tiberias, those of the west in Gaza, and those of the south in Zo'ar. Humiliation of the Jews reached its peak during the Byzantine period, when the Stone of Foundation, the site of the Holy of Holies mentioned in the Bible – or the Rock of the Temple Mount, as it was called in the Moslem period – was covered with refuse.

Jerusalem in the Later Persian Period (614–629 c.e.)

During the Persian occupation in the early seventh century, there were some 20,000 Jews in a special Jewish division of the Persian army. An alliance between Persians and Jews was mutually beneficial, since the Jews hoped for a return to Jewish rule in the Land of Israel and the reconstruction of the Temple, while the Persians needed Jewish aid in conquering the Near Eastern countries; they regarded the Jews as a decisive local element, due to their connections and ties with the Holy Land.

With the Persian occupation of Jerusalem (614), Jewish rule was reestablished the city and ritual was renewed. 37,000 Christians were exiled from Jerusalem to Persia. However, three years later the Persians went back on their promises to the Jews and helped the Christians to banish the Jews from

Jerusalem, returning it to Christian rule. The Jewish exiles fled to Jericho and the Judean Desert, hoping for an eventual return (*Sefer Zerubabel*).

The Byzantine emperor Heraclius took Jerusalem back from the Persians in 629 and exiled the Jews to a distance of 5 km from the city. In 638 the city fell to the Moslem armies led by Omar. The Byzantine Christians surrendered on condition that the Jews should not be allowed inside the city, but Jews were later permitted to settle in Jerusalem.

Jerusalem in the Early Moslem Period (638–1099)

> *I have set watchmen upon thy walls, O Jerusalem, they shall*
> *never hold their peace day or night; ye that are the Lord's*
> *remembrances, take ye and give Him no rest, till He establish,*
> *and till He make Jerusalem a praise in the earth.*
>
> Isaiah LXII, 6–7

The army of 'Omar, which took Jerusalem from the Byzantines, included Jews in its ranks, and they were allowed to re-establish settlements in the Land of Israel and in Jerusalem. 'Omar believed that the Moslems originally came to the land by reason of their kinship with the sons of Abraham. However, thirty years later the Moslems took the lands belonging to Jews and forced them to serve in the army. At the time of the Moslem conquest, Arab writers noted the presence of stones on the Temple Mount, prepared by the Jews for the re-building of the Temple. At first the Moslems handed over the Temple area to the Jews, and the festival of *Sukkoth* was celebrated on the Mount. The Karaites noted that the Moslems gave the Jews a place in Jerusalem in which to live, and that many Jews came to Jerusalem to study and pray. (Sahl Ben Matzliah, *Sefer Hamitzvot, Hamelitz*, 1879, p. 640.) After the Arab conquest, Jerusalem did not become an Arab city, either in appearance – the city remained Byzantine in plan and buildings – or in the composition of its cosmopolitan population. Jerusalem was a provincial city, from the Arab conquest in 637 to the end of the Turkish rule (1917), in a kingdom in the centers of which were Damascus, Baghdad, Cairo and Constantinople.

Jerusalem is in fact sacred to three religions, but not equally so to all three. What the Land of Israel was to Judaism and Christianity, all Arabia was to Islam. Never was the entire country sacred to Islam. The land was a province of a larger empire, and Jerusalem did not serve as the capital city of the province of Palestine. Its strategic importance became evident only thirty years

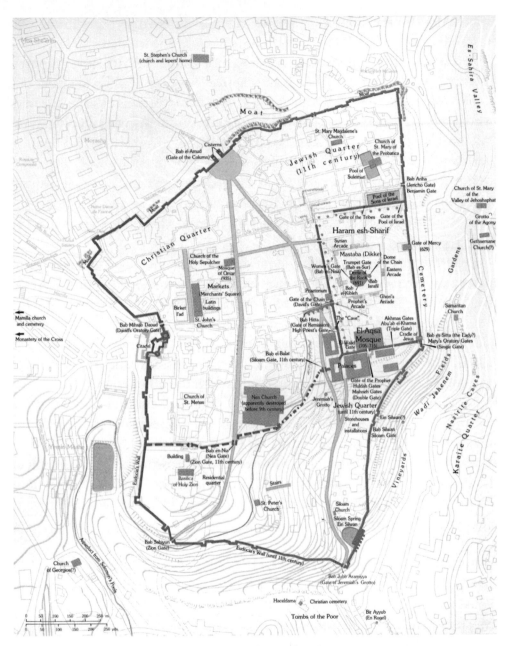

Jerusalem in the Moslem Era

before the Crusades. During the Moslem period holders of radical opinions were exiled to Jerusalem; it did not serve as a cultural center for Moslems. The Arabic name for Jerusalem, *el-Quds*, "the holy," was taken from the Hebrew appellation for the Temple, "the Holy City," mentioned 37 times in the Old Testament; only later did the city become holy for the Moslems.

The Caliph 'Omar visited Jerusalem shortly after its conquest, accompanied by Jewish sages from Tiberias and captive Jews from Homs and Damascus. Omar declared the Temple Mount to be a place of prayer, thus pleasing the Jews, who regarded this as foreshadowing their redemption. Omar asked the Jews: "'Where would you wish to live in the city?' And they answered, in the southern part; and that is the marketplace of the Jews. Their intention was to be close to the Temple and its gates, as well as the waters of Siloam for ritual bathing. The Emir of the Believers granted this to them" (*Sefer Hayishuv*, p. 18).

According to B. Dinur, the Jewish quarter was near the Wall, which the Jews regarded as holy (*Yisrael Bagolah*, p. 54).

In the first years after its conquest, Arab Jerusalem had a Yemenite appearance; Yemenite Jews apparently came to the city along with the Arabs from Yemen. The attitude of the Moslem rulers toward the inhabitants of the country was apparently determined by religious, economic and strategic considerations. There were three population groups at the time of the conquest: Christians, divided into sects; Jews and Samaritans. Christianity, previously the official religion, was given equal status with the other religions, and Jews were allowed to develop an independent religious, cultural and social life within the law. The Arabs who entered the country were not numerous; the majority served as a garrison, and only a few settled on the land.

The first Umayyad caliph, Mu'awiya, was crowned in 660. Jerusalem, however, was not the capital of any Moslem state. The two Umayyad caliphs connected with the land of Israel, Mu'awiya and Suleiman, were not overly concerned with Jerusalem.

Jerusalem During the Umayyad Dynasty (660–750)

In 661 c.e., Ali, the husband of Fatima – the daughter of Muhammad – and his cousin, was murdered, and Mu'awiya was appointed as the fourth caliph of the Moslems. Then the Arab empire split because of the caliphs' inheritance wars. Mu'awiya, who was an outstanding officer when conquering Syria and the Land of Israel, and the governor of the Syrian county, founded the Umayyad Dynasty, proclaimed himself a Moslem caliph in 661, and took over Egypt. Mu'awiya expanded the Moslem empire's borders in army campaigns in the east up to central Asia and northwest India, and conquered the countries of North Africa up to the Atlantic Ocean in the west. He was the first caliph to set his seat and capital outside the Arabian borders – in Damascus. Mu'awiya was appointed by the families of the Kuraish tribe – the tribe of Muhammad.

Syria and the Land of Israel were the center of the Moslem world during the Umayyad dynasty. The rulers were in Damascus, and the great "Umayyad Mosque" became holy to the Moslems. 'Abd al-Malik (685–705) built in Jerusalem the Dome of the Rock in 691–692 as a shrine and not as a mosque. However, since Mecca was distant from Syria and the Land of Israel, the Moslems celebrated their festivals in Jerusalem. The El-Aqsa mosque was built by Al-Walid, the son of 'Abd al-Malik, in 705–715. Umayyad palaces were discovered during the excavations of Professor Mazar, south of the Temple Mount. 'Abd al-Malik's second son, Suleiman, who ruled from the Land of Israel, built Ramleh and made it the provincial capital of Palestine as well as a commercial center situated at an important junction. Jerusalem at this time was secondary to Ramleh. (It is worth noting that the name Palestine has no connection with Islamic culture or history, and stems from the references of Greek historians to the region of Philistia, on the coast. It was Hadrian who wished to erase the name of Israel, and changed the name of the country from Judea to Palestina. The Arabic name of the country might well have remained Israel, just as Syria inherited the name of Assyria, and Lebanon, Egypt, Jordan, Arabia, Yemen and Persia bear the names of ancient peoples and lands, some mentioned in the Bible.)

Arabs were not numerous in the country at that time and did not aspire to settle on the land. Jews were living in Tiberias and its vicinity, in Dan (= Banias), Haifa, Jaffa, Jerusalem and Hebron and their environs. The town of Eilat was Jewish, according to Arab writers. The other cities had mixed populations, Persians and Samaritans, as well as Arabs.

At the time of Mohammed, the founder of Islam, Jerusalem was relatively unimportant. Mohammed instructed his followers to face Jerusalem during prayer; the Jewish and Christian inhabitants of the city were monotheists, while the Arabs were pagan, and he hoped in this way to attract Jews to Islam. But according to the *Koran*, after eighteen months of scant success, he instituted the custom of facing Mecca (*Sura B* 136, 139). Jerusalem is not mentioned in the *Koran,* and later oral tradition connected it with Mohammed's nocturnal journey to the El-Aqsa (in Arabic, the farthest or external) mosque; the precise site of the El-Aqsa is unidentified, and one opinion is that it is at El-Ja'aranah in the vicinity of Mecca, where there were two mosques, El-Adna and El-Aqsa. The Land of Israel is not mentioned in the *Koran*. The only link between Mohammed and Jerusalem is to be found in the legend of his ascent to Heaven. There are three traditional versions of this legend (according to Professor H.Z. Hirschberg).

1. Mohammed arrived from Arabia and returned to it, to the farthest mosque, riding the Burak, a mare with wings, a woman's face and a peacock's tail; he then ascended a ladder to the seven heavens, accompanied by Gabriel.
2. Mohammed ascended to heaven directly from Mecca as Mecca is the center of the upper world.
3. Mohammed saw the ascent to heaven in a vision. In the third *Sura*, Mohammed proclaimed the connection between the patriarch Abraham and Mecca; the land promised to Abraham was Arabia and not the Land of Israel. Pilgrimages to Mecca are based on the divine command to Abraham, and the imprint of Abraham's heel is shown to this day on the Ka'aba, in Mecca.

The Jewish community of Jerusalem gained strength after the Arab conquest and soon became the largest in the country. The Jewish center, previously in Tiberias, was transferred to Jerusalem (*Sefer Hayishuv*, 2, p. 9). The Jews of Jerusalem suffered at the hands of the Christians and the Moslem officials, but did not leave the city. They settled at first in the south of the city, near the Temple Mount, and after an earthquake in 1033 they moved to the quarter north of the Temple area.

Jerusalem During the 'Abbasid Dynasty (750–969)

The 'Abbasids center was in Baghdad, and Persians as well as other nationals were of considerable importance to the dynasty. Jerusalem declined in significance because of its distance from Baghdad, and Moslems made pilgrimages to Mecca. The Caliph Haroun al-Rashid made this pilgrimage every two years, but he never went as far as Jerusalem. The 'Abbasids neglected Jerusalem, except for the repairs to the Temple area buildings commissioned by Al-Ma'mun, the son of Haroun al-Rashid. Famine and locusts plagued the country during his reign (813–833), and most of the city's Moslem inhabitants left. The caliphs of the 'Abbasid dynasty and their successors, the Fatimids, ruled the country from their administrative capital in Ramleh.

In 868 Syria and Palestine were annexed by Ahmed ibn-Tulun, who, on behalf of the Abbasids, ruled in Egypt. There was extensive warfare between the Egyptian rulers and their masters in Baghdad; Jerusalem is not mentioned throughout this period.

Shelomo ben-Meir, the head of a *Yeshivah*, reports that the courtyard of the Temple served as a meeting place for the Jews in the time of Rabbi Mosy, during the first half of the ninth century (B. Dinaburg, *Zion 3*, 1929, pp. 69–70).

Jerusalem During the Fatimid Dynasty (969–1071)

> *Zion, once a desiccated tree, shall bear fruit once more.*
> *May your humblers be humbled,*
> *never more to call you a rebellious nation.*
> *Shemuel HaNaggid (993–1056)*

The Fatimids conquered Mecca and Medina, Egypt, Palestine and Syria with Bedouin aid. The Caliph Al-Hakim, who ruled in Egypt, ordered the destruction of synagogues and churches in Jerusalem (1009), although he later allowed Christians and Jews to build places of worship. Salomon ben-Yeroham, the Karaite, reports (in the middle of the tenth century) three stages in the existence of places of prayer in Jerusalem:

1. On the appearance of the kingdom of Ishmael the people of Israel were allowed to enter (Jerusalem) and live there for many years and the courtyard of the Temple was given to them for prayers.
2. Over the years the area granted to Jews on the Temple Mount was gradually restricted.
3. The Jews were expelled from the Temple area (B. Dinaburg, *op. cit.*, p. 72).

It was said of Rabbi Shemuel Hanagid (993–1056) that he helped the Jews in Spain, Africa, Egypt, Sicily, the religious schools of Babylon and the Holy City. He benefited all students of the Law in these places, bought many copies of the Bible, the *Mishnah* and the *Talmud*, and in addition supplied olive oil every year for the synagogues of Jerusalem.

In the middle of the eleventh century, Jerusalem gained in importance, apparently because of the depredations of the Bedouin at Ramleh and the increase in pilgrimages to the Holy City. In 1065, 12,000 Christian pilgrims arrived in the city from southern Germany and Holland. There were also many Jewish pilgrims, according to the report of Rabbi Shelomo ben Yehuda, one of the *Geonim*, who was head of the *Yeshivah* in Jerusalem. Jews prayed in synagogues on the Mount of Olives during the pilgrimages in the month of Tishrei, placating the stones of the city by comforting the earth, circling the gates and prostrating themselves in prayer and consolation.

The Seljuks conquered Jerusalem in 1071, laying waste to the surrounding country. The population was depleted in the course of the struggles between Seljuks and Fatimids (Y. Prawer, *Yehudim be-Mamlechet Yerushalaim Hatsal-banit, Zion 2,* 1946; B. Dinaburg, *Letoledot Hayehudim be-Eretz Yisrael Bimei Masa Hatzelav Harishon, Zion,* 2, 1923). Al-Muqaddasi, the Arab historian who lived in Jerusalem in the tenth century, wrote in 985 A.D. that, after 400 years of Arab rule, "there were no sages of the law or educated laymen. The Christians and the Jews prevailed, and the mosque was empty of students and believers in prayer." (*Yakut*, Vol. 5, p. 596, according to *Sefer Hayishuv* 2, p. 23.) *Yakut* stressed the religious significance of Jerusalem for Jews and Christians. Sahl ben-Matzliah (who lived in Jerusalem at the end of the tenth century) wrote that Jerusalem was a place of refuge, of rest and of peace.

Rabbi Bar-Hiyya notes that there was a synagogue in the Temple Mount area up to the Crusader conquest of Jerusalem, "and in addition, the kings of Ishmael treat us well, and have allowed the Jews to come to the Temple and build there a place of worship and study. All the Jews exiled near the Temple make pilgrimages on the holidays and festivals, and pray there, and their prayers are a replacement for the sacrifices" (*Sefer Hayishuv* 2, p. 20).

From the time of the Seljuk conquest, up to the twentieth century, Arabs no longer ruled the Holy City.

It is interesting to note that most of the Jews who immigrated to Jerusalem before the Crusades were from Islamic countries; later, immigration began from Europe and western countries.

Jerusalem in the Early Crusader Period (1099–1187)

> *Jerusalem! May your oppressors drink the cup of bitterness!*
> *Yehuda Halevi, 1075*

In 1099, Jerusalem fell to about 15,000 Crusaders who attacked from the north at Herod's Gate and at the site of the present-day New Gate, and from the south, through the Zion Gate. Siege was laid and victory was gained at points unprotected by a moat. Crusader Jerusalem was considerably smaller than the pre-1033 eras; its walls were mainly built on the same alignment as the present Turkish walls, which are about 4 km long. Godfrey of Bouillon, notifying the Pope of his conquest of Jerusalem, called the country "Terra Israel."

The Crusaders, having taken Jerusalem after a fierce battle with Moslems and Jews, proceeded to massacre the inhabitants. They then began to settle the quarter nearest the Church of the Holy Sepulcher (which they reconstructed) and the Tower of David. The Christian inhabitants of Jerusalem, most of whom were Europeans, were freed from taxation. The Jewish Quarter, at that time north of the Temple Mount, was burned down; one synagogue was set aflame with its worshipers inside. The Crusaders sold Jews into slavery in the Christian countries of Europe. Thus the Jews of Acre, Haifa and Caesarea were oppressed, and the Jewish communities of Ramleh were destroyed. Villages of the Galilee which surrendered were left intact, as the Crusaders needed their produce. Settlement of Moslems and Jews in Jerusalem was expressly forbidden, since this was desecration, and the Jewish Quarter north of the Temple Mount was taken over by Syrian Christians. In spite of this, two Jews leased a dye-shop, and Benjamin of Tudela, writing in 1170, recorded that some 400 Jews were living in the city. At the same time the Jewish communities of Tyre, Ashkelon, Ramleh and Tiberias slowly came to life again.

During the reign of Saladin the Ayyubid, permission was given for Jews and Moslems to settle the hill regions, and the ban on Jewish settlement in Jerusalem was lifted. Jews from Ashkelon came to live in the city, and with the arrival of the Ramban, the Jewish community in Jerusalem revived, especially after 1267. The Ramban, is considered the father of the modern Jewish community of Jerusalem. In a letter to his son, he wrote that there were very few Jews, most of them having fled or been killed. He found only two brothers, dyers both. Together with them he located a ruined building, with marble columns and a handsome dome, and made it into a synagogue; the city was lawless, and ruined buildings were available for the taking.

The repairs to the building were made voluntarily. Once the repairs were begun, messengers were sent to bring Scrolls of the Law from Shechem, since these scrolls came originally from Jerusalem and had been sent north at the time of the Tatar invasion (1260). The scrolls were placed in the synagogue, where prayers were held. Many Jews visited Jerusalem from Damascus, Tzova and all the regions of the empire to see the place where the Temple had stood

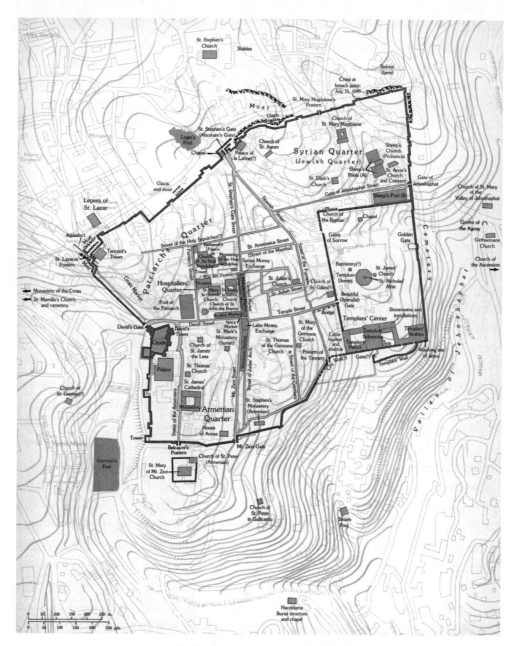

Jerusalem in the Crusader Era

and to lament its destruction (Rabbi Joseph Schwartz, *Tevuot Ha-aretz*, Jerusalem, 1845). One of the students of the Ramban wrote in his book about the Land of Israel that many Jews believed the time of the Messiah was near, since the nations were treating Israel so harshly. Jews settled near Mount Zion, and there life was concentrated around the Ramban synagogue, which the Moslems tried to take away from them.

It is noteworthy that the Tower of Hippicus (nowadays called David's Tower), built by Herod during the Second Temple period and used as a Roman fort in the time of Titus and Hadrian, became the stronghold of the foreign Crusades, and the hostile Turkish regime also established itself there.

Jerusalem was a religious and spiritual center for the Crusaders; they identified the El-Aqsa mosque with the Temple of Solomon and built churches that were maintained by the military orders of the Knights Templar (of the Temple). They established hospices for pilgrims, run by Hospitallers. Nevertheless, the city was of no special economic or political value during this period, except for a short time before its conquest by Saladin. Jerusalem was a well-fortified city, and the Crusaders maintained permanent bases there for their armies, in preparation for an invasion of Moab and Edom.

Jerusalem in the Late Crusader Period (1187–1260)

> *Speak unto the heart of Jerusalem*
> *That all who wish may to her return*
> *The remnants of Ephraim shall come from Egypt and Assyria*
> *And the dispersed shall be gathered from the four corners of the earth*
> *To dwell within her borders.*
>
> *Yehuda Alharizi, 1215*

When the Crusaders recaptured Acre, in 1191, Saladin repaired the walls and fortifications of Jerusalem, and built towers on the western side. He also built *madaress* (religious colleges) north of the Temple area and in other sections of the city. In 1219 the ruler of Syria and Palestine, al-Malik al-Mu'athem 'Issa, demolished the walls and towers, fearing the Crusaders might entrench themselves in Jerusalem. In 1221 the Crusaders demanded that the Moslems repair the walls, and when this demand was not met, the struggle between them was renewed (*'Aref el-'Aref, Tarikh al-Quds*, p. 172).

Saladin and his successors wished to attract settlers to Jerusalem, and favored the arrival of Jews and Christians of the eastern sects. The rights of the Jews to the land were recognized, along with an appreciation of their fighting alongside the Arabs against the Crusaders. Yehuda Alharizi (1170–1235) notes that Saladin made a proclamation calling on the Jews to settle in Jerusalem, whereupon "three hundred rabbis" immigrated from France and England;

the Jews coming from North Africa were accompanied by North African Moslems.

Two Hebrew inscriptions were found in the As'ardiya *madrasa*, north of the Temple Mount (in the tomb of Mujir al-Din). According to Professor L.A. Mayer, these were apparently inscribed in stone by Jewish pilgrims. The inscriptions read as follows:

> *Mossi David Amran Kayuma*
> *The sons of Mossi Saliman*
> *God, the Lord of Hosts,*
> *Build this House*
> *In the Lives of Ya'akov the son of*
> *Yosef and Theopolektus*
> *And Sisina and Anastasia*
> *Amen ve'Amen Sela.*

Many Hebrew names were found this way. This inscription was found inside the Golden Gate.

> *The traveler, Rabbi Benjamin of Tudela, noted of the Western Wall*
> *that all the Jews wrote their names on the Wall.*
> *North of the Temple Mount are the remains*
> *of ancient Jewish buildings, going back to the beginning of Islam,*
> *with their Hebrew names Birket Bnei Israil,*
> *Bab al-Asbat (the tribes), Zawiyat el-Lawi.*

After the destruction of the walls by al-Malik al-Mu'athem 'Issa, the inhabitants fled to Transjordan, Syria and Egypt, fearing to live in an unfortified city. The city passed again to Christian hands in 1229, with only the area of the *Haram* (Temple Mount) remaining in the hands of the Moslems. The entire city came under Moslem rule in the days of the Ayyubids. However, when the Crusaders captured the Egyptian port of Damietta, the rulers (al-Kamil and the successors of al-Salih) were ready to concede Jerusalem in return for the port, a situation which demonstrates the difference in the degree of holiness between Mecca-Medina and Jerusalem, as far as the Moslems were concerned.

The coastal cities were Christian at the time, and most of the inland towns were Moslem. Jewish immigrants from Europe settled in the coastal cities, and the Jews were active in commerce and economic life. A large Jewish community developed in Acre, which included the Sages of Acre. Jews also settled in Jerusalem (B.Z. Dinaburg, *Yisrael Bagolah 2*, p. 175).

Jerusalem During the Mameluke Period (1250–1516)

After the battle of Mansura in 1250 Jerusalem came under Mameluke rule, from Cairo. The Mamelukes had originally served as guards to the Ayyubid sultans, then overthrew their masters and ruled in their stead. During this period the Maghrebians (Moslems from North Africa) came to settle in Jerusalem. At this time the country was invaded by Mongols, who caused much death and destruction among the inhabitants; many fled from Jerusalem, returning only after the Mongols had been defeated. There was also considerable emigration from provincial Jerusalem to Damascus and Egypt, and to Turkey in the latter half of the fifteenth century. Natural disasters, such as earthquakes, pestilence, drought, locusts and famine, led to considerable emigration, as did the tyranny of the rulers of Cairo and the minor powers of Syria, combined with the cruelties of local young emirs in the smaller cities. This resulted in anarchy, revolts on the part of the farmers, and Bedouin invasions of the land (J. de Haas, *History of Palestine, The Last Two Thousand Years*, ch. xv). Arab writers noted that the Mamelukes were aware of the tie between the people of Israel and their land, and realized the necessity for negotiations with the Jews in order to restore their country to them. Nevertheless, the Jews were ordered to wear yellow caps, Samaritans red caps and Christians blue, while Moslems wore white headgear. (L.A. Mayer, *Sefer Hazikaron 1*, L. Magnes, pp. 161–167). The local Moslems also suffered at the hands of the Mameluke rulers; a contemporary description notes that slaves fared better than the farmers. According to Professor A. Ashtor,

> *The calculated policy of the Mameluke government toward Jerusalem was in keeping with its intention of curtailing the development of large towns in Palestine, leaving the country in partial ruin. It was no coincidence or negligence that caused the sultans of Cairo to repair the mosque of El-Aqsa and the water devices, but to do no more to reconstruct the Holy City and bring it to economic prosperity.*
>
> Yerushalaim Bimei Habeinayim Hameucharim,
> *Jerusalem, Mossad Harav Kook, 1955, p. 3*

In 1490, Felix Fabri wrote of Jerusalem that the city was desolate and the buildings destroyed, without inhabitants.

A Dominican monk terms it "city of destruction and ruin." Fabri notes that there were some 1,000 Christians and over 500 Jews. Rabbi Obadiah of Bertinoro (1450–1510) wrote that Jerusalem was largely destroyed and desolate; it was not walled; there were about four thousand families, 70 of them Jewish, poor, and without means of sustenance. The general standard of living was low, and anyone possessing enough food for a year was termed rich. There were also many widows, from various countries, seven women for each man (A. Ya'ari, *Mas'ot Eretz Israel*, p. 127). He also notes that all of Transjordan, the lands of the tribes of Rueben and Gad, the Ammonites, Moabites and the hills of Edom were desolate, without a single populated city. The desert Arabs would sweep periodically through the land, up to the gates of Jerusalem, stealing everything. No one could stop their robberies, and the entire land was fallow, with no farmers working the soil (A. Ya'ari, *Iggerot Eretz Israel*, pp. 135–136).

Rabbi Meshulam of Volterra wrote (1481) that Jerusalem was not walled, except for a short stretch on one side. There were then about 10,000 Arab families and 150 Jewish families. Rabbi Moshe Basola (1522) mentioned three gates in the wall on Mount Zion, one of which was in Jewish hands (A. Ya'ari, *Mas'ot Eretz Israel*, pp. 59–60).

The population of Jerusalem was small due to the ravages of plagues and disease and as a result of the Mameluke policy of leaving the city partly ruined and decreasing its population, in order to prevent a Christian invasion. The city remained poor and unfortified, and its inhabitants were exploited and heavily taxed by the Governor.

Through the efforts of Rabbi Obadiah, who settled in Jerusalem, the lot of the Jews was improved, and immigration then began from Spain and Portugal; by 1496 the Jewish population had increased to 1,600 (*Iggerot Eretz Israel*, p. 157).

During the Mameluke period Syria and Palestine were divided into seven provinces: Aleppo, Hammat, Tripoli, Damascus, Safed, Gaza and Kerak. Jerusalem belonged to the province of Damascus, along with Lydda, Kakun, Shechem and Beth-Shean in Cisjordan, and Edrei, 'Ajlun and Balka in Transjordan. Gaza and Safed were the chief cities. Jerusalem, far from being the center of political life, became the place of exile for ministers and commanders who were dismissed or out of favor with the government.

Jerusalem did not witness any event of political importance to Islam;

it was not the capital of any Arab state, or even the capital city of the entire country. During the Moslem period, the towns of Emmaus, Ramleh, Lydda and Gaza served as provincial centers in Judea, those of Safed and Acre in Galilee, and Kerak in Moab. The shrines of Islam in the country – despite the holiness of the mosque of El-Aqsa – were of local significance, and Jerusalem did not complete with Mecca and Medina.

Jews clung to Jerusalem tenaciously, despite the difficulties of life and the inimical attitude of the inhabitants and government. Mount Zion was holy in Jewish tradition, and was taken over by the Moslems. The synagogue of David's Tomb was converted by the Christians to a chapel commemorating Jesus' Last Supper; the Moslems later established their rule over it, as they did with Rachel's Tomb, the Cave of Machpelah (the burial place of the Patriachs at Hebron), and the Tomb of Samuel. The building at David's Tomb was turned into a mosque, and both Jews and Christians were denied entry until 1948. The architect J. Pinkerfeld wrote (1949–1951) that the synagogue of David's Tomb was established in the first centuries after the destruction of the Second Temple, and the niche for the Holy Ark faced north, toward the City and the Temple Mount, as in Eshtemoa, south of Hebron. The synagogue was apparently established on the site because of the tradition that King David had brought the Ark of the Covenant there from Beth-Shemesh and Kiryat Yearim, before the Temple was built. Groups of Jews returned to settle in Jerusalem, from the time of the Bar-Kochba revolt until the Arab invasion of the city. The Traveler of Bordeaux (333 C.E.) notes that only one of the seven synagogues remained standing, the others having been ploughed under and the area cultivated. Epiphanius, who lived in Jerusalem in the second half of the fourth century C.E., mentions one synagogue. It may thus be assumed that the synagogue on Mount Zion near David's Tomb was repaired in the period of Julian the Apostate. In 1428 the Jews wished to buy the Tomb of David, whereupon the Pope and the Doge of Venice forbade Christian ship owners to transport Jews to Palestine. The conquest of Constantinople by the Ottomans, the termination of Byzantine rule, together with the expulsion from Spain, constituted a major turning point in the history of the Jewish community of Palestine and led to considerable immigration.

Jerusalem in the Ottoman Period (1516–1917)
In the middle of the fifteenth century, Rabbi Isaac Sarfati, who lived in Turkey, wrote a letter to the Jews of the Diaspora, calling on them to return to the land

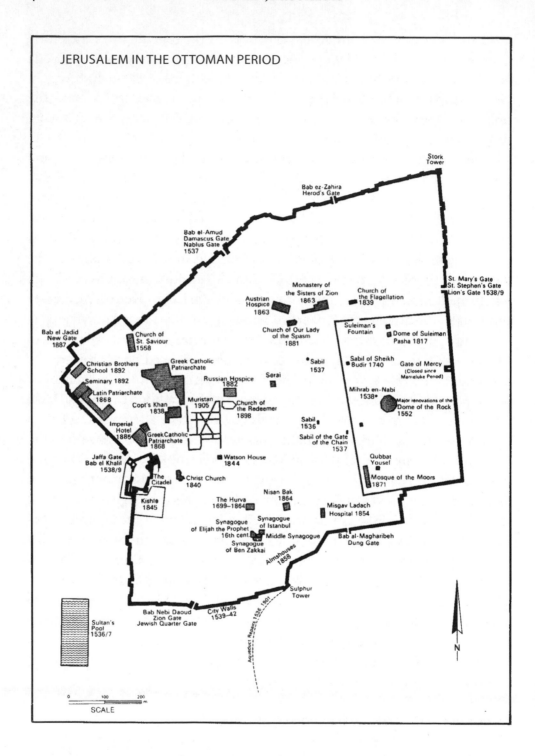

JERUSALEM IN THE OTTOMAN PERIOD

Stork Tower

Bab ez-Zahira
Herod's Gate

Bab el-Amud
Damascus Gate
Nablus Gate
1537

St. Mary's Gate
St. Stephen's Gate
Lion's Gate 1538/9

Monastery of
the Sisters of Zion
1863

Church of
the Flagellation
1839

Austrian
Hospice
1863

Church of Our Lady
of the Spasm
1881

Suleiman's
Fountain

Dome of Suleiman
Pasha 1817

Bab el Jadid
New Gate
1887

Church of
St. Saviour
1558

Sabil
1537

Sabil of Sheikh
Budir 1740

Gate of Mercy
(Closed since
Mameluke Period)

Christian Brothers
School 1892

Greek Catholic
Patriarchate

Russian Hospice
1882

Serai

Mihrab en-Nabi
1538

Major renovations of the
Dome of the Rock
1552

Seminary 1892

Latin Patriarchate
1868

Copt's Khan
1838

Muristan
1905

Church of
the Redeemer
1898

Sabil
1536

Imperial
Hotel
1885

Greek Catholic
Patriarchate
1868

Sabil of the Gate
of the Chain
1537

Qubbat
Yousef

Jaffa Gate
Bab el Khalil
1538/9

The
Citadel

Watson House
1844

Mosque of the Moors
1871

Kishle
1845

Christ Church
1840

Nisan Bak
1864

The Hurva
1699–1864

Misgav Ladach
Hospital 1854

Synagogue
of Elijah the Prophet
16th cent.

Synagogue
of Istanbul

Middle Synagogue

Bab al-Magharibeh
Dung Gate

Synagogue
of Ben Zakkai

Almshouses
1858

Sulphur
Tower

Sultan's
Pool
1536/7

Bab Nebi Daoud
Zion Gate
Jewish Quarter Gate

City Walls
1539–42

Aqueduct Repairs 1536, 1901

N

0   100   200
                m
SCALE

of their forefathers and to renew the religious ritual on the Temple Mount, because the Turks were fulfilling the prophecies of redemption (S. Rosanes, *Divrei Yemei Yisrael be-Togarmah* 1, p. 16). Don Isaac Abarbanel, writing in 1500, also dealt with the messianic movements, prophesying that not only would all the Jews leave their countries of exile and return to the Land of Israel, but all those who were forced to renounce their religion (by the Spanish Inquisition) would also be gathered together on holy soil. Hopes that the Messiah was at hand were also expressed by Rabbi Isaac ha-Cohen Sholal of Jerusalem (1521), writing after the Spanish Jews had emigrated to Palestine; he tells of a weekly fast day, with two shifts of fasting each week. The unseasonal rainstorm accompanied by violent winds, which occurred on the eleventh day of the Omer in Jerusalem, was taken as a sign of the approaching redemption (I. Ben-Zvi, *Eretz-Yisrael ve-Yishuvah Bimei Hashilton Haotomani*, Jerusalem 1955). Turkish rule lasted 400 years, from 1516 to 1917, with one interval of rule from Egypt by Mohammed Ali, (1831–1840). As in the early Moslem period, the country was not given autonomy, but the Turkish period saw Palestine enter into world trade and transport.

At the end of the Mameluke period, Jews were settled mainly in Jerusalem and Safed. In the coastal plain, Gaza was the center of Jewish settlement. There were smaller communities in Shechem and Hebron, and in a few villages.

During the Ottoman period, Jerusalem was a remote town but cosmopolitan in nature, due to the influence of Christian pilgrims and the Jewish inhabitants, who spoke many different languages. The Turkish Sultan Bayazid II encouraged Jewish settlement at the end of the fifteenth century; Spanish Jews settled in Salonica, Constantinople, Adrianople and other Turkish cities. The Judaeo-Spanish community developed during his rule, especially in Tiberias, Safed and Jerusalem, and the country again became the spiritual center of Judaism. The Ottoman sultan was Selim I, the son of Bayazid, who crowned himself "Ruler of Jerusalem" in 1517 and imposed a personal tax on non-Moslems. During the reign of his son, Suleiman (1520–1566), the Ottoman Empire attained its greatest power and reach. Suleiman repaired and rebuilt the walls and gates of Jerusalem (1537), reconstructed David's Tower and ensured the reliable supply of water to the city. In his time the country enjoyed peace and security. Both Selim and Suleiman were served by Jewish court physicians. The arrival of refugees from Spain increased the Jewish population of the country, and they were the dominant factor in the Jewish community during the next 400 years. There were four Jewish communities in Jerusalem: the Ashkenazim, living there since the time of the Ramban, and those driven out of Spain; Sephardi refugees from Spain; Maghrebis from North Africa; and Musta'arabs (Moriscos), local inhabitants; who had not come from the Diaspora. About 2,000 Jews lived in Jerusalem in the sixteenth and seventeenth century, composed of Sephardim, Maghrebis and Spanish refugees, as well as Ashkenazi immigrants from Europe, and Karaites. Their chief occupation was study of the *Torah*, and they subsisted on donations from the Jews in the Diaspora.

However the Jewish community of Jerusalem began to diminish as a result of the heavy taxation and the confiscation of property; eventually only the poorest were left in the city. The Ottomans set the Jews a personal tax, a guard tax, a monthly tax, imposed on them gifts for holidays, a tax for government aid, and a land tax. An 1806 document tells of the suffering in Jerusalem, likening the inhabitants to doves in pain. Usury and interest led to a debt of 250,000 aries (the income of the entire Jewish community was 200,000 aries), besides the debts to Jews. The strife between local rulers increased bloodshed, and each day was worse than the one before.

In view of the situation, the Jews of Jerusalem united and created four funds, using the donations received from abroad: a fund for scholars; a fund for the poor; a sick fund; and a fund for orphaned girls.

After the massacre of Jews by Cossacks in Russia in 1648–1656, Jews began to arrive from Poland and Russia. In 1700 Rabbi Judah he-Hassid led a group of 1,500 to Jerusalem. Some 500 of them were lost en route, and the remainder came to the Holy City in order to hasten the Redemption. Rabbi Judah bought a plot of land in Jerusalem; in the Ramban's time it had probably been the site of a synagogue, which was later destroyed by the Arabs, and thus know as the *Hurvah* (ruin). After the death of Rabbi Judah, a synagogue was built on the spot and was called the *Hurvah* of Rabbi Judah he-Hassid. Arabs burnt down the synagogue with its forty scrolls in 1721, and the Ashkenazim used the Ben-Zakkai Synagogue for their prayers. The *Hurvah* was rebuilt in 1837. According to A.M. Luncz (*Yerushalaim*, 5; p. 190) "the Sephardi Jews of Jerusalem were divided into three groups: scholars and students who lived on charity from abroad; craftsmen and laborers, largely natives of the country, who lived on their earnings; and the rich, who came to spend the remainder of their days in the Holy City and be buried in its soil."

Rabbi Gedaliah of Siemiatycze wrote in his book *Sha'alu Shelom Yerush-alaim* of the great difficulties of the Jerusalem community, and of their oppression by the Ishmaelites.

The mystics studying the *Kabbala* in the Beth-El synagogue founded communes in the middle of the eighteenth century, swearing to live together as brothers, with communal property, to strengthen the love of God and the *Torah* (E. Tcherikower, *Di Komune fun Yerushalaimer Mekubalim, Yivo Historische Schriften* 2, p. 155). In 1777 the Hassid, Rabbi Menachem Mendel of Vitebsk, came with 300 followers from the Ukraine, Lithuania and Romania to Safed and Tiberias, and later went on to Jerusalem. In 1799 Napoleon called upon the Jews of Africa and Asia to rally to him, in order to re-establish ancient Jerusalem. The Turks thereupon began to fear a connection between the Jews of Jerusalem and Napoleon. Up to the nineteenth century, Arabs robbed the Jews of Jerusalem of their money till robbery became a tradition, just as they stole the places holy to Judaism and turned them into places holy to Islam. Still the Jews clung to the city, and it was written of them that they lived a life of poverty and misery, but with an overwhelming desire to rebuild Jerusalem. (*Sefer Meah Shanah*, quoted by M. Salomon in *Sheloshah Dorot beYishuv*, Jerusalem, 1939).

Montefiore's visits to the country, in the first half of the nineteenth century led to an improvement in the lives of Jerusalem's Jews and to an expansion of the area where they lived. The first Hebrew press in Jerusalem was established by Israel Bak in 1842, with the aid of Montefiore; it produced prayer books, Kabbalist works and books praising Jerusalem. Montefiore also set up a weaving shop and a windmill, west of the city. The quarters of Mishkenot Sha'ananim (1856–1860), Nahalat Shivah (1869), Meah Shearim (1873) and Mishkenot Yisrael (1875) were established, and educational institutes were founded and developed both by the local community and on the initiative of Jews abroad: the Laemmel School (1856), the Alliance Israelite School and the Mikveh Yisrael Agricultural School (1857). Hospitals were founded: the Rothschild (1854), Bikkur Holim (1857), Misgav Ladakh (1879). The first Hebrew paper in Jerusalem, *Ha-Levanon*, appeared once a month in 1863 (for one year only); *Havatzelet*, monthly in 1865; *Ha-Ariel* in 1874; and *Yehuda Viyerushalaim* in 1877, biweekly. At the end of the century, there were sixty Jewish quarters in Jerusalem. Jews arrived from Mesopotamia, Yemen, Persia, Bukhara, Kurdistan, Georgia, Daghestan, Aleppo, Damascus and Egypt, as well as from eastern Europe, England and the United States.

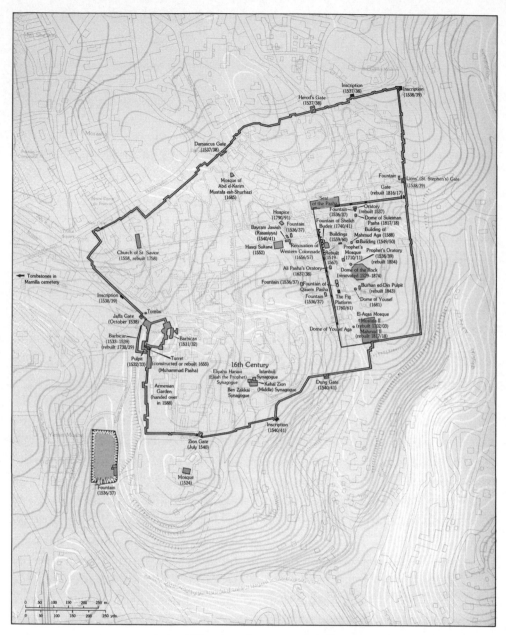

The Old City and its environs today

During the nineteenth century the country's significance increased considerably in the eyes of the world, and other nations demanded their rights at the holy places. The Jewish community of Jerusalem began to restore the ruined synagogues; the population increased until living quarters outside the city walls became necessary. The organization *Hevrat Yishuv Eretz Yisrael* (Society for the Settlement of the Land of Israel) was founded in Germany and Turkey. In 1863 Rabbi Yehudah Alkalai of Belgrade published a detailed plan for a return to Zion, dealing with the road to redemption, a national organization, political efforts, settling the land, financial problems and cultural matters (stressing the Hebrew language), the political regime of the country and even its defense. These ideas undoubtedly influenced Herzl in his work *Der Judenstaat* (B. Dinaburg, *Sefer Hashanah Shel Eretz Yisrael*, pp. 471–479).

Yitzhak Ben-Zvi wrote that "although there were periods of destruction and ruin, as in Safed, the Jewish population of Jerusalem overcame the difficulties; Jewish settlement never ceased in the city, even for short periods (as in Tiberias) or for several years (as in Safed)." (*Eretz Yisrael ve-Yishuvah*, p. 206).

In no other city in the country did the Jews maintain a community for two thousand years, after the destruction of the Second Temple, in the face of religious and economic persecution, with the fear of death and the overthrow and destruction of the city hanging over them. None of the chief rulers during the Moslem period were Arabs: the Seljuks, who ruled after the Fatimids, were Turks; Saladin, who captured the country, including Jerusalem, from the Crusaders, was a Kurd, and until recently his nation was subjugated by Iraqi rulers; the Mamelukes were also Turks, as were the Ottomans, who ruled the land for 400 years. None of these rulers had any historical connection with the land, and it was not the center of government. The ethnic composition of the country's inhabitants during the Turkish period may be learned from the names of the various quarters in cities: in Jerusalem, the North-African Maghrebi quarter; in Hebron and Safed, the Kurdish quarters; in Gaza, the Kurdish and Turkmen quarters; and in Ramleh, Egyptian and Turkmen quarters. Thus, a considerable part of the country's inhabitants were not Arabs. It should also be noted that Palestinian Arabs never ruled the country; it was always ruled by foreign Moslems, throughout the Moslem period and after. During the Ottoman period the Turkish rulers treated the Arabs of Jerusalem, who were Moslems and Christians, cruelly. After the War of Independence in 1948, the ruler of eastern Jerusalem was an Arabian Bedouin, who reigned over Transjordan. On the other hand, Jews had never left the country, least of all Jerusalem, permanently; they regarded themselves as the rightful redeemers of a land that had been taken from them by force. Under foreign rule Jerusalem was never a great city, but was even more reduced; only under Jewish rule did it grow both in area and in population, Jewish and non-Jewish together.

The Population and Area of Jerusalem Through the Ages

And the eternity – this refers to Jerusalem.

Berakoth 58

The Jerusalem that Melchizedek ruled in the time of the Patriarchs, and the city of the Amorites in Joshua's time, was the capital of the southern province of the Judean Mountains and the Shephelah. Jebusite Jerusalem had an area of forty dunams (ten acres); during Solomon's time, when the city was the capital of Eretz Yisrael, and during the rule of the Judean kings, the area of the Upper and Lower Cities amounted to 650 dunams.

The size of the city decreased during the Persian period and increased again under Hasmonean rule. It was greatest at the end of the Second Temple period, reaching about 1,800 dunam (almost two square kilometers), with a population of 100,000. This was also the period of greatest development of the water supply and of the agriculture practiced in the vicinity. After the death of Herod, during the rule of the Roman procurators and up to the time of the revolt, Caesarea became the capital, and residence of the rulers. Following Hadrian, the area of Jerusalem shrank to 850 dunams. There were 1,300,000 Jews in the country before the destruction of Betar, and only 700,000–800,000 afterward, about one-quarter of the country's total population. Half of the Jewish population was in Galilee.

During the Christian-Byzantine period, Caesarea was the capital of the country, despite the sacred nature of Jerusalem, whose population numbered only 80,000. At the end of the Byzantine period, there were 150,000–200,000 Jews in the country, constituting 10–15% of the general population (according to Professor Avi-Yonah).

Jerusalem declined so much in importance after the Arab conquest that Emmaus was first designated as the capital. Later, after an occurrence of plague, a new Moslem capital was built at Ramleh. During the Fatimid period in the eleventh century, when Jerusalem reached its peak under Moslem rule, there were 30,000 people living there; its walls were four km long, and its area no more than one sq. km; i.e., less than half the area of the Second Temple period.

There were 30,000 Jews and Arabs at the time of the Crusader conquest. The population fell to 3,000 after the conquest; this number included the Christian Syrians and the Christian Bedouin brought to Jerusalem by Baldwin, encouraged by the fact that the Crusader authorities levied no taxes on Christians, in order to induce them to settle in the Holy City. At its peak, Crusader Jerusalem numbered 30,000 (the Crusader population in the Land of Israel was 100,000). Although Jerusalem was sacred to the Crusaders (Moslems and Jews were forbidden to settle there), their political and economic center was Acre. The Crusaders fortified themselves along the coasts of Syria and Palestine at Antioch, Tyre, Acre, etc., mainly because of the proximity of these ports to Europe; the Moslems, on the same principle, maintained the capitals of their states far inland in places such as Cairo, Damascus and Aleppo, at a secure distance from the sea and its enemy peoples. Crusader Jerusalem had an area similar to that of Hadrian's Aelia Capitolina. The fertile land was laid waste during the Mameluke period, as a result of robberies, looting and systematic exploitation (according to Professor Heyd, *Yerushalaim Bimei Hamamelukim ve-Haturkim, Yerushalaim-le-Doroteha*, Israel Exploration Society (IES), Jerusalem 1969).

According to Professor Ashtor, there were no more than 10,000 inhabitants in late fifteenth-century Jerusalem (*Yerushalaim Bimei Habienyaim Hameucharim*, Jerusalem, Mossad Harav Kook, 1955, p. 3). From the end of the Mameluke period and throughout the Ottoman period, till the eighteenth century, the population of the city ranged between 10,000 and 15,000; it exceeded 70,000 only on the eve of World War I.

According to the censuses made by the Turks in 1525–1573, and quoted by Yitzhak Ben Zvi in his book (*Eretz Israel ve-Yishuvah Bimei haShilton haOtomani*, p. 35), there were very few villages in the province of Jerusalem – 168, compared with 210 in Gaza and 275 in Safed. The population of the country was about 300,000, of whom roughly 270,000 were Moslems, 15,000 Christians and 18,000 Jews. In 1741 there were 10,000 Jews in Jerusalem. This increase in population led to harsh edicts against the Jews, and in 1770 they numbered only 5,000. In 1782 the Jews were forbidden to bury their dead in the cemetery on the Mount of Olives, and large sums of money were required to abolish this ruling.

Selim, the Ottoman sultan, conquered the country in 1516, and Turkish rule lasted for 400 years. There was no development of the country during this period. No roads were laid or new settlements built, although there were no wars with foreign powers or invasions until Napoleon's campaign in 1799. At the end of the nineteenth century the population of the country was

200,000 and population density was the lowest since the Canaanite period. The desolation was such that Napoleon was not even concerned about first taking Jerusalem.

The increase of the Jewish population in Jerusalem may be assessed on the basis of the censures taken. Montefiore counted about 3,000 Jews in 1839. Moore, the British Consul, counted 8,000 Jews in a general population of 15,000 in 1864, i.e., over 53%. In 1874 the Jews numbered 10,500 out of a population of 20,500. According to Luncz, in 1876 there were 14,000 Jews, in a general population of 20,500, i.e., 68%. In 1895 there were 28,000 Jews; and in 1905, 50,000 Jews out of 75,000. In 1912 Jews numbered 45,000 out of a general population of 70,000. The city's area was then 12,720 dunams (12.72 sq km) and 95% of the population lived in the new city.

The number of Jews engaged in commerce and crafts increased from 1839 on. In 1830, 80 Sephardim and 7 Ashkenazim were merchants; in 1872 the number had risen to 241 Sephardim and 251 Ashkenazim. Crafts and other occupations provided the livelihood for 299 Sephardim and 251 Ashkenazim in 1839, while the respective numbers had risen to 390 and 579 by 1872. Religious observances were kept by 545 Jews. These facts are evidence of the partial emergence of Jerusalem's Jews from dependence on charity and the donations of the rich.

The Jews of Jerusalem underwent periods of development alternating with humiliation, all in keeping with the political situation in Turkey and its international status. An improvement in the Ottoman regime led to similar developments in the Jewish community, and a deterioration of the government resulted in rioting against the Jews and a decrease in the Jewish population.

Jewish quarters began to be established outside the city walls in 1860, as well as Christian quarters. Jerusalem was connected with the telegraph system, and a paved carriage road led to Jerusalem from Jaffa and other towns. The first railway line in the country was laid in 1892, from Jaffa to Jerusalem; this was one of the first railways in the Middle East.

Toward the end of Turkish rule in the country, in the late nineteenth century, Jerusalem had a general population of 25,000. Zionist-impelled immigration increased the population to 75,000, two-thirds being Jewish. Since 1864, Jews have constituted the predominant element in Jerusalem. Since then the Arab population has also increased, not only in Jerusalem, but in villages that had lain waste in the mountains of Judea and Jerusalem and in the rest of the country, including Transjordan.

At the end of the nineteenth century Jerusalem had 25,000 inhabitants, 60% of the entire Jewish community of the country. At the end of World War I the Jews of Jerusalem numbered 21,500; in 1922 – 34,000; in 1931 – 53,800; in 1939 – 80,800. Between 1922 and 1936 the Jewish community tripled in Jerusalem, compared with a seven-fold increase in the entire country, an eleven-fold increase in Tel Aviv and a thirteen-fold increase in Haifa. The Jewish community of Jerusalem then constituted only 17% of the community in the country, as compared with 41% previously.'

The Jewish Population of the Country According to the Historic Memoranda of the Va'ad Leumi, 1947

Settlement	1830–40	1850	1870–80	1890	1914
Jerusalem	4,000	10,000	14,000	24,000	55,000
Safed	1,200	2,100	—	7,150	12,500–13,000
Jaffa	30	400	1,200	3,000	12,000
Tiberias	650	1,514	2,047	3,200	7,000
Hebron	500	400	600	1,420	1,000
Haifa	150–200	100	175	1,000–1,400	3,500
Sidon	300	300	500	780	800
Gaza	—	—	150	75	175
Acre	100	120	140	130	50
Shechem	150–200	40	120	31	—
Beth-Shean	—	—	—	13	80–100
Ramleh	—	—	—	100–166	20
Beersheba	—	—	—	—	130–150
Lydda	—	—	—	14	10–15
Peki'in	100	50	100	96	90
Shfar 'Am	60	60	30	45	15
Total	**7,240**	**15,084**	**19,062**	**44,054**	**92,375**
Jewish Population of Jerusalem as a percentage of total Jewish population of the Country	55.2%	66.3%	73.4%	60.1%	59.5%

In 1948, toward the close of the British Mandate, the population of Jerusalem stood at 165,000: 100,000 Jews, and 65,000 Arabs and others, 33,000 of them in the Old City. The Jewish city had an area of 25.76 sq. km, double its area at the beginning of the twentieth century. The area of the Arab city was then 2.6 sq. km, with the Old City constituting one-third of it. Twenty years later, in 1968, the population of Jewish (Western) Jerusalem had doubled, and reached about 200,000, similar to that at the end of the Second Temple period, while eastern (Arab) Jerusalem retained the same population as twenty years previously – 65,000, with 24,000 of these in the Old City; at the same time the populations of Shechem and Hebron, cities with no religious significance for the Moslems, were almost doubled.

The area of united Jerusalem after the Six Day War was 104 sq. km., and its population was the largest of any city in the country.

Development of Jewish Settlement in Jerusalem In the 19th and 20th Centuries

Year	Jews	Moslems	Christians	Total Population	Percent Jews
1844	7,120	5,000	3,390	15,510	45.9
1876	12,000	7,560	5,470	25,030	47.9
1896	28,112	8,560	8,748	45,420	61.9
1905	40,000	7,000	13,000	60,000	66.6
1913	48,400	10,050	16,750	75,200	64.3
1922	33,971	13,413	14,699	62,578	54.3
1931	51,222	19,894	19,335	90,503	56.6
1948	100,000	40,000	25,000	165,000	60.6
1967	195,700	54,963	12,646	263,309	74.3
1975	259,000	—	—	365,000	72.2
1978	272,300	103,700	—	376,000	72.4
1985	327,700	115,700	14,300	457,700	71.5
1993	406,400	140,500	14,900	567,100	71.4
1995	417,000	158,000	15,800	591,400	71.0
1999	436,700	189,700	14,100	646,300	67.6

CHAPTER II

JERUSALEM DURING THE SECOND TEMPLE PERIOD

A Visit to the Second Temple Model at the Holyland Hotel, Jerusalem

The Old City of Jerusalem is best visited after one has become familiar with the structure of the city and the functions of its walls and ancient buildings through a visit to the model at the Holyland Hotel. The plan of Second Temple Jerusalem was created with great precision by Professor M. Avi-Yonah, the archaeologist, and the architectural plan was made by his wife, Mrs. H. Avi-Yonah. The model was magnificently and painstakingly built by the artist, Mr. R. Brotzen, on a scale of 1:50. Each centimeter on the model represents 0.5 m in the actual city.

The structures in the model city all date from the Second Temple period, just before the destruction of the city in 70 C.E., as also the "Third Wall" built in 41–44 C.E. is represented. They were constructed from the materials used at that time, scaled to actual size. Few models of this type in the world are as useful.

A visit to the Second Temple model is thus the preliminary, preparatory stage for a visit to the Old City, and a prerequisite for a full understanding and appreciation of its sights.

Let us now combine our view of the model with a knowledge of historical events in Jerusalem at the time. The model should be viewed twice: once to look at the topographic layout of the city and the functions of its walls, citadels, towers and palaces (and to compare them with the present), and a

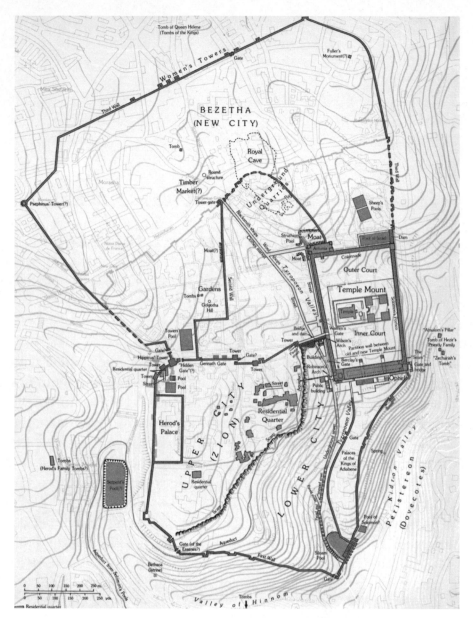

Jerusalem during the Second Temple period

second time to study the defensive positions of the besieged rebels and the phases of the Roman attacks, leading to an appreciation of the heroism of the zealots fighting to liberate their city and free their Temple.

We shall also learn something of everyday life in Jerusalem at the time, projects in time of peace and customs and feelings of the people during war.

From the following sources:
Ezra and Nehemiah; the *Letter of Aristeas* (third century B.C.E.); Hecateus of Abdera (the period of Alexander the Great); *Book of Hasmoneans*; *Mishnah*, Tractate *Middot* and its parallels, *Yoma, Tammid* and *Shekalim*; Simeon ben-Sira of Jerusalem (end of second century B.C.E.); Flavius Josephus' *Antiquities of the Jews* and *Wars of the Jews* (Josephus was a priest at the Temple, and his work provided the basis of the scientific work); the *New Testament*; Roman writers; ancient maps; archaeological excavations in Jerusalem.

Topography of the City and its Environs

Jerusalem is surrounded by mountains and its topography is typically mountainous. The ancient city was built on two spurs: the hill bearing the Lower City in the east, 747 m above sea level, in which the first settlement of Jerusalem as well as the site of the Temple were established and in the west, the hill of the Upper City, which became inhabited in the course of the city's expansion. This later hill is unjustifiedly known today as Mount Zion, and is 777 m high. A deep vale separated the two hills, and was know as the Cheesemongers' Valley (*Tyropoeon*, in Josephus); it served to drain the rainwater and sewage of ancient Jerusalem into the Kidron Valley.

The two hills are surrounded on three sides by deep valleys, which barred the route of attacking armies: on the south and west the Valley of Ben-Hinnom, and on the east the Kidron Valley, which includes the Gihon spring and Ein Rogel. The Ben Hinnom Valley debauches into the Kidron Valley at the southeastern corner of the city, and eventually a canyon is formed leading to the Dead Sea.

The internal topography of the city (but not the external) is precisely represented in the model, and the model is direction-orientated.

The following mountains and hills surround Jerusalem: on the east the Mount of Olives (830 m). It was planted with olive groves, which produced the oil for anointing the kings of Judah; it is also called the Mount of Anointing in the *Mishnah*. Southeast of the Mount of Olives lies the isolated Mount of Scandal (or Offense), which is the same height (740 m) as the Temple Mount. King Solomon erected places of worship on the mountain for his foreign wives, and the Bible calls it the Mount of Offence. In the south lies the spur of Abu Tor, which includes the Hill of Ananias (the High Priest at the Temple, mentioned by Josephus), 760 m high. The hill with the present YMCA building is in the west (780 m), and at its foot to the east is the grotto containing tombs believed to be of the House of Herod. The present Russian Compound is at the top of a hill to the northwest, 800 m high.

The deep Kidron and Ben-Hinnom (= Hennom) valleys constituted a natural line of defense for the city; their breadth made it impossible for enemies to approach and fire missiles; the Romans therefore used engines to hurl stones from a distance. The depth of the valleys prohibited the building of ramparts for the approach of the ramming devices; Titus laid ramparts only in the northwest and north, where there were no valleys. Due to the great height of the foundations of the walls above the valley floors, enemies were unable to tunnel under them. The Romans therefore built towers and suspended ladders and bridges to the tops of the walls in order to get into the city.

In ancient times, Jewish Jerusalem was thus protected by only one wall on the east, south and west; on the north, where there are no natural deep valleys, three successive walls were erected, as revealed by archaeological excavations since 1867. The city thus first expanded westward from the Lower City to the Upper City, which was protected and fortified; only later did it spread north and northwestward, where the slope is more gradual and there is no natural protection. The sages said of this area that it was the weak point of the city and made possible its conquest.

The Nucleus of the City and the Site of the Temple

What were the reasons that led David and Solomon to locate their capital city and Temple in the Lower City rather than on the higher hill later known as the Upper City?

Settlers of antiquity always looked for sites affording the greatest natural protection and power; the Lower City is situated in an eminently suitable spot. However, the paramount problem of any city in the semi-arid regions of antiquity was that of water, rather than protection (which could be augmented by artificial structures in case of need) or food (which could be stored for long periods of siege or war). Proximity to the Gihon spring, which is the richest of all the springs along the ridge of the Judean Mountains (with an average flow of 50 cu m per hour), determined the site of the city.

The Walls, Towers and Palace Built by King Herod

Why did Herod erect his palace in the northwestern corner of the Upper City and the three prominent, magnificent towers in its close vicinity?

Herod's palace was built at the highest spot of both cities, at 777 m. The site also happened to be the weak point in the defenses of the city. There were no deep valleys north of the palace, and Herod therefore built the three towers very close to it: Phasael, named after his brother; Hippicus, after his close friend; and Mariamne, named for his Hasmonean wife. All three of the northern walls of Jerusalem converged at the tower of Hippicus (the only one remaining today), the weakest point of the city.

The First Wall

The wall begins at the Hippicus Tower and was constructed by Herod along the route of an older wall, probably dating to the rule of the kings of Judah and the Hasmoneans; excavations at the Citadel revealed sherds from the late period of Judah. The wall turned east, towards the Hasmonean palace and the Chamber of Hewn Stone, seat of the Sanhedrin, to the Temple Mount, along the bridge known as Wilson's Bridge. The ashlars dating from Herod's time are large and dressed with double margins; the external margin is wide and the internal margin narrow, with a smooth boss in the center of the stone. Stones from the Hasmonean period have broad margins and a very prominent, rough boss. The wall had sixty towers, 50–100 m apart, and was 3,800 m long.

The Second Wall

This wall, built by Herod, began at the Hippicus Tower and turned by the Pool of Amygdalon northeast to the Antonia fortress, northwest of the Temple Mount, finally reaching the pool now known by the Arabic name Bani (= sons of) Israil, nearby. Remnants of this wall were probably revealed at the foundations of the present-day Damascus Gate. The wall was relatively short – 1,100 m – and included fourteen towers. This wall was also protected by three deep pools: the Pool of Amygdalon near the Jaffa Gate, Lacus Legerii, the date of which is not clear, near the Damascus Gate, and the Bani Israil near the Lions' Gate.

The Third Wall

The city grew too small for its inhabitants during the reign of King Herod, and Jerusalem spread northward, towards Bezetha, beyond the Second Wall. Agrippa I fortified the Third Wall between the years 41 and 44 C.E., raising it to a height of 12.5 m, but was unable to complete the work. The wall was ultimately finished during the Revolt, in 66 C.E. The Third Wall began at the Hippicus Tower and turned north to the octagonal Psephinus Tower. It then ran eastwards by the Women's Tower to the tomb of Queen Helena of Adiabene (dubbed nowadays Tombs of the Kings) beyond the city wall, reaching the Kidron Valley and the Temple Mount. The foundations of this wall consisted of small stones, mortar and quarry stones to a height of 80 cm, surmounted by large ashlars with an average size of 1.20 × 1.00 × 2.00 m, dressed in the manner typical of the Herodian period. The largest stone is 5.10 × 1.15 m. The few towers found along the route of the third wall project 8 m from the wall, and their width reaches 12 m. The Third Wall had ninety towers, 10 m high and 10 m wide, including stairs connecting the wall with the rooms, and water cisterns. The wall was 2,900 m long. In 1878 Schick, the archaeologist, discovered remnants of a wall 45 m long, in the northwestern corner (near the present-day Notre Dame building). In 1838 Robinson discovered part of the wall of the Psephinus Tower in the Russian Compound. Remnants of a wall were discovered in 1903 near the Italian Hospital, in the slope of the Street of the Prophets. The archaeologists Sukenik and Mayer uncovered another 500 m long section of the third wall in the years 1925–1927, in the vicinity of the Mandelbaum Gate. A further section, 65 m long, was later found leading to the Kidron Valley. The average width of this section was 4.0–4.5 m.

The general length of the outer wall of Jerusalem was 5,550 m. According to Josephus, the circumference of Jerusalem during the rule of Herod Agrippa was 33 stadia, i.e., 6,270 m (*Wars* v, 4;3) and its population was 120,000 (*Against Apion*, 122).

According to Josephus, the towers were among the most magnificent and best fortified in the world; they were built close to Herod's palace, for its protection.

Phasael Tower

Phasael, Herod's brother, was originally designated by his father Antipater as governor of Jerusalem and its vicinity. He was arrested when the Parthians came from Mesopotamia to aid Antigonus the Hasmonean against Antipater's family, and was exiled to Galilee, where he took his own life. The tower that Herod erected in his memory was the highest building in the city. Its base was 20 × 20 m, and its foundations rose to a height of 20 m. A large hall, 5 m high, was built over the entire area of the tower, covered by breastworks. Over this hall there was another tower, divided into magnificent rooms and a place for bathing. The overall height of the tower was 45 m, and in appearance it resembled the Tower of Pharos, near the port of Alexandria. No remnants of this tower have been discovered.

Hippicus Tower

This tower was named after a close friend of King Herod's. It too was square, each side being 12.5 m long, and its height 40 m. Beneath the tower was a reservoir, 10 m deep. Over this was a two-story building with many rooms, surmounted by two turrets. The foundations of this tower are still visible in the Old City, in the Citadel (David's Tower).

Mariamne Tower

This delicatelooking, magnificent tower was named after the Hasmonean wife of the king and was built of white marble. Its dimensions were 10 × 10 m, and its height was 25 m. It, too, has not yet been found.

Pool of Amygdalon

This pool, sometimes erroneously called the Pool of Hezekiah, was excavated on a high-lying site and was fed by a conduit leading from the present-day Mamillah Pool, which was supplied by rainwater flooding the head of the Ben-Hinnom Valley. The surplus waters of the Mamillah Pool flowed to the Pool of Amygdalon and the reservoirs of Herod's palace, and served to decorate the palace and its grounds by means of a series of fountains and pools, as well as being used for domestic purposes. Today the pool lies in a space among the buildings northeast of the Jaffa Gate. Its original name was the Pool of the Towers because of its vicinity to the above-mentioned towers. The name Amygdalon is Josephus Flavius' misnomer.

Herod's Palace

Herod built two large edifices described by Josephus as rivaling the Temple in magnificence. He named them after his ruler-friends: Caesarion, after Augustus Caesar, and Agrippeon, after the commander Agrippa, son-in-law of Augustus.

The palace was encircled by a wall, 15 m high, bearing many towers, which were accessible by staircases. The numerous rooms of the palace contained

Herod's palace and the Temple Mount

gold and silver plates, and were surrounded by colonnades. The floors were of precious stones, imported from many lands. Here Herod received honored guests. The foundations of the palace and the surrounding buildings were honeycombed with water cisterns and reservoirs, which were probably supplied from the Pool of Amygdalon; the same water source served the fountains, which were made of copper. The pools were surrounded by dovecotes, possibly housing carrier-pigeons for communication with Herod's forts. This palace was apparently also the home of the later Hasmonean kings, as well as of the Roman procurators after Herod. The foundations of the palace have recently been revealed. The area is today occupied by the police barracks near the Citadel, and the Armenian Seminar. All the major institutions of the city were built near the palace, in the Upper City.

Upper Market

The chief market of the city was located near Herod's palace, and the commercial buildings of the Upper City were also known as the Upper Market, due to the importance of the market and the functions of its buildings.

Hananiah's (Ananias') Palace

The palace of the High Priest, Hananiah, was built northeast of the Upper Market; during Hasmonean times this was close to the Chamber of Hewn Stone. Hananiah was High Priest at the time of the Roman revolt.

Chamber of Hewn Stone

The chamber was built of hewn stones (ashlars) and served for public meetings. Opposite was the *Sanhedrin* building, containing the Court of the *Sanhedrin*. Here, northwest of the Western Wall Praying Plaza, was the great court of *Beth-Ya'azek*, where the witnesses gathered to announce the New Moon. The *Sanhedrin* also served as the local council of Jerusalem as well as the national *Sanhedrin*, the judicial and legislative institute and a place of study. The *Sanhedrin* concerned itself, *inter alia*, with the proclamation of the New Moon, and intercalation to fix the calendar and festivals. Sages from the entire country and from the Diaspora came to the Chamber of Hewn Stone in Jerusalem for judicial proceedings and decisions of Jewish law.

The First Wall passed near the Chamber of Hewn Stone, starting from the Hippicus Tower, crossing the Cheesemongers' Valley, and ending near the bridge known today as Wilson's Bridge leading up to the Temple Mount. The Temple Archive was near the Chamber of Hewn Stone.

The Theater

Every Hellenist or Roman city boasted its theater. The Jerusalem theater was in the Upper City, southwest of the Upper Market; the slope from the Upper City to the valley was suitable for the purpose. The theater was divided into three parts: benches for the spectators in the upper part, the orchestra, a flat space below the benches where the dancing chorus performed, and the stage at the front of the theater, which was a wall two or three stories high, with niches for the statues of the rulers, and doors at its foot for the entry and exit of the actors. It was never found by archeologists and its place is unknown.

Palace of Caiaphas

Joseph Caiaphas, the High Priest during the rule of Pontius Pilate, at the end of the Second Temple period, lived in this palace, located south of Herod's palace. The palace is now identified south of the Zion Gate, near the Church of the Dormition, at the church named "Petrus in Gallicantu."

Launderers' Quarter

Yarn and fabric made of wool produced by the abundant sheep and goats raised in the Judean Desert were laundered in this area. Troughs and basins for washing are visible, and posts for hanging the washing out to dry.

"David's Tomb"

The builders of the model have included the traditional "Tomb of David," east of the palace of Caiaphas, for orientation. The historical tomb of David is in the Lower City.

Cheesemongers' Valley and the Industrial Quarter

On the way from the Upper City to the Lower, we come across one of the central arteries of the city, the Cheesemongers' Valley (Tyropoeon). The head of the valley was known as the *Mishneh* (second) and the lower part as *Makhtesh* (deep valley) (see *Zephania* 1:10). In the Bible the Cheesemongers' Valley is called simply The Valley, since it was the central, most important valley in the city. Its central location between the Upper and Lower Cities was ideal for commerce and for defensive purposes, since it separated the two parts and constituted the lowest point in the entire city. The Valley also served for the collection of water, draining most of the rainwater of the city. The low-lying situation of the Valley and the scant security it offered, and the fact that it was in the path of the northwestern winds, which carried foul odors, turned it into a low-class neighborhood. The poor, as well as industrial workers, lived in crowded hovels, with flat or domed roofs, with cisterns in their yards. The Valley was an industrial center since floodwaters were collected in five pools along it: the Pool of the Launderers' Field, the Upper Pool, the Lower Pool, the Pool of Hezekiah, and the Pool of Siloam; these supplied ample water for industrial purposes. In the model the long buildings of the industrial quarter lie along the bottom of the Valley and on both its sides.

The following industries were developed in the Valley: pottery-making (the Clay Gate, in Hebrew *harsit*, mentioned in the Bible, was nearby); wool manufacture (this was the site of the biblical "Launderers' Field"); slaughtering and tanning, as well as harness-making (the Pool of Siloam, or Shelah, in *Nehemiah*, III, 15; the Hebrew *shelah* implies animal hides, and the Septuagint renders *shelah* as *kodion*, meaning the hide or wool, or both, of a sheep).

There was also a soap industry; this was the site of the "potash pit," where the soda from the Dead Sea was collected before being mixed with the oil from the Mount of Olives to produce soap. A perfume industry flourished, its raw materials being brought from the plantations of the Jericho Valley and the Dead Sea, as well as from the nearby Kidron Valley. There were also blacksmiths and silversmiths. Josephus mentions the blacksmiths' workshops.

Cheesemongers' Valley

Wilson's Bridge and Robinson's Arch

Wilson's Bridge is named after the British archaeologist who was the first to describe it in 1865 (although Tobler had discovered it in 1835). It traverses the Cheesemongers' Valley from east to west and was apparently built originally during the Hasmonean period, in the form of arches, and completed by Herod in order to link the Upper City with the Chamber of Hewn Stone and the

Temple Mount, through the Gate of the Priests. The bridge was 90 m long, its arches reaching a height of 22 m. Its remains, 14 m thick, are visible today in a subterranean hall northwest of the Western Wall, having been cleared of accumulated debris.

Robinson's Bridge bears the name of the American scholar who discovered it in 1838. In the course of the excavations of Professor Mazar, it became clear that it was in fact not a bridge at all, but one arch only (as already suggested by Sir Charles Warren in 1867). Herod built it during his enlargement of the Temple courtyard, to give direct access to the royal portico (stoa) from the palace in the Upper City. The spring of the arch can be seen today, jutting out at the southwestern corner of the wall of the Temple Mount, south of the Western Wall. Recent excavations have uncovered a staircase descending from the arch to the south, supported by a series of small arches. The staircase was probably used by the royal family, who went up to the top of the arch and entered the royal portico through a special gate. The arch was 20 m high and 15.5 m wide.

The Hippodrome

Like every Hellenistic and Roman city, Jerusalem possessed a hippodrome. It was built by Herod in the Cheesemongers' Valley, following the pattern according to which the hippodrome was located in a valley rimmed by hills on two sides. It was used for races and other athletic performances, as well as for circuses and horse racing. One end of the hippodrome was flat – the starting and finishing points for the races – and the other was rounded. The slopes on three sides were covered with rows of benches. Some archaeologists believe the stadium must have been further north up the valley, as no remnants of it have come to light in the recent excavations around the Temple Mount.

Pool of Hezekiah and Pool of Siloam

After excavating the tunnel to conduct the waters of the Gihon spring beneath the Lower City to the Valley, King Hezekiah of Judah built the pool bearing his name. The Upper Pool was above it, so named because it collected the surplus floodwaters of the Cheesemongers' Valley. The Upper Pool was northwest of the Western Wall.

The Lower Pool was called the Siloam Pool; the waters of the Gihon reached it through a conduit along the Kidron Valley, irrigating the royal gardens at the junction of the Ben Hinnom Valley with the Kidron. This was also the lowest point in the Cheesemongers' Valley, and a gate was therefore built at this spot.

Gate of the Essenes

This gate was at the southern tip of the valley, and is included in Josephus' description of the line of the First Wall. It is called the Gate of the Essenes, since the members of this sect, who were mainly concentrated in the Dead Sea area, entered the city through this gate.

The Lower City

The Lower City was built on a spur sloping from north to south, between the Kidron Valley in the east and the Cheesemongers' Valley in the west. The spur was widest in the north, in the Temple area, and narrowed southward.

This is the oldest part of the city, and the site of the following major foundations:

The City of David and the Ophel

Before its conquest by David, the city was known as the "City of the Jebusite." During David's rule it was variously known as the City of David, Zion, and Mount Zion. The citadel of Zion was on the upper, northernmost part of the hill, near the southern wall of the Temple Mount, and was probably also called the Ophel, i.e., tower; this was the historical Tower of David. Archaeologists have been searching for the Ophel vicinity of the Huldah Gates, south of the Temple Mount. Josephus is ambiguous on the matter, stating in one place that the Ophel was south of the Temple Wall, and elsewhere that it lay west of the wall, near the Chamber of Hewn Stone.

Synagogue

A synagogue, ritual bath and pilgrims' hostel (to accommodate the travelers making their pilgrimage to Jerusalem from fourteen countries in the Mediterranean region and the Near East) were built in the southern part of the city during Herod's rule, as is evident from an inscription found there.

Queen Helena's Palace

Helena, queen of Adiabene in Mesopotamia, and her family adopted the Jewish religion in 50 C.E., apparently due to the influence of Babylonian Jews, and purchased estates and burial plots in Jerusalem (Tombs of the

Kings). The royal family made its home in Jerusalem, and even participated in its defense during the Great Revolt (Josephus mentions the valor of Chagiras the son of Nabataeus of Adiabene). Helena and her family erected palaces in the Lower City, near the Temple Mount. The queen made many contributions to the Temple, and brought grain from Alexandria, as well as dried figs from Cyprus, to distribute to the poor of Jerusalem in years of drought.

Tomb of the Prophetess Huldah

Huldah the prophetess, one of four mentioned in the Bible, prophesied in the time of King Josiah of Judah in the seventh century B.C.E., and lived in the *Mishneh* (quarter at the top of the Valley) in Jerusalem. The *Talmud* notes that she was kin to the prophet Jeremiah.

Huldah Gates

The two southern gates of the Temple were named for Huldah, since they were close to her tomb. Many pilgrims, arriving in the Lower City from the Mount of Olives, congregated in the square just in front of the southern wall, and entered the Temple Mount through the Huldah Gates.

The Temple Mount and the Western and Southern Walls

The Temple Mount (Old Testament Real Mount Zion)

The area of the Temple Mount and Herod's Temple was originally broader in the north and narrower toward the south, due to the topography of the site. The area of the Temple Mount is 144 dunams (36 acres), and the Temple was one of the greatest known to antiquity. Herod carried out the building of Jerusalem and its Temple in the fifteenth year of his reign, under Caesar Augustus, after ten years of peace and economic growth. He doubled the area of the Temple court. Since the terrain was not flat, it was necessary to buttress the courtyard of the Temple Mount with ashlar blocks, 5 m thick; some of these stones were 12 m long, 2.1 m high, 3 m wide, and weighed about 100 tons. Herod filled in the valley northeast of the Temple Mount and erected a wall standing 38 m above the bedrock. The valley at the southwest corner of the Temple Mount was also filled in, and a wall built to a height of 32 m. The wall at the southeast corner went down to a depth of 43 m below the level of the courtyard; the overall height of the wall at this point is 48 m from the bedrock.

The western wall of the Temple Mount was 488 m long, and the eastern wall 465 m; the northern wall was 320 m long, and the southern wall 290 m. The total length of the Temple Mount walls was approximately 1,550 m.

Ten thousand workmen constructed the Temple Mount and the Temple, using 1,000 carts for carrying materials. Of the workmen, 1,000 were priests, who worked on the Temple itself; the rock-cutters and woodworkers wore special priestly garb. Josephus reports that the building of the Temple took ten years (the *Talmud* notes that over the entire period rain fell only at night, so as not to interfere with the work). The New Testament mentions that the building of the walls, palaces and towers of Jerusalem required forty-six years (*John*, 2:20).

Temple Courtyard

On the east, north and west the square was surrounded by a roofed portico with two rows of columns. The columns were monolithic, of marble, 12.5 m high. The portico also served as a passageway, and was called "The Street of the House of God." In the south there was a "portico inside a portico," that is, four rows of columns. The two inner rows formed a central hall, two stories high and roofed over, with two lower rows, one on each side, one story high. This southern portico was 15 m wide, and included 162 columns with Corinthian capitals. (Josephus, *Antiquities*, xv, 11). Herod and the royal entourage were spectators from this portico during the festival rituals at the Temple. In front

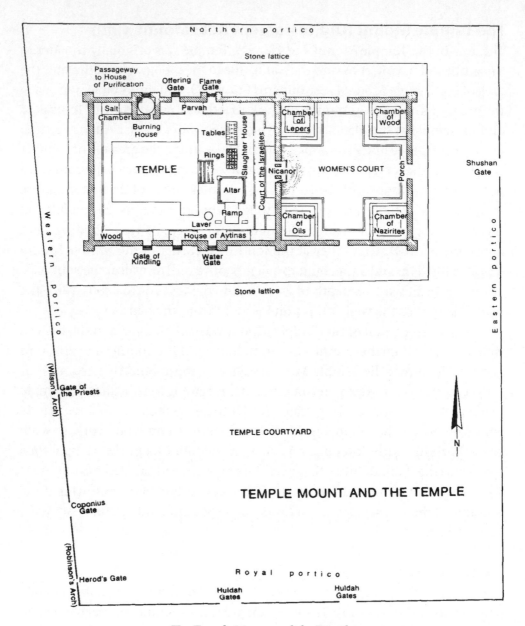

The Temple Mount and the Temple

of the columns were slabs of stone, which served as benches; the *lulavim* (palm branches) were placed on these benches when the eve of *Sukkoth* occurred on the Sabbath. Two loaves, ritually unfit for any other purpose, were put on top of the portico on the eve of Passover; the removal of one signified that eating leavened bread was now forbidden. And the removal of the second was the sign for the ritual burning of leftover leavened bread. The porticos were the scene of popular gatherings; preachers, money-changers and vendors of pigeons (for sacrifices) set up business there. The total length of the porticos along three sides of the Temple was 900 m.

There were five gates in the wall of the Temple Mount: in the south, the two Huldah Gates, serving the traffic to and from the Lower City; in the west, the Coponius Gate, named after a benefactor who contributed it and not after the Roman procurator in the years 6 to 9 c.e., and used for passage to and from the Valley and the Upper City; in the north, the Tadi Gate, apparently named for the generous Theodos. (This was not a public gate and was used solely by Herod and his armed forces going in and out of the Antonia fortress. It was probably on the site of the present-day *Bab el 'Itam, Dark Gate*, or nearby.) The eastern wall was entered by the Shushan Gate and was also used by the High Priest on his way to the Mount of Anointing for the ritual burning of the Red Heifer. The name is probably derived from a representation of the Persian Capital of Shushan, and the location was apparently south of the present-day Golden (Mercy) Gate.

According to Josephus, the pilgrims making sacrifices and assembling in the Temple square numbered 255,600, as reckoned by the number of sacrifices at Passover. These were made by heads of families only; the total number of people gathering in Jerusalem on the festivals reached a million.

The Courtyard and Hall of the Temple
The building was divided into three sections surrounded by the Partition: the Court of the Women, the Israelites Court and the Temple proper.

The Partition (of stone latticework) was 1.5 m high, surrounding the consecrated area at a distance of some 10 m; it was separated from the actual Temple by a moat. Plaques with Greek and Latin inscriptions were attached to it, forbidding the entry of strangers past that point on pain of death.

The Court of the Women
The wall of the Temple proper lay beyond the Partition; it was 20 m high, and enemy spoils were displayed upon it during the Hasmonean and Herodian periods. The Court of the Women was entered through the eastern gate, known as the Beautiful Gate in Christian sources, and the staircase, and women were only allowed as far as this court, which was 67.5 m square. There were four chambers in the court: that of the Nazirites in the southeast, where the

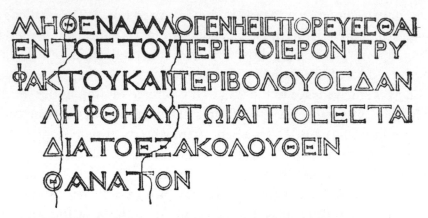

*Greek inscription reads: "A gentile man must not enter inside the partition
that surrounds the Temple and the courtyard within it. And he who will be
apprehended, his soul will be charged and his verdict will be death."*

Nazirites cut their hair and prepared their sacrifices; the Oil Chamber in the
southwest, used for storing oil for the Temple; in the northeast a chamber for
storing wood, which was cleaned for the Temple Service by ritually impure
priests; and in the northwest the Lepers' Chamber. From the Court of the
Women, Nicanor's Gate led to the Court of the Israelites.

Nicanor's Gate

West of the Court of the Women there were fifteen steps in the form of a semi-
circle (seen in the model near the Shushan Gate in the Temple Mount wall),
leading up to Nicanor's Gate and the Court of the Israelites. These were the
steps on which the Levites stood with their musical instruments (*kinnor, nevel*
and *metziltaim*) and recited the fifteen psalms (Songs of Ascent) 120 to 134.
The Levites also read seven psalms, one on each day of the week (24, 48, 82, 94,
81, 93 and, on the Sabbath, Psalm 92) to symbolize the days of the Creation.

The seven gates of the Temple were covered in gold, except for Nicanor's
Gate (named after a generous Alexandrian), which was made of Corinthian
brass. It was therefore also known as the Corinthian Gate; the beauty of the
workmanship led the New Testament to refer to it as the "Beautiful Gate."
Every gate had two doors, 15 m high and 7.5 m wide, but Nicanor's Gate was
25 m high, and its doors were 20 m high. (The 19th century archaeological
excavations on Mount Scopus revealed the tomb of Nicanor's family.) The
Talmud tells of a miracle which befell Nicanor: while bringing the gates by
sea from Alexandria, the ship nearly foundered. The doors were cast away,

but the sea cast one of them back again. To commemorate this miracle the gate was left ungilded.

The Temple Proper
In Herod's day, temples were not intended as places for prayer, but rather as the dwelling places of the gods or of their symbols; the Temple was therefore also known as the House of God. The consecrated area was entered through the following two courts:

The Court of the Israelites and the Court of the Priests
The Court of the Israelites was part of the Court of the Priests, and only men were permitted to enter. Its area was 67.5 × 5.5 m. Ordinary Israelites (those who were not priests) entered the Court of the Priests only for the purpose of "laying their hands" on the head of the animal being sacrificed, for its slaughtering, and for the waving of the sacrifices.

The Court of the Priests was 67.5 × 93.5 m in area, and it surrounded the Temple on three sides. There were nine gates overlaid with gold in the Temple wall. In this court were the altar, the copper basin (holding 80 cu m, weighing 30 tons, and with twelve taps for washing the hands and feet of the priests), a pit for the ashes of the burnt offerings, and the slaughter-house.

The crowning glory of this part of the Temple Mount was the Temple itself. Its construction took eighteen months. The façade was 50 m wide, and narrowed down to 35 m at the rear. It was built of marble and gold, and the dome was surmounted by golden spikes to prevent birds from alighting and soiling the building.

The Temple was divided into three parts: the hall, which served as the entrance; the sanctuary, where the ritual was performed; and the Holy of Holies. The hall was entered by twelve steps and separated the sacred from the unhallowed. There were two columns – Yachin and Boaz – at the front, both 2 m in diameter. In Solomon's Temple these pillars were made of copper. One opinion holds that the pillars were commemorative obelisks, and others believe they were altars, enormous lamps or "trees of life." However, it seems reasonable to assume that the names are derived from the biblical verses telling of the establishment (*kinun*) of the House which was built with power (*uz*), and the pillars were symbols of the pillar of fire and the pillar of cloud, which accompanied the Tabernacle in the desert. Professor S. Yeivin assumes that Solomon wanted to perpetuate the names of the Royal House, calling one pillar after Boaz, an ancestor of King David, and the other after Yachin, one of the priestly families in David's time (*Chronicles I* XXLV, 17). Herod affixed the Roman eagle over the gate, but when he fell ill the zealots removed it.

The doors of the gate were 27.5 m high and 8 m wide. Just inside the gate was a curtain, its colors symbolizing the four elements; scarlet for fire, brown for earth, blue for air and purple for water.

The sanctuary was 30 m high, 20 m wide and 30 m long, and was completely covered with gold. Some of the stone blocks of the sanctuary were 22.5 m long and 3 m wide. Within the sanctuary was the seven-branched candelabrum, representing the seven planets; the table of the shewbread, where twelve loaves were placed for the twelve signs of the Zodiac and the months of the year; and the altar and shovel, where the thirteen types of incense used in the ritual were kept. The incenses came from the sea, the desert and the inhabited areas, symbolizing the world in its entirety, the gift of God.

The Holy of Holies was 10 × 10 m in area, and contained nothing but the Rock of the Foundation. Pompey, capturing Jerusalem in 63 B.C.E., entered the Holy of Holies and was amazed that the ritual of the Jews would be centered around an empty hall. Only the High Priest, appointed by the *Sanhedrin*, was allowed to enter the Holy of Holies on the Day of Atonement.

The golden gates of the Temple glittered and shone at sunrise, and had the appearance of a burning fire. The white, clear marble looked like snow from a distance. The sources say: "Whoever has not seen Herod's building has not seen a handsome edifice. What was it built of? Rabbah says: of green and white marble, and some say, of blue, green and white stones."

The highest point of the Temple Mount was the Antonia fortress.

The Antonia Fortress

The fortress was built on a hill 25 m high, in the northwest part of the Temple Mount, as a defense for it. The length of the fortress, from east to west, was about 115 m; on the western side its width from north to south was 35 m and in the east 42 m.

During the time of Nehemiah this was the site of the Tower of Hananel, also called *Birah*, i.e., tower; it was also probably known as the Tower of the Hundred. Nehemiah appointed Hananiah commander of the *Birah*. The Hasmoneans called the fortress *Baris*, and Herod named its successor *Antonia* in honor of Mark Antony, ruler of Rome, who appointed Herod king over the Jews; it was as splendid as the royal palace.

At the base of the fortress Herod built a wall of huge stones to hamper enemy attempts to ram it. There were four towers at the corners of the fortress; the two western towers were 25 m high, and the two eastern ones 35 m. They afforded an excellent vantage point over the Temple Mount and the Upper and Lower Cities.

The fortress contained many rooms, bathhouses, army barracks, halls and courts. The towers were manned by Roman soldiers, particularly during festivals, to prevent any rebellion against Herod and Rome, and underground passages connected the fortress with the Temple Mount. A large cistern (the *Struthion*) was dug at the base of the fortress, visible today in the Western Wall tunnel and in the Ecce Homo basilica on the Via Dolorosa. Water was brought to this pool by a conduit leading from the Lacus Legerii (north of the present-day Damascus Gate), which was filled by the floodwaters at the head of the Cheesemongers' Valley. The Convent of the Sisters of Zion, at the Ecce Homo basilica, is built near the ruins of the ancient Antonia fortress.

Pool of Bethesda – Beth Zetha

This pool, northeast of the Temple Mount, was filled by the waters of the Bezetha Valley, draining the northeastern part of the New City. The pool was 120 m long, 50 to 60 m wide and 10 to 15 m deep. Because of its great length it was divided in two. The name Bethesda implies mercy (*hessed*).

In the time of Jeremiah, the Gate of Benjamin was nearby, since this was the beginning of the road leading north to Anatot and the land of Benjamin. In the Bible this gate is called the Gate of Ephraim because the land of Ephraim lay to the north. During Nehemiah's time it was known as the Gate of the Sheep, since the sheep intended for ritual sacrifice at the Temple were apparently washed in the pool. The New Testament recounts miraculous cases of healing by Jesus, and the Pool of Bethesda is sacred to Christians. Nowadays the pool is in the courtyard of the Church of St. Anne, near the Lions' Gate. Surplus waters from this pool probably flowed to the pool of Bnei Israil (now silted up) just northeast of the Temple Mount, near the present-day Gate of the Tribes.

Monument to Alexander Janneus

A monument to Alexander Janneus was erected near the Pool of Bethesda. This was the Hasmonean king during whose reign (103–76 B.C.E.) the frontiers of the country were greatly extended and took in parts of Transjordan.

Bethesda Pool and Church of Saint Anne

Bethesda

The growing population of Jerusalem at the end of the Second Temple period led to its expansion northward, towards Bethesda, meaning New City, or Beth Zetha, where olive trees grew, or where olive oil was gathered. This quarter was also known as "the suburb of Jerusalem." It did not enjoy the natural defenses surrounding the Upper and Lower Cities and was vulnerable to attack from the north until the Third Wall was built. On the other hand, the northwestern part of Bethesda was on a relatively high hill (800 m) which stretched to the present-day Russian Compound. It was possible to see the Temple Mount from this hill.

Bethesda was also an area of gardens. During the reign of Agrippa I, Bethesda was surrounded by a wall which was completed in the early stages of the Roman revolt. In the model, the entire Second (Herodian) Wall may be seen near the Third Wall, and also the present-day Damascus Gate, where remains of Herod's wall were found.

Towers of the Women
The Towers of the Women are mentioned by Josephus along the route of the third wall, which began at the Psephinus Tower (see below) at the northwestern corner and continued through the Towers of the Women to the tomb of Queen Helena in the Kidron Valley. This was also the site of the gate to the Towers of the Women.

Wood Market
The wood market was in Bezetha, near the Second Wall. The wood was used for heating during the winter and for cooking and for the altar rituals all the year round.

Markets
The major commercial and artisan markets of the city lay between the Antonia Fortress and the present-day Damascus Gate. The markets are mentioned by Josephus and in the *Mishnah* as dealing in wool, clothing, fattened animals, and blacksmiths' work.

Psephinus Tower
This was located at the highest point of Bezetha (800 m) in the northwestern corner of the third wall, near the present-day Russian Compound. It was octagonal in shape and 35 m in height. At sunrise the Mediterranean was visible from it, and at sunset the mountains of Gilead and Moab.

According to Josephus, the site was known as the Camp of the Assyrians, since the army of Sannecherib camped there during the campaign against King Hezekiah of Judah. It was also Titus' base camp during the Revolt of the Jews.

Monument to Yohanan (John) Hyrcanus

Yohanan Hyrcanus, a scion of the Hasmoneans, was *Nasi* (Ethnarch) as well as High Priest from 135 to 104 B.C.E. The monument stood between the second and third walls, north of the towers and the pool of Amygdalon.

Revolt and Destruction

The Greeks of Caesarea provoked the Jews during their Sabbath worship. When the Jews complained to the Roman procurator, Florus, in Sebaste (Samaria), the latter set off to rob the treasures of the Temple. This marks the beginning of the Revolt against the Romans.

Florus' Trip to Jerusalem

Florus, the cruelest of all the Roman procurators, breached Jerusalem through Bezetha, pillaged the Upper Market, and killed 3,600 Jews. The Jews resisted, and the Zealots destroyed the northern portico, which connected with the Antonia fortress, thus preventing Florus from reaching the Temple. He was eventually driven from the city. Elazar ben-Hananiah, the High Priest, persuaded the priests not to offer the sacrifice to the health of the Emperor; this signal from the Temple sparked off the Revolt. (*Wars of the Jews II*, chaps. 14, 2, 4 and 15).

The Battle Between the Rebels and Agrippa II

At the outset of the revolt, the more peaceable faction, together with the priests, and aided by the forces of Agrippa II (a descendant of Herod) gained control of the Upper City. The rebels, led by Elazar, took over the Lower City, and civil war raged. Agrippa gathered the people together in the Chamber Hewn Stone, in a futile effort to restore peace. The rebels set fire to the house of Hananiah, the High Priest, and to the palaces of the king and his sister Berenice near the Chamber of Hewn Stone. Agrippa fled from Jerusalem. The rebels then captured the Antonia fortress and Herod's palace from the Roman forces of Agrippa and burned the fortress. (*Wars* II, 17:7)

The Civil War

Menahem the Galilean, who had plundered the arms stored at Masada, arrived in Jerusalem and killed Hananiah the High Priest and his brother Hezekiah. The Zealots, commanded by Elazar, hunted Menahem; he fled to the Ophel, where he was caught and killed. Thus began the tragic civil war in Jerusalem. The city was divided under two commands; Shimon bar-Giora controlled the Upper City and part of the Lower, including the Acra; Yohanan ben-Levi of Gush-Halav (John of Gischala) took charge of the Temple Mount and the Antonia. The two factions fought bitterly. Bar-Giora had 10,000 fighters at his command, as well as 5,000 Edomites; John of Gischala had 6,000 men plus 2,400 Zealots (of Elazar's men). Three factions eventually fought one another within Jerusalem. (*Wars*, III–VI)

The Journey of Cestius Gallus to Jerusalem

Cestius Gallus, procurator of Syria, attacked Jerusalem in 66 C.E. in an attempt to quell the Revolt. He set up camp on Mount Scopus and entered the city, where he burned the wood market and Bezetha. He then camped near the royal palace, but he was unable to capture the Temple Mount and retreated hurriedly by way of Mount Scopus and the ascent of Beth-Horon. Bar Giora's soldiers harassed the retreating forces at the rear and captured all their arms. The rebels were then given a respite for four years, until the siege of Titus, and were meanwhile able to complete the third wall.

Destruction of the Food Stores, and the Famine in Jerusalem

The struggles between the factions of Bar-Giora, John of Gischala and Elazar's Zealots eventually led to the destruction of all the food stocks laid in for the Revolt. The rebels began to break into the homes of the populace, robbing them of food. The inhabitants of Jerusalem died of hunger and bloated bodies lay in the streets. The famine finally caused the betrayal of the city to the Romans. (During the reign of Zedekiah, king of Judah, the city also fell as a result of famine, to the king of Babylon, as noted in *Jeremiah* LII, 6–7: "…the famine was sore in the city, so that there was no bread for the people of the land. Then a breach was made in the city and all men of war fled, and went forth out of the city by night.")

Titus' Siege of Jerusalem

The siege of Jerusalem lasted four and a half months. Titus arrived from Caesarea with two legions (the Twelfth and the Fifteenth) and reached Mount Scopus by way of Givat Shaul. This was an excellent vantage point overlooking Jerusalem. Another legion (the Fifth) came from Emmaus, and yet another (the Tenth) was moved from Jericho to the Mount of Olives.

Titus approached Jerusalem and set up three camps: one on the Mount of Olives, the second near the Camp of the Assyrians near the Psephinus Tower, and the third in the north-west, near Herod's palace, outside the city. Titus waged his campaign in four stages.

Symbol of the Tenth Roman Legion

1. The Battle for the Third and Second Walls

First of all Titus circled the city, searching for a likely place to breach the wall. The Third Wall was breached near the Hyrcanus Monument, north of the present-day Jaffa Gate, since it was low at that point and was not joined to the Second Wall. Titus attempted to sweep through directly to the Temple Mount, but the Zealots attacked from the Towers of the Women in the Third Wall. They blocked the route of the army from the Psephinus Tower to Queen Helena's Monument in the Kidron Valley, causing considerable losses to the Romans. Titus later captured the new city, breached the Second Wall, and took the wool and clothing markets, finally halting at the Antonia fortress.

In the Upper City, near the Yohanan Hyrcanus' Monument at the Hippicus Tower, Titus faced the forces of Shimon bar-Giora. Titus built siege ramps in four places, against the fortress and the Hycranus Monument. John of Gischala attacked Titus from the Antonia fortress; Bar-Giora's rebels and the Edomites fought the Romans from the Hyrcanus Monument and broke out of the siege ring near the "Hidden Gate" at the Hippicus Tower, destroying the Roman weaponry and burning down their ramparts.

2. The Siege Wall

Since Titus was unable to break through the Antonia Fortress and the walls of the Upper City, he laid a siege wall around the city in three days, along a course of 7,350 m, with thirteen forts. This wall was intended to cut the city off completely, causing its surrender through lack of supplies. It started at the Hyrcanus Monument, crossed the Kidron valley to the Mount of Olives, passed by the Shiloah Pool to the Monument of the High Priest Hananiah (Abu Tor, today) and turned back through Herod's Tomb (probably south of the location of today's King David Hotel) to rejoin the Hyrcanus Monument.

3. Capture of the Antonia Fortress and the Destruction of the Temple

John of Gischala commanded the Temple Mount and defended it, fighting the Romans from the Antonia fortress, the northern wall of the Temple Mount, and the Alexander Janneus Monument.

After a cruel, hard siege, Titus breached the foundations of the Antonia on the seventeenth day of Tammuz (*Wars* VI, 2:9; 4:1) and built ramparts to the Temple Mount. The final assault was made from the Antonia Fortress, and the Temple was burned on the ninth day of Av. The civil war between the rebels raged unceasingly all this time. The Romans also burned the Lower City, and the fire reached the palace of Queen Helena (*Wars* VI, 5:3).

4. Capture of the Upper City

After the destruction of the Temple, Titus' four legions began to attack the Upper City. On the twentieth day of Av the Romans set up their war engines west of the Upper City, laid ramparts against the Chamber of Hewn Stone and the Tower of Shimon bar-Giora, near the Chamber, and burned them down. Eighteen days later, on the eighth of Ellul, one month after the destruction of the Temple, the Romans breached the walls of the Upper City. The Zealots then barricaded themselves in the three towers near Herod's palace (*Wars* VI, 8:4; VII, 8:4)

The Zealots fled through the subterranean passages leading from the towers. Bar-Giora was taken prisoner; the entire Upper City was taken on the eighth of Ellul, having been set afire, and the Zealots were massacred without mercy. Josephus reports that they: "…blocked up the streets with the dead, and deluged the whole city with blood, so that in numerous instances it extinguished the flames." (*Wars* VI, 8). This was the last chapter of the desperately brave battle waged by the Zealots who, as Josephus says: "…despised death, having rightly preferred it to slavery; … while they breathed, they would inflict every possible injury on the Romans" (*Wars* V, 9:2).

The strength of the defenses of the Second Temple and the bravery of the Zealot rebels may be deduced by comparing the numbers of fighters on each side and their methods of warfare.

There were 24,000 Zealots, starving and with few arms, involved in a cruel, tragic civil war at the same time (Josephus reports that "the sedition subdued the city and the Romans the sedition" (*Wars* v, 6:1), against four legions (out of the total of twenty-five legions of the Roman Empire, stationed in Europe, North Africa and Asia), i.e., 80,000 well-seasoned Roman soldiers, the finest of the ancient armies, equipped with war, siege and breaching engines. The Romans fought for six successive months, from the fourteenth day of Nissan to the eighth day of Elul. Titus' speech to his soldiers is ample evidence of the bravery of the Zealots: "The Jews, whom desperation alone directs, do every thing with forethought and circumspection, carefully arranging their stratagems and ambuscades: fortune, moreover, favors their enterprises, because of their obedience, and their kindly feeling towards one another, and their fidelity; while the Romans, to whom even fortune, and prompt submission to their officers, has ever been a servant, now fail under an opposite line of conduct and are defeated through their own intemperate proceedings." (*Wars* v, 3:4).

According to Josephus (*Wars* vi, 9:3) there were 110,000 dead and 97,000 prisoners in Jerusalem. After the city was captured, Titus razed the buildings and walls to their foundations except for the three towers – Hippicus, Phasael and Mariamne – which were left to glorify his prowess and show following generations the strength of the city that he had captured. The towers also served as quarters for the Roman garrison. Titus never realized that the remains of the city would fan the spark of hope in the hearts of Jews through the generations, feed the yearning to renew the glory of old, and bind the nation to its past up to this very day; for in the path of suffering comes redemption.

Conscription notice from the king at a time the Land of Israel was in danger of annihilation.
Excerpt is from the Temple Scroll of the Scroll Sect, according to Yigal Yadin

Chronological Table of the Events of the
War Between Jews and Romans in Jerusalem
According to Josephus

Month of	3826 A.M./66 C.E.
Nissan	*Cestius Gallus, procurator of Syria, arrives in Jerusalem and hears the complaints of the Jews against the procurator Florus (Wars II, 14).*
Iyar	*The Roman Emperor rules in favor of the Greeks of Caesarea and against the Jews in a trial concerning the government of the city; the revolt begins (II, 14).*
Iyar (on a Sabbath)	*The Greek citizens of Caesarea harass the Jews at prayers; the Jews flee with the Scrolls of the Law to their land at Narbata, east of the city (II, 14).*
Iyar	*The procurator Florus sends messengers to take some of the Temple treasures and causes confusion in the city (II, 14). Florus attacks Jerusalem by way of Neapolis (Shechem), destroys the Upper Market and kills 3,600. The Zealots are aroused (II, 14–15).*
Iyar	*The Jewish king, Agrippa II, attempts to quiet the Jews, fails, and leaves Jerusalem (II, 17).*
Iyar	*The Zealots take Masada from the Romans. The High Priest Eleazar ben Hananiah stops the sacrifices to the health of Caesar, and the revolt against the Romans officially begins (II, 17).*
Av	*Agrippa II sends 3,000 cavalrymen to Jerusalem to aid the peaceable faction; a civil war breaks out (II, 17).*
Av	*The rebels overpower Agrippa's forces, beat them back to the royal palace, and burn the houses of the aristocracy (II, 17).*

Av	*The rebels take the Antonia Fortress after a two-day siege (II, 17).*
Ellul	*Menahem the Galilean, leader of the rebels, takes the palace, frees the Jewish soldiers of Agrippa, and forces the Romans back to the three towers of the palace (II, 17).*
Ellul	*Hananiah, the High Priest, and his brother Hezekiah are killed by the rebels, and Menahem the Galilean is killed by the followers of Eleazar ben-Hananiah (II, 17). The forces of Eleazar ben-Hananiah enter into a pact with the Romans besieged in the towers and later kill them. The Greeks of Caesarea take revenge and kill 20,000 Jews there; Florus sells the remaining Jews into slavery (II, 17–18).*
3827 A.M./66–67 C.E.	
Tishrei	*Jews living in the cities of Syria and in Alexandria are massacred (II, 18). The commander Cestius Gallus sets out to attack Judea and razes Lydda. The Jews of Jerusalem meet him at Gibeon and kill many of his troops (II, 18–19).*
Tishrei	*Cestius Gallus encamps on Mount Scopus and hopes for the rebels' surrender. When this does not occur, he returns to Jerusalem through Bethesda and camps before the Temple Mount (II, 19).*
Heshvan	*Cestius Gallus besieges the Temple Mount for five days, fails, and retreats to Mount Scopus (II, 19).*
3828 A.M./67–68 C.E.	
Winter and Spring	*Civil war breaks out between the Zealots and the citizens (IV, 3). The zealots hold the town and the Idumeans fighting with them kill the priests (IV, 4:6). John of Gischala rules the city (IV, 7).*
3829 A.M./69 C.E.	
Nissan	*Shimon bar-Giora enters Jerusalem and fights John of Gischala and the Zealots (IV, 9).*

3830 A.M./70 C.E.	
Winter	*The three factions, headed, respectively, by John of Gischala, the Zealots, and Shimon bar-Giora, fight one another and burn down granaries (v, 1).*
Nissan	*The forces of Titus fight around the city (v, 2).*
14 Nissan	*Civil war during Passover; murder in the court (v, 3). Titus leaves his base on Mount Scopus and camps near the city wall (v, 3; v, 13).*
Nissan to 7 Iyar	*The Romans lay ramparts against the new wall – the third – and ram it with engines. The Zealots almost succeed in destroying the ramparts, but the Romans take the new wall (v, 6–7).*
7–15 Iyar	*The Romans lay ramparts again the First Wall and later take the Second Wall; they are driven off, but recapture the wall and destroy it (v, 7–8).*
20 Iyar	*Titus sends Josephus to exhort the Jews to make peace (v, 9). Famine grows worse in the city (v, 10).*
29 Iyar to 2 Sivan	*The ramparts against the old wall are ready: John of Gischala destroys the ramparts near the wall of the Upper City (v, 11).*
Early Sivan	*Titus lays a wall around the city, intensifying the famine. He builds new ramparts against the Antonia fortress (v, 12; VI, 1).*
1 Tammuz	*John of Gischala attempts to destroy the ramparts around the Antonia Fortress and fails; Titus orders the fortress attacked with battering rams (VI, 1).*
5 Tammuz	*The Antonia Fortress is captured by the Romans, who try to break through to the Temple Mount, but are forced back by the Zealots (VI, 1). Fierce fighting for the Temple Mount ensues (VI, 2).*

17 Tammuz	*The daily sacrifice in the Temple ceases. Josephus tries to speak to the Jews again. Many Jews defect to the Romans (VI, 2).*
22–28 Tammuz	*The rebels burn down the northeastern hall of the Temple, and the Romans burn the northern hall (VI, 2); the rebels draw the Romans to the western hall and set it afire (VI, 3).*
8 Av	*The ramparts are set against the wall of the Temple. Titus attempts to break through to it but fails; he then orders the court to be set afire (VI, 4).*
9 Av	*Titus commands quenching of the fire in the court (VI, 4).*
10 Av	*The rebels are overcome by the Romans and flee to the Temple. The Romans burn down the Temple (VI, 4) and the Lower City is then destroyed (VI, 5).*
19 Av	*The Romans build ramparts against the Upper City (VI, 8).*
7–8 Ellul	*The Upper City is captured and burned down (VI, 8; VII,8).*

CHAPTER III

"WALK ABOUT ZION AND GO ROUND ABOUT HER"

Psalm XLVIII, *13*

The Kidron Valley

The Kidron Valley is the largest and most important valley in Jerusalem and its vicinity, and was the scene of many decisive events. The valley as a whole and its several parts had a significant effect on the citizens' way of life, and on the city's economy, roads and ritual.

The head of the Kidron Valley extends from the northeast of Jerusalem to the east, near the country's water-divide, where the water flowing west to the Mediterranean runs down Nahal Sorek, and that flowing east to the Dead Sea passes through the Kidron Valley. Both these valleys served as roadways; the western one connected with the Sea Road (Via Maris) and Jaffa, and the eastern one led to Rabbat Ammon and the King's Road. The prophet Zechariah says of this water divide: "And it shall come to pass in that day, that living waters shall go out from Jerusalem; half of them toward the eastern sea (Dead Sea) and half of them toward the western sea (Mediterranean); in summer and in winter shall it be." (*Zechariah* XIV, 8). The "living water" he refers to is probably the Gihon spring in the Kidron Valley, and the waters of Naftoah (*Lifta*) in the Sorek Valley. The water divide passes near the neighborhood of Sanhedriyah in Jerusalem, at a height of 820 m above sea level. The valley is plateaulike at its head, and widens from Givat-Hatahmoshet and the Mount of Olives in the northeast and east to the Beth-Israel and Bukharian quarters

89

Southern Jerusalem, Kidron River, Hinnom Valley and the King's Garden.
At right: Silwan neighborhood

in the west. On the plateau the breadthwise roads cross the lengthwise ones, leading to Beth-El and Nablus in the north and to Bethlehem and Hebron in the south. Southward the valley bed deepens and reaches the point where the Valley (Cheesemongers' Valley) and the Ben-Hinnom Valley merge into it, between the Pool of Siloam and the well of Ein Rogel. At this point the valley lies at a height of 600 m, having traversed a distance of 4 km. The Kidron Valley then flows east, twisting and turning, until it reaches the Dead Sea, south of the Qumran ruins.

The Kidron is the lowest-lying valley in Jerusalem, and the nearest to the Judean Desert; its heat is oppressive, and its lower course is consequently known in Arabic as Wadi Nar, the Valley of Fire (this connotation links up with the Hebrew root *qdr*, meaning piercing heat).

The name is sometimes explained by the word *qederah* (bowl), which in Hebrew, as in Arabic and Aramaic, suits the bowl-like shape of the valley where the Ben-Hinnom Valley joins it. Another explanation is based on the root *qdr* meaning darkness; the low-lying cirque is surrounded by mountains and is consequently the first part of the city to darken at nightfall.

The several sections of the valley were also variously named in different periods. The water-divide area is known in Jewish sources as the Valley of Beth Miqlah – grain parched with fire – where grain was cultivated. A valley known in Arabic as Wadi Joz, i.e., Valley of Nuts (in Hebrew: the Valley of Simon the Just), joins the upper part of the valley. This section stretches up to the tomb of Simon the Just. The valley deepens from this point on. Its continuation is called Wadi Sitt Miriam (named after the mother of Jesus), since, according to Christian tradition, Mary was buried in the valley. This section continues east of the Lions' Gate, north of Gethsemane, where it deepens and collects the water from the area known in antiquity as Bezetha, as well as a considerable part of the rainfall from the Mount of Olives. The next section, further south, is known as the Valley of Gethsemane, of significance in the life of Jesus; it stretches to a point opposite the Mercy Gate. The valley widens slightly in this part, since the chalk rock is softer and more easily eroded; these rocks are also suitable for the cultivation of olives. The next section is considerably deeper, and is called the Valley of Jehoshaphat (God has judged), as, according to *Joel* (IV, 2; 12), the judgment of the nations will take place there. This is the site of the tomb complexes known as Absalom's Tomb and Zechariah's Tomb. The deep incision of the valley is implied by *Joel* (IV, 14): "Multitudes, multitudes in the valley of decision or incised valley (the root *hrz* denotes incisive action) for the day of the Lord is near in the valley of decision." The next section is called the Valley of Shiloah, since the spring of Gihon, popularly called the Shiloah, flows there. The Arabs call this part Silwan, after the village on the eastern side of the valley. The lowest part of the Kidron Valley is called Wadi Nar – valley of fire – since the heat is great and oppressive in summer, due to its proximity to the Judean Desert. This section begins after the Ben-Hinnom and Cheesemongers' Valleys debouch into the main course. *Zechariah* calls the Kidron "valley of the mountains" (xiv, 5).

Various events and activities took place in different parts of the Kidron, which had a deep-reaching effect on the life and economy of the city. These were reflected in the various names for the valley and its sections. Below we shall present some of the roles filled by the valley in its different sections.

The Fields of Kidron

King Josiah of Judah speaks of "the fields of Kidron" (*II Kings* xxiii, 4) refer-ring to the grain fields of the Kidron Valley. *Jeremiah* (xxxi, 40) says: "And the whole valley of the dead bodies, and of the ashes, and all the fields unto the brook of Kidron, unto the corner of the horse gate toward the east, shall be holy unto the Lord." *Isaiah* (xxxvii, 27) says: "Therefore their inhabitants were of small power, they were dismayed and confounded; they were as the grass of the fields, and as the green herb, as the grass of the housetops, and as a field of corn before it is grown up," and according to *Habakkuk* (iii, 17), "For though the fig tree shall not blossom, neither shall fruit be in the vines; the labor of the olive shall fail, and the fields shall yield no food; the flock shall be cut off from the fold, and there shall be no herd in the stalls."

The "fields of Kidron" seem to have been in the upper plateau – like part of the Kidron Valley, between Sanhedriya and the Mount of Olives in the north and Bezetha and the Valley of Nuts in the south. The meal-offerings in the Temple consisted mainly of grain: "All other meal-offerings consist of wheat, but this consists of barley. The meal-offerings of the *Omer*, although consisting of barley, was in form of groats, but this was in the form of coarse flour" (*Sotah* 2, 1). It is reasonable to assume that the *Omer* was brought to the Temple from this area, as stated in the *Mishnah*: "The precept of the *Omer* is that it should be brought from what grows nearby" (*Menahot* 10, 2). The *Omer* was reaped on the sixteenth day of Nissan, and had to be brought to the Temple in the morning. The *Tosephta* reports that the *Omer* was brought from the Valley of Beth Miqlah (House of Parched Wheat) in the Kidron Valley, which had a southerly aspect, and yielded about three *se-ah*; it received the early sunlight as well as the late, and was kept half sown and half fallow. The Valley of Beth-Miqlah was probably in the part which connected Givat-Hamivtar and the Mount of Olives with the Valley of Nuts. This southerly slope is warmed by the sun most of the day and produces the earliest barley crop in Jerusalem. The name comes from the root *qlh* meaning roasting or parching, since the grains of barley were parched with fire. (The valleys of Lower Galilee were also called in accordance with their type of produce: the *Valley of Beth Kerem* had vineyards; the Valley of Netofa was swampy, and was used for summer crops and cattle-raising; pomegranates grew in the Valley of Beth Rimmon and irrigated crops in the Valley of Ginossar.) Grain was cultivated in this part of the Valley of Beth Miqlah up to the early years of the British Mandate; the city proper has only recently expanded into this formerly agricultural area. In years when the crop did not ripen in time, the citizens of Jerusalem were forced to bring the first fruits from afar: "The precept of the *Omer* was that it should be brought from (what grows) nearby. If (the crop) near Jerusalem was not yet ripe it could be brought from any place. It once happened that it was brought from Gaggoth Zerifin, and two loaves from the plain of En Sokher (which is near Shechem). What was the procedure? The messengers of the *Beth Din* (court) used to go out on the day before the festival and tie the unreaped corn in bunches to make it easier to reap. All the inhabitants of the towns nearby assembled there so that it might be reaped with much display… They reaped it, put it into the baskets and brought it to the Temple Court. Then they parched it with fire to fulfill the precept that it should be parched with fire" (*Menahot* 10, 2–4); "After the *Omer* was offered they used to go out and find the market of Jerusalem already full of meal and parched corn" (*Menahot* 10, 5). The upper part of the Kidron Valley was thus known as the Valley of Beth Miqlah. The *Omer* was also brought from Michmas: "All the offerings of the congregation or of the individual may be offered from produce in the Land (of Israel) or outside the Land, from the new (produce) or from the old, excepting the *Omer*-offering and the Two Loaves, which must be offered only from the new produce and from (produce grown) in the Land. All (offerings) must be offered from the choicest produce, and which is the choicest? Michmas and Zanoha rank first for the quality of their fine flour" (*Menahot* 8, 1).

Valley of Rephaim

Another broad field for grain crops was the Valley of Rephaim, of which Isaiah said: "And it shall be as when the harvestman gathereth the standing corn, and reapeth the ears with his arm; yea it shall be as one gleaneth ears in the Valley of Rephaim" (*Isaiah* xvii, 5).

The Valley of Rephaim stretches from the water-divide, east of the Jerusalem railway station, at a height of 750 m, to Nahal Rephaim, south of the Mekor Haim quarter (at 700 m), which eventually joins Nahal Sorek. This valley was the site of one of the major roads from the Shephelah to the mountains; the Philistines used it when attacking David at his citadel in Jerusalem: "But when the Philistines heard that David was anointed king over Israel, all the Philistines went up to seek David; and David heard of it, and went down to the hold. Now the Philistines had come and spread themselves in the Valley of Rephaim" (*ii Samuel* v, 17, 18), and further (*ii Samuel* v, 20, 21): "And David came to Baal-perazim, and David smote them there; and he said: 'The Lord hath broken mine enemies before me, like the breach of waters.' Therefore the name of that place was called Baal-perazim. And they left their images there, and David and his men took them away."

Where then was Baal-perazim, the scene of the battle?

Professor B. Mazar, who carried out archaeological excavations on the hill of Ramat Rahel (1930) found relics of the Canaanite period, and assumes that this was the site of Baal-perazim. (This is also the opinion of Dalman; see *Ramat Rahel* and *Khirbet Salah, Journal of the Palestine Exploration Society 1935*, pp. 4–18.) The hill of Ramat Rahel is the highest south of Jerusalem (820 m). It was the scene of Baal worship, and the Philistines left their images behind at that place. The hill is isolated and wind-swept, and this may have contributed to its name.

According to another opinion, Baal-perazim is Givat-Hananiah (Abu Tor), south of the Upper City (760 m), since it is close to David's citadel; the Bible says of David that "he went down to the hold," and the hill of Ramat Rahel is 4 km from the City of David.

Defense of Jerusalem

The Kidron Valley drains the Mount of Olives and Mount Scopus in the east and north, and a considerable part of the Old and New Cities in the west. It is thus the lowest valley in the vicinity of Jerusalem, reaching a depth of 120 m near the Mount of Olives, and 70 m near the Temple Mount. The valley is also deeply carved out because of the soft rock, which is easily affected by rain and floodwaters. The powerful flow of floodwater and the abundant silt prevented the establishment of pools in the valley except for the Pool of Simon the Just, which is completely silted up. The power and importance of this, the greatest of Jerusalem's valleys, is legendary. It is described as holding all the rainwater falling in Jerusalem. This deep valley therefore constituted a formidable line of defense against invaders; its exceedingly steep slopes provided protection in the east. This is mentioned in the time of King Hezekiah of Judah, when Sennacherib besieged Jerusalem, apparently from the west: "And it came to pass, when thy choicest valleys were full of chariots and the horsemen set themselves in array at the gate" (*Isaiah* xxii, 7).

The Kidron Valley was the borderline between the tribe of Benjamin in the north and Judah in the south, as well as the northern boundary of the city. King Solomon warned Shimei ben-Gera: "For on the day thou goest out, and passest over the brook of Kidron, know thou for certain that thou shalt surely die; thy blood shall be upon thine own head" (*1 Kings* 11, 37).

The most important mountain in Jerusalem, adjacent to the Kidron Valley on its eastern side, is the Mount of Olives, formerly covered with olive trees.

The Mount of Olives

The Mount of Olives is so called because its chalk rocks, unique in the Jerusalem Mountains, are suitable for planting olive trees. The harder limestone rocks in the western part of the city cannot support olives, except for the slopes where the soil layer is deeper. During the period of Ezra the trees on the Mount of Olives were used as a source of branches for the *Sukkoth* booths in Jerusalem (*Nehemiah* viii, 15). The Mount of Olives is also mentioned by Josephus. In the New Testament the valley immediately below the mountain derives its name Gethsemane (oil-press) from the rich oil pressed out of the olives. The olive oil was used to anoint kings, and the mountain was therefore also known as the Mount of Anointing.

The Mount of Olives has three peaks, running from north to south: the northernmost, popularly known as Mount Scopus, the original site of the Hebrew University, rises to 826 m; the central peak, with the quarter of A-Tur, is 800 m (these two are higher than Jerusalem proper); and the southernmost, known as *Jabal Baten el-Hawa* (747 m) is identified with the Mount of Scandal, or Offense. It is the site of a monastery named after Father Abraham and is the same height as the Temple Mount.

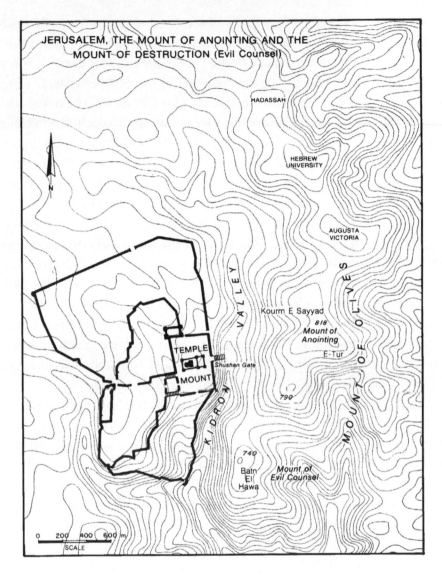

The Mount of Olives is mentioned in connection with the flight of David from Absalom: "And David went up by the ascent of the Mount of Olives, and wept as he went up, and he had his head covered, and went barefoot; and all the people that were with him covered every man his head, and they went up, weeping as they went up" (*II Samuel* xv, 30). The ascent was probably east of the City of David, near the village of Silwan. The southern peak of the Mount of Olives was apparently known as "the top" (*II Samuel* xv, 32): "And it came to pass that when David was come to the top of the ascent, where God was wont to be worshipped..." This gave rise to its sacred character, which is also attested to by *Ezekiel*: "And the glory of the Lord went up from the midst of the city, and stood upon the mountain which is on the east side of the city" (XI, 23). The southern peak, close to the City of David, was used by Solomon to build high places of worship for the gods of his gentile wives (*I Kings* XI, 7, 8): "Then did Solomon build a high place for Chemosh, the detestation of Moab, in the mount that is before Jerusalem, and for Molech, the detestation of the children of Ammon. And so did he for his foreign wives, who offered and sacrificed unto their gods." (It is noteworthy that *Baten-el Hawa* affords an excellent view of the mountains of Moab and Ammon.) This gave rise to the name of the Mount of Corruption during the reign of King Josiah, who purified Jerusalem (*II Kings* XXIII, 13): "And the high places that were before Jerusalem, which were on the right hand of the mount of corruption, which Solomon the king of Israel had built for Ashtoreth the detestation of the Zidonians, and for the Chemosh the detestation of Moab, and for Milcom the abomination of the children of Ammon, did the king defile." In *Targum Yonathan* the "Mount of Corruption" is called "Mount of Olives," and the identification of the site was made accordingly. *Rashi*'s explanation is that the Mount of Corruption is the Mount of Olives, and the name was changed for the worse after the foreign gods had been worshipped there.

After the destruction of the Second Temple, the Jews and Karaites used to celebrate the festival of *Sukkoth* on the Mount of Olives. The Gaon Rabbi Meir wrote to the Sages of Babylon at the beginning of the Arab period, saying that prayers were held on the Mount of Olives, opposite the site of the Temple, in view of the gates, when the people of Israel gathered to celebrate the festival of *Sukkoth* (*Sefer Hayishuv*, II, p. 21, and Y. Braslavi, *Aliyot-regalim beHar ha-Zeitim, Eretz Yisrael le-Dorotehah*, 1969, pp. 120–144.)

Jews also made pilgrimages to the Mount of Olives on the other Jewish holidays, and indeed all the year round, in order to pray opposite the Temple, for the Western Wall was concealed by rubbish and earth. The Mount of Olives was bare, since the Romans had cut down the trees all around Jerusalem for a distance of 100 *stadia* (15 km) and thus the olive trees had been destroyed (Josephus, *Wars* VI, 2, 7).

The Mount of Olives was chosen as a hallowed place of prayers for the following reasons: the Glory of God was upon it (*Ezekiel* XI, 23) – the High Priest used to burn the Red Heifer there, and the site was therefore considered as an altar and a place of worship; the entire Temple area, with the gates, could be seen from it, and thus it became a suitable place for lamenting the

Destruction. Jews from the Land of Israel gathered on the Mount together with Jews from the Diaspora during *Sukkoth*, and on *Hosha'ana Rabbah* they circled the mountain seven times.

The Mount of Olives is about 80 m higher than the Temple Mount, and it was therefore a lookout point and one of the sites for lighting beacons.

Mountain of Beacons

The Mishnah (*Rosh Hashanah* 2, 4) states: "Whence did they carry the (chain of) beacons? From the Mount of Olives (in Jerusalem) to Sartaba, and from Sartaba to Grofina, and from Grofina to Hauran, and from Hauran to Beth Biltin." The *Tosephta* mentions the mountains of Machaerus and Gador. The flares from the Mount of Olives were thus directed to Samaria, to Mount Sartaba (Alexandrion, opposite the present-day Damia Bridge) over a distance of 40 km, and thence to Galilee, the Hauran and Babylon, and also westward across the Jordan to Machaerus, 45 km from the Mount of Olives, and to Gador (Salt), visible 25 km from Sartaba.

The Ceremony of Hallowing the Month

According to the *Talmud*, hallowing (fixing) the new month was celebrated in Jerusalem while the Second Temple was in existence; the ceremony was probably unchanged after the Destruction, when the blessing and intercalation were done by the *Sanhedrin* at Yavneh and later transferred to Galilee.

The month was hallowed as follows: "There was a large court in Jerusalem called Beth Ya'azek. There all the witnesses used to assemble, and the *Beth Din* used to examine them." At first any man could bear witness, but when heretics became more common the witnesses had to be known to the court. Once the testimony had been accepted "the head of the *Beth Din* says 'sanctified,' and all the people repeat after him, 'sanctified, sanctified,' " (*Rosh Hashanah* 2, 5).

The hallowing of the month and intercalation of the year were done by three elders (sages). The *Nasi* of the *Sanhedrin* apparently had a special court, qualified by the Great Court to hallow the month. The ceremony of intercalation attracted many spectators. The negotiations between the sages would last all night, in a closed session, and sometimes aroused the suspicions of the Roman government. Because of the fear of revolt, intercalation of the year was sometimes forbidden.

After the *Sanhedrin* moved to Galilee the *Nasi* used to send scholars to Ein Tav, between Lod and Yavneh, to hallow the month in Judea, because of

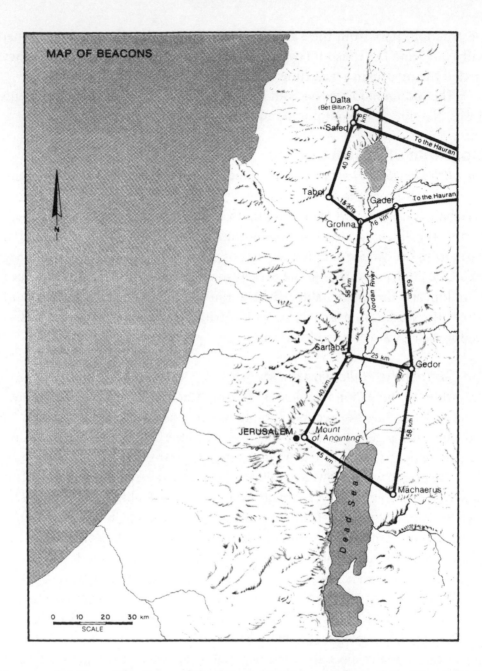

its sacred nature. The Jews of the Diaspora were notified of the New Moon by beacon signals. "How did they light the beacons? They used to bring long poles of the cedar and reeds and olive-wood and flax fluff, which they tied to the poles with a string, and someone used to go up to the top of a mountain and set fire to them, and wave them to and fro and up and down until he saw the next one doing the same thing on the top of the second mountain, and so, on the top of the third mountain. Whence did they carry the chain of beacons? From the Mount of Olives (in Jerusalem) to Sartaba, and from Sartaba to Grofina, and from Grofina to Hauran, and from Hauran to Beth-Biltin. The one on Beth-Biltin did not budge from there but went on waving to and fro and up and down until he saw the whole of the Diaspora before him like one bonfire" (*Rosh Hashanah* 2, 3–4). What was the "bonfire"? Each of the Babylonian Jews would light a flare and go up to his roof, so that the signalers at Beth-Baltin would know the signal had been received.

The signal of the New Moon was awaited at the various mountaintops, but the Roman government suspected the signalers of transmitting rebellious or seditious messages, since the Parthians, Rome's enemies, lived in Babylon. In the course of time the various sects, such as the Samaritans, began to light signal flares at the wrong times, to confuse the distant communities, and flare signaling was no longer regarded as the chief source of information. The method continued in use, however, until the second century C.E. Rabbi Yehudah *haNasi* ordered the practice to be stopped, apparently on Roman instructions; the New Moon was thereafter proclaimed by messenger. The *Mishnah* says: "Originally they used to light beacons. When the Cutheans (Samaritans) adopted evil courses they made a rule that messengers should go forth" (*Rosh Hashanah* 2, 2).

Not every month was proclaimed thus, but only the months of the Jewish festivals: "There are six New Moons for which messengers go forth (from Jerusalem to the Diaspora): (the New Moon) of Nissan, on account of Passover; of Ab, on account of the Fast; of Elul, on account of the New Year; of Tishri for the adjustment of the Festivals; of Kislev, on account of *Hanukah*; and of Adar, on account of *Purim*" (*Rosh Hashanah* 1, 3).

The leaders of the communities in the Diaspora awaited the instructions about the New Moon eagerly, since this was indispensable for determining the times of the festivals, and depended on the Land of Israel. It was therefore ruled that the year could not be intercalated outside the country, and any intercalation done abroad, when it could have been done in the Land of Israel, was consequently invalid. This recognition of the authority of the *Nasi* in the Land of Israel led to unity of the people with their spiritual leaders, as well as national discipline. When the Jewish community in the country grew sparse and its connections with the Diaspora weakened, Hillel the Second devised the fixed calendar, in 359 C.E.; it is in use to this day.

Which was the Mount of Anointing, where the flare signaling started? Most scholars identify it with *Baten el-Hawa*; this seems rather unlikely, however, as this low hill, today the site of a monastery named The Field of Abraham and surrounded by pine groves, does not afford a view of Mount Sartaba (Alexandrion), in the central Jordan Valley opposite the Damia Bridge.

The site of the Mount of Anointing may be determined by studying the site of the Red Heifer, the ashes of which were used for purification and cleansing, as laid down in *Numbers* xix: "A causeway was made from the Temple Mount to the Mount of Olives, being constructed of arches above arches, each arch placed directly above each pier (of the arch below), as protection against the Tomb of the Void, whereby the priest who was to burn the Heifer, the Heifer itself, and all who aided in its preparation went forth to the Mount of Olives" (*Parah* 3, 6).

According to this source, the Mount of Olives was beyond the causeway, which was apparently near the Kidron Valley. Elsewhere in the *Mishnah* we find: "...the Eastern Gate, over which was a representation of the Palace of Susa, and through which the High Priest who burnt the Red Heifer, and all who assisted with it, used to go forth to the Mount of Olives" (*Middot* 1, 3). It is thus apparent that the High Priest approached the Mount of Olives through the Gate of Susa (*Shushan*), the eastern gate of the Temple Mount. The Mount of Olives was obviously one of the peaks of what is known today as the Mount of Olives, probably north of A-Tur, since this is the only spot from which Sartaba is visible. Rabbi Ishtori Hapharhi (fourteenth century) writes that the Mount of Olives is in the eastern part of Jerusalem, and tradition places it north of the Tomb of Huldah, but slightly lower down. (He identified the Tomb of Huldah on the Mount of Olives, north of the present-day Intercontinental Hotel.) More precise information may be found in the *Mishnah*: "All the walls of the Temple were high, except the eastern wall, so that the High Priest who burnt the Red Heifer might while standing on the top of the Mount of Olives, by directing his gaze carefully, see the door of the *Heikhal* at the time of the sprinkling of the blood" (*Middot* 2, 4).

According to this source, the Mount of Anointing is lofty, and lies east of the entrance to the Temple Sanctuary.

The northern part of the Mount of Olives is higher than the south, and served as a lookout point over the Temple Mount and Jerusalem, for watching both pilgrims and possible invaders.

Mount Scopus

Mount Scopus is popularly identified today with the hill on which the original Hebrew University buildings stand, but the sources do not bear this out. Josephus describes the location of Mount Scopus when writing of the Roman campaigns: "Caesar, being joined during the night by the legion from Ammaus, moved the next day from thence and advanced to Scopus, as it is called, the place from which the city first became visible, and the stately pile of the sanctuary shone forth: whence it is that this spot – a flat adjoining the northern quarter of the town – is appropriately called Scopus" (*Wars* v, 2). This was the site of the camp of Cestius Gallus, the Roman commander, at the outset of the Roman revolt in 66 c.e. (*Wars* ii, 19). The site of Scopus is thus on the main road from Givat-Shaul (present-day *Tell el-Full*) toward Jerusalem. Today travelers coming south have their first view of the Temple Mount from the vicinity of Givat-Hamivtar (at a height of about 815 m). Alexander the Great and Simon the Just probably met at this spot (*Antiquities* xi, 8; *Yoma* 9).

Mount Scopus is mentioned in the *Talmud* in connection with the Destruction: "Once again they were coming up to Jerusalem together, and just as they were coming to Mount Scopus...they fell a-weeping" (*Makkoth* 24). The *Tosephta* characterized Mount Scopus as the spot from which there is an uninterrupted view southward.

The Israel Defense Forces attacked Jerusalem by way of the historical Givat-Shaul (*Tell el-Ful*) and Givat-Hamivtar in the Six Day War.

Necropolis Hills

Rock-cut graves were in use in the Middle East from earliest antiquity, since burning of the dead was forbidden to Semitic peoples. Family graves are implied in phrases such as "and he was gathered to his people"; "and he slept with his fathers"; "and he was buried in the grave of his fathers." The family burial plot was thus of great significance, as was the case in the story of the Cave of Machpelah, in Hebron.

The necropolis of the Jewish people lies along the Mount of Olives and its western slopes. Joel's prophecy (iv, 2) of the future judgment of the nations includes the following: "I will gather all nations and will bring them down into the Valley of Jehoshaphat..." and also (iv, 12): "Let the nations be stirred up, and come up to the Valley of Jehoshaphat, for there will I sit to judge all the nations round about." The Jewish necropolis stretched over an area of 6.5 km, covering the Mount of Olives and its slopes, and the length of the Kidron Valley, from Wadi Nar near the junction of the Ben-Hinnom Valley with the Kidron, up to the western slopes of the village of Sha'afat, at the tomb of Umm el-'Ammud. The vast majority of the graves are east, north and south of the city, since the rocks in the west are more brittle and fissured, and the prevailing westerly winds would have borne evil odors to the city. There are three major areas of graves: the Kidron Valley, the slopes of the Mount of Olives and the Sanhedriya vicinity.

The Royal Family of Judah buried their dead within the City of David at first, but the graves were later transferred because of the holiness of the Temple.

Tombs of the House of David

The graves were researched by Ch. Clermont-Ganneau in the eighties of the 19th century; K. Galling in 1900–1908; A.L. Sukenik and N. Avigad in the fifties and sixties of the 20th century.

About 800 graves were discovered from the First and Second Temple periods, six kilometers around Jerusalem, in the valley's cliffs and the hill's slopes around the city, most of which were in the east. In front of about half of the graves, an open courtyard was carved out in the rock of the hill, and sometimes stone benches were placed and a purifying *mikveh* for visitors. In 450 graves from the Second Temple period, niches were carved in the majority, as well as a rectangular entrance. In very few there was found a round, rolling stone that moves on a permanent track to close the grave. In a quarter of the graves were small niches for gathering bones, and there are those who were placed in sarcophagus in sub-graves.

Most of the graves were carved out in the second century B.C.E., until the destruction of the Second Temple. Many of the sarcophagi were decorated with engravings and painted yellow or red. The most common patterns are the shape of rose (rosette), and also acanthus leaves, tree and palm branches, fruit and other geometric patterns, tiers of granite and more.

Nehemiah (III, 16) says: "After him repaired Nehemiah the son of Azbuk, the ruler of the district of Beth-zur, unto the place over against the sepulchers of David, and unto the pool that was made, and unto the house of the mighty men." The Tomb of David was thus apparently near a pool in the Valley (the Cheesemongers' Valley) i.e., in the City of David. The three series of the Tombs of the House of David were discovered by R. Weill in 1913–1914 in the southern part of the city of David, some 100 m northeast of Hezekiah's Pool at the end of the tunnel. Two deep, rounded, burial caves were found; the western one 16 m deep, 1.80 – 3 m high and about 3 m wide, and the eastern one 12 m deep, 1.70 – 3 m high and about 3 m wide. Weill ascribed them to the Tombs of the House of David, but in Hadrian's day the place was used as a quarry, and stones were taken from there for the city buildings, thus largely destroying the series of ancient tombs. Excellent examples of ancient quarrying methods are shown by the scars in the various rock strata.

The family of the House of David, as well as some of the prophets, and a priest, were buried there. David and Solomon were buried in the City of David itself, so was King Uzziah of Judah, as described in *II Kings*, XV, 7: "And Azariah (Uzziah) slept with his fathers, and they buried him with his fathers in the city of David." Also interred there were the kings of Judah, Ahaz (*II Kings* XVI, 20) and Hezekiah (*II Chronicles* XXXII, 33): "And Hezekiah slept with his fathers, and they buried him in the ascent of the sepulchers of the sons of David, and all Judah and the inhabitants of Jerusalem did him honor at his death"; Menasseh "slept with his fathers, and was buried in the garden of Uzza" (*II Kings* XXI, 18), probably the tomb of Uzziah king of Judah. The priest Jehoiada, who served in the time of King Joash, and made repairs to the Temple, was also buried there: "And they buried him in the city of David among the kings, because he had done good to Israel, and toward God and His House" (*II Chronicles* XXIV, 16). Jewish sources also place the graves of the prophet Isaiah and the prophetess Huldah in these tombs.

The Jewish Sages gave reasons for the continued burial of the kings in the House of David within the city, despite its sacred nature. *Avot d'Rabbi Nathan* gives the following explanation: "No graves may be kept up there excepting the graves of the House of David, and of Huldah the prophetess, which were there since the days of the early prophets. And when (all other) graves were cleared away, why were these not cleared away? They say: There was a tunnel there which gave passage to the uncleanness into the brook of Kidron." A second version states the only dead allowed in the city were the kings of the House of David, and Isaiah and Huldah. The theory of the tunnel bearing away all the uncleanness recurs in the *Tosephta* (*Baba Bathra* 1). A Byzantine source (354 C.E.) recounts the burial of the prophet Isaiah with great pomp, in the vicinity of the Siloam spring, close to the tombs of the kings, which lay west of the graves of the Jews. These royal tombs originated in the time of King Solomon, who hewed David's Tomb out of the rock in the east.

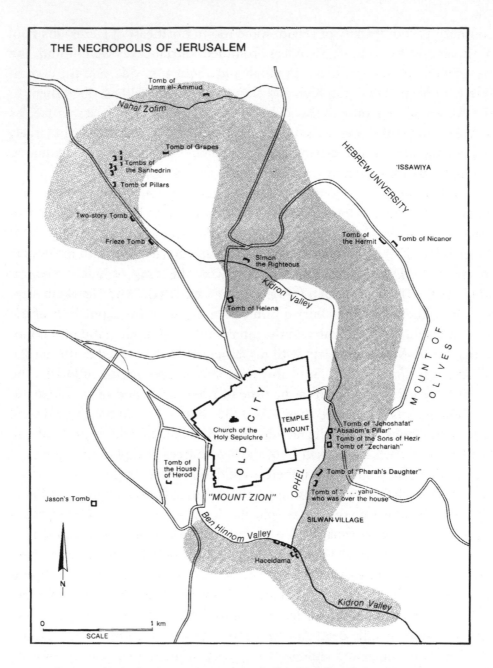

THE NECROPOLIS OF JERUSALEM

Tomb of
Umm el-Ammud

Nahal Zofim

Tomb of Grapes

Tombs of
the Sanhedrin

Tomb of Pillars

Two-story Tomb

Frieze Tomb

HEBREW UNIVERSITY

'ISSAWIYA

Tomb of
the Hermit

Tomb of Nicanor

Simon
the Righteous

Kidron Valley

Tomb of Helena

MOUNT OF OLIVES

Church of the
Holy Sepulchre

TEMPLE
MOUNT

OLD CITY

Tomb of
the House
of Herod

Tomb of "Jehoshafat"
"Absalom's Pillar"
Tomb of the Sons of Hezir
Tomb of "Zechariah"

Tomb of "Pharah's Daughter"

OPHEL

Tomb of ". . . . yahu
who was over the house"

Jason's Tomb

"MOUNT ZION"

SILWAN-VILLAGE

Ben Hinnom Valley

N

Haceldama

Kidron Valley

0   1 km
SCALE

Yohanan (John) Hyrcanus opened the Tomb of David and removed 3,000 talents of silver, in order to pay ransom to Antiochus who was besieging Jerusalem (*Antiquities* XIII, 8; *Wars* I, 2). Herod similarly removed "many ornaments of gold and precious goods that were laid up there" (*Antiquities* XVI, 7). The tombs were thus common knowledge up to the end of the Second

Temple period, and were used as quarries by Hadrian's builders for the walls
of Aelia Capitolina.

The excavations of Professor B. Mazar in 1971 at the southwest corner
of the Western Wall have revealed a series of tombs resembling Phoenician
tombs on the shores of Nahariyah. Professor Mazar ascribes these tombs to
the royal family of Judah.

The Mount of Olives was suitable for excavating rock tombs and erecting monuments, due partly to its proximity to the City of David, but mainly
because of its soft, easily cut rock. During the period of the expansion and
fortification of Jerusalem, beginning with the repairs to the walls carried out
by the Hasmonean kings and culminating in the monumental building projects initiated by Herod, hard rock for construction became a necessity. Many
quarries were then opened, mainly in the upper part of the Kidron Valley
where the rock is hardest and less broken up. After quarries were abandoned,
they were sold as gravesites, mainly to the rich and influential of the city.

Tombs of the Sanhedrin

The graves of the Kidron Valley and the Mount of Olives are dealt with in the
comprehensive work by Professor N. Avigad, *Matzevot Kedumot beNahal
Kidron*. The burial chambers in the Sanhedriyah area were discovered in the
early seventeenth century. The western chamber contained sixty-six sepulchers
and therefore became known as the Tombs of the *Sanhedrin*. (The *Sanhedrin*
still used to assemble in the time of Judah the Maccabee in the Chamber of
Hewn Stone in Jerusalem, with seventy members and the *Nasi*.) The site was
earlier known as "Head of the Vineyards" or "Field of Graves."

In 1949, 21 graves were discovered; 20 more were found at the top of a
hill further south. Many other graves have yet to be excavated. These burial
chambers, mostly located in abandoned quarries, were used by the rich of the
city, possibly by the *Sanhedrin*, from the middle of the second century B.C.E.
to the middle of the first century C.E.

Jews of the Diaspora wished to be buried in the Holy City, and the
remains of Jews who had died in other countries were brought in coffins
to Jerusalem and interred there. All of the burial chambers of Sanhedriyah,
including the courtyards, are rock-cut. A courtyard was formed out of an
ancient quarry, and the burial chamber was excavated at one end of it. Most
of the courtyards lack seats, but the courtyard of the Tombs of the *Sanhedrin*
(with quarrying scars all around it) contains benches hewn out of the rock for

visitors. The uncleanness of the dead precluded any visits to the actual graves. Some burial chambers contain a trough, which was filled by rainwater flowing through a conduit cut in the rock. This water served for ritual purification. The courtyard leads into a smaller court, enclosed on three sides. The passage into this court at the Tombs of the *Sanhedrin* has a pediment decorated with plant motifs: acanthus leaves in a lyre shape, with tendrils growing out of them, and further acanthus leaves, interspersed with pomegranates and figs. This is evidence of the high level of Judaeo-Hellenistic decorative and burial art, which developed in the Land of Israel during the first century C.E.

The inner entrance to the small courtyard, relatively large in size, is decorated with a design of acanthus leaves. The opening was closed by a stone door, and was used for placing additional sarcophagi in the tomb. The openings of the burial chambers are usually small, 50 × 60 cm, and just adequate for inserting a sarcophagus. On the right side of the courtyard is a deep cavity with a room for a single grave; one sarcophagus was found there.

There are three types of burial chambers: chambers without burial recesses; chambers with burial recesses; and chambers with burial recesses and vaults.

Jews adopted two modes of burial: burial in a stone sarcophagus, placed in a recess, or interment in a stone ossuary, placed in a vault. The vault containing a sarcophagus was 2 m long and 0.5 m wide, while one containing an ossuary was rock-cut, with an arched roof, 2.2 m long, 1.2 m high and 0.5 m wide. The ossuary contained the remains of the body, collected about a year after burial, during which time the corpse lay on the floor of the burial chamber. The source of this custom is unknown; it was not traditional among Semitic peoples and, in fact, constituted a disturbance of the dead. The custom is mentioned in the Jerusalem *Talmud*.

The Tombs of the *Sanhedrin* include chambers with burial recesses in the basement of the complex. One of the graves contains a sarcophagus decorated with a relief of lilies.

A magnificent burial chamber of the first century C.E. was discovered on the western slope of the village of Sha'afat, near the Sorek Valley, northwest of Sanhedriyah; it was popularly known as Umm el-'Ammud (Mother of Pillars), after the Ionic and Doric pillars of the façade, which is now largely in ruins. The masonry is Herodian, with wide, flat margins and a prominent central boss, and the entrance is arched, 2.6 m high and 3.2 m wide. Four burial recesses were hewn in the front room, and an additional recess in the center, leading to a courtyard with four burial recesses, is now blocked up. The western wall contains five recesses, and there are three more in the east, with a vault 2.4 m high and 1.9 m wide. A flat cistern for the use of visitors lies 20 m east of the tomb series.

Tomb of Simon the Just

About 500 m northeast of the Mandelbaum Gate, east of Wadi Joz and near the riverbed, is a tomb popularly ascribed to Simon the Just, High Priest during the Second Temple period. He "…was one of the last survivors of the Great Synagogue. He used to say: upon three things the world is based – upon the Torah, upon the Temple service, and upon the practice of charity" (*Aboth* 1, 2). The tomb is entered through a building, and steps lead down to the burial chamber. The southern wall contains a small pool. This type of tomb is known in archaeology as a trough tomb.

Oriental Jews celebrate *Lag Ba-Omer* and the day following the festival of *Shavuoth* in memory of Simon the Just; they make pilgrimages to the tomb, lighting candles and laying requests before it. These are also dates of pilgrimages to the tombs of Rabbi Meir Baal Ha-Ness in Tiberias, and of Rabbi Simeon Bar Yohai and his son, Rabbi Elazar, at Meron. The visitors pray at the tombs, making requests and petitions, and entire families spend the day there, eating, drinking, singing and dancing. The tomb of Simon the Just and the area surrounding it are Jewish property. The tomb dates to the second century C.E., and according to a Latin inscription it is that of a woman, Julia Sabina.

Tombs of Queen Helena and the Royal Family of Adiabene

These tombs are 350 m southwest of the Tomb of Simon the Just, in the upper part of Wadi Joz and at the northern corner of Saladin Street, near its junction with Nablus Road. They were discovered by de Saulcy in 1863 and excavated by Clermont-Ganneau in 1867. Originally the tombs were erroneously identified as the Tombs of the kings of Judah, and are known to this day as the Tombs of the Kings. Jewish medieval custom also identified the site as the Tombs of the Kings, although it was also known traditionally as the Tomb of Kalba Savua, Rabbi Akiba's wealthy father-in-law, who, according to legend, used to provide poverty-stricken guests with sumptuous meals (*Gittin* 56a). The site is known in Arabic as Qubur al-Salatin or Qubur al-Muluk, graves of the sultans or kings.

The tomb is of the family of Queen Helena of Adiabene, in Mesopotamia,

Courtyard of Queen Helena's tomb

who converted to Judaism in 50 C.E. and came to live in Jerusalem. The entrance corridor contains 23 rock-cut stairs, and is 30 m long and 9 m wide. Two conduits are hewn along the sides of the corridor, bringing rainwater to two pools, which were used for purification and washing. The main courtyard is 26 × 27 m in area, and its walls are 8 m high. A rock-cut cistern in the west of the courtyard supplied water for the burial ceremony.

Josephus (*Antiquities* xx, 4) mentions three pyramids rising above the façade of the tomb. The remnant of one capital was found in the excavations. The façade itself is slightly damaged. The pediment of the façade is beautifully decorated, with a bunch of grapes at the center, flanked by sheaves of palm leaves and acanthus. The wreath of intertwined leaves, fruit and cones is continued down along the side of the entrance. The decorations are in the Judaeo-Hellenistic style, as in the Tombs of the *Sanhedrin*. The façade also had two pillars resembling the monumental pillars of the tombs at Umm el-'Ammud, and the Tombs of Nicanor and the Sons of Hezir (see below).

The entrance to the chamber was closed by a circular rolling stone, operated mechanically by a rope moved from a pit in the courtyard, and connected with another pit in the outer hall (M. Cohen, *Sefer Kivrei ha-Melachim*). This burial chamber has eight rooms, with burial recesses and vaults. Several sarcophagi were found, one decorated in a lily pattern. One had a two-line carved inscription in Hebrew-Syriac square lettering, followed by a line in Aramaic. The inscription (which reads: "This is the sarcophagus of Zedan the Queen") refers to a queen; de Saulcy identified the name as that of King Zedekiah's queen, thus reaffirming the name of Tombs of the Kings. Euting discovered an inscribed sherd, which he read as "Helene," in Hebrew script. In Professor Avigad's opinion, based on the inscription on the sarcophagus, the sherd and the architecture of the site, the art is Jewish, of the first century C.E. Josephus (*Antiquities* XX, 4) strengthens this case: "But Monobazus sent her bones, as well as those of Izates, his brother, to Jerusalem, and gave order that they should be buried at the pyramids which their mother had erected; they were three in number, and distant no more than three furlongs from the city Jerusalem." Elsewhere (*Wars* V, 2) Josephus says that the Tomb of Queen Helena was near the gate of the Towers of the Women in the Third Wall, i.e., near the Kidron Valley.

Graves at Givat-Hamivtar and French Hill

In 1968 four Jewish burial chambers were discovered at Givath-Hamivtar, from the end of the Second Temple period. Ossuaries decorated with lily and palm leaves were found, one of which contained ankle bones nailed together, evidence of a crucifixion; the ossuary bears the name of Yohanan the potter. Another ossuary bears the name of Simon who built the Sanctuary, presumably one of the artisans who worked on Herod's Temple. A coin was found from the second year of the Revolt, and an Aramaic inscription from the period of the Second Temple, in Samaritan calligraphy instead of the Jewish square lettering. The inscription tells of one *Abba bar Kahana Eleazar bar Aharon Rabbah*, who was born in Jerusalem, exiled to Babylon, and returned bearing with him the bones of *Mattati bar Yahud*, which he interred in this chamber, which he had bought.

Prof. E. Oren discovered many ossuaries on French Hill (north of Jerusalem, on the Ramallah road) from the late Hasmonean period to the first century C.E., just before the destruction of the Second Temple. The dating is based on the finds of bottles, pottery lamps, vials and cooking pots. An oil-press with a device for crushing and pressing olives in the northeastern corner of the hill, as well as a winepress with a treading-floor, pipes and pits for collecting the wine. The area was settled during the Hasmonean period; most of the structures are Byzantine, dating from the fifth and sixth centuries C.E., when the farm of a monastery existed there. Dr. G.P. Strange found six chambers with recesses, part

of a Jewish cemetery of the late Second Temple period. The cover and recep-
tacle of the ossuary bear the name of *Yehoseph bar-Haggai*, written three times.
Herodian lamps, cooking pots and other vessels were also found there.

Tomb of Nicanor and Tomb of the Nazirite

The Tomb of Nicanor was discovered in 1903 on Mount Scopus. It is located
near the Hebrew University buildings, north of the Botanical Garden and
opposite the former National Library, east of the road. Professor Sukenik
excavated it in 1928–29. The tomb consisted of four burial chambers, and
contained several ossuaries, one with a Greek inscription, which, according
to Professor Avigad, marked the burial place of Nicanor the Alexandrian who
made the doors. This refers to the copper doors of the Temple, brought by
Nicanor from Alexandria (*Yoma* 38, 1). The inscription ends with "Nicanor
Alexa," the Hebrew names of the owner of the tomb.

Two pioneers of the *Hovevei Zion* (Lovers of Zion) movement, I.L. Pin-
sker, who died in 1891, and M. Ussishkin, who became president of the Jewish
National Fund and died in 1941, were interred in a burial chamber nearby.

Nicanor's Cave is complex; the wide courtyard leads through a façade
built of stone piers into four series of chambers with wide vaults. The central
series has an arched ceiling and contains several stories of vault and chambers.

Another tomb was discovered in 1967, near the former National Library,
about 60 m southwest of the Rosenblum building, and was called by Professor
Avigad the "Tomb of the Nazirite." The Tomb is Herodian and consists of four
rock-hewn chambers. The walls, arches and facades are built of ashlar blocks.
Ten ossuaries were found, some damaged. One of them bears a relief of two
bunches of grapes, tendrils and lilies, resembling those found in the Tomb of
Queen Helena and the House of Herod.

Cave of Huldah

The cave is just east of the road from the Russian Convent at A-Tur, on the
Mount of Olives, in the direction of the Intercontinental Hotel. It contains
two chambers, the upper one larger, leading down into the courtyard and to
the lower chamber, where there is a monument to the prophetess Huldah. The
sources report that the grave of Huldah was in the City of David; the belief
that it was on the Mount of Olives springs from folklore and is not founded
on fact. The tradition is mentioned by Rabbi Moses Basola, who visited Jeru-

Rocky terrain of Israeli mountains before the construction of agricultural terraces by the Israeli inhabitants (M. Har-El)

The Israelite and Roman path from Tekoa to Ein Gedi (A. Erev)

Threshing floor in an Arab village (M. Har-El)

Pilgrim's path to Jerusalem in the Second Temple period from the west to the Western Wall

Western Wall tunnel, built-up ceiling and aqueduct (A. Erev)

Wilson's Arch at the Western Wall (A. Erev)

The village of Beitar and Wadi Sorek in Jerusalem (M. Har-El)

Wine press in Jerusalem (M. Har-El)

Agricultural terraces and towers in the Jerusalem hills (M. Har-El)

Wine press in the biblical city of Giv'on (M. Har-El)

Israeli oil press, from the excavations by H. Makne. (M. Har-El)

Wadi Perat of Jeremiah the Prophet outside Jerusalem (M. Har-El)

Tower in a Jerusalem vineyard (M. Har-El)

Path to Beit Horon (M. Har-El)

salem in the sixteenth century. He describes a large building atop the Mount of Olives, where the prophetess Huldah was buried in a marble edifice. The custom was to light candles at the grave, after first paying the Arab guard (*Masa'ot Eretz Yisrael*, p. 154). Rabbi Simha bar Yehoshua wrote of his ascent to the Mount of Olives, where the grave of the prophetess lay; the Arabs had erected a mosque and forbade the Jews entrance, which could, however, be gained by bribing the guards. He goes on to say that conditions have improved considerably regarding access to the tomb (*Ahavat Zion* 60, 19). Yehoseph Schwartz reports that this was the tomb of a gentile woman from Antiochia, Margarita Pelagia, originally a singer and theater dancer, who converted to Christianity (from paganism) in 453 C.E., came to the Land of Israel and built herself a little hut on the Mount of Olives. She was buried there as a saint, and a place of worship was erected on the spot. When the Moslems conquered Jerusalem, they buried their holy woman, Bint Hassan el-Masri, in the same place (*Tevuot ha-Aretz*, Jerusalem, 1900, pp. 350–51).

Tombs of Silwan

A survey made by Prof. D. Ussishkin and Dr. G. Barkai in the summer of 1968 showed that the First Temple burial caves on the slope of the Mount of Olives were damaged during the Roman-Byzantine period, probably in the fifth and sixth centuries C.E., when Christian hermits used them for dwellings. Each cave was altered to suit the needs of its occupant, and the changes were destructive. In the course of settling the village of Silwan on the slope of the mountain the tombs were almost completely destroyed and the caves put to use as water cisterns, sewage pits, storerooms, chicken coops and sheep pens. Travelers in the nineteenth century noted that the villagers of Silwan lived in rock-cut caves and that the village was a robbers' lair.

Ussishkin found three groups of ancient tombs on the Mount of Olives: tombs with gabled roofs, tombs with flat roofs, and monolithic tombs similar to the tombs of "…*yahu* who was over the household," and of the Daughter of Pharaoh, which were hewn out of the rock, and stood separate from it.

Tombs with Gabled Roofs

Prof. D. Ussishkin surveyed seven graves of this type, all hewn out in the escarpment under the lowest row of houses in the village. These are handsome tombs, hewn painstakingly and with great precision. Most of the tombs are single or double, but one contains three burial shelves. The openings, high above ground level, are small (0.5 × 0. 6 m), and entry is only possible by a ladder. The ceiling inside the chamber is gabled (triangular); only one ceiling is rounded. The burial rooms are small, the largest being only 2.4 m long and 1.3 m wide. The walls below the gable are 2.1 m high, and the height of the room at its center is 2.55 m. The burial shelf, trough-shaped, is either to the right or the left of the entrance, and a stone pillow is left projecting at one end to take the head. In two of the tombs there is a wide double burial trough, apparently for husband and wife. The length of the trough varies from 1.75 m to 2.10 m; they were thus apparently prepared before death. Ussishkin regards this mode of burial as non-Jewish, and basically Phoenician; the tombs were probably made by the slaves of King Hiram of Tyre and their descendants. The style of the single tombs is evidence of the prominence and wealth of those buried there.

Monolithic Tombs

These tombs are all above ground, hewn out of the rock but standing completely apart from it. They consist of a monument made of one mass of rock, containing a grave (examples are *Absalom's Monument* and *Zechariah's Tomb*, of the Second Temple period). Three monolithic tombs, dating from the time of the kings of Judah, were found in the village of Silwan. The best known is the Tomb of Pharaoh's Daughter.

Tomb of "…Yahu Who Was Over the Household"

This tomb is at the northern tip of the village of Silwan (*Shiloah*), opposite the Ophel hill, some dozen meters south of the Tomb of Pharaoh's Daughter. It is rock-hewn, square, and contains one room with a gabled ceiling. Its façade is 8 m in length, and the dressed façade is 4 m high. Today an Arab house stands on top of it, but originally it had a pyramid in pure Egyptian style. The left side of the façade had an opening 1.9 m high and 1.44 m wide. The chamber inside is 2.25 × 4.65 m in area, and 2.95 m high. The walls are plastered because the chamber was used as a water cistern by the inhabitants of the house. Today it serves as a storeroom.

The tomb was discovered by Clermont-Ganneau in 1870. He noted a three-line inscription in ancient Hebrew letters in the lintel stone, and another line over the window in the front. The inscriptions could not be deciphered by Clermont-Ganneau, except for one word meaning "house." He therefore suggested that this be read "who was over the household." The stones were removed and sent to the British Museum. Professor Avigad deciphered the inscription in 1945–47 to read as follows: "This is (the grave of...) *yahu* who was over the household; there is no gold and silver (save) only (his bones) and the bones of his bond maiden with him; cursed be the man who opens this."

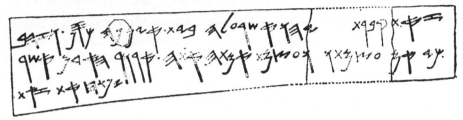

Tomb of "...Yahu Who Was Over the Household"

On the basis of the designation "who was over the household," Professor Avigad assumes that this was the grave of an important personage: the Bible mentions seven persons bearing this title. On the basis of the title, and the suffix "*yahu*" to the name, the tomb dates from the First Temple period, before the Babylonian exile. Professor Avigad believes that this was the Tomb of Shebna, the scribe of Hezekiah King of Judah, mentioned in Isaiah's prophecy (*Isaiah* XXII, 15–16): "Go, get thee unto this steward, even unto Shebna, who is over the house: What hast thou here? And whom hast thou here, that thou hast hewest thee out here a sepulcher, thou that hewed thee out a sepulcher on high, and gravest a habitation for thyself in the rock?" The Bible and Hebrew seals include other forms of this name, such as Shevaniah and Shevanyahu. This grave is therefore early, from the seventh century B.C.E. Ussishkin believes that the builders of monoliths were influenced by Phoenician culture, and he is of the opinion that Shebna, to whom Avigad ascribes the tomb of "*yahu*," was himself Phoenician, for the title of "treasurer," given by Isaiah, was common among Phoenicians.

Tomb of Pharaoh's Daughter

This is in the northern part of the village, some 60 m northeast of the Tomb of "*yahu* who is over the household," and about 100 m northeast of the Silwan spring. The tomb was acquired by the Russian Archimandrite at the end of the nineteenth century, and was fenced in, thus protecting it from destruction.

The popular name of the tomb stems from Arab tradition, which named it *Qabr bint Fara'un*, or Tomb of the Daughter of Pharaoh; it was known thus from the end of the thirteenth century. De Saulcy discovered it in 1865 and

Professor Avigad investigated it in 1945–47. Avigad thinks that the tomb is in Egyptian style; its pyramidal form served as a monument to the soul of the dead. The tomb is a square monolith, 8.40 × 9.30 m, 4 m high. The ledge is complete on three sides but missing on the fourth. The front entrance is slightly right of center, 1.6 m high and 0.68 m wide, and its threshold is 1.16 m above the rock. A small cavity on the right shows the position of the door hinge. Rectangular niches on both sides of the lintel originally contained inscriptions. In 1844 Clermont-Ganneau found an ancient Hebrew inscription in the left-hand rectangle, but it was undecipherable. The entrance leads into a corridor and thence into a burial chamber, almost square (2.13 × 2.20 m), with a gabled ceiling. A shelf was hewn on one side, for the actual burial. The shelf was destroyed, according to Avigad, by the Byzantine hermit who lived in the tomb; he hollowed out some niches in the wall and also enlarged the entrance, in the process destroying the inscription on the lintel stone. At present only one letter remains, to the left of the opening, and part of another letter preceding it. The tomb was surmounted by a pyramid, which was part of the monolith, as in Zechariah's Tomb. In Ussishkin's view the pyramid was used as a stone quarry; the signs are visible on the roof of the monolith. Some investigators believed that the building was a small Egyptian temple used by Pharaoh's daughter to worship after her marriage to King Solomon; others think it was a Hasmonean tomb.

According to Avigad the calligraphy is similar to that on the nearby Tomb of "*yahu* who was over the household" and the architecture is not Hellenistic. He therefore concludes that this was the tomb of dignitaries of the late First Temple period, who were denied burial within the City of David, near the royal tombs, because of the sanctity of the city. They were buried opposite the kings, east of the Kidron Valley, fairly high up the slope of the Mount of Olives. Several other graves resembling the Tomb of Pharaoh's Daughter were found in the village of Silwan. Gabled tombs have also been found in Anatolia and Etruria.

The Third Monolith

This monolith was discovered by Ussishkin north of the Tomb of "*yahu.*" Its workmanship is superior to that of the other tombs. Today a house is built over it, and only the façade of the tomb is visible. The opening of the monolith is blocked, and it is being used as a water cistern; the new opening is in the courtyard above it. Byzantine hermits who lived there destroyed the opening and roof of the tomb. Its width is 5.25 m, and a height of 4.23 m is preserved. The center of the façade has a deep niche 2.42 m high, 1.5 m wide and 0.5 m deep. This was the site of the original opening. The façade above the niche was smoothed out, and the burial inscription incised in it. The inscription, of three lines, has largely been destroyed but it apparently resembled that on the Tomb of *"yahu."* The upper line has the words "grave of z…" presumably the name of the owner. The second line has the equivalent of "Who will op…" which should be completed as "open," and is apparently a warning to grave-robbers, as in the Tomb of *"yahu."* The inscriptions on the monoliths, resembling those of the Gihon tunnels, and a sherd of a stele discovered in Samaria bearing the word *"which* is," prove, in Ussishkin's view, that the tombs are of the eighth century B.C.E.

Tombs With Flat Roofs

Most of these tombs are on the western slope of the village, and the village houses are built over them. The tombs are thus all part of the houses, and most are destroyed. They are relatively large, and some contain more than one chamber. Ussishkin found varying traditions in the architecture of the tombs; one has a gabled ceiling. The actual burial places are also of varied types: shelf graves, vaults (typical of graves in the Judean Mountains), as well as the troughs found in the tombs with gabled ceilings, and even a rock-hewn sarcophagus.

The magnificence and high quality of the dressing of these tombs led Ussishkin to conclude that they were the Tombs of the House of David. In our opinion, however, the Bible affords evidence that the royal tombs were within the City of David. Avigad divides the ancient tombs of the Valley of Jehoshaphat into two periods: the tombs of Silwan village, along the slope of the Mount of Olives, belonging to the rich and powerful citizens of the First Temple period; and the monuments on the lower slopes of the mountain, close to the bed of the Kidron Valley, from the Second Temple period.

Tomb of Zechariah

At the foot of the Mount of Olives, near the bed of the Kidron Valley and north of the Shiloah spring, is a group of monuments and tombs. In order, from south to north, they are: the Tomb of Zechariah, the Tomb of the Sons of Hezir, Absalom's Monument, and the Cave of Jehoshaphat.

Zechariah's Tomb is the southernmost of these tombs. It was partly cleaned in 1924 by Professor Slouschz, fully excavated in 1960 by Professor Stutchbury, and surveyed in Avigad's book.

Jewish medieval tradition identified this as Zechariah's grave, because of the apocryphal vision in his prophecy (Chapter XIV). Its significance made it a favored burial area for Jews over the generations.

Its structure is better preserved than that of all the others. The monolith is almost square, 5.5 × 5.6 m; the height of its lower portion is 7.5 m. Its corners have half-columns with Ionic capitals, and the monument is surmounted by an Egyptian pyramid 4.7 m high. A small cell is hewn out of the rock at the bottom of the façade. One view is that Zechariah's Tomb is the *nefesh* (soul), i.e., the tombstone, of the nearby Tomb of the Sons of Hezir. Avigad, however, believes that this is a separate tomb. The monument is in a combined Hellenistic-Roman style, common to the architecture of Jewish graves of the late Hellenistic period and the early Roman period, i.e., the end of the Second Temple period. The investigator believes that the descendants of the priestly family of Hezir built this burial chamber later and joined it to the tomb of their ancestors.

Tomb of the Sons of Hezir

The tomb is north of Zechariah's Tomb, between it and Absalom's Monument, at the foot of the Mount of Olives. Avigad investigated it in 1945–47, and determined the style as mixed Egyptian-Hellenistic. The façade, supported by two pillars, is Doric, and this tomb is therefore distinct from the other tombs built in the mixed Hellenistic-Roman style. This is the earliest of the Second Temple tombs found in Jerusalem; it is built in Greek architectural style and dates to the beginning of the Hasmonean period, in the middle of the second century B.C.E. Over the lintel of the entrance, between the pillars, is a Hebrew inscription from the beginning of the first century B.C.E., written by the priestly family of the Sons of Hezir, the seventeenth by lot of priests in the Temple (*1 Chronicles* XXIV, 15).

זה קבר והנבש · שֶׁל אלעזר חניה ווֹעֹזֵר ויודה שמעון ווחנן
בני יוסף בן עוביד יוסף ואלעזר בני חניה
כהנים מבני חזיר

The inscription is written in three lines, beginning: "This is the grave and the *nefesh* (monument) of..." It then gives the names of the members of the family buried there. The *nefesh* mentioned is a pyramidal monument, which formerly existed, according to Avigad, on the left, north of the pillar-façade opening; its base is visible today. A pillar-façade and pyramid are found in the graves of Thebes in Egypt. The burial chamber has a central hall and three burial rooms, with nine niches, and a room with three arches. The cave is entered through a staircase of thirteen steps leading down from the north end. A long corridor joins this complex with the Tomb of Zechariah to its south, by an ascent of ten steps.

Jewish tradition identifies this burial cave with the "house set apart" in which King Uzziah dwelt after he was stricken with leprosy (*II Kings*, xv; *II Chronicles*, xxvi, 21). Medieval Christians regarded the Tomb of the Sons of Hezir as the refuge of the apostle James from the time of the Crucifixion until the Resurrection. They therefore called it after St. James and erected a church (Which no longer exists) in his name.

"Absalom's Monument"

"Absalom's Monument" is first mentioned in the Bible: "Now Absalom in his lifetime had taken and reared up for himself the pillar which is in the king's dale, for he said, I have no son to keep my name in remembrance; and he called the pillar after his own name: and it is called Absalom's Monument unto this day" (*II Samuel*, xviii, 18). It is also mentioned by Josephus: "Now Absalom had erected for himself a stone marble pillar in the king's dale, two furlongs distant from Jerusalem, which he named Absalom's Hand" (*Antiquities* vii, 10). The site of this pillar is unknown. The Pilgrim of Bordeaux (333 c.e.) describes two monuments in the Kidron Valley, which he ascribes to Isaiah and Hezekiah. In 1170 Benjamin of Tudela wrote that the Gate of Jehoshaphat led to the Valley of Jehoshaphat, the "Desert of the Nations," where the monument of Absalom and the Tomb of King Uzziah were located (A. Yaari, *Mas'ot Eretz Yisrael*, 1946, p. 40) All these identifications were erroneous. In 1884 Warren and Conder thought that Absalom's Monument was the Tomb of Alexander Janneus, but this tomb was known to be in Bezetha, northeast of the Temple Mount.

What, then, is this edifice? Clermont-Ganneau cleaned it out and studied it in 1871, followed by Professor N. Slouschz in 1924. Professor Avigad investigated it in 1924–25 and summarized his views in his book. He regarded the monument as being in mixed Egyptian-Greek style.

The building is almost square, 6.80 × 7 m, and 20 m high. It consists of two main portions, differing in structure. The lower part is a monolith, 8.17 m high, built on a projecting ledge. The upper part is built of ashlar blocks, its roof in the form of a concave cone. The southeastern corner of the monument had a water cistern, used by the Jews of Jerusalem as a depository for defective *Torah* scrolls. The monument was damaged by grave-robbers who broke into it from the east, north and west.

The monument is divided into four sections, horizontally:

1. The threshold, which is 1.50 m high in the west and slopes down towards the east. It measures 7.80 × 7.50 m.
2. The monolith, a square room, 2.43 × 2.44 m, 2.48 m high. A gap in the southern wall was used by medieval hermits. The monolith has two vaults, which were the actual burial places.
3. On top of the monolith is a square structure, with sides 6 m long and a height of 2.15 m. It consists of a course of large blocks and a molding of low stones. A square opening in the southern wall was used to insert the coffin.
4. The whole monument is topped by a cylinder, 5.82 m in diameter and 2.65 m high, bearing the concave cone roof; its lower diameter is 6.10 m, and at the top it is 0.80 m, with a height of 5.85 m.

The roof is decorated with a stone carved in the shape of a lotus flower, with six leaves (partly broken). This stone is 0.80 m high and 0.72 m wide. A similar stone was found in the Tomb of Queen Helena.

Avigad regards this as an example of mixed Egyptian-Hellenistic architecture, as in the Tomb of Zechariah. The Hellenistic element is itself a combination of Doric and Ionic influences, as well as Roman; there are Ionic pillars, with Doric capitals beneath an Egyptian molding, with a cone roof in the Hellenistic-Roman mode. Thus there are in the Kidron Valley three similar buildings, with the style of the later ones influenced by that of the earlier ones. The monolith of the Tomb of Pharaoh's Daughter is the earliest, with its pure Egyptian pyramid; the Tomb of Zechariah, which copied the shape of the Daughter of Pharaoh, with the addition of Ionic columns; and "Absalom's Monument," whose builders inserted, between the concave Egyptian cone and the Greek pillars, Roman capitals decorated with a spiral pattern and discs, and exchanged the Egyptian pyramid for a Hellenistic cone.

Inside the monument there are two vaults, each 2.25 m long. From this Avigad concluded that the building was not simply a monument, such as that of the Sons of Hezir, but that the monolith at the bottom was used for burial, while the *nefesh* was built above it in a rounded form. He assumes that the complex of Absalom's Monument and the Cave of Jehoshaphat was built by a rich family of some standing. The Cave of Jehoshaphat was thus the burial place for the many children of the family, while "Absalom's Monument" was reserved for the family elders.

Tombs similar to "Absalom's Monument" have been found in the Middle East, and the most typical of the kind are in Petra. Avigad therefore fixes the period of the building in the Roman period, at the beginning of the first century C.E.

The Cave of Jehoshaphat

This cave lies behind "Absalom's Monument," to its northeast. Christian tradition fixes it as the Tomb of King Jehoshaphat of Judah, although the Bible places his grave within the City of David (*I Kings* XX, 51; *II Chronicles* XXI, 1). It was excavated by Professor N. Slouschz in 1924, and investigated further by Professor Avigad in 1945–47.

The direction of both monuments runs parallel. The entry to the cave is wide, with a decorated gable, and is approached by stairs. The opening is 2.5 m wide by 3.38 m high, and the doorposts are 1.37 m deep. The center of the pediment is decorated with an acanthus motif, lyre-shaped, with tendrils spiraling between reliefs of various fruits and lilies. This gable resembles those of the Tombs of the Sanhedrin in decoration and is in the Greek-Hellenistic style developed by Jewish art in the Land of Israel. The cave is contemporary with "Absalom's Monument," i.e., from the first century C.E., under Roman rule.

The cave contains eight subterranean burial rooms: the first one is the entrance hall to the burial cave, and the second is arched and contains a burial recess, as do the other rooms. During the Middle Ages the cave was used as a depository for worn-out religious articles.

Tombs in the Ben-Hinnom Valley

The Ben-Hinnom Valley was one of the chief sources of building material for Second Temple Jerusalem, on account of its proximity to the city, as well as to the softness of the rock, which facilitated quarrying (compared to the rock in the area of the Tombs of the Sanhedrin, which was too hard for the purpose).

The Valley contains many tombs, of early and late periods, especially in the lower part. One of the caves has two parallel arched rooms, unique among the burial series of Jerusalem. These tombs are highly decorated; their walls bear reliefs of doors, and one central door is decorated with a shell relief. According to Avigad, this series and others date to the end of the Second Temple period.

Haqal Dama at the Convent of St. Onophrius

A many-branched complex of tombs is to be found at the southeastern end of the Ben-Hinnom Valley, just before it joins the Kidron Valley. Most of the tombs were originally stone quarries, which became burial plots during the Second Temple period. Christian tradition identifies this as the site of the potter's field mentioned by Judas Iscariot in connection with the betrayal of Jesus. Judas gave the priests the silver he received for the betrayal: "And the chief priests took the silver pieces and said, it is not lawful for to put them into the treasury, because it is the price of blood. And they took counsel, and bought with them the potter's field, to bury strangers in. Wherefore that field was called the Field of Blood, unto this day" (*St. Matthew* xxvii, 6–8). A Greek Orthodox monastery now stands on the site of a Crusader church (of St. Mary) built in 1143 and given to the Hospitallers of St. John. The church was built in an ancient burial cave; the courtyard of the church contains many two-storied grave series, with burial recesses and vaults. At the center is a cave named after the Apostles, since Christian tradition identifies this as the place where the Apostles hid during and after the trial of Jesus. The courtyard of this cave is now entered by a new staircase. At the front of the cave are two new pillars, and beyond it is a courtyard, to the left of which is the grave of the monk Cyril, who came from Bithynia in Cappadocia and died in 1903. Beyond the courtyard is an entrance hall with a triple pediment over its entrance. Its eastern (left-hand) wall bears a Greek inscription. The hall has a round dome of dressed blocks; three pillars protrude from the walls, and there are three entrances at a height of 1.65 m. The burial chambers have recesses and vaults, the latter containing the collected bones and skulls of medieval pilgrims, but in one of the rooms there is a grave in the floor. One of the burial chambers has two stories. The early Christians originally used the rooms as graves, later turning them into dwellings.

In 1874 the Greek Church rebuilt a monastery and church on the site, named after St. Onophrius (famous chiefly for his long beard), whose portrait is in the church. The entrance cornice bears decorations of grapevines, lilies, leaves and wreaths, incised in square medallions. The walls and ceiling of the church have frescoes of saints, and the central ceiling has a painting of Jesus flanked by John the Baptist and Mary, with the angels Gabriel and Michael at their sides. The southern wall included burial recesses and two vaults. The floor of the church has a water cistern with a small opening, 0.25 cm in diameter.

Below the monastery, closer to the eastern road, are tomb complexes with large openings and decorations. The southern cave, with its entrance of 1.2 × 2.2 m, includes a hall with a lily-like flower 3 m in diameter, with thirty-two petals, carved out of the ceiling. To the right of the hall and north of it, there are three deep, shell-shaped vaults, which are rare in Jerusalem.

Ben-Hinnom Valley – Valley of Topheth

The valley head is in the quarter of Mekor Baruch, near the western entrance to Jerusalem, and is 810 m above sea level. It continues along Jaffa Road to Independence Park and Mamillah Pool, through the Sultan's Pool and the Sham'a quarter. It joins the Kidron Valley at the foot of Givath-Hananiah, at 600 m. The valley is 3.1 km long, and in Arabic it is known as Wadi Rubabah – Valley of the Violin, apparently because of its shape, narrow at the head and widening towards its junction with the Kidron Valley. It is mentioned as the boundary between the territory of Judah in the south and Benjamin in the north. "And the border went up by the Valley of the son of Hinnom unto the south side of the Jebusite southward – the same is Jerusalem – and the border went up to the top of the mountain that lieth before the Valley of Hinnom, westward, which is at the uttermost part of the Vale of Rephaim northward" (*Joshua* xv, 8).

The Valley of Ben-Hinnom was viewed by the prophets as the source of uncleanness, since it was a place of pagan worship. The sites of worship were apparently at the junction of the Ben-Hinnom and Kidron Valleys, since this region was beyond the sphere of influence of the city proper, lay close to the water sources required for the ritual and sacrifices, and was a crossroads and way station for the many pedestrians traveling between the Judean Desert in the east, the territories of Ephraim and Benjamin in the north, and the territory of Judah in the south.

The kings of Judah who were faithful to the tenets of the Law persecuted the pagans, shattered their ritual vessels and threw the remnants into the Ben-Hinnom Valley and its tombs, in order to emphasize the vessels' impurity. Asa, king of Judah, "…put away the Sodomites out of the land, and removed all the idols that his fathers had made. And also Ma'acah, his mother, he removed from being queen, because she had made an abominable image for an Asherah; and Asa cut down her image and burnt it at the brook Kidron" (*1 Kings* XV, 12, 13). Hezekiah also called on the tribes of Asher, Manasseh and Zebulon to make the pilgrimage to Jerusalem during the Passover and cleanse it of the idols: "And they arose and took away the altars that were in Jerusalem, and all the altars for incense took they away, and cast them into the brook Kidron" (*11 Chronicles* XXI, 14). Josiah also burnt the idols in the Ben-Hinnom Valley and strewed the ashes over the cemetery of the Kidron Valley: "And he brought out the Asherah from the House of the Lord, without Jerusalem, unto the brook Kidron, and burned it at the brook Kidron, and stamped it small to powder, and cast the powder thereof upon the graves of the common people … and he defiled Topheth, which is in the Valley of the son of Hinnom, that no man might make his son or daughter to pass through the fire to Molech" (*11 Kings* XXIII, 6, 10; *Jeremiah* VII, 21, 22; XIX, 5–14, XXXII, 35).

Tomb of the House of Herod

This lies southeast of the King David Hotel, and was discovered by Schick in 1891. The identification of the tomb is almost positive, since it is twice mentioned by Josephus, first in recounting the siege of Jerusalem: "…and thus the whole space from Scopus to the monuments of Herod adjacent to what is called the 'Serpents' Pool' was reduced to a level'" (*Wars* V, 3). The Serpents' Pool is identified at Birket el-Sultan, at the western foot of Mount Zion, and the location of the tomb is virtually certain. Josephus next mentions it in the description of the siege wall Titus laid around the city: "…he ascended by the monument of the High Priest Ananus, and taking in the mount …passing which, he enclosed Herod's monument, and once more united it to his own camp at the point where it commenced" (*Wars* V, 12).

The necropolis was concentrated in the east of the city rather than the west, as noted above, because of the prevailing westerly winds, which would have been malodorous, and the fissured, broken, conglomerate rocks, which were unsuitable for building monuments. Herod's Tomb is one of the few built in the western part of the city, probably due to the proximity of the site to the royal palace and the towers of Mount Zion. Herod apparently devoted this tomb to his Hasmonean wife, Mariamne, and his close relatives.

The tomb was not hewn in an abandoned quarry, nor made in a natural cave, as were other tombs, but was built according to a plan. It is divided into three parts: the monument (*nefesh*), the courtyard, and the tomb. The monument was north of the tomb, and only one layer of the structure still stands. The stones are dressed in a delicate, serrated style, and have been plundered over the years. The monument measured 13.5 × 13.9 m. The courtyard was surrounded by a wall of dressed stones, also completely destroyed. The main entrance to the tomb was sealed by a circular stone, which was upright and rolled along a groove. The tomb was opened after the buttressing stone, which was under the rolling stone, had been removed – "What is the buttressing stone? That upon which the covering stone [that seals the grave] is supported" (*Oholot* 2, 4) – and the round sealing stone rolled back to the left. The grave was sealed by rolling the sealing stone back into position and securing it by the buttressing stone. Such an arrangement was evidently very costly, since it has only been found (apart from Herod's Tomb) in the Tomb of Queen Helena and in two tombs near Kibbutz Ma'aleh haHamisha west of Jerusalem.

The tomb has a unique cruciform plan, with four symmetrical rooms on four sides of a central room with an arched ceiling. The walls of the chambers are covered by slabs of ashlars dressed with the same delicate serration, and their entrances had stone gates. The walls were covered because the local rock is not easily worked, being friable and ugly. The graves contained two sarcophagi decorated with plant motifs: acanthus, tendrils and lilies. During the British Mandate this tomb was used to store the arms of the British headquarters at the King David Hotel.

Jason's Tomb

Another tomb was discovered in the western part of Jerusalem, on Alfasi Street in the Rehavia quarter, and was studied by L.Y. Rahmani. It consisted of two courtyards, a corridor and two burial chambers. The façade has one Doric pillar. The tomb was surmounted by a pyramid, several stones of which were found in the excavation. The wall of the corridor bears a mourning inscription in Arabic, mentioning one Jason; hence the name of the tomb. Charcoal drawings of two ships were also found. The tomb is dated to the first century B.C.E.

The Mount of Olives Today

Jews of the Land of Israel and the Diaspora always yearned to bury their dead on the Mount of Olives, near the Temple Mount, in an area sanctified by the proximity of the graves of Zechariah the prophet and Jehoshaphat king of Judah, as well as the apocryphal visions. The Mount of Olives therefore bears tens of thousands of Jewish graves. The majority (50,000 of the 70,000) was desecrated by the Arabs during the nineteen years of Jordanian rule in eastern Jerusalem. Christian tradition has also sanctified the mountain, because of certain events, which took place in the life of Jesus, and from the Byzantine period churches began to be erected there. These were mainly on the heights of the mount and along the western slope, among them the churches of A-Tur and Gethsemane in the Valley of Jehoshaphat. After Moslem tradition had sanctified the Dome of the Rock and the Mosque of El-Aqsa, Moslem cemeteries were established near the city gates, in three main locations near sources of water: in the west near the Jaffa Gate, by the Mamillah Pool (graves of Arab mystics and religious warriors—*mujahidoon*—who died fighting the Byzantines in 636 and the Crusaders in 1187 under Saladin); in the east near the Mercy (Golden) Gate and the Lions' Gate (during the Middle Ages many Jewish graves still existed there); and in the northwest on a hill near Herod's Gate.

Water in Jerusalem

> *Waters are described as living …*
> *Aboth d'Rabbi Nathan, 31a*

In the arid lands of the Middle East, water was of considerably greater significance than were the other necessities. Food could be stored in unlimited amounts within a city in case of emergency; a settlement could be fortified by thick, high walls and strong, lofty towers, or by deep moats, to hinder the approach of the enemy and his battering rams. Water, however, could only be collected from sources, which in this part of the country were mostly poor, and special installations were vital to ensure the purity of the collected water and to prevent evaporation. The storage of water was thus difficult, and dependent on the building of expensive water systems. This was especially true in the mountain regions, where the natural water sources are generally found on the slopes and in the valleys. Eusebius, who lived in the fourth century C.E., notes, quoting Timochares, that water flowed throughout Jerusalem, and even gardens were irrigated with running water brought from outside the city. And yet, many historians, from the fifth century C.E., and up to the time of William of Tyre, during the Crusades, note that Jerusalem never experienced a serious lack of water, despite the droughts and sieges, which befell it.

The development of water sources for cities in arid or semi-arid countries was the factor that determined that city's growth and development. The available water sources, within the city or near at hand, as well as those at some distance, were partially or fully exploited, depending on the size of the city. When the population decreased, only part of the water sources were exploited, primarily those inside the walls and nearby. This was the case in Jerusalem. While the city was small its inhabitants used the water from one or two sources; in times of expansion and development, the water from all five types of sources was used: springs, wells, cisterns, pools and aqueducts.

The Gihon Spring

The Gihon spring flows in the Kidron Valley, east of the Lower City, 450 m southwest of Absalom's Monument. This source is unique in the Judean Hills, being of a cretaceous nature, i.e., it is supplied by groundwater flowing from the more distant, more rain-drenched mountains in the west. Jerusalem lies in a saddle of the Judean mountains, between the anticline of the mountains of Beth-EI in the north and that of the Hebron Mountains in the south. The rainwater from these heights flows down to the mountains of Jerusalem. The spring supplies an average of 50 cu m per hour, varying with the seasons. It flows intermittently, and is therefore called Gihon, for the water gushes forth (*gah*) strongly when the underground tunnels are full, and the flow lessens when the pressure in the tunnels is lower. The upper Gihon is mentioned in *II Chronicles* xxxii, 30; *II Kings* xx, 20; and *Isaiah* xxii, 11, and the Gihon in *I Kings* i, 33. In Arabic the spring is called *Umm el-Daraj* because of the sixteen upper stairs and the fourteen lower stairs leading to the spring. (*Daraj* is the Arabic word for stair).

Its flow is the greatest of all the springs in the Judean Mountain ridge, and therefore determined the location of the ancient Cana'anite and Jebusite town, on the lower hill of the City of David. The spring was then the only large source of water for the city. Warren's excavations in 1867 revealed a shaft sunk by the Jebusites from within their city, reaching down to the level of the Gihon waters; this made it possible to draw water from within the city in time of war.

Access to Water in the City of David

Access to the Warren Shaft is through the foyer and proceeds from there to the tunnel hewn in rock, which in the beginning is graded and then continues horizontally for 41 m. The shaft drops down a level, and Hezekiah's tunnel descends to the depth of 12.3 m. In the tenth century B.C.E., before digging Hezekiah's tunnel, Jerusalemites drew their water from a spring by a rope and bucket, from within the city, to obviate the need to go outside the city walls. From the excavations of Y. Shilo and the geologist D. Gil, it seems that the tunnel and the shaft are part of a natural, karstic burrow and are not man-made. Additional hewing aided the city's inhabitants in approaching the shaft.

The apparently miraculous flow of the spring caused it to become sanctified in antiquity, and Solomon, the builder of the First Temple, was anointed at the Gihon: "And Zadok the priest and Nathan the prophet have anointed him king in Gihon, and they are come up from thence rejoicing, so that the city is in an uproar" (*1 Kings*, 1, 45). The *Tosefta* notes that a king should be anointed at the spring, it is explained in the *Baraitha*, so that their reign should endure.

The purity and clarity of the water made the spring an important place

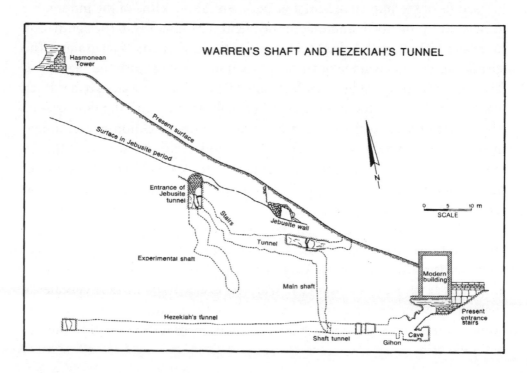

for ritual immersions. At the bottom of the stairs, near the head of the spring, there is a pool 1.6 × 3.5 m in area, called the Bath of the High Priest Rabbi Ishmael, who officiated at the end of the Second Temple period; immersion in it is practiced to this day. It is mentioned in the book *Tosefta, Menahot* 1, 9 as having very cold water, which has a beneficial effect on eye diseases, and even non-Jews immersed themselves in it. The pure water was used for drinking: "Had you been worthy, you would be dwelling in Jerusalem and drinking the waters of Shiloah, whose waters are pure and sweet" (*Introduction to Lamentations Rabbah*). The spring water is no longer fit for drinking, having been contaminated by the sewage of Silwan village; the water now contains 300 mg chlorine per liter. The water was used in antiquity for the water libation during the festival of *Sukkoth*. "How was the water libation (performed)? ...A golden flagon holding three *loogim* was filled from the Siloam. When they arrived at the Water Gate they sounded a *Tekiah* (long blast), a *Teruah* (tremulous note) and again a *Tekiah* ...As was its performance on weekdays so was the performance on the Sabbath, save that on the eve of the Sabbath an unhallowed golden barrel was filled from the Siloam, and placed in a chamber" (*Sukkah* 4, 9–10, and see also 5, 1–4; *Sanhedrin Yerushalmi* 2, 5; *Ta'anith Babli*, 2, 72; *Sukkah* 48b; *Zevahim* 110b). Another tradition is that "on Tabernacle's judgment is passed in respect of rain" (*Rosh Hashanah* 1, 2), and that the libation of water promises a year of beneficial rains (*Rosh Hashanah* 16b). The libation of water before God is mentioned in the story of David's Campaign against the Philistines in Bethlehem: "And David longed, and said, oh, that one would give me water to drink of the well of Bethlehem, which is by the gate! And the three broke through the host of the Philistines, and drew water out of the well of Bethlehem, that was by the gate, and took it, and brought it to David; but David would not drink thereof, but poured it out unto the Lord" (*1 Chronicles* xi, 17–18). According to *1 Samuel* vii, 6, the libation of water is a type of atonement sacrifice (see R. Patai, *Ha-Mayim* p. 48 ff).

The spring became sacred to Christians, for the New Testament tells of the miraculous healing of a person blind since birth. "And said unto him Go, wash in the Pool of Siloam. He went his way, therefore, and washed and came seeing" (*St. John* ix, 7). The pool is known as St. Mary's Pool, after the mother of Jesus. Archaeological excavations by Bliss and Dickie from 1894 to 1897 disclosed a fifth century Byzantine church, built at the Pool of Siloam to commemorate the miracles worked there by Jesus. Herod built baths on the spot and apparently enlarged the pool. At present there is a mosque over the remnants of the church and baths.

Pool of Siloam

Before the Israelite monarchy, the water of the spring flowed freely outside the city walls. Eventually the riverbed became silted up to a height of ten meters. The water flowed in a conduit at the eastern foot of the Lower City, outside the walls, as noted in *Isaiah* VIII, 6: "…the waters of Shiloah that go softly…" The waters of the spring were conveyed to the pool from the period of King Solomon and the early kings; the pool was at the southern tip of the Cheese-mongers' Valley in the Lower City, outside the city at that period.

Josephus provides another report of the building of this pool during the reign of Solomon (*Wars* v, 4) – "…and advanced with a southern aspect above the fountain of Siloam, whence it again inclined, facing the east, towards Solomon's reservoir."

The Drainage Channel

The drainage channel was apparently built in the Middle Bronze period and improved upon by King Solomon to irrigate the king's gardens from the waters that had entered the King's Valley through the Kidron River. A portion of this channel was discovered to be open and another portion, hewn into the tunnel. In the eastern partition of the channel, the Y. Shilo team found openings leading to water, which irrigated cultivated plots of the Kidron River and the king's garden. The Y. Shilo team cleaned this channel from 1978–1982 to the length of 120 meters. The waters of the channel reached 400 meters to the pool, or the king's pool, where it collected the water and also watered the king's garden. The disadvantage of this channel is that it was hewn totally outside the city walls and used by enemies in times of war.

The pool is also mentioned in *Nehemiah* III, 15: "…and the wall of the pool of Siloah by the king's garden, even unto the stairs that go down from the City of David." The place is called the Pool of Shelah, i.e., pool of the ditch: it may also imply that tanneries existed there, since the root of the word also means animal hide. The pool and spring were called Shiloah also, because their waters were used for irrigation in the King's Garden, where the Ben-Hinnom Valley debouches into the Kidron (*II King's* XXV, 4; *Jeremiah*

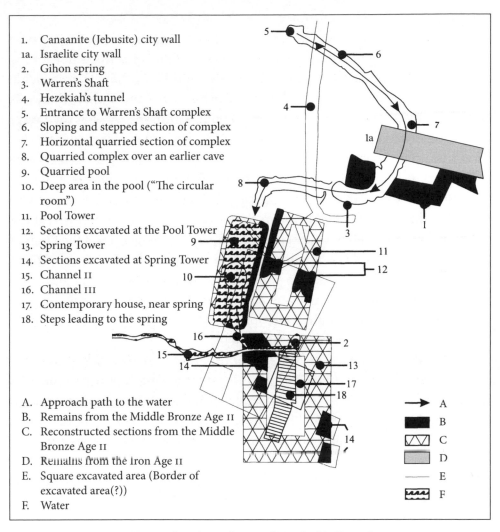

1. Canaanite (Jebusite) city wall
1a. Israelite city wall
2. Gihon spring
3. Warren's Shaft
4. Hezekiah's tunnel
5. Entrance to Warren's Shaft complex
6. Sloping and stepped section of complex
7. Horizontal quarried section of complex
8. Quarried complex over an earlier cave
9. Quarried pool
10. Deep area in the pool ("The circular room")
11. Pool Tower
12. Sections excavated at the Pool Tower
13. Spring Tower
14. Sections excavated at Spring Tower
15. Channel II
16. Channel III
17. Contemporary house, near spring
18. Steps leading to the spring

A. Approach path to the water
B. Remains from the Middle Bronze Age II
C. Reconstructed sections from the Middle Bronze Age II
D. Remains from the Iron Age II
E. Square excavated area (Border of excavated area(?))
F. Water

New archaeological sites of Hezekiah's Tunnel

XXXIX, 4; LII, 7). The pool, built by the early kings of Judah, and the conduit constructed by Solomon were also called "the pool of the king" (*Nehemiah II*, 14), since its waters served to irrigate the King's Garden. The Gihon waters were thus drawn for drinking at their source; the water was then conducted into a pool and collected to facilitate drawing by the inhabitants of Jerusalem: and surplus waters were used for irrigation in the King's Garden. This pool, the earliest in Jerusalem, was called by *Isaiah* "the old pool" (XXII, 11).

The Tunnel

In the reign of Hezekiah (727–698 B.C.E.), when Sennacherib came up against Jerusalem, the King of Judah conceived the plan of bringing the waters of the Gihon through an excavated tunnel into the middle of the city to provide fresh water for the besieged inhabitants. The outward flow of the Gihon was sealed up, and the water carried to a pool built within the walls of the Lower City, as recounted in *II Chronicles* XXXII, 2–4; "And when Hezekiah saw that Sennacherib was come, and that he was purposed to fight against Jerusalem he took counsel with his princes and his mighty men, to stop the waters of the fountains which were without the city, and they helped him. So there was gathered much people together, and they stopped all the fountains and the brook that ran through the midst of the land, saying, 'Why should the kings of Assyria come, and find much water?'" Hezekiah's great work is also mentioned in the Book of Ben Sira, and the pool is alluded to in *II Kings* XX, 20: "Now the rest of the acts of Hezekiah, and all his might, and how he made the pool, and the conduit, and brought water into the city, are they not written in the book of the chronicles of the kings of Judah?"

According to M. Hecker (*Water Supply in Antiquity [Haspakat hamayim bimei kedem] Sefer Yerushalayim*, pp. 191–218), the length of the tunnel was 533 m, its height between 1.1 and 3.4 m and its width 0.58–0.65 m. Its maximum depth below the top of the hill is 52 m, and its gradient is 2.18 m, i.e., about 4%. According to the geologist, Dr. Gil, the tunnel incline from beginning to end is 35 cm, i.e., a gradient of 0.2 thousandths. In 1880 Schick discovered a Hebrew inscription six lines long on the tunnel wall at a point six meters from the pool. The inscription, today in the Istanbul Museum, Turkey, was deciphered as follows:

"This is the story of the boring through: whilst (the tunnelers lifted) the pick each towards his fellow, and whilst three cubits (yet remained) to be bored (through, there was heard) the voice of a man calling his fellow, for there was a split in the rock on the right hand and on (the left hand). And on the days of the boring through, the tunnelers struck, each in the direction of his fellows, pick against pick. And the water started to flow from the source to the pool, twelve hundred cubits. A hundred cubits was the height of the rock above the head of the tunnelers."

The tunnel gives rise to several questions. Why did the tunnelers work on a winding course along 533 m, when the distance between

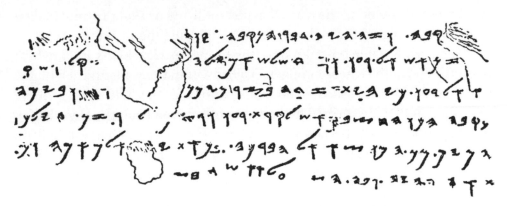

The Hebrew inscription of Hezekiah's Tunnel

the two ends of the tunnel is only 320 m as the crow flies? How did the two gangs of workers, hewing from opposite ends, meet as the inscription states? The inscription says explicitly, "And on the day of the boring through, the tunnelers struck, each in the direction of his fellows." How did Hezekiah's engineers plan the work in a tunnel of this depth, and achieve such a minimal gradient? How was the supply of fresh air ensured for the workmen?

Hecker believes that the sinuous course of the tunnel was dictated by the differences in rock strata encountered in the course of the work; hard rock was bypassed and the work continued in a softer stratum. This does not, however answer the other queries. The theory of H. Sulley, also held by Prof. R. Amiran (*Kadmoniot*, Vol. 1, 1968, pp. 13–18) provides possible solutions to all these problems. According to this theory, the tunnel followed the route of a natural cretaceous fissure, created by the dissolution of the calcium in the limestone by the carbon dioxide in the rainwater. This is the meaning of the phrase "for there was a split in the rock," i.e., there was a natural split or fissure in the rock before Hezekiah's gangs started work. Such cretaceous phenomena are not uncommon in the country; their lower levels are usually horizontal. Supplementary evidence is provided by the height of the tunnel ceiling, which reaches 3.4 m in some places, and was obviously not man-made. The short period of time required for the tunneling provides further support for this theory: the tunneling was carried out hastily under the threat of siege, and the presence of a natural fissure was vital, since there was obviously no time to plan such a project in its entirety. The work thus proceeded from both sides of the tunnel at once, along the natural fissure, utilizing its slight natural incline. Fresh air also entered through this fissure, supplying the workers.

The spring water flowed along this tunnel to Hezekiah's Pool, which was at the end of the Cheesemongers' Valley, within the walls and at a higher level than the Shiloah (Siloam) Pool (also known as the "Old Pool"). Guthe, excavating in 1881, discovered baths apparently dating from the Herodian or Roman period. The site became holy to Christianity, and a church was built on it. The water was used primarily for drinking by the inhabitants of the city.

Another important source of drinking water was the well of Ein Rogel.

Ein Rogel – Bir Ayoub

Ein Rogel is mentioned as a border point between the territories of the tribes of Judah and Benjamin, standing, as it does, at a crossroads where the Ben-Hinnom road leads to the territory of Judah, and the Kidron road goes north to the land of Benjamin and east to the Judean Desert, Rabbat Ammon and Gilead (*Joshua xv, xviii*, 16). The spring is also mentioned in connection with Absalom's pursuit of David; Jonathan and Ahimaaz the priest set out from Ein Rogel on the orders of Hushai the Archite, David's counselor, to inform him of Absalom's plans. This was the borderline between the cultivated lands in the west and the wilderness of the east (*ii Samuel xvii*, 17). Ein Rogel was of considerable significance, since Adonijah the son of King David and Haggit was crowned there (*i Kings* i, 9, 18).

At present Ein Rogel is only a well, 38 m deep. The well is built of ashlar blocks to a depth of 20 m, with fieldstones for a further 12 m, while the bottom 6 m are hewn from the rock. The biblical word *ein*, however, denotes a spring. Where, then, is the spring of Ein Rogel?

Scientists believe that the spring vanished as a result of the earthquake during the reign of King Uzziah of Judah, mentioned in *Zechariah xiv*, 5. "And ye shall flee to the valley of the mountains; for the valley of the mountains shall reach unto Azel; yea, ye shall flee, like as ye fled from before the earthquake in the days of Uzziah, king of Judah…" This earthquake was also recorded by *Amos* i, 1: "…two years before the earthquake." Josephus says the earthquake rent the mountain at the place called Ein Rogel (*Antiquities ix*, 10). The generally accepted view is therefore that the spring disappeared in this earthquake, and Uzziah, who dug many wells (*ii Chronicles xxvi*, 10), excavated a well at the site of the former spring of Rogel.

In my opinion, however, it is more likely that Ein Rogel was a flowing spring as long as the waters of the Gihon reached it along the Kidron Valley, since Ein Rogel was fed mainly by the Gihon. After the early kings of Judah built the Pool of Shiloah, using the Gihon waters to irrigate the King's Garden, and especially after Hezekiah excavated the tunnel, and the waters were conducted to Hezekiah's Pool, the spring disappeared. The present well is of a much later date and is known as Bir Ayoub to the Arabs. A similar phenomenon of the disappearance of springs occurred in modern times in the Beth-Shean Valley. Formerly the springs of the terrace east of the city of Beth-Shean were fed by the water of springs and swamps on the western terrace. The swamps were drained after the establishment of the State of Israel, and the springs of the western part of Beth-Shean were led into the regional water system. Most of the eastern springs then ran dry and eventually completely disappeared, along with the springs that fed them in the west.

Bir Ayoub, today supplying the inhabitants of Silwan village, is a well, supplied by the floodwaters of the Kidron, Ben-Hinnom and Cheesemongers' Valleys. It was the second source of drinking water in the city. The third, very important, source was provided by the water cisterns.

Water Cisterns

Archaeologist Professor W. Albright regards the collection of rainwater in cisterns as an Israelite invention. The Israelites were the first nation to inhabit the mountain region, with its hard rocks and sparse sources of water. The other nations living in the mountainous areas (Hivites, Amorites, Hittites and Jebusites, among others) mostly settled in sites with available springs. The Israelites, forced by the reality of the political situation and for reasons of security to settle the mountains, discovered the technique of waterproofing rock-cut cisterns with mortar, and were thus able to settle wherever the soil was suitable for agriculture, or along the main highways.

The excavation of cisterns in the hard limestone areas to the north and west of Jerusalem (west of the Ben-Hinnom Valley) is difficult, but easier in the softer chalky rock of the Upper City, west of the Temple Mount to the Ben-Hinnom Valley and in the Bezetha quarter, north of the Temple Mount. Cisterns were excavated in the courtyards, inside the houses and in the foundations. The indoor cisterns collected water for drinking, while the water in the large paved courtyard cisterns was generally used for washing and laundering. Cisterns were hewn out and built in every type of soil, regardless of the topography; there were even cisterns in the many towers of the Second

Water cistern in the Old City of Jerusalem

Temple wall, as Josephus wrote: "Over the solid altitude of the towers, which was twenty cubits, were sumptuous apartments, and above these again upper rooms, and numerous cisterns therein to receive the rainwater" (*Wars* v, 4). The Hippicus Tower had a cistern 10 m deep, and the Phasael Tower even had a bathhouse (*Wars* v, 4). The lives of Jerusalem's inhabitants thus depended to a considerable extent upon rainwater.

Water for the Pilgrims

The *Mishnah* distinguishes between a "public" cistern and a "private" one (*Erubin* 2, 4). The private cistern was built within the domain of a private person, in his house or yard, while the public cistern was dug in a public place, such as a street or square. Workers constructing the cisterns were given the title of "cistern digger" (*Shevi'it* 8, 5). There were thirty-eight cisterns in the Temple Courtyard containing 16,000 cu m of water, and the person in charge of the Temple cistern diggers is mentioned by name, Nehunia (*Shekalim* 5, 1). Jerusalem had to supply water for the multitudes of pilgrims, whose numbers reached one million a year by the end of the Second Temple period. The *Tosefta* tells of preparing for ritual baths, cisterns, pits and aqueducts for purification (*Ahiloth* 18, 13). The *Mishnah* says: "…roads, broadways, and pools may be put in order and all public needs may be performed" (*Moed Katan* 2a). Maimonides explains a ruling of the Jerusalem *Talmud* to mean that the cisterns, normally kept locked all the year round, were opened to the public during pilgrimages. Twenty-five of the thirty-six cisterns of the Temple Mount are still in use: eight around the Dome of the Rock, seven near the El-Aqsa Mosque, six west of the courtyard, three in the east and one in the north. The largest cistern on the Temple Mount, known as "the Sea," is in the southern part, just north of the El-Aqsa. It was probably supplied by the aqueduct front Ein 'Arrub, and constituted the chief source of water for pilgrims coming through the Gates of Huldah in the south of the Mount or through the Coponius Gate in the west.

The ease of excavation in the friable chalk rock, which is impervious to water, led to the excavation of many cisterns in the Judean Desert. The inhabitants of Jerusalem therefore started sheep-raising, which depended chiefly on desert and meadow vegetation. The cisterns made it possible for Jerusalem to enjoy the benefits of a rich agricultural hinterland, from which milk, fat, meat and wool were supplied throughout the mountain region bordering the desert.

Jerusalem required additional sources of water to supply its developing industry. This problem was overcome by means of pools.

Pools

The Israelites had collected water in pools since the time of their desert wanderings. Existence in the desert is only possible if floodwaters can be gathered in reservoirs for use at a later date. The natural location of reservoirs in the desert was along the slopes of the small, low valleys; the deeper valleys were flooded by powerful streams, which usually swept away the dams. When the Israelites settled in the mountains, they began to dig out pools and reservoirs in the low-lying parts of their towns. These may still be seen in Arab villages, where most of the pools are remnants of ancient settlements.

Jerusalem, built on three hills – the Lower City, the Upper City and Bezetha – was surrounded by deep valleys and dissected by many small vales. It was therefore more suitable for the collection of rainwater than any other city in the mountain region. However, while the waters of springs, wells and cisterns served mainly for drinking, pool water was used for washing, laundering, irrigation, construction and industry.

During the Second Temple period there were fifteen pools in Jerusalem, most of them quite large. Twelve were fed by rainwater flooding the vales, and three received spring water by special aqueducts. These pools were as follows:

Two pools outside the wall in the Ben-Hinnom Valley, dating from the Roman period: the Mamillah Pool (east of the present-day Hechal Shlomo and Independence Park) 60 × 89 m and 6 m deep; and the Serpents Pool (Birket el-Sultan) west of Mount Zion, 67 × 169 m, and 12 m deep.

Another pool, the Pool of Simeon the Just, was located outside the city wall in Wadi Joz (which debouches into the Kidron in the Sheikh Jarrah quarter,) and is now filled in.

There were five pools in the Valley, or the Cheesemongers' Valley: Lacus Legerii, part of which is visible northwest of the present-day Damascus Gate; the Upper Pool, northwest of the Western Wall, now stopped up and built over. (It was apparently located near the Fish Gate [Ephraim], and was supplied by the waters drained from the Street of David, in the Old City); the Lower Pool, west of the Tombs of the House of David (unidentified), also fed by the course running down from the Upper City, and apparently situated near the Gate of the Valley; Hezekiah's Pool, at the end of the Siloam Tunnel; and the Pool of Shiloah, (outside the wall), at the end of the Cheesemongers' Valley, near the Kidron Valley south of Hezekiah's Pool. The Shiloah Pool is now used for irrigating fruit orchards and market gardens, and is called in Arabic Birket el-Hamra (the pool of clay), probably echoing the ancient name of Sha'ar haHarsith (Clay Gate).

There are four pools in the Bethesda Valley: Birket el-Hajj, north of Herod's Gate, now built up; the Pool of Bethsaida, or Bethesda, northwest of the Lions' Gate, partially visible at present in the courtyard of the Church of St. Anne; Birket Israil, southeast of the Bethesda Pool and northeast of the Temple Mount wall, but now filled in; and the Pool of Sitt Miriam, outside the wall, north of the Lions' Gate and still visible.

Three pools were supplied by secondary pools higher up the valley courses: the Pool of Amygdalon, lying among the buildings northeast of the Jaffa Gate, and known to the Arabs as Birket Hammam el-Batrak, i.e., the Pool of the Patriarch's Bath, as the Patriarchal Residence is nearby. This pool was fed by an aqueduct from the Mamillah Pool. It is 44 × 73 m in area, the southern and eastern walls are built of ashlar blocks, and the western wall is rock-hewn. The Struthion Pool by the Antonia Fortress can be partially seen in the foundations of the Ecce Homo Basilica on the Via Dolorosa, in the Old City. This pool is supplied by an aqueduct from Lacus Legerii. The Pool of Sitt Miriam was apparently fed by an aqueduct carrying the surplus waters of the Bethesda Pool. All these pools were excavated near the ancient city gates of the First and Second Temple periods.

It would be of interest to determine the dates and purposes of these pools. They seem to have been built chiefly during two periods: in the rule of the kings of Judah, when the city spread westward, towards the Upper City, and in the Second Temple period, mainly in the reign of Herod.

The Series of Pools in the Cheesemongers' Valley

It is reasonable to assume that the early kings of Judah (perhaps it was King Solomon) built the Pool of Shiloah first. This pool was known in the Bible as the King's Pool (*Nehemiah* II, 14) or the Old Pool (*Isaiah* XXII, 11). It was built to collect the waters of the Gihon, which until then flowed freely into the Kidron Valley. At a later date, apparently before the days of Isaiah, in the eighth century B.C.E., three additional pools were excavated in the Cheesemongers' Valley, from north to south as follows:

1. The Upper Pool, mentioned in the Bible: "And the king of Assyria sent Tartan the chief eunuch…unto Jerusalem. And when they were come up, they came and stood by the conduit of the upper pool, which is in the highway of the fuller's field" (*II Kings* XVIII, 17). This pool was probably west of the Western Wall of the Temple Mount.

2. The Lower Pool, mentioned in *Isaiah*: "And ye saw the breaches of the city of David, that they were many; and ye gathered together the waters of the lower pool" (XXII, 9). The lower pool may have been located

north of Hezekiah's pool, where the valley descending from the Upper City opens into the Cheesemongers' Valley. This may have been the pool mentioned by *Nehemiah* (iii, 16): "…unto the place over against the sepulchers of David, and unto the pool that was made, and unto the house of the mighty men." The Tombs of the House of David were indeed discovered in the Lower City, northeast of Hezekiah's Pool.

3. Hezekiah's Pool, the remnants of which are visible at the end of the tunnel, situated south of the Lower Pool, and north of the Shiloah Pool dug during Isaiah's lifetime.

It is thus clear that during the First Temple period there were four pools in the valley for the collection of rainwater. The Cheesemongers' Valley drained the three hills of ancient Jerusalem, and the four western gates of the Lower City were built along it: the Fish Gate (Ephraim), the Mishneh Gate (the corner), the Valley Gate and the Dung Gate (also known as the Clay Gate, or Between the Two Walls). The water of the Upper Pool served mainly for the ritual of the Temple, and the three lower-lying pools were used by the inhabitants of the Lower and Upper Cities. The deep upper pool also served as a moat to protect the Temple Mount. Sennacherib's armies were in fact stopped at this point, as recorded in *ii Kings* xviii, 17: "…they came and stood by the conduit of the upper pool." The Lower Pool and the Shiloah Pool were deterrents to possible invaders of the City of David on the Lower Hill. The valley also served to connect the three parts of the city; it was the focus of the city's economic and commercial life, as well as its industrial and marketing center.

Pools of the Second Temple Period

The other pools of Jerusalem were constructed during the Second Temple period, chiefly in Herod's reign. They were intended to supply the ever-growing needs of the city, which was undergoing unprecedented expansion. The rock excavated from the pools was used in building the city walls, while the water collected in the pools was also used for construction purposes. The pools provided a defense for the city walls and gates, serving as moats which prevented the approach of battering rams.

The Series of Pools in the Ben-Hinnom Valley

The Mamillah and Serpents' (Sultan's) Pools were built part-way down the valley instead of at its end in order to prevent possible damage by floodwaters as well as silting up. The rock excavated from these pools and from the Pool of Amygdalon appears to have been used in the construction of parts of the wall on Mount Zion, and for Herod's palace and the towers of Hippicus, Phasael and Mariamne. Positive proof of the Second Temple date of the Mamillah Pool was provided by the aqueduct discovered by Robinson in 1838, and again the entire length in the 1990s. It leads from the Mamillah Pool to the Pool of Amygdalon, northeast of Jaffa Gate. The surplus waters of the Mamillah Pool flowed to the pool of the Hippicus Tower, and may have had sufficient power to operate the fountains of Herod's palace (*Wars* v, 4). The Pool of Amygdalon must also have been used in the construction of the royal palace and towers. The Serpent's (Sultan's) Pool was built in the shallow bed of the Ben-Hinnom Valley in order to provide a moat round Herod's palace. This pool was repaired during the reign of the Sultan Barquq (1398 C.E.), and again under Suleiman the Magnificent (1538). The Pool of Amygdalon was also built to try and prevent possible invasion from the north, which did in fact take place during the battle between the Zealots and the Romans.

The Series of Pools at the Head of the Cheesemongers' Valley

Lacus Legerii was also apparently built during Herod's reign, since it was excavated near the Herodian city wall, just north of the present-day Damascus Gate; remnants of the wall were discovered in the foundations of the modern gate. The pool was located at the head of the Cheesemongers' Valley, among other reasons for the defense of the towers and the northern gate, and in order to supply building materials for the wall and towers. (Stone quarried from Zedekiah's Caves, which reaches a depth of 220 m, was also used for this purpose.) The chief reason, however, for the position of the pool was its convenience for collecting surplus waters and conveying them along an aqueduct to the Struthion *Pool* near the Antonia Fortress, the chief fortress of the Temple Mount and of the Temple itself (*Wars* v, 11). The pool known in the Crusader Period as Lacus Legerii was thus contemporary with the fortress that it supplied. The rocks excavated from the Struthion Pool were probably used in building the Antonia Fortress. The surplus waters of the Struthion Pool flowed to the Birket Israil Pool, east of the fortress.

The Series of Pools in the Bethesda Valley

This series, which includes four pools, was apparently also built during Herod's time or later. The Pool of el-Hajj (nothing is known about the date of this pool) was near the present-day Herod's Gate, an area which was unwalled until the Second Temple period. The pool defended the gate and its towers and the rock dug out of it was used in building the wall. The Pool of Bethsaida-Bethesda is mentioned in the New Testament (*John* v, 2), and ancient artifacts were found dating to the Hasmonean and Herodian periods. The pool was thus obviously built during the Second Temple period. It was 120 m long, 50–60 m wide and 10–15 m deep. The pool was used mainly to supply building materials and water to the Antonia fortress and to the wall of the Temple Mount during construction, and later to provide the fortress with water. The Pilgrim of Bordeaux (333 C.E.) mentions two large pools within the city, named Bethsaida, used for fish-breeding. There was probably an aqueduct (the date of which is unknown) from this pool to the Pool of Sitt Miriam east of the wall; the surplus waters of the Bethsaida-Bethesda Pool flowed to Birket Israil.

Birket Israil was of impressive dimensions: it was 110 m long, 38 m wide, reached a depth of 21 m, and contained more than 100,000 cu m of water. Its size is evidence of the chief purpose of this pool – to provide a moat in defense of the Temple Mount at the northeastern corner, its weakest point. (The northwestern corner was defended by the Antonia Fortress). The Hasmonean kings, as well as Herod, therefore made every effort to create a long, deep barrier at this point. The stone quarried in the excavation of this pool undoubtedly served in the construction of the Antonia Fortress and the Temple Mount wall. It was the chief reservoir for the Temple Mount, and was supplied by the overflow from the Bethsaida Pool. These surplus waters were filtered at the el-Hajj Pool and the silt was deposited in the two pools of Bethsaida. The water of the Birket Israil Pool was thus clear and pure. The surplus water of the Struthion Pool also flowed downhill to this point. The Crusader historian William of Tyre noted that the Pool of Birket Israil was filled by water flowing along conduits from a distance. The Jerusalem municipality filled in the pool during the 1930s, since sewage from the surrounding houses was being deposited in the pool, causing epidemics.

The Pool of Simon the Just in Wadi Joz, now filled in, provided, together with the many quarries around it, raw materials for the nearby walls of Jerusalem. The water collected in the pool was also used originally for construction purposes. Wilson and Warren note in their book, *Recovery of Jerusalem* (p. 18), that this was probably the largest pool in the vicinity of the city. The municipality filled in the pool during the time of the British Mandate for fear of drowning accidents and malaria.

To summarize: each of the internal valleys of Jerusalem (such as the Cheesemonger's Valley and Bezetha) contained four or five pools. These valleys have small drainage basins, and there was no danger of strong floods rushing down the valley and destroying the pools or silting them up. Larger valleys, such as the Ben-Hinnom, had only two pools, while the great Kidron Valley, with its large drainage basin, contained no pools at all, because of the destructive force of its floodwaters. The historian Aristeas (200 or 250 B.C.E.) wrote: "The water supply is inexhaustible, for an abundant natural spring pours forth within the Temple area, and there are furthermore marvelous underground reservoirs passing description, to a distance of five stades, as was pointed out, round the foundations of the Temple; of these, each had innumerable pipes, so that the various channels converged at the several reservoirs. The floors and sides of these reservoirs, they explained, were overlaid with lead, and above them a great mass of plaster was laid, everything being made secure… I am myself convinced of the system of reservoirs, and I shall show how my belief was confirmed. They took me more than four stades out of the city, and at a certain place bade me bend over and listen to the noise of the meeting of the waters." (*Letter of Aristeas*, pp. 89–91).

Several of the pools were also fed by rainwater, as well as by aqueducts conveying water from considerable distances.

Aqueducts from Distant Sources

Aqueducts bringing water over considerable distances in the country date from the Second Temple period and later. Aqueducts symbolized the stability and wealth of government, as well as the size and expansion of a city. There were aqueducts in the arable and settled areas, as well as in the wilderness.

The majority of the aqueducts were built in low-lying settlements, utilizing the obvious inclines. These settlements were along the coast (at Acre, Athlit, Caesarea, and elsewhere) or in the valleys (such as Zippori, Tiberias, Beth-Shean). The aqueducts drew from abundant water sources and were intended to serve irrigated agricultural areas, as well as domestic use in bathhouses, etc. Some aqueducts led to the Jordan Valley and the Dead Sea region, rich agricultural lands mentioned in the Bible: "And Lot lifted up his eyes, and beheld all the plain of the Jordan, that it was well watered everywhere …like the garden of the Lord, like the land of Egypt," (*Genesis* XIII, 10). The aqueducts of the Jordan Valley were constructed at Banias, in the northern part of the Huleh Valley; in the Ginnosar Valley west of Kinneret; in Qarwa (Coreae), at the mouth of the

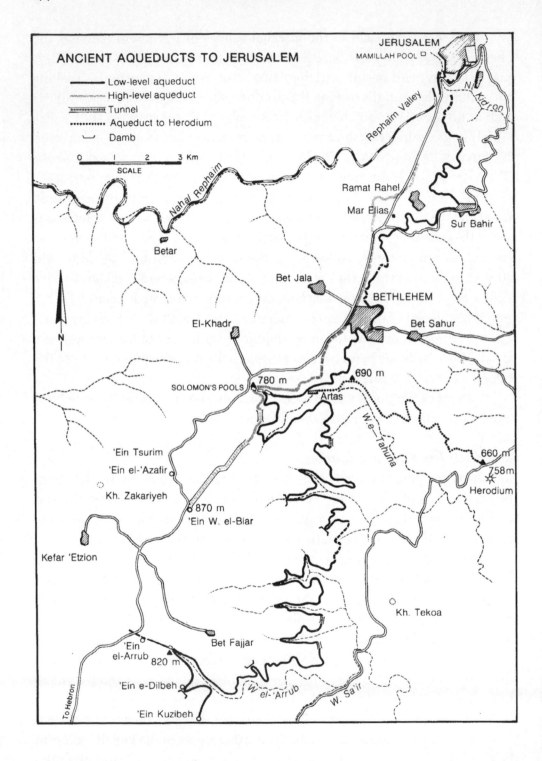

ANCIENT AQUEDUCTS TO JERUSALEM

——— Low-level aqueduct
····· High-level aqueduct
▨▨▨▨ Tunnel
········· Aqueduct to Herodium
⌣ Damb

0   1   2   3 Km
SCALE

JERUSALEM
MAMILLAH POOL □
N. Kidron
Rephaim Valley
Ramat Rahel
Mar Elias
Sur Bahir
Nahal Rephaim
Betar
Bet Jala
BETHLEHEM
El-Khadr
Bet Sahur
N
SOLOMON'S POOLS 780 m
690 m
Artas
W. e-Tahuna
'Ein Tsurim
'Ein el-'Azafir
660 m
758m
Herodium
Kh. Zakariyeh
870 m
'Ein W. el-Biar
Kefar 'Etzion
Kh. Tekoa
Bet Fajjar
'Ein el-Arrub 820 m
'Ein e-Dilbeh
W. el-'Arrub
W. Sa'ir
To Hebron
'Ein Kuzibeh

Far'a Valley, where it debouches into the Damia Valley at the ruin of Archelaus, led by springs of the Samarian mountains; at the ruin of Archelaus, fed by the springs of the Auja stream, between the mountains of Judea and Samaria; at Na'aran, supplied by the springs of 'Uyun Duyuk, north-west of Jericho; at Herodian Jericho, its water flowing down three conduits from the Qelt Valley springs: at Ein Gedi, supplied by three watercourses from the David and Arugot streams; and finally at Ein Bokek, which utilized the water rising nearby.

The Judean Desert had aqueducts leading mostly to forts built during the Second Temple period, carrying mainly rainwater floods. Such aqueducts are found at Alexandrion (Sartaba) in the central Jordan Valley; at Horkania (*Khirbet Mird*) north of the Kidron Valley and Mar Saba monastery; at Khirbet Qumran, northwest of the Dead Sea, and at Masada, half-way down the Dead Sea coast. Two of these forts utilized spring water: Herod's fort of Kipros, at the mouth of the Perat stream (Qelt), south of Jericho, and Herodion, southeast of Bethlehem, which was supplied by an aqueduct from the Artas springs.

The crowning glory of the water systems of the country were, however, the two aqueducts to Jerusalem: the low-level aqueduct, which led from the 'Arrub springs north of Hebron, and the high-level aqueduct, which ran east of the Etzion area, south of Bethlehem. Surprisingly, the engineers of the period constructed an aqueduct at a height of 820 m ABOVE SEA LEVEL (ASL), along a distance of 68 km, to the Temple Mount at 750 m ASL. The difference in height is 70 m, a gradient, that is, of only 1%. It is even more amazing to find that the low-level aqueduct led from the pool at Ein 'Arrub, as said at 820 m ASL, to "Solomon's Pools," the central pool being at 800 m ASL. The distance of 44 km spans a height difference of 20 m; the gradient is 0.45%. The distance as the crow flies is only 8 km. The planning and construction of these aqueducts was complicated, due to the great distances they traversed, and the lie of the land, which precludes any view of Jerusalem from the water source. The aqueducts originate at a source in a dry region south of Jerusalem. The springs are poor compared with sources along the coast and in the Jordan and Dead Sea Valleys. Their gradient is the smallest of all the known aqueducts. Why were two aqueducts built at this time, originating in the same area, constructed by different methods and taking parallel routes? Who initiated the construction work? When were they in use, and when was their use discontinued?

There is no information extant on the instruments used for measuring such small gradients, less than 1%. (The water level was the only instrument known to be available at the time). Modern engineers are amazed at the precision of measurements along a distance of 68 km, with a gradient of one percent, while the distance as the crow flies is only 20 km. It should be borne in mind that Jerusalem is the lowest lying of all the important towns of antiquity in the Judean Mountains. Its height is 750 m ASL, compared with 780 m ASL at Gibeon, 840 m ASL at Givath-Shaul, 850 m ASL at Mizpah, 900 m ASL at Beth-El and 950 m ASL at Hebron.

The Low-Level Aqueduct

The springs of Wadi 'Arrub were the starting point of the aqueduct, three km southeast of Kfar Etzion, east of the Jerusalem–Hebron road. Several springs flow into a pool 48 × 68 m in size, 6–8 m deep, and with a capacity of 20,000 cu m. The springs, from west to southeast, are: Ein Fureidis, Ein el-Mazra'ah, Ein el-Bas, Ein el-Fawwar, Ein el-Baradeh, Ein e-Dilbeh and Ein Kusibah. They supply 60 cu m per hour.

The lower aqueduct

The mountains north and south of Wadi 'Arrub are rugged and rocky, with many fissures, down which the soil disappears along with the rainwater. The subsoil consists of impermeable, yellowish clay and marl rocks, which provide suitable conditions for springs. The soil is yellowish-brown, shallow and fertile, and favorable for viticulture. Most of the vineyards between Bethlehem and Hebron grow on this type of soil.

The water from the Ein 'Arrub pool flowed along a conduit partly excavated out of the rock and partly built. Its average width was 60–70 cm and its depth 70–100 cm. The walls and base of the conduit were plastered with lime and roofed with stone slabs (many of which were later plundered). The aqueduct twists and turns along 44 km, up to "Solomon's Pools," circumnavigating 15 large valleys in order to maintain its incline. The water flowed into the two lower of "Solomon's Pools." The ruins of the aqueduct are barely visible today south-east of "Solomon's Pools," below the high-level aqueduct, which is still virtually intact. The ruins can also be seen near the Lower Pool, northwest of it and south of the road; a clay pipe, dating from the Mameluke or the Ottoman period, has been built into it. Another aqueduct is to be found north of the Middle Pool; this is the high-level one, which turned east to Bethlehem. Its ruins can be seen just north of the road.

"Solomon's Pools," 780–810 m ASL, were excavated in a tributary of the Artas Valley, to accommodate the waters of the four nearby springs: Ein

"King Solomon's Pools:" Lower Pool

al-Burak, Ein Salih in the upper part, near the Turkish fort, Ein Farruja at the foundations of the Lower Pool, and Ein 'Itan in the valley south of the Lower Pool. The Jerusalem *Talmud* reports that the aqueduct to the Temple began at 'Itam (*Yoma* 49, 1). The water of the two upper springs, as well as of Ein Farruja and Ein 'Itan, first flowed to the low-lying aqueduct. The foundation of the pools consists of clay and marl rock, impermeable to water and thus highly suitable for the purpose.

Lower water tunnel

The Upper Pool is 71 × 118 m, and its depth 10–12 m. The Middle Pool is 135 × 50–76 m, and its depth 10–12 m. The Lower Pool is 179 × 46–61 m and is 8–16 m deep. The capacity of the three pools is 160,000 cu m. The low-level aqueduct emerges from the Lower Pool through a tunnel, and from there the water flows north of Artas village to Bethlehem by way of an underground tunnel. The tunnels have shafts to ensure a fresh air supply and to allow cleaning of the aqueduct. At Bethlehem there is a special shaft to provide water for the

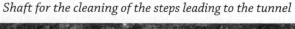

Shaft for the cleaning of the steps leading to the tunnel

local inhabitants. The aqueduct passes north of Bethlehem along the eastern road and continues in the open to the village of Sur Bahir. Clay pipes, 20–22 cm in diameter, were built into the aqueduct along this stretch in the Ottoman Period. From Sur Bahir the aqueduct passes south of Talpiyoth, where it enters a tunnel, 250 m southeast of the memorial to soldiers of the Jerusalem Division fallen in the Six Day War. This tunnel also contains remnants of the Turkish clay piping. The tunnel crosses the level of the U.N. Headquarters Road. The openings of three shafts are visible 150 m apart. The tunnel is flanked by two aqueducts leading to Givath-Hananiah and Abu Tor. The aqueduct crosses the Ben-Hinnom Valley in the west and east, reaching the Serpents' Pool and circling "Mount Zion" from the south and the east. Its ruins in this section, containing clay pipes of a later date, are visible in four places above the southwestern road of "Mount Zion," as well as west of the Western Wall, halfway up the staircase leading to Yeshivat haKotel. The aqueduct entered the Temple Mount through the Gate of the Chain, over a bridge. It supplied the Serpents' Pool, the Upper Pool and Birket Israil. The section between Solomon's Pools and Jerusalem is 24 km long, and traverses relatively few valleys.

The production of the underground spring is, as stated, 50 cu m an hour on a yearly average. Assuming that this was also the amount of water produced from the spring in ancient times, it had to quench the thirst of 32,000 people during the First Temple period, according to the calculations of the daily consumption of 40 liters of water per person daily, which was a large amount in those days. If we divide the spring yield to 120,000 inhabitants of Jerusalem in the Second Temple period, we will receive 10 liters of water per person daily.

Why therefore, was water in the Second Temple period drawn from guaranteed water wells that are north of the Hebron Mountain towards Jerusalem?

According to Jehosophat, the priests decided the number of Passover sacrifices, which amounted to 255,600 (*Wars* IV, 11, 2). If we double the number by four, which is presumably the average amount for a family going up to Jerusalem in order to celebrate the Passover feast, there were about a million souls. How is it possible, therefore, to explain the amazing fact, that amongst hundreds of thousands of the ascendants, who sacrificed an astounding quarter of a million animals, plagues didn't break out due to contamination, which almost certainly must have been caused by the blood, the waste and the excretions that remained after the sacrificed animals?

The *Mishnah* refers inadvertently to this question: "Ten miracles were given to our fathers in the Temple: a woman never miscarried from the smell of the Temple meat, the Temple meat never stank, and a fly was never seen on the altar…" (*Avot* 5:7). Here is a clear hint that the many waters of the springs washed the blood and the waste of the sacrifices and from the manure house and flushed them through the Haggai or the Cheesemonger's Valley toward the Kidron Valley.

In other words, in the courtyard of the Temple Mount, 38 ancient and later wells were quarried holding 40,000 cubic meters of water. Among them were three giant wells, of course from Herod's time, that held 25,000 cubic meters of water – i.e., 25 million liters. In other words they had 25 million liters of water. These wells were filled from the aqueduct waters of the springs, even before the ascent to Jerusalem. If a million pilgrims need three liters of water per person per day to drink, i.e. three million liters of water a day, the large wells of the Temple Mount were sufficient for all the pilgrims for a period of eight days or more. Thus during the holy days, the aqueduct of spring water supplied all the needs for purification of the sacrifices and washing of each pilgrim, and after that the water flowed to the Kidron River, to water the incense and perfume gardens.

The low level aqueduct is largely destroyed today. Its roofing slabs have been widely utilized for building by villagers along the way. The low-level aqueduct from Solomon's Pools to Jerusalem is mentioned by the Arab and Persian historians Muqaddasi (985) and Nasir-i Khosrau (1047). The aqueduct underwent many repairs, by el-Malek el-Adal (1202), al Malek el-Zaher Baybars (1266), Emir Tankiz e-Nasiri (1328), Sultan Barquq (1382), Sultan Khushqadam (1460), Sultan El-Ashraf Qait Bei (1483), and Sultan Suleiman the Magnificent (1537). Sultan Mohammed IV, the Ottoman, repaired the fort at Solomon's Pools in 1622. The aqueduct was further repaired by Kanj Ahmad Agha in 1812, by Kamal Pasha in 1856 and by Thuraya Pasha in 1860.

The High-Level Aqueduct

This begins at Ras el-'Id, in Wadi el-Biar, east of the Etzion area. The name signifies a permanent flow of water, and the spring is called Ein Wadi el-Biar, or the spring of the Valley of Wells, because of the many shafts along the tunnel from which water could be drawn. The spring is about 2 km northeast of the junction between the Jerusalem–Hebron highway and the road entering

Upper water siphon

Kfar Etzion, and some 600 m northeast of the dirt track going east from the highway to Tekoa. The spring on the eastern bank of Wadi el-Biar may be reached about 120 m down a path, which leaves the road eastward. Another group of springs flows to Wadi el-Biar: the springs of Ein el-Fa'ur, about 1.5 km north of Ras el-'Id and south of Khirbet Hamidieh, a spring at Khirbet el-Qat, and Ein el-'Asafir.

The beginning of the high-level aqueduct at Ras el-'Id in Wadi el-Biar is 870 m ASL. The spring waters flow along an underground tunnel down Wadi el-Biar, for 2.5 km, underneath fruit orchards; shafts along the way are used for drawing water as well as for cleaning the tunnel. Wadi el-Biar and the shafts can be reached two km down the road southwest of the junction of "Solomon's Pools" with the Hebron highway. An open conduit then leads north for about one km, passing into a tunnel one km long until it reaches Kal'at el-Burak at "Solomon's Pools." This aqueduct, which receives the water from the higher springs at Solomon's Pools, Ein Salih and Ein el-Burak, stretches along the main road to Jerusalem, south of the low-level aqueduct. The high-level aqueduct runs along a less winding course than the low-level one, since its source lies higher; it is also shorter than the low-level one, being largely underground. In the section northwest of Bethlehem and south of Rachel's Tomb it goes through a syphon 1,200 m long, constructed of stone piping. This is visible over an area of 40 m, just east of the road, underneath the local dwellings. Each link is 90 cm high by 90 cm long, with an internal diameter of 38 cm. One link has a connecting protrusion, seven centimeters long, and the next has a corresponding concavity; the stone links were joined together by the pressure of clay on mortar, rendering them proof against water pressure. These pipes were made in order to traverse the Bethlehem valley, since the aqueduct had to reach the Upper City of Jerusalem. Remnants of the aqueduct near the Mar Elias monastery are clearly visible to passers-by, south-west of Ramat Rahel, and other sections in the Valley of Rephaim and near Givat-Hananiah (Abu Tor) are also seen in parts. The water flowed to the Mamillah Pool and thence to the Jaffa Gate and Herod's palace or Hezekiah's Pool. The high-level aqueduct from Solomon's Pools to Jerusalem was 13 km long, compared with the 24 km of the low-level aqueduct, that is to say, 11 km shorter. The high-level aqueduct from Ras el-'Id at Wadi el-Biar to the Upper City was 18 km long, and its gradient from a height of 870 m ASL at its source to 780 m ASL in Jerusalem was 90 m, or five percent.

The aqueducts were roofed with stone slabs in antiquity, to prevent evaporation and pollution, as well as silting from the torrents pouring down the mountain slopes. Most of these slabs were plundered over the centuries. Today the high-level aqueduct still carries water to "Solomon's Pools," and during the winter the floodwaters of the mountain slopes also flow along it. It is therefore still necessary for the aqueduct to be cleaned out every autumn. "Solomon's Pools" also receive the floodwaters of the hills around them.

Stages in Building the Aqueducts

What was the reason for the existence of two aqueducts? When were they constructed, used, and abandoned?

It would appear that the water of the low-level aqueduct was conducted to the Temple Mount and the Lower City, while the water of the high-level aqueduct was conducted to the towers of Phasael (the present-day Tower of David), Hippicus and Mariamne, on the heights of the Upper City. The high-level aqueduct apparently stretched from Rachel's Tomb to the western part of the hill at present occupied by Kibbutz Ramat Rahel, and thence through the western parts of what are now the Yemin Moshe and Mishkenot Sha'ananim quarters and the King David Hotel to the Mamillah and Amygdalon pools.

Details of the technique of excavating the conduits and tunnels, with their dates, are given in the work of M. Hecker (*Haspakat haMayim biYerushalayim Bimey Kedem. Sefer Yerushalayim*, pp. 191–218), as well as in an account of investigations made after the Six Day War. Alexander Jannaeus may have been the first to excavate ditches to bring water to his desert strongholds.

Herod, however, appears to have been the first to convey water over great distances, using techniques developed by the Romans. During his rule Jerusalem expanded considerably, and its growing population required increasing amounts of water. Herod's first project was the construction of an aqueduct from a high point near Bethlehem to a lower point in the Judean Desert. Water was taken from the Ertas springs, east of Solomon's Pools, to Herodion. The springs supply 43 cu m per hour. The aqueduct, which starts at a height of 690 m ASL, is visible along the Artas Valley, and runs for eight km to Herodion. The pool at the foot of the fortified hill is 660 m above sea-level; the gradient therefore was 3.75%. This work is mentioned by Josephus, who notes the distance of the water source and the expense of the construction (*Antiquities* XV, 9). Herod built another aqueduct from the Qelt Valley to the fort of Kipros (Which he named after his mother), on top of a hill at the mouth of the Qelt Valley, on its southern bank. Remnants of this aqueduct are also visible today.

It is reasonable to assume that Herod's engineers gained in experience in the course of building these aqueducts, and the scope of their efforts widened. They planned and constructed the low-level aqueduct from Ein el-'Arrub to "Solomon's Pools" and thence to the Temple Mount, where one million pilgrims gathered on the Jewish festivals. The Jerusalem *Talmud* mentions the spring of Ein 'Itam by name, giving the difference in height between it and the Temple forecourt, clear evidence that the waters of Ein 'Itam were conveyed to the Temple Mount. The engineers of the period obviously had instruments, which measured the differences in height between sites distant from one another. Ein 'Itam is 760 m ASL, that is, some 17 m above the Temple Mount.

Some scholars believe that the low-level aqueduct was built by the Roman procurator Pontius Pilate (25–35 C.E.), since Josephus recounts in *Wars* II, 9, that, "He subsequently occasioned another tumult by expending the sacred treasure, called Korban, in the construction of an aqueduct. He brought the water from the distance 400 furlongs" (or 400 stadia). According to Hecker, this is a distance of 74 km, corresponding to the distance between Ein ʿArrub and Jerusalem.

We believe a project of this magnitude to be more typical of the imagination of Herod, the king who constructed a magnificent Temple, great towers and palaces, enlarged the city and built aqueducts elsewhere rather than that of a foreign procurator, who is not mentioned specifically as having built the aqueduct, but only as having planned or repaired it. The aqueducts are mentioned in connection with the Revolt: "On the day following, the High Priest Ananias was discovered, hiding in an aqueduct, and with his brother Hezekiah was executed by the brigands" (*Wars* II, 17). Josephus also mentions the zealots killed in battle by the Romans within the tunnels in the city, where two thousand corpses were found, and where Simon bar-Giora and Yohanan ben-Levi were caught (*Wars* VI, 9). More light will no doubt be shed on the matter when the underground tunnels of Jerusalem are discovered. In any case, no evidence of Roman construction was discovered along the low-level aqueduct (as distinct from the high-level aqueduct).

Josephus reports that Titus razed the Temple and the city walls, leaving the towers of Phasael, Hippicus and Mariamne intact, as well as the western wall, for the use of the Roman garrison (*Wars* VII, 1). During Hadrian's reign the Romans inhabited Aelia Capitolina and the Upper City, and the Tenth Legion made its stronghold in the region of the towers. The low-level aqueduct was thus unsuitably located for the needs of the Romans, and the Roman military engineers therefore constructed the high-level aqueduct, with its water reaching the western hill and the Upper City. Hecker notes that syphons were common in aqueducts in other parts of the Roman Empire; as noted above, several links of a syphon were found in the high-level aqueduct, bearing Roman names and the stamp of a Roman centurion. According to Hecker, the high-level aqueduct was used in the Byzantine period as well. A Greek inscription was found near the aqueduct, forbidding planting or sowing for a distance of fifteen feet on either side of the conduit, for fear of possible damage by plant roots.

From the Byzantine period onward, the use of both the high- and low-level aqueducts depended upon the power and stability of government in the city. During periods of growth the aqueducts were activated, but during decline their use was discontinued.

At the end of the Second Temple period Jerusalem had about 100,000 inhabitants and the low-level aqueduct was in full use, its water flowing to the Lower City and the Temple Mount. The water was originally conveyed only from Solomon's Pools; the water of the Ein 'Arrub springs was added later. Maintenance of the aqueduct, including the repair of cracks and cleaning of the silt borne by floodwaters, was costly. After the destruction of the Second Temple, the Romans constructed the high-level aqueduct, which conveyed water to the towers of the Upper City.

The city had about 80,000 inhabitants during the Byzantine period, and the high-level aqueduct was in use, since the inhabited areas were mainly in the vicinity of the Holy Sepulcher and the towers. There is no information on the working of the low-level aqueduct at this time. Moslem Jerusalem had only 30,000 inhabitants at most. The high-level aqueduct was cut off during this period, and probably the low-level one as well, since farmers living along the routes damaged the conduits and drew off the water, which increased the costs of upkeep. At this time the inhabitants of the city apparently used only the waters of the Gihon, Ein Rogel, and the cisterns and pools.

During the Crusader occupation (eleventh to thirteenth centuries) the population of Jerusalem at first dropped to 3,000, but eventually grew again to a maximum of 30,000. It is reasonable to assume that the Crusaders did not use the aqueducts. An Arab historian recalls the lack of water suffered by the Crusaders besieging the city, while the besieged inhabitants had an ample supply. During the Ottoman period, the fort of Kal'at el-Burak was built northwest of Solomon's Pools, 100 × 150 m in size, with four towers at its corners. The fort was built to watch over the carrying of water through the low-level aqueduct from the pools to Jerusalem. The depredations of the local farmers continued, however, and in 1620 the Ottoman rulers inserted clay piping within the low-level aqueduct. These pipes were only 20–22 cm in diameter, since the city was less densely populated, and are visible today north of Bethlehem, along the eastern road to Sur Bahir. These pipes were also damaged. In 1902 the Moslem Waqf laid an iron pipe, 20 cm in diameter; part of this pipe was laid within the low-level aqueduct, but from north of Bethlehem it follows a shorter route than the aqueduct. Water pressure in the iron pipe caused its eventual damage and destruction. The British Mandate government established a motor pump at Solomon's Pools, with a purifying device, including pressure filters and chlorinating equipment, to convey the water to Jerusalem. In 1928 additional pumps were set up at Ein Farah; in 1931 at Ein Fawwar; and in 1935 at Ein Qelt, in Wadi Qelt, north of Jerusalem. About 1,000 cu m per hour were pumped up to French Hill, east of Givath-Hamivtar, and flowed by force of gravity to the city proper. In 1936 Jerusalem began to receive water from the sources at Rosh Ha'ayin, in the coastal plain, through a pipe 60 km long and 45 cm in diameter. There were four pumping stations along the route: Rosh Ha'ayin, Latrun, Sha'ar Hagai and Shoresh. After the War of Independence, Jewish Jerusalem was supplied by wells in the Shephelah, and eventually through the National Water Carrier pipeline, 60 cm in diameter, in unlimited amounts.

After the War of Independence, eastern Arab Jerusalem was supplied by the waters of Wadi Qelt and "Solomon's Pools," pumped to the city twice a week; the balance was provided by cisterns. United Jerusalem is today provided with water by the National Water Carrier, and the water of "Solomon's Pools" is pumped to Bethlehem.

Two reservoirs were established on the heights of the modern city, in Bayit Vegan and in Romema; their water flows through the city by force of gravity. In 1964 the Jerusalem area had an annual requirement of 16 million cu m, and in 1975, 25 million cu m, and the forecast for 1980 is 30 million cu m.

No other city in the Judean Mountains enjoyed geological and topographical conditions as favorable for the supply of water by various means as those of Jerusalem. The capital city possessed a copious spring, a rich well, soft rocks favoring the excavation of water cisterns, numerous vales suitable for damming and for collecting rainwater in pools, and a central, low topographic location, which facilitated the construction of aqueducts for the bringing of water over considerable distances. Few cities of antiquity, given the same conditions as Jerusalem, devoted such effort and ingenuity to solving the problem of water supply. All resources and means seem to have been aimed at the collection of water at every possible site. The entire structure of the city and its environs was planned for maximum utilization of sources of water, above and below the ground. Rainwater was collected from rooftops by pipes leading into rock-cut cisterns; water was collected in the pools excavated and constructed by damming the internal vales of the city, and tiled drains throughout the city trapped every drop of water, conducting it into pools. Water from sources outside the city was conveyed through carefully-inclined conduits, and distributed through a complicated system of subterranean tunnels which brought the water from the Upper City to the Lower, and to the Kidron Valley, while preserving its purity. During recent centuries this water has become contaminated; according to Wilson and Warren there were, in 1867, 13,000 cases of intestinal infection requiring hospitalization (about half the inhabitants of the city) due to pollution of the water by sewage.

Jerusalem has thus never wanted for water, in times of war or peace. It appears that the practice of utilizing water sources in arid countries developed and reached a high degree of sophistication in the Land of Israel. It originated with the Israelites and reached its greatest development during the Second Temple period, when large quantities of water were required to fulfill the tenets of Judaism, such as the laws of purification, and to meet the needs of the multitudes of pilgrims.

The King's Garden

The Bible mentions the King's Garden when describing the flight of Zedekiah king of Judah from the Chaldean army: "And it came to pass that when Zedekiah the king of Judah and all the men of war saw them, then they fled, and went forth out of the city by night, by way of the king's garden, by the gate betwixt the two walls; and he went out the way of the Arabah" (*Jeremiah* xxxix, 4). Nehemiah reports, in connection with the rebuilding of the city wall, that the Pool of Shiloah and the King's Garden were linked with each other: "And the wall of the pool of Shelah by the king's garden even unto the stairs that go down from the city of David" (*Nehemiah* iii, 15). The Pool of Shiloah is also mentioned in Nehemiah as the King's Pool: "Then I went on to the fountain gate, and to the king's pool" (*Nehemiah* ii, 14). This is evidence of the connection between the King's Pool and the King's Garden. According to this, the King's Garden seems to have been situated south of the Shiloah Pool (King's Pool), and lower-lying, at the meeting-point of the Kidron, Ben-Hinnom and Cheesemongers' Valleys. The garden was irrigated by the Waters of the Shiloah spring.

Gardens in the Bible

The word *gan* (garden) in the Bible denotes a location rich in water, as in the *Song of Songs* (iv, 15), "a fountain of gardens, a well of living waters," and always appears in connection with irrigated agriculture, supplied by the waters of a spring or river, rather than a vineyard or field of corn, which is dependent on rainfall: "And a river went out of Eden to water the garden" (*Genesis* ii, 10), or "As the valleys stretched out, as gardens by the riverside" (*Numbers* xxiv, 6). An area of irrigated agriculture is also called the Garden of God, as in *Genesis* xiii, 10: "And Lot lifted up his eyes, and beheld all the plain of Jordan, that it was well watered everywhere…like the garden of the Lord, like the land of Egypt, as thou goest into Zoar." The vegetable garden is mentioned in *Deuteronomy* xi, 10. "For the land, whither thou goest in to possess it, is not as the land of Egypt, from whence ye came out, where thou didst sow thy seed, and didst water it with thy foot, as a garden of herbs." The vineyard of Naboth the Jezre'elite was evergreen, thanks to the proximity of the spring of Jezre'el nearby: "And Ahab spake unto Naboth, saying, Give me thy vineyard, that I may have it for a garden of herbs, because it is near unto my house" (*1 Kings* xxi, 2). The *Mishnah* says: "…wild herbs and garden herbs that have been uprooted in order to be planted elsewhere" (*Ukzin* 1, 2). The *Midrash* legend also describes a watered garden as having a dark-green color, and becoming paler when the water runs dry (*Leviticus Rabbah* 16). The lushly irrigated garden is also mentioned: "…and thou shalt be like a watered garden, and like a spring of water, whose waters fail not" (*Isaiah* lviii, 11). The garden is the site of orchards and fruit trees: "I made me gardens and parks, and I planted trees in them of all kinds of fruits" (*Ecclesiastes*, ii, 5), and the garden is indeed destroyed when the spring supplying it runs dry: "For ye shall be as the terebinth whose leaf fadeth, and as a garden that hath no water" (*Isaiah*, i, 30).

A garden, therefore, requires water; but even more does it require soil. Where, in the vicinity of the Temple Mount, was deep soil available?

Location of the King's Garden
As noted above, the most likely location of the King's Garden was at the junction of the three valleys of Jerusalem, where the alluvial accumulation was deepest. Orchards and vegetable gardens are cultivated there to this day over a relatively small area (120 dunams = 12 hectares or 30 acres). The location has several advantages: new alluvium is deposited on the site and refertilizes it annually; the floodwaters rushing down the three valleys all reach this point; the bowl-shaped valley is very deep, lying at an altitude of 600 m ASL, i.e., 200 m below Jerusalem itself; its proximity to the Judean Desert brings high temperatures. The garden contained citron trees, and was irrigated by the waters of the Gihon spring and the Shiloah Pool, as well as by the nearby waters of Ein Rogel.

Why was this relatively small garden dignified by the name of the "King's Garden"? The king obviously had sufficient land in other areas around Jerusalem, or in the Jordan Valley.

The soil of this valley, however, was the richest of all, since the three prerequisites for high yields of irrigated agriculture were present: soil, water

The King's Garden at the Kidron Valley; in the south – Temple Mount wall

and warmth. The soil was also fertilized by the Temple drain, which conveyed the remains of sacrifices and blood to the garden: "Both mingled together in the channel and flowed away into the brook Kidron, and it was sold to gardeners as manure, and the law of sacrilege applied to it" (*Yoma* v, 6). The combination of these conditions led to the creation of a tropical-type enclave in Jerusalem, which was suitable for cultivating the perfume and incense crops required for the Temple service. Dates, which require a warm climate, were also grown there: "There are two palm trees in the Valley of Ben-Hinnom and between them smoke rises ... and this is the gate of Gehenna" (*Erubin* 19a). The valley was thus also known as the King's Valley.

Perfumes

Perfumes and the ingredients of incense were traditionally supplied by tropical countries, such as India, Yemen, and Africa and, in the Land of Israel, by the Jordan Valley and the Dead Sea region, where temperatures are high, and fresh water is plentiful in the oases. This is made clear in the important book by Professor J. Feliks, *Olam Ha-tsomeah ha-Mikra'i, Tsimhei Noi, Besamim uKetoret*, Masada, 1957.

Perfumes were very costly, since they were grown in few places throughout the world; a single plant yielded only a very small amount of the aromatic juices, and that by a laborious process. The aromatic substance was usually mixed with high quality olive oil. Professor Feliks mentions Theophrastus' comment on the extraction of balsam sap oil: "One man can gather in a day only enough to fill a conch shell."

The holy anointing oil consisted, according to *Exodus* xxx, 23–26, of four tropical perfumes: "Take thou also onto thee the chief spices, of flowing myrrh five hundred shekels, and of sweet cinnamon half so much, even two hundred and fifty shekels, and of sweet calamus two hundred and fifty shekels, and of cassia five hundred, after the shekel of the sanctuary, and of olive oil a hin; And thou shalt make it a holy anointing oil, a perfume compounded after the art of the perfumer; it shall be a holy anointing oil. And thou shalt anoint therewith the tent of meeting, and the ark of the testimony." The *Song of Songs* mentions the following perfumes: "…Henna with spikenard plants, spikenard and saffron, calamus and cinnamon, with all trees of frankincense; myrrh and aloes, with all the chief spices" (iv, 13–14). According to Professor Feliks, myrrh, balsam, camphor and saffron grow in the country. The most important perfume was balsam, which was cultivated at Ein Gedi.

Ingredients of Incense

The ingredients of incense are detailed in the Bible (*Exodus*, xxx, 34–36): "And the Lord said to Moses, take unto thee sweet spices, stacte, and onycha and galbanum; sweet spices with pure frankincense; of each there shall be a like weight. And thou shalt make it incense, a perfume after the art of the perfumer, seasoned with salt, pure and holy. And thou shalt beat some of it very small, and put of it before the testimony in the tent of meeting, where I will meet with thee, it shall be unto you most holy." Almost all these perfumes were used in the incense at the Temple altar. The *Talmud* also mentions many perfumes. According to Professor Feliks, 264 kg (about 500 Libras) of incense were used annually in the Temple.

The offerings and perfumes were prepared with olive oil, which was available close to the King's Garden, on the Mount of Olives. The offerings consisted mainly of wheat and oats cultivated at the head of the Kidron Valley, in the Valley of Beth Miqleh (as we have already seen) and in the Valley of Rephaim (see *Isaiah* xvii, 5): "And it shall be as when the harvestman gathered the standing corn, and reapeth the ears with his arm; yea it shall be as when one gleaned ears in the Valley of Rephaim." The meal-offerings were also brought from Michmas, north of Jerusalem, and from Zanoah in the Shephelah, where the climate was warmer (*Menahot* 9, 1). The meal-offerings were mixed with perfume and frankincense, taken in part at least from the King's Garden: "All (other) meal-offerings require oil and frankincense (*Sotah* 2, 1), and "These require both oil and frankincense: the meal-offering of fine flour, that prepared on a griddle, that prepared in a pan, the cakes and the wafers, the meal-offering of the priests, the meal-offering of the anointed High Priest; the meal-offering of a gentile, and the meal-offering of women, and the meal-offering of the Omer ...the shewbread requires frankincense but not oil" (*Menahot* 5, 3).

The Garden of Perfumes

The Queen of Sheba's visit to King Solomon is described as follows: "And she came to Jerusalem with a very great train, with camels that bore spices, and gold very much, and precious stones; ...and she gave the king a hundred and twenty talents of gold, and of spices very great store, and precious stones, there came no more such abundance of spices as these which the Queen of Sheba gave to King Solomon" (*1 Kings* X, 2, 10). King Solomon must also have received from the Queen seeds and saplings of spice plants, which he planted in the King's Garden. This is clear from the following, in connection with King Hezekiah, who lived about 250 years after Solomon, and showed the spices to the emissaries of the King of Babylon: "And Hezekiah hearkened unto them, and showed them all his treasure-house, the silver and the gold, and the spices, and the precious oil, and the house of his armor, and all that was found in his treasures, there was nothing in his house, nor in all his dominion, that Hezekiah showed them not" (*1 Kings* XX, 13). *Ecclesiastes* recounts: "I made me pools of water, to water therefrom the wood springing up with trees" (II, 6). Thus the King's Garden also included trees, possibly yielding aromatic juices. The *Targum* of Jonathan ben Uziel, dating from the late Second Temple period, implies as much. The *Song of Songs* (IV, 13) says: "Thy shoots are a park of pomegranates," and the Midrashic legend describes orchards around Jerusalem, each with camphor and other perfumes, used by the priests for the Temple service. The *Letter of Aristeas* also describes the service of the priests as including the preparation of perfumes. The *Mishnah* (*Shekalim* V, 1) gives the following details about the preparation of the incense. "...these are the officers which served in the Temple ...the House of Abtinas was over the preparation of the incense." This priestly family was probably also in charge of cultivating the pure perfumes for the service. According to the

Mishnah (*Shevi'it* 7, 6) "The Sabbatical Law applied to the rose, henna, balsam, the lotus…" implying that they were cultivated in the country, obviously in the warm Jordan Valley and Dead Sea region. The balsam mentioned here was the chief perfume of the Jordan Valley and indeed of the country. It seems to us that perfumes were originally grown in the King's Garden, from the seeds and plants brought by the Queen of Sheba, and were then cultivated near the Dead Sea, and in the Jordan Valley, which had climatic conditions similar to those of the King's Garden, and also appears to have been royal property. The perfume beds in the King's Garden in Jerusalem are mentioned in the *Song of Songs*, as are also the vineyards of Ein Gedi.

Perfume Spices

The lily is mentioned in the Song of Songs as a perfume cultivated in the garden, obviously in the King's Garden: "My beloved is gone down into his garden, to the bed of spices, to feed in the gardens and to gather lilies" (vi, 2). The lilies grew in warm valleys: "I am the rose of Sharon, a lily of the valleys" (ii, 1). Ben Sira describes the lilies as growing along watercourses. The *Mishnah* mentions an important rose garden in Jerusalem: "Rabbi Judah said: It once happened in a rose garden in Jerusalem…" (*Ma'aseroth* 2, 5). This rose garden must have been in the King's Garden in the Kidron Valley. The *Mishnah* also says: (*Tohoroth* 3, 7): "If a child was found at the side of a graveyard with lilies in his hand, and the lilies grew only in the place of uncleanness, he is deemed nevertheless to be clean," implying that the lily garden was near the Kidron necropolis. The lily is also known as the "king's lily": "Iris, ivy and the king's lily, likewise all manner of seeds are not *Kil'ayim* in a vineyard" (*Kil'ayim* 5, 8). The rose also served for anointing: "Royal children may anoint their wounds with roseoil" (*Shabbat* 14, 4).

Perfumes that Grew in the Country

Balm. This supplied local needs as well as being exported, as noted in *Ezekiel*: "Judah and the land of Israel, they were thy traffickers; they traded for thy merchandise wheat of Minnith, and balsam, and honey, and oil, and balm" (xxvii, 17). Professor Feliks identifies resin (*nataf*) with balm, and points out that according to Rabbi Simeon ben Gamliel there is also a connection between *nataf* and *kataf* (balsam). Since, according to the *Mishnah*, "the Sabbatical Law applies to the rose, henna, balsam, and the lotus… (*Shevi'it* vii, 6), it therefore follows that balm must have been grown in the country; it was a thorny bush growing in the oases of the lower Jordan Valley, and could quite easily have grown in the King's Garden in Jerusalem.

Myrrh. This perfume is mentioned in the tale of Joseph, whom the Ishmaelite caravan bore to Egypt with its load of myrrh: "…with their camels bearing spicery and balm and myrrh" (*Genesis* XXXVII, 25). Myrrh and balsam are counted among the fruits of the land, in the commands of Jacob to his sons, bound for Egypt: "…take of the choice fruits of the land in your vessel, and carry down to the man a present, a little balm and a little honey, spicery and myrrh, nuts and almonds" (*Genesis* XLIII, 11). Professor Feliks identifies the myrrh with the sap of the rock-rose, which grows wild in Asia Minor, Crete and Cyprus, and since the Sabbatical year also applies to the rock-rose, it follows that this too could have been cultivated in the King's Garden in the capital.

Henna (or Camphire). Henna is mentioned in the *Song of Songs*: "My beloved is unto me as a cluster of henna in the vineyards of Ein Gedi" (I, 14). Henna is one of the largest spice plants in the country, and the laws of *Shevi'it* apply to it. According to Professor Feliks, it is a bush or small tree whose sweet-smelling flowers grow in clusters of white or gold. Today it is grown in the Arab farms of the Shephelah and the Jordan Valley; from its roots and stems is extracted the red dye with which the Arab women paint their hands and nails. We assume it was also grown in the King's Garden in the Kidron Valley.

Saffron. This is mentioned in the *Song of Songs* (IV, 13–14) in connection with the garden of perfumes: "Thy shoots are a park of pomegranates, with precious fruits; henna with spikenard plants, spikenard and saffron, calamus and cinnamon. With all trees of frankincense; myrrh and aloes, with all the chief spices." Professor Feliks notes that saffron is mentioned in an early *Baraitha* as one of the kinds of incense used in the Temple service. Its delicate oil was used for dyeing and spicing foods, for perfume and for medicinal purposes. Seven species of crocus, from which saffron is extracted, grow wild in the country, and were undoubtedly cultivated in the King's Garden.

Balsam. In his book Professor Feliks quoted the Hebrew sources in which balsam is mentioned. From Josephus we learn where balsam grows: "…Jericho. This, the most fertile district of Judea, nourishes numbers of palm trees, the stems of which being cut with sharp stones, the juice is received at the incision, in drops like tears" (*Wars* I, 6) and "...even the plantation of palm trees at Jericho, where grows the balsam tree" (*Wars* I, 18), where mention is made of the gifts bestowed upon Cleopatra by Mark Antony, denoting the significance the Romans attached to balsam. Herod eventually had to lease the plantations at Jericho from Cleopatra (*Antiquities* IX, 4). The range of balsam cultivation in the Jordan Valley may be deduced from the *Talmudic* interpretation of *Jeremiah*: "But Nebuzaradan the captain of the guard left of the poorest of the land to be vinedressers and husbandmen" (LII, 16). The commentary runs: the vinedressers were assumed to be the balsam pickers from Ein Gedi to Ramata, northeast of the Dead Sea.

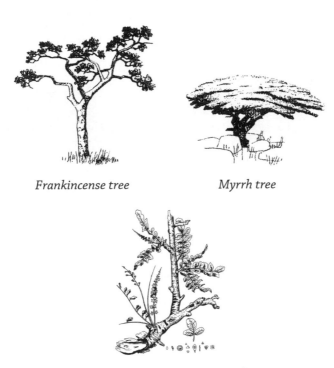

Frankincense tree   Myrrh tree

Branch of frankincense tree from an Arabian country

CHAPTER IV

THE LOWER CITY FROM THE FIRST TEMPLE PERIOD ONWARD

Jebusite Jerusalem

The Jebusite City was located on the southeastern spur of present-day Jerusalem, the lower hill of the city, and probably covered an area of 60 dunams (15 acres). The city was surrounded by valleys on three sides: the Kidron Valley in the east, the Valley (called the Cheesemongers' Valley during the Second Temple period) in the west, and the Ben-Hinnom Valley in the south. In the north the city was connected by a narrow saddle to the threshing-floor of Araunah the Jebusite; in all probability this is the Temple Mount. The road running at present along the southern wall of the Temple Mount to the Dung Gate is very near the saddle. S. Yeivin believes that in Jebusite times this saddle was bisected by a moat, three meters wide, which separated the city in the south from the threshing floor to its north. The Jebusite city occupied the southern part of the lower hill, since this area was naturally fortified by the valleys. About 60% of the mountain settlements during the Canaanite and Israelite periods were located on hill spurs, which provided defense on three sides; only about 40% were on top of hills and mountains. Archaeological excavations by K. Kenyon and her predecessors have revealed remnants of the early and middle (Jebusite) Canaanite periods, as well as of the First Temple period and the Kingdom of Judah.

Israelite Jerusalem

The Jerusalem of David and Solomon spread northward, to Araunah's threshing floor and the Temple Mount, and the total area of the city was 140 dunams. Later expansion occurred westward, and included the suburbs – the Mishneh and the Makhtesh – further up the valley. Its area then reached 230 dunams. The Shiloah Pool added ten dunams to the city area. Several archaeologists believe that the Upper City was included in the Jerusalem of this period, on the basis of remnants of masonry on "Mount Zion" and the Citadel. The total area

Jebusite wall in the eastern City of David, Jerusalem (above the treetop)

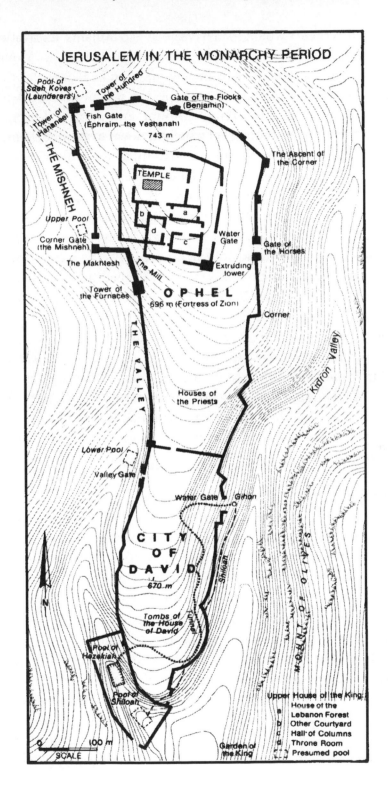

JERUSALEM IN THE MONARCHY PERIOD

Pool of
Sdeh Koves
(Launderers)

Tower of
the Hundred

Gate of the Flocks
(Benjamin)

Tower of
Hananeel

Fish Gate
(Ephraim, the Yeshanah)
743 m

THE MISHNEH

The Ascent of
the Corner

TEMPLE

Upper Pool

b   a

Corner Gate
(the Mishneh)

d

c

Water
Gate

Gate of
the Horses

The Makhtesh

The Mill

Tower of
the Furnaces

Extruding
tower

OPHEL
696 m (Fortress of Zion)

Corner

THE VALLEY

Houses of
the Priests

Kidron Valley

Lower Pool

Valley Gate

Water Gate   Gihon

CITY
OF
DAVID
670 m

Shiloah

MOUNT OF OLIVES

Tombs of
the House
of David

Pool of
Hezekiah

Pool of
Shiloah

N

0   100 m
SCALE

Garden of
the King

Upper House of the King
a   House of the
     Lebanon Forest
b   Other Courtyard
c   Hall of Columns
d   Throne Room
     Presumed pool

according to this theory would then have been 650 dunams. Excavations conducted by Professor Nachman Avigad in the Jewish quarter of "Mount Zion" revealed part of the wall of the Israelite city or of an Israelite palace.

The Lower City of the First Temple period was broad, at a fairly high altitude in the north, near the Temple Mount, and narrowed progressively southward, with a corresponding fall in height down to the Ben-Hinnom Valley. Its length, from north to south, was 1050 m; its maximum width, on the Temple Mount, was 320 m, and, at the center of the Lower City, was 70–100 m. At the upper part of the Temple Mount the altitude was 743 m, and the Ophel (the citadel of the city, south of the Temple Mount) was 696 m high; the lower part of the city, near the valley, was 670 m high. The very deep Kidron Valley ran along the entire eastern side of the Lower City. The western valley was flatter and wider in the north; this section was called the Mishneh, and was probably the site of the Upper Pool. The central part of the valley was deeper, and was known as the *Makhtesh* (crater), while the southern part was deep and narrow, draining the hill of the Upper City, as well as the Lower, by way of a small vale. Three pools were therefore built in it: the Lower Pool, Hezekiah's Pool, and the Shiloah Pool. The southern boundary of the city was the lowest part of the Ben-Hinnom Valley, where it merges into the Kidron. This point is at a height of 600 m. The difference in height between the point just south of the Temple Mount and the junction of the Kidron and Ben-Hinnom Valleys was thus 143 m.

Mount Zion, the Citadel and the City of David

After David's conquest of the Jebusite city, the hill of the Lower City was divided into several parts. The highest, northern part was the site of the royal buildings, and Solomon built his Temple there. This was the original Mount Zion, as mentioned in *Psalms* XLVIII, 2–3: "Fair in situation, the joy of the whole earth, even Mount Zion, the uttermost parts of the north, the city of the great king. God in her palaces hath made himself known for a stronghold," and in *Micah* IV, 1–2: "But in the end of days it shall come to pass that the mountain of the Lord's house shall be established as the top of the mountains, and it shall be exalted above the hills; and people shall flow unto it. And many nations shall go and say, Come ye and let us go up to the mountains of the Lord, and to the house of the God of Jacob; and He will teach us of His ways, and we will walk in His paths, for out of Zion shall go forth the law, and the word of the Lord from Jerusalem." This high place was probably the site of

Map of archeological excavations in the City of David

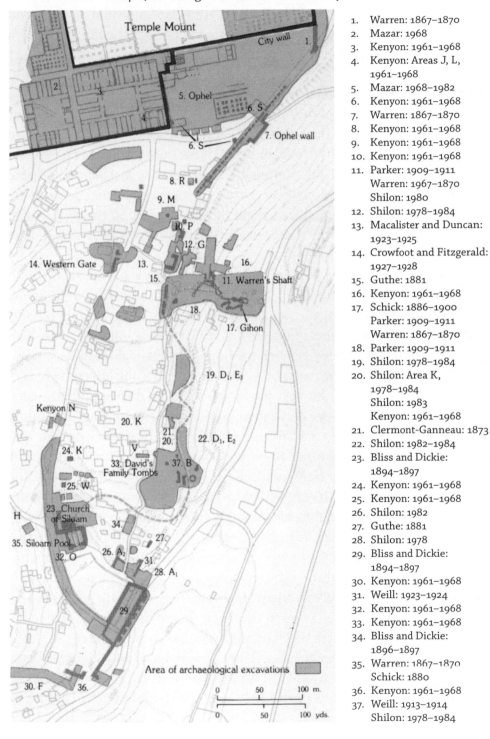

1. Warren: 1867–1870
2. Mazar: 1968
3. Kenyon: 1961–1968
4. Kenyon: Areas J, L, 1961–1968
5. Mazar: 1968–1982
6. Kenyon: 1961–1968
7. Warren: 1867–1870
8. Kenyon: 1961–1968
9. Kenyon: 1961–1968
10. Kenyon: 1961–1968
11. Parker: 1909–1911
    Warren: 1967–1870
    Shilon: 1980
12. Shilon: 1978–1984
13. Macalister and Duncan: 1923–1925
14. Crowfoot and Fitzgerald: 1927–1928
15. Guthe: 1881
16. Kenyon: 1961–1968
17. Schick: 1886–1900
    Parker: 1909–1911
    Warren: 1867–1870
18. Parker: 1909–1911
19. Shilon: 1978–1984
20. Shilon: Area K, 1978–1984
    Shilon: 1983
    Kenyon: 1961–1968
21. Clermont-Ganneau: 1873
22. Shilon: 1982–1984
23. Bliss and Dickie: 1894–1897
24. Kenyon: 1961–1968
25. Kenyon: 1961–1968
26. Shilon: 1982
27. Guthe: 1881
28. Shilon: 1978
29. Bliss and Dickie: 1894–1897
30. Kenyon: 1961–1968
31. Weill: 1923–1924
32. Kenyon: 1961–1968
33. Kenyon: 1961–1968
34. Bliss and Dickie: 1896–1897
35. Warren: 1867–1870
    Schick: 1880
36. Kenyon: 1961–1968
37. Weill: 1913–1914
    Shilon: 1978–1984

the threshing floor of Araunah the Jebusite, where David built an altar to God after his conquest (*II Samuel*, XXIV, 18–19): "And Gad came that day to David, and said unto him, Go up, rear an altar unto the Lord in the threshing-floor of Araunah the Jebusite. And David went up, according to the saying of Gad, as the Lord commanded." This is also mentioned in *II Chronicles* XXI, 18–19. "Mount Zion" was also called the holy mountain: "…and Jerusalem shall be called the city of truth; and the mountain of the Lord of hosts the holy mountain" (*Zechariah* VIII, 3). The height of the mountain of the Lord is implied in *Ezekiel* XL, 2: "In the visions of God brought He me unto the Land of Israel, and set me down upon a very high mountain, whereon was, as it were, the frame of a city on the south." The *Letter of Aristeas* gives the following description: "When we reached the region we beheld the city situated in the center of all Judea, upon a mountain which rises to a lofty height. Upon its crest stood the Temple in its splendor" (83–84).

The site of the citadel (known in the Second Temple period as the Birah (Baris in Greek) could have been either of two places, according to Josephus. One possible site was along the slope of the Lower City, near the Ophel citadel of the Biblical period (*Wars of the Jews*, V, 4): "Of these hills, that on which the upper town was situated is much the higher, and straighter in its length… The other, which bears the name of Acra, and supports the lower town, is of a gibbous form," and, in the next paragraph: "It then turned and advanced with a southern aspect above the fountain of Siloam, whence it again inclined, facing the east towards Solomon's reservoir, and extending to a certain spot designated Ophla, it joined the eastern colonnade of the Temple." The commander Yohanan ben Levi (John of Gischala), who held the Lower City during the Revolt, is mentioned in connection with the following (*Wars* V, 6): "John occupied the Temple, and the parts about it, to a considerable distance, with Ophla, and the valley called Kidron." Josephus also notes in *Antiquities of the Jews* that the Acra was in the Lower City. The *Book of Maccabees* (1, XIII, 32) mentions the citadel, but its location is unclear: "He fortified the Temple Mount near the citadel more strongly. He and his men dwelt there." Elsewhere (1, XIII, 52), it states: "In his time everything prospered in his hands, so that the heathens were expelled from their country, as well as those in the city of David, in Jerusalem, who had made a citadel for themselves, from which they used to go out and pollute the environs of the Sanctuary, doing great damage to its purity." The citadel was thus probably close by the Temple, in the Lower City.

The alternative possibility is the vicinity of the Chamber of Hewn Stone and the Council House, between the Upper City and the Temple Mount; this may be implied in *Wars* VI, 6: "Orders were then issued to the troops to plunder and burn the city, but on the following (day) they set fire to the residence of the magistrates, the Acra, the council chamber and the place called Ophla; the flames spreading as far as the palace of Queen Helena, which was in the center of the Acra."

It is reasonable to assume that while the city was small and located on the eastern, lower hill, the citadel of Ophel was south of the Temple Mount. After the erection of the Temple another citadel was built at the north-western corner of the Temple Mount, which was called Birah (*Nehemiah* VII, 2), during Herod's reign this was the site of the Antonia Fortress. During the Second Temple period the city expanded westward, to the upper hill, and northward to the new section of Bezetha; the Acra was then built to serve as a fortress guarding the Temple Mount against possible invasion from the Upper City, and buttressing the weakest point of the Lower City, its northern side. The Ophel of the Lower City became less important at the end of the Second Temple period, in view of the mighty defenses of the Temple Mount; the Acra was then built on the eastern slope of the Upper City, just above the Cheesemongers' Valley, which connected the three sections of the city.

Site of the City of David – Zion

The City of David was located on the lower hill; it was also known occasionally occasionally as Zion, or the City of Zion (*I Kings* VIII, 1–4): "Then Solomon assembled the elders of Israel, and all the heads of the tribes, the princes of the fathers' houses of the children of Israel unto King Solomon in Jerusalem, to bring up the ark of the Covenant of the Lord out of the city of David, which is Zion… And they brought up the Ark of the Lord, and the Tent of Meeting, and all the holy vessels that were in the Tent, even those did the Priests and the Levites bring up" (and in *II Chronicles* V, 2–5). *I Kings* IX, 24, also recounts that "Pharaoh's daughter came up out of the city of David unto her house which Solomon had built for her; then did he build Milo." (This is also mentioned in *II Chronicles* VIII, 11.) The City of David, Zion and "Mount Zion" were located on the lower hill, from which one ascends to the Temple Mount. The City of David is also mentioned in the *Book of Maccabees* (1, I, 33; 1, II, 31; and 1, VII, 32), and Zion in the *Book of Ben Sira* (XXIV, 10).

The name "Zion" appears 160 times in the Bible on account of the paramount importance of the site. The name "Mount Zion" denotes occasionally Mount Moriah, where the binding of Isaac took place and the Temple stood. The Bible also includes all of Jerusalem, and indeed the entire Land of Israel, in the name "Zion." It is often mentioned in the later history of the Jewish people, in poetry and prayer, signifying both the nation and the land. The name of the Zionist movement stems from this ancient name, and comprises political and national feelings. The love of Zion during the Revolt against the Romans is manifested in the inscription "for the freedom of Zion" on the coins of the period, and in the phrase "for the redemption of Zion" on the Bar-Kochba coins.

The Findings in the City of David

The team of Prof. Y. Shilo excavated in the City of David in Jerusalem in 1978–1984. (Y. Shilo, *New Encyclopedia for Archeological Excavations in the Land of Israel,* item Jerusalem, pp. 614–626, 1992, Jerusalem). The area of the City of David in the days of the Jebusites was approximately 80 dunams, in the time of Solomon 130 dunams, and that of Hezekiah, 650 dunams.

Professor Shilo's team uncovered 30 meters from the Jebusite wall. Portions of this 2.5 meter thick wall were used as a nucleus for the Israelite wall from the tenth century B.C.E., which has a thickness of 2.5 m. In the eastern part of the city, the team excavated structures from the thirteenth and fourteenth centuries B.C.E., which comprised of steps up to 25 m long and 8 m wide. This structure of steps was used as a basis for building the Jebusite (fortress) Acropolis. A few other sites from the Jebusite era of the twelfth and eleventh centuries B.C.E. in the City of David were also found.

Solomon built in Jerusalem the House of God, his own house, the Milo, and the Jerusalem walls (*I Kings* IX, 15) in Jerusalem. David's Citadel (*Isaiah* XXXII, 14; *II Chronicles* XXVII, 3; XXXIII, 14) was, according to Y. Shilo, built upon the Jebusite fortress in the City of David. The Milo, in Shilo's opinion, (*II Samuel* 5:9; *I Kings* 9:15; *II Chronicles* 32:5) was in the eastern slope of the City of David, between the City of David and the Mount of Olives. The "Milo House" (*II Kings* XII, 21) was, in the opinion of B. Mazar, the segment between David's Citadel and the Temple Mount, where the archaeologist A. Mazar discovered steps with walls the thickness of 1.40 m from the Iron Age (tenth to sixth centuries B.C.E.).

Cluster of grapes and grape leaves on coins from the period of the Bar-Kochba Revolt.
On the left: Grape leaves. Legend: Freedom of Zion.
On the right: Cluster of grapes. Legend: Year One of Israel's redemption.

There were two great building periods in the City of David, during the days of Solomon and Hezekiah. In the ninth to sixth centuries B.C.E., the city spread westward, and in the eighth century it reached its apex – an area of 650 dunams. During this period, Judah absorbed many Israelite refugees from Samaria, conquered by King Assur in 722, when Hezekiah was the king of Jerusalem (*II Chronicles* XXXII, 5).

Y. Shilo uncovered the 120 m western wall in the City of David. The non-uniform width of the wall, reaches up to 5 m, and in several places the wall was preserved to the height of 3 m. The quarries discovered in the southern part of the City of David were used, it seems, for the magnificent building projects during the period of Solomon.

The Y. Shilo team discovered building remnants on the main level on the western hillside of the City of David, which are 12 m wide, and 27 m long. Here, three main buildings were unearthed. The "Ahiel House," measuring 8 × 12 m, was in the central strip and was built in the style of the "four rooms house," which was one of a series of domestic structures among which was also discovered a bathroom – an unusual feature in this period. Here were found two ostracons engraved with the name "Ahiel." North of this, the "burnt room" was discovered from the remnants of the fire that broke out in the time of the destruction of the First Temple by the king of Babylon. On the second level, 5 m lower, was the "blockhouse." Here were found 51 clay blocks bearing stamps of Hebrew names, such as "Benayahu ben (= the son of) Hoshayahu," "'Azriyahu ben Halkiyahu," "Elshama ben Samachyahu;" and the name mentioned in the Bible "Gemaryahu ben Shafan," who was the court scribe of Jehoiakim, king of Judah in 604 B.C.E. (*Jeremiah* XXXI, 9–12). This was apparently a public archive of documents that were burnt during the destruction in 586 B.C.E. and the clay blocks remained as a reminder and proof. The destruction and the fire by the Babylonians were mentioned in detail in *II Kings* XXV, 8–9: "And in the fifth month and on the seventh day of the month, which is the nineteenth year of King Nebuchadnezzar, king of Babylon, came Benuzaradan, captain of the guard, a servant of the king of Babylon, unto Jerusalem. And he burnt the house of the Lord, and the king's house, and all the houses of Jerusalem, and every great man's house he burnt with fire. And all the army of the Chaldeans, that were with the captain of the guard, broke down the walls of Jerusalem round about." (Also in *II Chronicles* XXXV, 18–19).

The Second Temple Synagogue and Hostel in the City of David

Weill's excavations in 1923–1924 revealed an inscription south of the "royal tombs" dating from Herod's reign. The text is as follows: "Theodotus the son of Vettenus the priest and head of the synagogue, the son of the head of a synagogue and the grandson of the head of a synagogue, built this synagogue for reading the Torah and teaching the commandments, and the hostel, rooms and water installations for needy pilgrims from abroad; the [synagogue] was founded by his fathers and the elders and Simonides."

The numerous visitors to the Temple are mentioned in the *Acts of the Apostles* (II, 8–11), in the *Jerusalem Talmud* (*Maaser Sheni* 1, 2) and the *Tosefta* (*Shekalim* 2, 3).

Pilgrims from fourteen countries came to the Temple, from all parts of the Middle East and the Mediterranean: Parthia, Media, Elam and Mesopotamia in the north-east; Arabia in the east; Cappadocia, Pontus, Asia, Phrygia and Pamphylia in the north; Egypt and Cyrene in the south-west, Crete and Rome in the west. The pilgrimages were made on Sabbaths and at the New Moon (*Ezekiel* XLVI, 3; *Isaiah* I, 13; LXVI, 23), and during the three annual Festivals (*Ezekiel* XLVI, 9; *Lamentations* I, 4; II, 6; and *Isaiah* XXXIII, 20). The pilgrims came also from all parts of the country (*Jeremiah* XVII, 26; XXVI, 2; XLI, 5; *Psalms* CXXII 1–2), and made the various requisite offerings and sacrifices (*Erubin* 32a; *Pesahim* 80a). The synagogue, hostel and ritual bath were for the use of the pilgrims, and citizens of Jerusalem were forbidden to accept payment from them. Jerusalem, in fact, was not part of a tribal territory and did not belong to its inhabitants; it was the property of the entire nation.

The Gates of the City

"Violence shall be no more heard in thy land, desolation nor destruction within thy borders; but thou shalt call thy walls Salvation and thy gates Praise" (*Isaiah* LX, 18).

The long, narrow aspect of the Lower City and the important valleys which surrounded it made it necessary to include many gates in the city walls; eight of these have been identified. The line of the city wall and gates during the biblical period was ascertained from several sources: the distances and directions of the city wall as mentioned in *Kings, Jeremiah, Ezekiel, Zephaniah, Zechariah, Nehemiah* and *Chronicles*; the topographic structure of the Lower City; the water sources and installations; and the archaeological excavations carried out in the nineteenth and twentieth centuries.

Most of the gates were situated in the lower-lying parts of the wall, near the water sources and reservoirs, and at the heads of the highways connecting the city with the settlements around it. Three gates were located in the eastern wall, along the Kidron Valley: the *Horse (East) Gate*, east of the Temple, which led to the Mount of Anointing; the *Water Gate*, near the Gihon spring, leading to the Mount of Olives; and the *Fountain Gate*, near Ein Rogel, toward the southeastern road to Jericho. In the south, near the Ben-Hinnom Valley, there was one gate, variously known as the *Dung Gate*, the *Cheese Gate*, the *Gate Between Two Walls*, and the *Clay Gate*; this was near the Shiloah Pool, and from it led the highway to the Judean desert and the Dead Sea. The western slope, along the central valley, had two gates: the *Valley Gate* in the west, opposite the *Water Gate* near the Lower Pool, connecting with the Upper City in the north and the Hebron highway in the south; and the *Corner Gate* (or the Mishneh), opposite the *Horse Gate*, between the *Mishneh* and the *Makhtesh*, near the Upper Pool. This gate led to Jaffa, in the west. The northern wall had two gates: the *Fish Gate*, at the north-western corner near the Pool of the Fuller's Field (also known as the *Gate of Ephraim*, or the *Old Gate*), which led to the territory of Ephraim in the north and to Shechem (Nablus); and east of it the *Sheep Gate*, or the *Gate of Benjamin*, near the Sheep Pool, from which one went out to Beth-El and the territory of Benjamin.

The gates were flanked by towers, some of them well-known such as the

Tower of the Hundred and the Tower of Hananel on either side of the Fish Gate northwest of the Temple Mount.

The Horse (East) Gate

This is mentioned in *Jeremiah* (xxxi, 39): "*...unto the brook Kidron, unto the corner of the Horse Gate toward the east, shall be holy unto the Lord,*" and in *Nehemiah* (iii, 28): "Above the horse gate repaired the priests, every one over against his own house." In *Ezekiel* xliv, 1–2, it is mentioned as the East Gate and as the ancient gate of the Temple; it might be identified as the "east gate" to which there is an allusion in *Nehemiah* iii, 29. The "Horse Gate" was thus east of the Temple and near the hostel of the priests serving in the Temple; the High Priests used it when leaving to celebrate the rite of the Red Heifer on the Mount of Anointing.

The Water Gate

This gate is mentioned in *Nehemiah* iii, 26: "Now the Nethinim dwelt in Ophel, unto the place over against the water gate toward the east, and the tower that standeth out" (See also *Nehemiah* viii, 1, 3). *Nehemiah* viii, 16, also says: "...and in the broad place of the water gate and in the broad place of the gate of Ephraim," and, in xii 37: "And by the fountain gate, and straight before them, they went up by the stairs of the city of David, at the going up of the wall, above the house of David, even unto the water gate eastward." These verses place the Water Gate east of the Lower City, near the Ophel; it was so called because the water of the Gihon was the chief water source of the city at the time. The Water Gate of Nehemiah was discovered during Dr. Kathleen Kenyon's excavations in 1961–1967, near the Jebusite wall and tower. The base of the wall dating from the eighteenth century B.C.E. was four meters wide. Remnants of a wall of the kings of Judah, from the eighth century B.C.E., were also found, built over the Jebusite wall and in its vicinity. Duncan and Macalister, excavating in 1923–1925, found a wall with two towers, separated by a wall and glacis, at the eastern part of the lower hill some 70 m above the Gihon spring, to its west. At the time it was supposed that these were the Jebusite and Davidic defenses of the city. Later excavations by Prof. Kenyon have proved otherwise; the towers are now dated to the Hasmonean period, in the second century B.C.E., and the wall to the time of Nehemiah and the return to Zion, about 440 B.C.E. Seventh-century dwellings (First Temple period) were revealed under the Hasmonean tower, as well as buildings on the terraces leading down from the Hasmonean towers to the Jebusite tower further east. Prof. Kenyon ascribes these terraces and structures to the Biblical Milo (*1 Kings* IX, 24). This, however, does not seem very likely to us; the Milo should have been in the valley south-west of the Temple Mount, since it is mentioned in connection with the building of the Temple. The wall of the Water Gate was built by the Jebusites at the eastern foot of the hill, due to its proximity to the Gihon spring. The shaft called the *tzinnor* was dug at this point (*II Samuel* v, 8), to enable water to be drawn from within the city walls. The common practice in antiquity, however, was to erect the city wall at the top of the mound or hill, to give maximum protection against enemy attacks. The first kings of Judah continued to fortify the low Jebusite wall, until Hezekiah excavated the tunnel to bring the spring water inside the wall. Late rulers (Nehemiah, the Maccabees), built the eastern wall on the higher part of the city.

"Yehud" coin from the Return to Zion period

The Fountain Gate

This is mentioned in *Nehemiah* III, 15: "And the fountain gate repaired Shalun… and the wall of the pool of Shiloah (Siloam) by the king's garden even unto the stairs that go down from the city of David"; in II, 14: "Then I went on the fountain gate, and to the king's pool," and again in XII, 37 "And by the fountain gate, and straight before them they went up by the stairs of the city of David, at the going up of the wall, above the house of David, even unto the water gate eastward." These were probably the stairs discovered by Weill in 1913–1914. The Fountain Gate, leading to Ein Rogel, was located near the Shiloah Pool, by the stairs leading up to the City of David; it was at the southern tip of the Lower City spur, southeast of the pool collecting the water of Hezekiah's tunnel.

The Dung Gate (Cheese Gate, Between Two Walls, or Clay Gate)

The Dung Gate is mentioned in *Nehemiah* III, 14: "And the Dung Gate repaired Malchijah the son of Rechab, the ruler of the district of Beth-Hakerem," and also in XII, 31. The gate of *shephoth*, in *Nehemiah* III, 13, is translated as "dung": "The valley gate repaired Hanun and the inhabitants of Zanoah; they built it and set up the doors thereof, and a thousand cubits of the wall unto the dung gate." The *shephoth* gate was built at the end of the valley. The Hebrew name implies wedges of cheese or suckling calves; the Arabic *shafaya* means sweetened milk. The name is also connected with the Cheesemongers' Valley of the Second Temple period, as mentioned in *Wars of the Jews* v, 4. This was in the valley, and was the site of the city's milk products industry. The "Gate between Two Walls" is mentioned in II *Kings* XXV, 4, in connection with the conquest of the city by Nebuchadnezzar: "Then a breach was made in the city and all the men of war fled by night by way of the gate between two walls." In *Jeremiah* XXXIX, 4, there is the description of Zedekiah's flight from the Chaldean army: "Then they fled and went forth out of the city by night by the way of the King's Garden, by the gate betwixt the two walls, and he went out the way of the Arabah." This is repeated in *Jeremiah* LII, 7. The Gate Between the Two Walls was thus near the King's Garden, at the junction of the Ben-Hinnom and Kidron Valleys, near the Shiloah Pool (see section on the King's Garden at end of previous chapter). Bliss and Dickie, excavating in 1894–1897 in the Lower City, disclosed the remnants of the double wall surrounding the Shiloah Pool, which was itself between two walls. This was probably the "other wall" which Hezekiah fortified against Sennacherib (II *Chronicles* XXXII, 5). "And he took courage, and built up all the wall that was broken down and raised it up to the towers and another wall without." During the Second Temple period this was probably the gate known as the "Gate of the Essenes" (*Wars of the Jews* v, 4), used by members of this sect in their travels to and from the Judean Desert and the Dead Sea region. The *Harsith Gate* is mentioned in *Jeremiah* XIX, 2: "And go forth unto the valley of the son of Hinnom, which is by the entry of the gate Harsith." (The Hebrew word *harsith* means clay.) The fine alluvium of the valley floodwaters sank to the bottom of the Shiloah Pool, the southernmost pool of the valley, and the resulting clay was used for the potteries nearby. The *Harsith Gate* was therefore close to the Ben-Hinnom Valley. The Arabic name of the Shiloah Pool supports this view: *Birket el-Hamra* means the Pool of Red Clay Soil. The various names all designate the same gate, located at the southern tip of the Lower City. In 1923–1924 Weill revealed sections of a wall, gate and guard tower, south of the Lower City, which could well be connected with this Biblical gate.

The western gates are as follows:

The Valley Gate

This is mentioned in *Nehemiah* III, 13: "The valley gate… and a thousand cubits on the wall unto the dung gate." According to its name, the gate was in the valley; the verse gives the distance between the Valley Gate and the Dung Gate as 1,000 cubits, i.e., about 500 m. *II Chronicles* XXVI, 9 gives the following information: "Moreover Uziah built towers in Jerusalem at the Corner Gate and at the Valley Gate, and at the Turning, and fortified them." It may thus be assumed that the Valley Gate was between the Dung Gate in the south and the Corner Gate north of the valley, and was well fortified. The high-lying location of the Valley Gate is also implied in *Nehemiah* II, 15: "Then went I up in the night in the valley, and viewed the wall, and turned back, and entered by the valley gate, and so returned." On the basis of these sources, and other data, Crowfoot and Fitzgerald conducted excavations at the Lower City in 1927–1928, west of the *Water Gate* near the Valley. They revealed a Jebusite wall, which had remained in use, with a gate flanked by windowless towers eight meters thick. The Valley Gate was also used by the inhabitants of the Upper City during the Return to Zion and the Hasmonean periods. The city expanded westward at these times, and the western wall of the Lower City became included within the city.

The Corner Gate

This is mentioned in *II Kings* XIV, 13: "And Jehoash… came to Jerusalem, and broke down the wall of Jerusalem from the Gate of Ephraim unto the Corner Gate, four hundred cubits," and again in *II Chronicles* XXV, 23. Since the Gate of Ephraim was north of the Temple Mount, the Corner Gate must have been about 200 m away. The gate is also mentioned in *Zechariah* XIV, 10: "…unto the Corner gate, and from the tower of Hananel," and in *Jeremiah* XXXI, 38. The kings of Judah paid special attention to the fortification of these gates, since the Temple Mount was naturally vulnerable in the north; King Uzziah fortified the gates and built towers (*II Chronicles* XXVI, 9). The Corner Gate was thus at the south-western corner of the Temple Mount, opposite the Horse Gate, near the *Mishneh* and the *Makhtesh*. The *Mishneh*, which was a residential and commercial quarter, is mentioned in *Zephaniah* I, 10. "…a cry from the Fish Gate, and a wailing from the Secondary Quarter (*Mishneh*)." *II Kings* XXII, 14, describes how Huldah the prophetess "dwelt in Jerusalem in the Secondary Quarter (*Mishneh*)" as does *II Chronicles* XXXII, 22. *Zephaniah* I, 11, also describes the *Makhtesh* as an inhabited area: "Wail, ye inhabitants of *Makhtesh*."

The Fish (Ephraim) Gate

This gate is referred to in *Nehemiah* III, 3: "But the Fish Gate did the sons of Hassenaah build; they laid the beams thereof, and set up the doors thereof, the bolts thereof and the bars thereof," and also in *II Chronicles* XXXIII, 14: "Now after this he built an outer wall to the city of David, on the west side of Gihon, in the valley, even to the entrance at the Fish Gate, and compassed about Ophel, and raised it up a very great height." The Gate of Ephraim is mentioned in *II Kings*, XIV, 13. "And Jehoash…came to Jerusalem and brake down the wall of Jerusalem from the gate of Ephraim unto the Corner Gate, four hundred cubits," in *Nehemiah* VII, 16: "…and in the broad place of the Water Gate and in the broad place of the Gate of Ephraim," and further in *Nehemiah*, VII, 39 "And above the Gate of Ephraim, and by the Gate of the (*yeshana*, or possibly *Mishneh* – secondary) Old City and by the Fish Gate, and the tower of Hananel, and the tower of Hammeah, even unto the Sheep gate, and they stood still in the gate of the Guard." It is thus reasonable to assume that the Fish Gate, the Gate of Ephraim and possibly the Old Gate (*Nehemiah* III, 6) were identical, and located near the *Mishneh*, up the valley course, where the goldsmiths and apothecaries worked (*Nehemiah* III, 8); and again it is clear that this was a vulnerable point in the north of the city. During the monarchy there were thus two towers flanking the gate: the Tower of the Hundred (*haMeah*) east of the gate, and the Tower of Hananel west of it (*Nehemiah* III, 1; XII, 39; *Jeremiah* XXXI, 38; *Zechariah* XIV, 10).

Sheep Gate, or Gate of Benjamin

This gate is mentioned in *Nehemiah* III, 1: "And they built the sheep gate; they sanctified it, unto the tower of Hananel." There is a further reference in *Nehemiah* XII, 39. The name "Sheep Gate" implies its location north-east of the Temple Mount, near the Bezetha Valley, where there was a rainwater pool used for washing the sheep before sacrifice. This pool was known to Christian sources during the Second Temple period as the Pool of Bethesda; it is visible in the courtyard of the Church of St. Anne, near the Lions' Gate. The "Gate of Benjamin" is referred to in *Jeremiah* XXXVII, 12–13: "Then Jeremiah went forth out of Jerusalem to go into the land of Benjamin…. and when he was in the gate of Benjamin…", in XXXVIII, 7: "The king then sitting in the gate of Benjamin," and in *Zechariah* XIV, 10: "….from Benjamin's Gate unto the place of the first gate, unto the Corner Gate." Since the territory of Benjamin was north of Jerusalem, the gate must have been in the northern wall of the Temple

Mount. The length of this wall, probably 320 m, makes it reasonable to assume that the Sheep Gate and the Gate of Benjamin are identical, since it was not likely that such a short wall would have more than one gate, and the distance between gates of the Temple Mount wall was usually at least 200 m.

CHAPTER V

JERUSALEM IN THE SECOND TEMPLE PERIOD AND LATER

According to Josephus, the population of Jerusalem during the Second Temple period (in the reign of Herod Agrippa) reached 120,000 (*Against Apion* I, 22). The size and fortifications of such a populous city are worthy of special study.

Second Temple Jerusalem was divided into three main parts: the Lower City, on the eastern, relatively small hill, the site of the former Jebusite city, with a maximum height (on the Temple Mount) of 743 m ASL; the Upper City on the western hill, with a height of 777 m ASL, over which the city expanded during the latter period of the Israelite monarchy, and in the days of the Hasmoneans. Both the City of David and the Western hill enjoyed the natural fortification of deep valleys, which limited their area to a total of 650 dunams. The third part, on the other hand, known as Beth-zeta in Hebrew meaning olives orchard, or the new city, had no natural defenses of this type, and its expansion was thus not limited. It grew northward, and became the largest section of the city, with an area of 1150 dunams. Its greatest height, in the northwestern part of the city, at the Psephinos Tower (probably on the site of the present-day Russian Compound) was 800 m. The Kidron valley, which begins at that point, is very shallow and broad there. The total area of the city, at the peak of its northward expansion (at the end of the Second Temple period), was 1,800 dunams; it was surrounded by a wall with an average height of 10 m and a width of 4–5 m. This was the largest walled city in the country, and one of the greatest in the Middle East.

The City Wall During the Reign of Agrippa

At the end of the Second Temple period the city was surrounded by three walls on the north, all starting at the Hippicus Tower (the Citadel of today), near the present-day Jaffa Gate. All three walls began at this point, since north of the line from the Hippicus Tower to the Temple Mount there were no deep valleys to defend the city; the Ben-Hinnom, Tyropoeon and Kidron Valleys deepened south of the line, defending the city. The third wall was built during the reign of Agrippa I (41–44 C.E.), and was not completed for fear of the Roman Emperor who suspected rebellion (*Wars of the Jews* II, 11; *Antiquities of the Jews* XIX, 7). The Zealots completed the wall during the revolt, in 66 C.E. (*Wars* V, 4).

The third wall began at the Hippicus Tower and stretched northeast, along the line of the present-day wall, as far as the Psephinos Tower. Remnants of the third wall have been disclosed at two main points: in 1912, at the northwestern corner of the present city wall, near the New Gate, L.H. Vincent discovered a fort, known as *Kal'at Jalud* (Fort of Goliath), which was of considerable importance during the Crusader–Moslem fighting in Jerusalem. Stones of the third wall were found at its base. Archaeologists believe that the Tower of Psephinos, mentioned by Josephus (*Wars* V, 4) as being at the northwestern corner of the city, was at the site of the present-day Russian Compound. This wall passed along the water-divide of two drainage basins, beginning at the Russian Compound: the basin of the Ben-Hinnom stream, southwestward, and the basin of the Tyropoeon Valley ("the Valley") to the southeast. The wall then descended eastward steeply along the line of HaNevi'im Street, and turned east to the Kidron Valley, south of the Tomb of the Kings. Remnants of the wall, 200 m long and 4.5 m thick, were found at the foundations of the Italian Hospital (conspicuous on the skyline for its square tower), at the foot of HaNevi'im Street near Shivtei Yisrael Street in the direction of the "Mandelbaum Gate."

These remains were excavated by E.L. Sukenik and A.L. Mayer in 1924–25, (see the report published by the Hebrew University in 1931) and in 1940. The remnants of the wall are also visible on Nablus Street at the corner of St. George Street, some 450 m north of Damascus Gate. A section of the wall is fenced, and a further section to the east is open. Other archaeologists discovered a further total of 300 m of the third wall. Part of the foundations of the wall consists of a mixture of small stones and mortar, with fieldstones. These are topped by large ashlars, of an average size of 1.20 × 1.00 × 200 m, dressed in the Herodian manner, the largest being 1.15 × 500 m. The few towers revealed along the third wall project about 8 m, and are 12 m wide. Since there was no natural barrier, such as a deep valley, north of this wall, the city was vulnerable at this point during the Second Temple period, and this was indeed the point of attack. The *Tosefta* explains that the upper part of Jerusalem was not sanctified, because of its tactical weakness.

Building stones of the Third Wall

Walls of Jerusalem in Successive Periods

Jerusalem, the capital city of the land, saw many battles, and was taken by many conquerors. Different walls were built during ten major periods. The walls were located at different sites, depending on the rate of the city's expansion, development or decline.

1. ***Jebusite wall.*** This was the earliest wall, surrounding the lower part of the eastern hill. The area of Jerusalem was at its minimum during this period. Remnants of the wall and its towers were discovered in the eastern part of the city, west of the Gihon spring, west of the Lower City near the Valley Gate, and south of the Lower City. This wall was built of fieldstones, roughly dressed, and was quite thick.

2. ***Israelite wall.*** This was discovered in the east of the city, west of the Gihon spring, above it; south of the Lower City, near the Pool of Siloam; west of the Lower City near the Valley Gate; south of the Temple Mount wall; south of Mount Zion and at the Phasael Tower (the Tower of David). The wall was built of small ashlar blocks.

3. ***Post-exilic wall of the Return to Zion.*** This was discovered along the eastern ascent of the Lower City, at the upper part of the Gihon spring, and above the Jebusite and Israelite walls. The area of the city was smaller, as noted in *Nehemiah*. The stonework was erected carelessly and was of poor quality.

4. ***Hasmonean wall (the First Wall).*** This was revealed by two towers of poor masonry on either side of Nehemiah's wall in the Lower City. However, along the ascent to the Mount Zion, at the foundations of Bishop Gobat's School and in its courtyard, the workmanship improves; the stones used are larger than in earlier periods and are medium, well-dressed ashlar blocks, with narrow margins and very prominent, roughly smoothed bosses.

5. ***Herodian wall.*** This is visible around the Temple Mount platform, especially on its eastern, southern and western sides; at the lower courses of the Phasael Tower; and on by the western tower of the Damascus Gate. The present-day wall, between the Jaffa and Damascus Gates, projects north of Herod's wall, while the southern wall of Herod's city was almost impossible to discover, due to the massive destruction by Titus' army. The magnificently worked blocks of this period are enormous, over 10 m long. The blocks were beautifully dressed, by means of a comb-shaped tool. Herodian ashlars have a double margin: the outer margin is broad, and the inner one narrow, surrounding a slightly projecting flat center, finely tooled. (The stones of the building over the Cave of Machpelah, at Hebron, are from Herodian times.)

6. ***Wall of Hadrian and his successors, dating from Aelia Capitolina.*** The city bore the full name of the Emperor, Aelius Hadrianus, and as commemorated the three Capitoline gods of the Romans. The wall encompassed a smaller area at this time, and followed roughly the same line as the existing wall. The stones used were rather large, usually dressed smoothly and flatly, without bosses or margins. The blocks were generally laid over Herodian stones, after the destruction of the previous wall by Titus; part of the upper courses of the Roman wall was taken from

the Herodian wall. Stones of this period are visible at the western wall, as well as at the southern and eastern walls of the Temple Mount, at the small gate to the left of the Damascus Gate and at its foundation, and in the arch of the Ecce Homo Basilica, and in the Russian church near the Holy Sepulchre.

7. **Byzantine wall.** This stretched further south than Hadrian's wall, and took in considerable areas of the southern part of the Lower City and south of Mount Zion. The blocks are small and plainly worked. Remnants of this wall are visible at the Golden Gate, in the eastern wall of the Temple Mount, which is magnificently executed; at a low wall at the southeastern corner of the Temple Mount and its continuation; at the Ophel wall, known as Eudocia's wall, built in 443 C.E.; south of the Lower City near the Pool of Siloam; and at the new Latin cemetery on Mount Zion.

8. **Crusader wall.** Remnants of this have been found above the Hadrianic wall. Since Crusader days city walls have been erected roughly along the line of the boundaries of Aelia Capitolina. Remnants of this wall have been uncovered at the Citadel (David's Tower); at the southern wall of the Temple Mount southwest of the El Aqsa mosque, and single stones have been found in the Turkish wall and at its gates. The blocks are dressed ashlars, with prominent bosses and margins, resembling the Hasmonean stones, although smaller. The Crusaders dug moats wherever the area adjoining the wall was horizontal. Remnants of moats are visible, to the west, and in particular, to the south of the Citadel.

9. **Turkish wall.** This dates to the time of Suleiman the Magnificent and his successors. The wall surrounds today's Old City, with its total area of 940 dunams. It follows more or less the line and remains of the walls since Aelia Capitolina, and consists of a mixture of stones from all the preceding periods. Its characteristic style is noticeable at the different gates of the city, with their low pointed arches bearing Arabic inscriptions dating to the period of Suleiman, flanked by discs with flower carvings, and with turrets pierced by firing slits on top of the walls.

The walls were at their most magnificent during the period of Herod the Great and his successors; they were at their longest at that time, enclosing a total area of 1,800 dunams. They decreased in length from the time of Hadrian till the Turkish period, to the present area of the city (940 dunams). After the destruction of the Second Temple, the extent of the walls contracted towards the center, except during the Byzantine period. The walls were completely destroyed by Titus and rebuilt by Hadrian, when they roughly followed the line of the second wall; in the north the wall projected slightly, while in the south the wall was very close to the wall of the Temple Mount. The Roman city did not include the quarter of the Bezetha (the *new city*) or the southern slopes of the Lower and Upper Cities. The eastern and western walls of the city of the Second Temple period were largely left intact after the Destruction, being protected by the deep valleys of Kidron and Ben-Hinnom.

The Roman city of Hadrian and his successors had the typical two main streets intersecting at right angles; these are clearly depicted in the sixth-century Medeba map. These streets began at the chief gates of the city, running from the Damascus Gate to the Zion Gate, and from the Jaffa Gate to the Temple Mount and the Lions' Gate. The city was thus divided roughly into four quarters, a configuration which, with some minor alterations, remains to this day.

CHAPTER VI

THE GATES AND WALLS OF JERUSALEM IN OUR TIME

The Walls

After the destruction of the Second Temple the walls of the city were razed to their foundations. Since then the walls of the Old City have followed roughly the same line, with certain changes, from the time of Hadrian up to the Turkish period. They were repeatedly destroyed and rebuilt, receiving their present form in the reigns of Suleiman the Magnificent, as no battles were fought for Jerusalem during the 400 years of Ottoman rule. The present-day walls are thus a mixture of styles from Herodian times to the present.

Some believe, without any proof, that the Ottoman Sultan's wall was designed by the architect Sinan in the Istanbul court during the years 1535–1540. It was built and later renovated with Egyptian tax money collected by the Sultan's Jewish minister of finance, Rabbi Abraham Castro.

This Ottoman reconstruction was based on the fear of invasions by Christians from Europe, who, at that time, financed the Crusader campaigns to Israel. It was the first time in their entire history that Muslims built the walls of Jerusalem.

The wall today is roughly square, bearing turrets, and with a total length of four km. The northern wall is the longest, and the eastern one the shortest. Thirty-four projecting square towers were built into the wall. The area within the walls is 940 dunams, 140 of these being within the Temple Mount enclosure. This was also the area of the Herodian enclosure. The square shape

Northern and eastern Jerusalem walls and the Temple Mount. Below at right: Rockefeller Museum

and intersecting streets leading to the main gates of the city made the division into quarters on the basis of communities quite natural.

Length of the southern wall, from the south-east corner of the Temple Mount to the Dung Gate	425 m
From the Dung Gate to the Zion Gate	510 m
From the Zion Gate to the south-west corner near Mount Zion	165 m
Total length of the southern wall	**1,100 m**
Length of the western wall, from the south-west corner to the Jaffa Gate	450 m
From the Jaffa Gate to the north-west corner, near Tancred's Tower	425 m
Total length of the western wall	**875 m**
Length of the northern wall from the north-west corner to the Damascus Gate	566 m
From the Damascus Gate to Herod's Gate	415 m
From Herod's Gate to the north-east corner near the Stork Tower	300 m
Total length of the northern wall	**1,281 m**
Length of the eastern wall, from the Stork Tower to the south-east corner	762 m
The total length of the present-day walls of Jerusalem is therefore	**4,018 m**

The walls encompass an area of roughly 1 sq km. The average height is 10–12 m; in some parts it drops to 3 m and at other points exceeds 20 m. In most places the wall is 4 to 5 m thick. From the Crusader period onwards the northern and western walls, particularly at the corners, were defended by a moat, 5 m deep and 10 m wide. This moat is now filled in.

Since the Six Day War, the State of Israel has been developing archaeological gardens along the walls and a promenade between the Jaffa and the Lion Gates.

The Gates

There are eight gates in the wall of the Old City. Seven are open and in use, but one, the Golden Gate, which is the most beautiful, is blocked up. The western wall has one gate only, the Jaffa Gate. The northern wall has three gates: the New Gate in the west, the Damascus Gate in the center and Herod's Gate in the east. The eastern wall has two gates: the Lions' Gate in the north and the Golden Gate in the south. The southern wall also has two gates: the Dung Gate in the east and the Zion Gate in the west.

There were several reasons for locating the gates at the lowest-lying points of the wall: to facilitate incoming and outgoing traffic, since the gates were the terminals for highways leading out of town; for proximity to the pools, excavated in low-lying areas for the collection of rainwater; and because conduits and drains were built below the thresholds of the gates.

The pools at the city gates were favorite meeting-places for the inhabitants, as well as important trading points for merchants coming in to water their riding and pack animals. They were also laundering places.

From the Second Temple period Jerusalem has had four main gates, one in each direction: the Jaffa Gate, the Damascus Gate, the Lions' Gate and the Zion Gate. They were the starting points for highways leading to the main cities of each province: the road from the Jaffa Gate led to the port of Jaffa in the west; the road from the Damascus Gate led to Nablus (Shechem) in the north, and continued to Galilee and Damascus; the road from the Lions' Gate ran down to Jericho and continued across the Jordan to Rabbath Ammon in the east, and the road from the Zion Gate led to Hebron in the south and continued to Beersheba. The other gates were of secondary importance, and one of their main purposes was to connect the quarters within the wall with the suburbs outside it, as well as with the service areas such as water sources, arable land and pasture, quarries and cemeteries.

The Old City is divided into four quarters by the two main streets, which link the gates on opposite sides of the city, and cross the city, one lengthwise and the other breadthwise. Each of the four main gates thus marks the boundary of one of the quarters at the city wall. The Jewish quarter of today is in the southern part of the city, near the Temple Mount and the Western Wall, between the Dung Gate and the Zion Gate. Jews were settled here after the Crusader period, probably even later than the rule of Saladin, leaving their former quarter north of the Temple Mount. The quarter began to be settled intensively from the fourteenth century onwards. Large housing projects (*Battei Mahaseh*) were established in the quarter by the Dutch-German community in 1868. The quarter had many synagogues, which were destroyed by the Arabs after the 1948 War of Independence; the quarter then became inhabited by Arabs. Since 1967 the Jewish quarter and the synagogues have been rebuilt. The Armenian quarter lies between the Jewish and Christian quarters from the vicinity of the Zion Gate to the Jaffa Gate. Armenians have been immigrating to Jerusalem since the fifth century C.E. (It is worth noting that Jews and Armenians inhabited adjoining neighborhoods in several ancient cities of the Middle East, both communities being minorities.) The most prominent structure in the quarter is the Church of St. James, with its silver-covered dome. The Christian quarter is in the north-western part of the city, between the Jaffa Gate and the Damascus Gate. Christians have been living in this quarter since the eleventh century C.E., as it adjoins the site identified as the last Station of Jesus before the Crucifixion. Christians of many sects live in the area, which includes many churches and institutions, such as the Greek and Latin Patriarchates. Many bell towers and church domes punctuate the skyline of this quarter. The Moslem quarter is in the central and north-eastern sections of the city, stretching from the Damascus Gate to the Lions' Gate, adjoining the Dome of the Rock. Moslems from neighboring countries settled in the city from the seventh century onwards, and the quarter abounds with the minarets and domes of many mosques.

The Citadel ("David's Tower")

When Herod the Great fortified Jerusalem, surrounding its northern side with a wall, he built his palace in the highest and best-fortified position, 777 m above sea level. The palace extended over an area of 300 m × 300 m, probably covering the positions of the present-day police barracks, the Anglican Church, and the Armenian monastery south of Citadel and the Armenian Garden. The earliest remains in the pool date from the Byzantine period. The aqueduct from the south served only for the Temple's use. Only in the second century C.E. did the Romans build the shorter aqueduct into "Hezekiah's Pool."

Citadel of Jerusalem ("Tower of David")

The northern flank of the palace – the most vulnerable point in the city's defenses – was guarded by three towers. This was also the one point where the different walls of the city met. The towers were named after Hippicus (Herod's close friend), Phasael (Herod's brother) and Mariamne (Herod's Hasmonean wife), and guarded the palace and city. When Titus conquered Jerusalem he ordered the destruction of all the buildings in the city except the towers, which were used as barracks by the Roman garrison, and were kept to glorify the prowess of the conqueror. Josephus Flavius recounts, in his *Wars of the Jews* VII, 1: "Caesar ordered the whole of the city and the sanctuary to be razed to the foundations, leaving the three loftiest towers, Phasaelus, Hippicus and Mariamne, and that portion of the wall which enclosed the town on the west: the latter as an encampment for those who should remain there in garrison, the towers to indicate to future times how splendid and how strong a city had yielded to Roman valor. All the rest of the wall that encompassed the city was so completely leveled with the ground that there was no longer anything to lead those who visited the spot to believe that it had ever been inhabited."

The Citadel eventually fell into partial ruin, and was repeatedly destroyed and rebuilt in the Roman, Moslem, Crusader, Mameluke and Turkish periods. The tower of Hippicus then acquired the popular name of "David's Tower" and the fortress the "Citadel of Jerusalem," for the tower was the only one that survived to our days within Jerusalem's walls.

Herod had two other pools in use in the vicinity of the towers: the Pool of Amygdalon, still in existence north-east of the Jaffa Gate, and the Mamillah Pool, further west. The deep pool in the north-east was used for defense, as well as for supplying stone for building work; the water of the Mamillah Pool flowed into the Pool of Amygdalon and was used by the inhabitants of the city and the palace only in the Roman period and onwards.

History of the Citadel

The great tower to the right of the entrance gate is the sole relic of the towers built by Herod; archaeologists identify it with the Hippicus Tower, which reached a height of 45 m, as described by Josephus (*Wars* v, 4): "Its entire altitude was about ninety cubits; in appearance it resembled the tower of Pharos which serves as a lighthouse to those sailing to Alexandria, though it was much greater in circumference." The area of the tower is 22.60 m × 18.30 m. The eight lowest courses slope outward, forming a glacis from the thirteenth century C.E. to strengthen the foundations of the wall. Eight further courses are vertical. The Herodian blocks of the lower courses were chiseled with a fine tool and have double margins: the outer margin is wide, and the inner one narrow, with a prominent center. The upper courses are a later addition, probably Mameluke and Turkish.

During the reign of Herod, the highest point in the city of Jerusalem was the top of the Hippicus Tower, 827 meters above sea level. One can assume that from here there was signaling contact – southward, to Herodium and the Judean desert; eastward, to Machaerus and to Mount Nebo in the Moab hills; and northward, to Mizpah in Nabi Samuel and to the Benjamin and Ephraim regions.

The average size of the Hippicus Tower stones is 1.25 × 2.50 m and the height of each stone one meter. In the past, three of these fortress towers defended Herod's palace as well as the First and Second Temple walls which met close to the towers. Southwest of the Jerusalem citadel, under the Turkish wall, a wall from the Hasmonean period was discovered. They were not

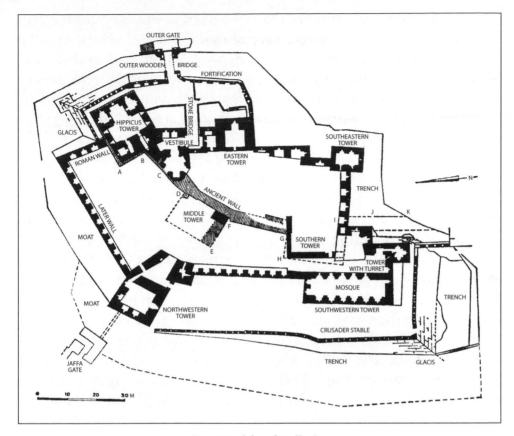

Zion Citadel and Jaffa Gate

from the time of the Moslem period when the tower was erroneously known as David's Tower, so named since the fifth century C.E.

From the Moslem period until the Crusader period and beyond, the tower was erroneously identified as "David's Tower." However, in the foundation of the Herodian tower, in the Hasmonean courtyard, and in archaeological excavations, no remains were found from the time of King David, only shards and pottery from the later Judean kings of the First Temple. The mistaken identification of "Mount Zion" with "David's Tower" is probably due to Josephus who dated the wall to the time of David and Solomon.

The archeologist C.N. Johns excavated at the site of the Citadel from 1934 to 1939, for the Mandate Department of Antiquities. He published his conclusions in an article, "Excavations at the Citadel," *Jerusalem, Palestine Exploration Quarterly*, April 1940, and more in QDAP in 1950.

The entrance gate is Turkish. The wooden bridge which existed there till the British conquest of 1917 replaced an earlier drawbridge, and led over to the outer defenses. The stone bridge is a British construction. The way then leads through a hall consisting of two right-angled turns; this was the main gateway of the Citadel. It was built probably in the fourteenth century C.E. (Mameluke period), and originally had both internal and external doors. Adjoining it is a lobby, from which stairs built by the British lead up the Hippicus Tower.

The Herodian wall of the city began at the Hippicus Tower and continued in a straight line for 18 m south-westward, to the central tower (B, C and D in plan). The wall was five meters wide and consisted of medium-sized ashlar blocks, with margins and rough-hewn, projecting bosses, and between them a filling of fieldstones. The masonry is Hasmonean, as confirmed by the latest excavations of R. Amiran and A. Eitan in the winter of 1969. Three stages of development can be traced in the Hasmonean stone-work: in the earliest, medium-sized ashlar blocks, smooth faced, are used; in the second, dating to the reigns of Hyrcanus and Jannaeus, there are larger stones, with very prominent centers and wide margins, the courses consisting of headers and stretchers respectively; the last stage dates to Herod's time and uses blocks with flatter centers and wide, double margins, and courses again consisting of headers and stretchers, respectively. During the excavations Hasmonean and Herodian coins were found. The south-western continuation of the wall was of inferior quality (D–F on plan). It served as the internal part of a tower, 18 m wide and projecting 10 m from the wall (the central tower on the plan). The line of the wall (G, H) is covered by later masonry. A third tower, projecting in similar manner to the second, was discovered (along the line H–I–J); a ditch in the courtyard contains courses of the ancient wall overlaid by a later wall, which apparently followed the pattern of the earlier tower. East of the Ottoman minaret, along the line K–L on the plan, the ancient wall seems to have continued towards the palace of Herod.

According to Johns, the beginning of the wall was Hasmonean, of the second and first centuries B.C.E.; part of it was removed to build a new tower, and was renewed under Herod. After the destruction of the Second Temple, the Romans left the towers, with the defending wall, as quarters for the garrison troops. Johns found clay water pipes, bearing the emblem of the Tenth Legion. These pipes were used to convey water along the high-level aqueduct from the Etzion bloc and Solomon's Pools. The city wall was continued to the north, to encompass the Roman city of Aelia Capitolina. Several Roman courses are preserved in this northern extension of the wall.

In the courtyard of the southern tower Johns discovered remnants of a wall and a round tower, which he attributed to the eighth century C.E. He therefore assumes that the Moslem Caliph al-Walid (705–715) utilized the ruins of Herod's palace for their center of government. The Citadel, destroyed and rebuilt repeatedly, served as a barracks for occupying powers up to Turkish times. It was also used by foreign governors of the city: Roman, Byzantine, Arab, Seljuk, Crusader, Kurdish Ayyubid, Mameluke Turk and Jordanian.

The twelfth century Crusader kings of Jerusalem used the building as a citadel, enlarging its limits and building new walls around it, for it was well placed strategically, as well as being near the Holy Sepulcher. The Crusaders divided the Citadel in two parts: an internal section, including the eastern towers, within the Old City wall, and an external one, with the western towers, outside the old wall. The fortress was destroyed in 1219 by one of Saladin's successors, to prevent the Crusaders from getting a hold there again, and was partially rebuilt by the Mamelukes in the early fourteenth century. The wall, which separated the two parts of the Crusader citadel, was torn down, and new buildings were erected over it. The basic form of the Citadel has remained unchanged since then, apart from the addition of structures by Ottoman rulers in the sixteenth and seventeenth centuries.

Stone balconies project from the north-west tower, opposite the Jaffa Gate, and from the south-west minaret; these were intended for the defense of the unfortified area at the foot of the wall. Stones were hurled down at attackers from these balconies. The wall balustrade and the window-frames were holed to enable the insertion of wooden beams supporting galleries for the defenders. These were constructed after the Crusader period. The minaret is Ottoman, in the Turkish style of round minarets.

The Crusader structures, possibly stables, were to the west of the south-west tower, near the Western Wall. In a sloping part of this wall one can see the upper part of a Crusader Gate, which opened outward. The Citadel was defended south of the western wall by a deep moat, which continued to the north-west tower, separating it from the present-day Jaffa Gate. The moat was filled up in honor of the visit of the German Kaiser in 1898, to facilitate the entry to Jerusalem of the royal entourage. The wall was opened up further north, and an entrance 12 m wide prepared and paved; this still serves as the western entrance to the Old City.

In 1927 the moat was filled in along the western side to provide a site for a taxi stand and gas station. A Turkish guard was stationed in the Citadel up to 1917, to watch over the safety of the city; every half-hour, to denote their diligence, the guard would sound their trumpets in the direction of the governor's residence, and the trumpeted answer would be heard.

Under the British Mandate the Citadel was repaired and renovated, and served as a museum for Jerusalem antiquities and Middle East folklore. After the reunification of the city, the museum was used for displays showing the development of the city over the ages.

Excavations at the Citadel

Excavations have been carried out since 1969 under the guidance of R. Amiran and A. Eitan. A Hebrew seal was found from the period of the monarchy, with the name "Matanyahu ben (= son of) 'Azaryahu." At the lowest strata of the excavation five floors were uncovered, containing sherds and broken figurines from the seventh century B.C.E. If these are indeed dwellings; this is further evidence of the expansion of the Israelite city during the monarchy. It is worth noting that during the excavations of Johns in the Citadel courtyard, as well as in the work of K. Kenyon, and, later, of D. Bahat and M. Broshi, in the courtyard of the Armenian Garden, some remnants of the Israelite period were found, and the city probably did in fact reach this area.

Pottery handles were found, with the stamp *yhd* (indicating the province of Judea) as well as a five-pointed star and the letters *yrshlm* (= Jerusalem). The city wall, a tower, and a dwelling of the Hasmonean period were found in the courtyard. Coins dating from the time of Herod and of the Procurators up to 58 C.E. were also found. At this time there were apparently a barracks, storehouses, servants' residences and workshops on the site.

In the fortress of "David's Citadel" and its surroundings, remnants of the wall from the First and Second Temple period were discovered by the K. Kenyon team (1962–1967), by D. Bahat and M. Broshi (1973–1978), and H. Geva in 1979–1980. M. Broshi uncovered the remnants of the Western Wall, 200 m long, under the Turkish wall. The width of the wall is 5 m, and within it were discovered four towers.

From the excavations carried out in the Citadel fortress and its surroundings since the Six Day War, it became apparent that here were discovered remnants of the wall from the First Temple period, the Hasmonean period and the Herodian period.

The Crusaders' Campaigns for Jerusalem

There is detailed scientific material available concerning the walls in the Crusader period, which we do not have for earlier or later periods. The following section is based on Professor J. Prawer's research (*Toledot Mamlekhet Ha-tzalbanim be-Eretz Yisrael*, Jerusalem 1963) with certain additions.

The first Crusaders' Campaign was in 1099. Their armies moved eastward from the coast through Rishpon and Ramleh, and covered the distance from Emmaus to Nebi Samwil in one night. At dawn the towers of Jerusalem were visible, drawing them onward. Moslem government in the region was divided at the time; the Egyptian Fatimids ruled the southern part of the country, while Syrians ruled the north. The Fatimids of Jerusalem trusted to the massive fortifications of the city, among the strongest known to the Crusaders. All Christians residing in Jerusalem were banished in preparation for the battle; the Moslem and Jewish inhabitants were given arms, and the cisterns outside the city were poisoned. It was the dream of the Crusaders to take Jerusalem because of its sanctity, but they also needed it for its strategic location as a fortified city in the center of the country. The battle for Jerusalem was therefore joined soon after their landing.

The Citadel, dubbed by them "Tower of David," was a fort within a fort, where the Fatimid commander of the city resided. The city wall was 12 m high, and the Fatimids had sufficient stores of food and water. The Crusaders, with an army of about 15,000 hungry, thirsty, soldiers were faced with the difficulty of fighting in coats of mail in the heavy summer heat. They therefore concentrated their fighting force in limited areas near the northern and north-west sections of the wall, where the lie of the land was suitable for the use of ramming towers and catapults. The movable towers, ladders and bridges were constructed of wood brought from the vicinity of Nablus, for the hills around Jerusalem had never recovered from the depredations of the Roman conquerors.

The Crusaders filled in the moats and attacked the city at four points along the northern wall and at one stronghold in the south (see map). The wall was first breached near Herod's Gate, from a base camp near the present-day Rockefeller Museum. Later breaches were made near the Zion Gate from the camp on Mount Zion, and near the New Gate, in the area of "Tancred's

Tower," from the camp near the present-day Russian Compound. The victorious Crusaders massacred the inhabitants indiscriminately, Jews and Moslems, men, women and children alike, and even burned down a synagogue with the Jews praying inside. The inhabitants also fled to the Temple Mount, where they were finally caught and killed. The Egyptian commander surrendered at the Citadel and was allowed to leave with his men, being amongst the few survivors of the battle.

The Crusaders founded in Jerusalem military orders: the Hospitallers, who looked after sick pilgrims and whose hostel was near the Church of the Holy Sepulcher; the Templars, who assured the safe passage of pilgrims from the coast to the city and the Jordan Valley and were concentrated at the El-Aqsa mosque, which they turned into their center; and the Knights to King Cane of the Lepers, who were located north of Tancred's Tower, near the present New Gate.

Saladin the Ayyubid attacked Jerusalem in 1177, but were defeated en route, at Gezer. After his victory at the Horns of Hattin and the conquest of the rest of the country, Saladin again attacked Jerusalem, in 1187, having proclaimed a holy war to free the land of the infidel. This was the final stage of his victorious campaign, since Jerusalem was of negligible strategic value at this period. The mountain road was of secondary importance, since the Crusaders had their bases along the coast of Syria, while the Moslem centers were in Cairo, Baghdad and Damascus. Saladin's first efforts were directed against the Citadel. After the failure of this attempt he adopted the Crusaders' tactics, attacking the northern wall along its entire length, from the Stork Tower in the east to Tancred's Tower in the west. However, unlike the Crusaders, who built towers with which to batter at the walls, Saladin tunneled underneath the walls at the Damascus Gate and Tancred's Tower to bring them down. From the vantage point of the Mount of Olives his armies were able to aim arrows and catapults at the densely inhabited area within the city. The Crusaders eventually surrendered, as a result of loss of morale, before the walls were actually breached. The Moslems did not massacre the Christians, but banished the Franks after payment of ransom; the local Christians were allowed to stay. Moslems and Jews returned to the city. Mosques, which the Crusaders had turned into churches, resumed their former status, and in fact most of the Crusaders' churches also became mosques; the frescoes were plastered and the mosaic inscriptions destroyed. The historian Mujir e-Din (1496) recounts the rebuilding of the wall by Saladin, from the Jaffa Gate to the Damascus

Gate, and the renewal of the moat around it. Crusaders' attempts to reestablish their rule in Jerusalem from the end of the twelfth century were unsuccessful; each attempt was answered by a massacre of Christians. A considerable part of the city walls was destroyed in the course of these abortive campaigns by the Moslem ruler Al-Mu'atham 'Issa in 1219, to prevent the Crusaders from getting a foothold again. The Crusaders tried to make the Moslems repair the walls in 1221; their refusal caused renewed fighting. In 1229 a treaty was signed between the Egyptian Moslems and the Crusader Frederick II, against the Moslems of Transjordan and Damascus. This treaty ensured co-existence of the two religions in the Holy City – Moslems on the Temple Mount and Christians in the city and the Church of the Holy Sepulcher. The treaty was broken when the Christians began to fortify the city, and was renewed later, until a further massacre of Christians finally drove the Crusaders from the country, during the Khwarizmian conquest of 1244.

The wall was partially repaired during the reign of King El-'Adel Zein e-Din in 1295, and again under the rule of El-Melek el-Mansur Qalaoun in 1330. Suleiman the Magnificent carried out massive reconstruction work from 1536 to 1540, and added several towers. Inscriptions of the period placed in the gate structures are evidence of the work done.

The Jaffa Gate

The gates of the Old City were mentioned by several travelers, in particular by the three Moslem historians, Al-Muqaddasi, writing in the year 985, Idrisi in 1154, and Mujir e-Din in 1496, from whom we learn their names, descriptions and numbers. The gates underwent certain changes between the times of these three writers, due to the attacks by the Crusaders, by Saladin and by the Mamelukes. A few gates were left at their traditional Second Temple sites, but most were destroyed and rebuilt elsewhere. Certain gates were blocked up, while new ones were opened.

The Jaffa Gate, the only one on the west (in a wall 875 m long), is not on the site of the Second Temple western gate. The ancient gate, which Josephus mentions as being "scarcely discernible" (*Wars* v, 6) was close to the Pool of Amygdalon and the Hippicus Tower, some 100 m east of the present gate. The pool was intended, among other things, to protect the gate from the battering rams of the enemy, and thus to prevent him from laying siege to the gate. A similar method was used at the fortress of Horkania in the Judean Desert, where pools were excavated west of the fortress as a shield for the only gate.

Jaffa Gate and the Citadel of Jerusalem

Horse-drawn carriages travel from Jerusalem to Jaffa and back. End of 19th century.

The Zealots of Jerusalem used the western gate to destroy the Roman arms at the beginning of the Revolt (*Wars* II, 6).

The gate is situated at a low point in the wall, at a height of 770 m, between the Upper City ("Mount Zion") at 780 m, and Tancred's Tower, near the New Gate, at 790 m. The position was chosen to facilitate movement in and out of the city. The aqueduct mentioned above must have passed underneath the concealed gate and conveyed the water of the Mamillah Pool, far to the west, into the Pool of Amygdalon (*Wars* V, 7), known today in Arabic as Hammam el-Batrak. During the Roman period, and later, in the Middle Ages, when the wall was moved westwards to its present position, the Jaffa Gate was built. It took its present form during the rule of the Turk Suleiman the Magnificent. The Byzantines knew this gate as David's Gate, because of the nearby Hippicus Tower, or David's Tower, on account of the mistaken identity of the Tower of David. The Jerusalem historian el-Muqaddasi noted that the gate was known as Bab Mihrab Daud (the gate of the prayer niche named after David). The Crusaders called it David's Gate, because of its proximity to the Tower.

The gate stands at a road junction between the Armenian quarter in the south and the Christian quarter in the north. One highway led west, to the Jaffa road, hence the name of the gate. The other way led east, along the line of the ancient wall through David Street and the Street of the Chain, bisecting the town and reaching as far as the Temple Mount; it ended in the vicinity of the Lions' Gate. Another street crossed this one, running from the Damascus Gate in the north to the Zion Gate in the south. Thus, since Roman times the city has been divided into four quarters. The Romans paved the ancient road to Jaffa; its remains are visible in the west of Jerusalem, in the valley between Har Hamenuhot at Givat-Shaul and the suburb of Ramat Motza. The Romans established military colonies along the highway to ensure safe passage for the caravans. These were at Colonia (where Mevasseret Yerushalaim is now situated), Castellum (now Ma'oz Zion, known in Arabic as Kastel), and at the village of Abu Ghosh. The Roman road led through Sha'ar ha-Gai and the valleys of Ayalon, Gezer and Lod to Jaffa. *Lamentations Rabbah* mentions the Jaffa Gate as the western gate, leading to Lod. The new road connecting Jaffa and Jerusalem was paved by the Sultan 'Abd el-'Aziz in 1864, and completed in 1869 in honor of the Emperor Franz Josef of Austria who visited the country, entering Jerusalem by way of the Damascus Gate, on the occasion of the opening of the Suez Canal. Traffic between Jaffa and Jerusalem had till then been by means of camel, donkey and mule, and the mail was delivered on horseback. The Jaffa Gate was connected with the Citadel by a narrow bridge over the moat of the Tower of David until the turn of the century. In 1898 an opening was made in the wall between the Jaffa Gate and the Citadel, an entrance 12 m wide was prepared, and the moat filled in to honor the visit of the German Kaiser Wilhelm II. A start was also made in paving the internal streets. In December 1917 General Allenby entered Jerusalem through the Jaffa Gate at the head of the British troops. The square near the Citadel was the scene of Allenby's proclamation of civil and religious freedom for the inhabitants of the city. The Jaffa Gate was attacked by the Israel Defense Forces during the War of Independence, but without success.

The road to Jaffa passed close to the quarter of Mahane Israel, near the Mamillah Pool, one of the earliest residential areas outside the wall, built by North African Jews in 1867. The road then passed by the Russian Compound, north-west of the Jaffa Gate, built by the Russian Orthodox Church in 1860–64, and one of the first groups of buildings to be put up outside the walls. The Compound was intended for the use of pilgrims from Russia and included hostels, a church, hospital, and the offices of the Russian Consulate. The Jewish quarter of Nahalat Shiv'ah was built south of the Russian Compound and the Jaffa Road; it commemorated the seven elders of Jerusalem's Jewish community (*Shiv'ah* means seven) who founded it in 1869, after first leasing the area for the cultivation of wheat for the special unleavened bread for Passover. After the Jerusalem–Jaffa Road had been paved, additional Jewish quarters were established along it: Mishkenot (in 1875), Even Israel, Beth-Ya'akov, Mahane Yehuda and the Nahalot Zichron quarters adjoining it. Mahane Yehuda became the site of a fruit and vegetable market for the inhabitants of the new quarters, who until then had been completely dependent on the merchants of the Old City. A carriage terminal was established in the Beth-Ya'akov quarter for a carters' service to the Old City and daily carriages to Jaffa. Jerusalem maintained commercial ties with Hebron, Shechem and Jericho, while the road to Jaffa made possible communication with the country's rulers abroad, and with world Jewry; this was of considerable political importance.

In the nineteenth century the Jaffa Gate was the scene of the ritual rending of clothes carried out by Jewish pilgrims as a sign of mourning for the Destruction of the Temple.

The gate is known in Arabic as Bab el-Khalil (Hebron Gate). The Arabic words mean literally "Gate of the Friend," denoting the connection with the Patriarch Abraham, for the road leading south from the gate links the two cities. Benjamin of Tudela mentions that the Crusaders knew this gate as Abraham's Gate: Hebron was more important than Jaffa to the dwellers of the hill region. The road ran through the Ben-Hinnom Valley, at the foot of the Serpents' Pool (Birket e-Sultan), near the quarter of Mishkenot Sha'ananim west of the pool opposite "Mount Zion." This quarter, with its long buildings, was established by Sir Moses Montefiore in 1860, and was actually the first Jewish quarter (or second, after Mahane Israel) outside the city walls. Montefiore began building the quarter in 1856, but the Turkish rulers stopped the work because of the rule that buildings could not be erected less than 1.5 km away from a walled city. However, after the Russian compound was built Montefiore received permission to continue. The residents paid no rent: they were in fact paid to live in the buildings at first. Montefiore erected a windmill in the quarter (to this day one of Jerusalem's landmarks) to serve the inhabitants, but it soon fell into disrepair. Directly north of Mishkenot Sha'ananim, Montefiore built Yemin Moshe (1894). The cholera epidemic, which affected one-quarter of Jerusalem's inhabitants, was a major reason for the Jews deciding to leave the confined areas within the walls. The road passed through the German Colony, built in 1874 by Christian farmers in the Valley of Rephaim, south-west of the railway station. The establishment of the railway terminal stimulated the development of the area, and another quarter, the Greek Colony, was built. The Hebron Road then turned south, west of Talpiyoth (1922) and Kibbutz Ramat Rahel, founded in 1925 by members of Gedud Ha'Avodah. The Bethlehem–Hebron Road was widened by the government after the Six Day War, to facilitate tourist traffic. During the Mandate period the area just south of the Jaffa Gate was the site of a bus and taxi terminus, serving Bethlehem and Hebron; today it is the site of a city bus station.

The gate assumed its present form after the repairs instituted by Suleiman the Magnificent in 1538–39; a plaque on the gate extols the great Sultan who commanded the wall to be built in the year 945 C.E. The door is of iron, and the opening is L-shaped, to forestall a sudden rush by an invading force. The façade is decorated in Turkish fashion, influenced by Crusader and Mameluke art. It is characterized by an arch neither rounded in the Romanesque style nor narrowly pointed in the Gothic, but slightly rounded and descending on either side in a shell pattern. To the right of the gate a column is inserted horizontally; the disc created by its base is carved with the flower pattern typical

At the bottom: the neighborhood of Mishkenot Sha'ananim. At the top: Dormition Abbey.

of Ottoman art. The arch is crowned with a small turret, through which the defenders of the city poured boiling oil and tar on their enemies.

The gates of Jerusalem were locked at night, for fear of robbers, and were opened at dawn. Latecomers had to sleep outside the walls. Travelers arriving at dusk had to carry candles or lanterns, so that they could be identified. The city was also locked up every Friday between eleven and one o'clock, for fear of an invasion while the Moslems were at prayer. The pioneering Hebrew newspaper *HaLevanon* describes the security situation and the attitude towards the Jewish minority: "The city is unsafe, within and without, with robbers and murderers abounding. An Ishmaelite wishing to be important rides roughshod over the poor Jew, spewing forth and spitting down at him" (No. 5, Iyar, 1863). After the first quarters were built outside the city, the gates remained unlocked day and night. In the time of the British Mandate many shops were built west of the Jaffa Gate and along the wall, to accommodate tourists. Most of these shops were destroyed on the eve of the War of Independence in November 1947, and the ruins were cleared after the reunification of the city in 1967.

A footpath (protected by railings) leads along the top of the wall from the Jaffa Gate to the gates on the north and west of the city, as far as the Lions' Gate. This path was laid by the Ottoman rulers for the use of the guards patrolling the wall. Another path leads along the wall from the Dung Gate to the south-west corner of the wall at "Mount Zion." A walk along these paths is richly rewarding, since it affords a unique viewpoint of the city and its environs. The staircase to the top of the wall is at the left side of the gate.

The New Gate

The northern wall of the city (with an overall length of 1281 m) has three gates: the New Gate in the west, the Damascus Gate in the middle, and Herod's Gate in the East. Research scholars think (without any proof) that Herod's wall did not extend as far as the north-west corner of the present wall, near the New Gate, but passed within the present confines of the city, near the Church of the Holy Sepulcher, at which point it turned north towards the Damascus Gate.

The main gates were opened at low-lying positions along the walls, but the New Gate was built at the highest point of the present wall, at 790 m. There is no information about any gate at this point before the time of the Crusaders. The latter apparently maintained a small gate, named after St. Lazarus, for the use of the soldiers stationed at Tancred's Tower (Goliath's Tower) and for the Leper's order knights also quartered there. The gate may well have been opened after the Crusader occupation of 1099, since one of their armies, led by Tancred, breached the wall near the tower later named after the commander; the breach may have been converted into a gate. After Saladin's victory of 1187 the gate was probably sealed up, and this may have been the Gate of the Serbian Monastery, used by the Franciscans during the sixteenth century while they were building the Church of St. Salvatore.

The French monastery of Notre Dame was built outside the wall in 1887, along with a hostel and hospital for pilgrims, following the example of the Russians 23 years earlier. The French government approached the Sultan, Abdul Hamid, in 1889, requesting access for them and for their pilgrims to the Church of the Holy Sepulcher from their monastery outside the wall. The gate known as the New Gate was then installed by piercing the wall; it is also called the Gate of the Sultan or the Gate of Abdul Hamid.

North of the gate and the nearby Zahal Square lies Shivtei Yisrael Street, leading to other Jewish quarters built outside the Old City in the previous century: Meah Shearim (1874) consisted of 140 houses with four iron gates which, until 1911, were locked every night for fear of robbers. This, the first planned quarter outside the walls, was designed by the architect, C. Schick. The buildings formed a wall around a wide, oblong courtyard, contained a religious school and synagogue, and had two cisterns excavated in its foundations. Fifteen years later, with the increase in population, rows of houses were built within the oblong, at right angles to its sides. There are two explanations of the name: one is, that the original intention was to build 100 houses, and the other, that the founders first convened on the fifth day of Kislev, when the biblical portion of the week describing the hundred measures of grain reaped by Isaac is read. Another old quarter is the Bukharan, built in 1893 with wide streets and spacious houses.

The Damascus Gate

The site of the present gate served this purpose as far back as the Second Temple Period as part of the Second Wall of the city: this is the only gate still located as it was in antiquity. It was built later as a victory gate by the Romans with three entrances: the central one – wide and high – and two smaller ones on its sides. Among the two gates, only the left one remains in its original form, and on both sides of the gates towers were built attached to the wall.

Northern wall of Jerusalem and the Damascus Gate at its center

The gate is situated in the lowest part of the district, at 755 m, at the head of the Tyropoeon Valley, which lies between the two parts of the city, from north to south. The Romans constructed a paved street along this central valley, from the Damascus Gate in the north to the vicinity of the Zion Gate in the south, dividing the city into the Lower City in the east (including the Temple Mount) and the Upper City, with Herod's palace and the towers in the west. The Emperor Hadrian built a new city over the ruins of Jerusalem in the year 131 C.E., calling it Aelia Capitolina. The city was built on the classical plan of the times, with a square and two intersecting streets. This basic plan still exists in the Old City.

The Damascus Gate is the busiest of all the gates, since it is strategically placed and at the hub of business. It has been the chief gate since the Middle Ages. It has many names, deriving from its location in the central valley and the fact that many important roads begin there. Since the Arab Conquest the gate has been known in Arabic as Bab el-ʿAmmud – Gate of the Pillar – because of the stone column bearing a statue of Caesar, set up by Hadrian or his

successors. According to Antonius of Piacenza, in the Byzantine period the column was surmounted by a cross instead of a statue, and was regarded as the center of the world. This was probably the column that served as the base for milestones and for measuring distances throughout the country. The Pilgrim of Bordeaux records that the gate was known to the Romans as the Neapolis Gate, from the Roman name of the city built at the site of Shechem (hence the later Arabic name of Nablus) as the road to that city started at the gate. A branch of this road led from Gofna, north of Ramallah, to Antipatris (Aphek) and Caesarea, the capital of the province. Since Mandate times there has been a taxi stand at the gate, and the bus terminal for Shechem and Jericho is nearby. During the Byzantine period the gate was also called the Galilee Gate, since the road leading north eventually reached that part of the country. In those days it was also called after St. Stephen; according to the *Acts of the Apostles* (VII, 58–59) Stephen was stoned by the inhabitants of the city, and appealed for help to Jesus, who had appeared to him in a vision outside the gate. In 460 C.E. the Byzantine Empress Eudocia erected a basilica to the memory of St. Stephen some 300 m north of the Damascus Gate. The church was destroyed by the Persians when they took the city in 614 C.E. A small chapel was built in the ninth century, reconstructed by the Crusaders in 1099, and finally razed by Saladin in 1187. Dominican monks acquired the site in 1881, and their excavations revealed the site of the fifth century basilica. The present church was built by the Dominicans in 1900 over the ruins of the Byzantine church, and the aisle floors include remnants of the ancient mosaic. The church and monastery today house the Dominican Biblical and Theological School.

A pool, probably dating from Herod's times and known to the Crusaders as Lacus Legerii, was dug some 200 m north-west of the gate. The pool was intended as a moat adding to the defenses of the city on the north, as well as a source of water, which was conveyed by way of a conduit underneath the gate to the Struthion Pool in the Antonia Fortress (still visible in the Ecce Homo Basilica); surplus water flowed from the Beth-zeta creek to the pool known as Birket Israil, now filled in. The stone quarried during the construction of the pool was probably used for the gate and wall, while the water collected in the pool served for construction, washing, laundering and for watering the domestic animals in the northern quarter of the city.

The Damascus Gate, situated between the Christian quarter in the west and the Moslem quarter in the east, was also, after Ch. Warren and before M.

Magen, excavated by R.W. Hamilton, of the Department of Antiquities of the British Mandate Government (1937–38). The gate and its environs developed over four main periods of building: the foundations date from Herod's time; the characteristic Herodian masonry, although in secondary use, with marginal draft and boss, is visible on the inner and outer faces of the gate (near the public toilets). The lower gateway, left of the gate, is Roman, part of Aelia Capitolina, as shown by the inscription above the key stone of the arch;

COL(ONIA)

AEL(IA)

CAP(ITOLINA)

D(ECRETO)

D(ECARIONUM)

which indicates that the gate was dedicated to the city Aelia Capitolina by the City Council (R.W. Hamilton, *Quarterly of the Department of Antiquities*, Palestine 10, 1944, pp. 22–23). Each of the towers flanking the wall includes four columns inserted horizontally for added strength, their cross-sections appearing disc-like among the blocks of the wall. This appears to be typical of Ottoman art. The present gate dates to the reign of Suleiman the Magnificent, as proved by the style (resembling that of the Jaffa Gate) and the following inscription found over the gate: "Our Lord the great Sultan and brilliant governor, Sultan of the strangers, Arabs and Persians, has commanded the construction of this blessed gate… Suleiman the son of Salim Khan, may Allah preserve his reign and his kingdom."

The Damascus Gate is the most strongly fortified and the most beautiful of Suleiman's gates. The entrance has a double angle, to prevent the sudden inrush of an attacking force. The gate is protected on both sides by a high tower; it is decorated by an Ottoman arch, with the characteristic almost flat arch, flanked by two discs of columns inserted horizontally; these discs are carved with a typical Ottoman flower pattern. The columns run the width of the wall and give it added strength. Above the gate are four flat discs of Mameluke columns, probably being re-used, since the upper portions of the gate are Turkish. The tops of the gates and towers are ornamented with pointed turrets, Turkish additions that are found at this place in the wall, and the outer gate of the citadel also dated from Suleiman's time.

The staircase leading to the roof of the gate is on its eastern side. The view from the top is magnificent, affording an excellent insight into the structure of the city and its various sections. The Tyropoeon Valley is visible from its top, outside the wall at the ruins of Lacus Legerii, now converted into a parking lot, in the north, to the middle of the valley in the south. To the southeast the Lower City can be seen, with the Temple Mount, the Western Wall, the gilded Dome of the Rock and the leaded dome of the El-Aqsa Mosque, and the probable site of the high-lying Antonia Fortress. The Upper City and the Citadel lie to the southwest. To the right of the Temple Mount are the Jewish quarter, and the Armenian quarter, with the silvered dome of the Church of St. James to the left of the Citadel. Further to the right is the Christian quarter, with the dark domes of the Church of the Holy Sepulcher, the large dome of the Byzantine basilica and the smaller dome of the Crusader chapel. To the left is the prominent square white bell-tower of the German Lutheran church, built over the ruins of a Crusader church and consecrated in 1898, during the visit of Kaiser Wilhelm II. Left of the Holy Sepulcher rises the dark, pointed tower of the Franciscan church of St. Savior, originally built in 1559, as well as the minaret of the Omariyah Mosque, identified in Islamic tradition as the site of the Caliph Omar's first prayer on entering Jerusalem. The square minaret is evidence of the pre-Turkish date of construction (Turkish mosques have round minarets), of the fifteenth century C.E. The observer also looks out over houses and roof-tops; the oldest buildings were constructed with domes, to bear the weight of the Jerusalem snowfalls, among other reasons, and to be able to convey the precious rain-water down through drainpipes to the cisterns; later buildings have red tiled roofs, with metal gutters, while the most recent structures are flat-roofed, with metal tanks for storing water.

Some 50 m east along the footpath on the wall, the north and west lines of the third wall, Agrippa's, may be discerned. This wall surrounded the new city, Beth-zeta, at the end of the Second Temple period. The wall started at the north-west corner of the present wall, leading to the Russian Compound, its green domes conspicuous on the skyline, in the west; on to the Italian Hospital in the north-west, with its unique square tower at the crossing of HaNeviim and Shivtei Yisrael Streets; onwards to the School of St. George with its low square tower, in the north; and eastward to a spot north of the Rockefeller Museum, where it meets the Kidron Valley.

The Jews of the Old City did not build on the northern side of the city, except for the quarter of Shimon haTzadik, near what is traditionally thought to be his tomb. This neighborhood, and Nahalat Yitzhak, became the home of Jews too poor to live in the better-protected quarters.

Zedekiah's Cave (Royal Caves)

Some 150 m east of the Damascus Gate, about 6 m below the wall, is the enormous complex of caverns known as Zedekiah's Cave. Tradition has it that this was the cave to which King Zedekiah of Judah fled from the forces of Nebuchadnezzar, king of Babylon, a flight which finally ended in his capture in Jericho (*II Kings* xxv, 4; *Jeremiah* xxxix, 4–5; lii, 7–8). Rashi and Radak give the legends relating to this cave, describing the parallel flights of Zedekiah within the cave and of a deer above it; the Chaldeans chased the deer and caught the king as he emerged from the opening at Jericho. *Numbers Rabbah* ii refers to the cave thus: "One who observed the Sabbath in a cave, even though it be like the cave of Zedekiah, which was eighteen miles long, may walk through the whole of it…" Josephus, describing the third wall, mentions the Royal Caves: "and extending through the royal caverns, was inflected at the corner tower," (*Wars* v, 4). The cave, discovered by European investigators in 1825, is known in Arabic as Migharat al-Kitan (Cotton Cave), and was used in antiquity for the storage of cotton. The actual length of the cave is 200 m and its maximum width 100 m. It was originally a quarry for stone used in constructing the walls and towers of the city; the chisel marks are clearly visible, as are the columns left standing to support the roof. Herod and the later rulers of Jerusalem needed great quantities of stone to fortify and expand the city, and quarries were dug in faraway regions such as Sanhedri-yah and Beth-Hanina. Stone was also brought from nearby, from the Kidron and Ben-Hinnom Valleys, from the pools around the walls, from the quarry known as Jeremiah's Grotto, (behind the bus terminal opposite the Damascus Gate), and, in particular, from Zedekiah's Cave, where the *melekeh* stone was conveniently stratified, and suitable for building purposes.

Herod's Gate

Herod's Gate is best reached along the wall by the footpath from the Damascus Gate. It was probably non-existent during the Second Temple period, since archaeologists have determined that the city wall ran west of the present gate, and south-east of it. This gate was also opened at a low-lying part of the wall (760 m), in the Beth-zeta Valley. The rainfall in the new city drained through the gate, and to the Birket el-Hajj pool (the Pool of the Mecca Pilgrim), which was located north of the gate, further up the valley. This pool, probably also Herodian in origin, was dug to serve as a moat, its stones being used for construction and its waters for domestic use and for watering animals. The surplus water flowed to the pools of Bethesda and Birket Israil, south of Herod's Gate, near the north-east wall of the Temple Mount. Birket el-Hajj is now built over.

The gate is known in Arabic as Bab e-Sahirah, and is mentioned by the historians El-Muqaddasi (985 C.E.) and Mujir e-Din (1496). The name means "the place where people stay awake." The Persian traveler Nasir i-Khosrau (1047) was of the opinion that the name was derived from the Moslem cemetery on the hill opposite, where warriors and pilgrims to Mecca are buried. According to Moslem tradition these people will be resurrected at the end of time. This tradition is also mentioned by Mujir e-Din (G. Le Strange, *Palestine under the Moslems*, Khayat, Beirut, 1961, p. 220). Cemeteries of Moslem heroes and holy men are also to be found near other pools and gates of Jerusalem, near the Mamillah Pool, in the vicinity of the Jaffa Gate, near the Lions' Gate close to the Pool of Miriam, and near the Golden Gate.

The gate was known to medieval pilgrims as Herod's Gate because just within it, near the Antonia fortress, is a Greek Orthodox church named Deir el-'Adas; pilgrims connect it with the time of Herod Antipas, because of the passage in *St. Luke* XXIII, 7 – "...and he sent him to Herod, who himself was also at Jerusalem at that time." The Crusaders, led by Godfrey of Bouillon, broke into the city at this point from their base at the site of the Rockefeller Museum, destroying the Jewish quarter (until then in that area), and not till the end of the fourteenth century was it reestablished on its present site adjoining Mount Zion. The Crusaders built four churches in the previous Jewish-Syrian quarter, all of which became Moslem institutions after Saladin's conquest.

The gate has a low-pointed arch in the Ottoman style, flanked with the discs of horizontal columns carved in a Turkish flower pattern. E. Robinson wrote in 1838 that the inhabitants called it Bab e-Zahirah (Flower Gate). Possibly the name, which sounds like Sahirah, was changed in Turkish times, since the meaning was so much pleasanter. Robinson reports an additional name, Bab e-Zahariyeh, which means Gate of Glory.

The gate was blocked up with stones during the 1880s and was reopened after the population outside the walls had increased considerably. The Lions' Gate can be reached along the wall path by way of the Stork Tower (Burj a-Laqlaq) at the north-east corner of the wall. This tower is 26 m long from north to south and 19 m from east to west. It affords an excellent view of Mount Scopus, the Mount of Olives, the Kidron Valley and the northern neighborhoods of Jerusalem.

The Lions' Gate

The eastern wall of the Old City, 762 m long, is built up of masonry of varying periods. The southeastern corner includes Hasmonean, Herodian, Roman, Byzantine and Crusader stones. Further north and at the Golden Gate the wall is Roman and Byzantine, while at the Lions' Gate it is Turkish. In the southeast corner the wall reaches a height of 48.2 m including the underground part, the thirty-five lowest courses rising to 42 m. The wall continues underground, consisting of great Herodian ashlars, each over 1 m high. The twenty upper courses are much more recent. The base of the visible wall at the south-east corner lies at an altitude of 694 m. A "seam" joins Herod's addition to the Temple Mount enclosure, at the southern tip of the eastern wall. In Herod's Temple this was the site of the royal portico, which was connected to the Upper City in the west by way of the arched staircase known as Robinson's Arch. This southern section of the Temple Mount was used for purposes of commerce, including money-changing. The royal portico can be seen in the Second Temple model at the Holyland Hotel.

The Lions' Gate is the only entrance open in the eastern wall. It could not have replaced any gate of Herodian times, since the second wall never went that far. There are three ancient pools near the gate: one north of the gate outside the present wall, known as the Pool of Miriam, after the mother of Jesus; a second, northwest of the gate, within the wall, the Pool of Bethesda (in the courtyard of St. Anne's Church); and the third, now filled in, just south-west of the gate and along the north-east wall of the Temple Mount, known as Birket Israil. The pools excavated during Herod's reign were all outside the walls, and served for defense purposes, so the Lions' Gate was probably constructed during the reign of Agrippa, at the end of the Second Temple period, when the third wall approached the line of the present wall. South of the gate, near the Temple Mount wall, there are remnants of an ancient tower, which guarded the Temple Mount. The Gate of Benjamin mentioned in the Bible (*Jeremiah* XXXVII, 12–13; *Zechariah* XIV, 10) was probably nearby; it was also known as the Sheep Gate (*Nehemiah* III, 1; XII, 39) since the sheep were washed in the Sheep Pool (Bethesda) before being sacrificed. The Sheep Gate was probably still in existence during the Second Temple period.

The gate is 735 m above sea-level, on the way to the Mount of Olives and Jericho, and is at present one of the lowest-lying gates of the city. The gate was also called Gethsemane, since it is near the olive groves of Gethsemane in the Kidron Valley, which were a meeting place for Jesus and his disciples

Lions' Gate in the eastern part of the Old City

(*St. Matthew* XXVI, 36). In Arabic the gate is called Bab Sittna Miriam (Gate of Our Lady Mary), after the mother of Jesus, whose tomb, according to tradition, is further down the valley. The pool north of the gate also bears the name of Mary. The gate is named in the *Acts of the Apostles* (I, 11–12) as the Galilee Gate, since after the Ascension of Jesus the men of Galilee came down from the Mount of Olives and entered Jerusalem through this gate. The gate is mentioned, but not by name, by the Pilgrim of Bordeaux (333 C.E.) During the Arab period it was known, according to al-Muqaddasi (985) as Bab e-Riha (Jericho Gate), since at this point the road turns towards Jericho. The modern carriage road to Jericho was paved in 1887. Al-Muqaddasi mentioned that the gate was also named Bab Birket Bani-Israil (Gate of the Pool of the Children of Israel), after the pool north of the Temple Mount wall, now filled in. The Crusaders added a name to the gate, calling it the Gate of Jehoshaphat (the Valley of Jehoshaphat adjoins the Kidron Valley). During the Middle Ages it was known as the Gate of the Tribes. Shams e-Din e-Suyuti (1470), recording the name, mentions that the Israelites used this gate to enter the Temple Mount for prayers. Mujir e-Din (1496) also gives it this name. Another name for the gate is Bab el-Ghor (Gate of the Jordan Rift Valley), indicating the road to the Jericho and Jordan Valleys.

The inscription above the gate records its construction by Suleiman the Magnificent in 1538–39. However, the lions, which flank the gate and gave it its Hebrew name are characteristic of the reign of the Mameluke sultan, Baybars (1260–77), who ruled from Egypt and placed the symbol on the forts he built along the highway connecting Damascus with Egypt. These lions are also found on the wall of the fort at Khan Yunis, near Gaza, and beside the Ayalon (Jindas) Bridge north of Lod, dating from 1273. The gate was built under Suleiman. The architecture (according to M. Rosen-Ayalon, in conversation with the author) is a combination of styles: the apex of the archway is Ottoman, while the inner arch of the gate is flat, in the Mameluke mode. The two tiny arches over the lions are carved in the Crusader fashion of "'pillow" arches, which the Mamelukes were fond of imitating. The flat discs under the lions are probably also Mameluke. Above the lions and on either side are firing slits; above these are flat discs in Mameluke style, and above these again are discs carved in the Turkish flower pattern. The Turks thus probably completed the upper portions of the wall and gate, while the lower portions bear signs of Mameluke or pre-Ottoman style. The upper archway and the turrets on top of the wall are Ottoman.

The paratroopers of the Israel Defense Forces entered Jerusalem through this gate on 7 June 1967, completing the unification of the city. The gate was damaged in the course of the fighting, and the Jerusalem Municipality carried out repairs in 1969. Each of the iron doors weighs three tons.

There is a complex of historical buildings close to the gate. They are described below and are worth visiting.

Pool of Bethesda and Church of St. Anne

The Pool of Bethesda is about 80 m north-west of the Lions' Gate. It is mentioned in *St. John* (v, 2–4) as the site of Jesus' miraculous healings when the water was troubled: "Now there is in Jerusalem by the sheep market a pool, which is called in the Hebrew tongue Bethesda, having five porches. In these lay a great multitude of impatient folk, of blind, halt, withered, waiting for the moving of the water. For an angel went down at a certain season into the pool, and troubled the water: whosoever then first after the troubling of the water stepped in was made whole of whatsoever disease he had."

According to the archeologist P. Benoit, who studied the site, the name Bethesda was found on a parchment at the Qumran ruins on the Dead Sea shore, telling of a double pool near the Temple called the Beth-Eshtadain* Pool, and the smaller pool housed a treasure (P. Benoit, *Tagliyot Arkeologiyot Bi-vrekhat Beit Hisda, Yerushalaim le-Dorotehah*, Israel Exploration Society, Jerusalem 1969). Since the days of Eusebius (300 C.E.) these pools have been identified as the Pools of Bethesda, north of the Temple Mount. For about 700 years, from the Middle Ages to modern times, tradition has located the Pool of Bethesda (which was actually silted and filled up) at Birket Israil, adjoining the northern wall of the Temple Mount, which was in use until quite recently; the Jerusalem Municipality filled it in during the 1930s. El-Muqaddasi reports three pools in the city: Birket Bani Israil, Birket Suleiman, and Birket 'Iyad. Le Strange identified the Pool of Suleiman with the Pool of Bethesda, and the Pool of 'Iyad with the Pool of Amygdalon near the Jaffa Gate. Barclay (*City of the Great King*, London, 1858, p. 301) writes that, according to the Crusader historian William of Tyre, Birket Israil was filled by water flowing through distant conduits. In 1509 the Franciscan Friar Anselm reported that Birket Israil was filled with water, and a similar account came from Felix Fabri in 1490. George Sandys (1670) described water flowing in 1610 from the northern wall of the Temple Mount into the courtyards of the Temple area.

The pool has several names: Bethesda implying the mercy shown to the sick who were healed (*hesed* means mercy), and also the Pool of Probatique (= of the sheep); it was also known as the Pool of Bezetha, either after the olive trees in the vicinity (*zayyit* is an olive) or the name of the new part of the city in the Second Temple period. The White Fathers discovered the two basins of the original pool in 1914, and since 1956 excavations have been carried out by M. Rousee. The excavations have revealed a Temple of Healing, two basins and the Byzantine basilica, which orginated in the First Temple Period.

---

* The parchment alluded to is not clearly noted; if this is the Copper Scroll, the pools are Beth-Ha'ashuhin according to B. Z. Luria, *Megillat Ha-Nehoshet Mimidbar Yehuda,* Jerusalem 1964, p. 121.

Temple of Healing

This was found east of the pool basins, in front of the over-lying Byzantine church. The temple existed for two main periods: during the Hasmonean period up to the Destruction in 70 C.E., and in Roman times, from the second to the fourth centuries C.E. Hasmonean pottery resembling that at Khirbet Qumran was found, and coins up to the year 66 C.E. Five natural caves were discovered, plastered and made usable, all with stairs and basins for bathing. It is therefore believed that they were used for healing purposes, but it is not clear whether the baths were supplied by a spring which later ran dry, or by the floodwaters of the nearby Bezetha Valley. It is generally believed that the miracles of healing attributed to Jesus took place here, but in my opinion this is difficult to prove.

Edifices from the Roman period (third to fourth centuries C.E.), with mosaic floors and frescoed walls going down to a depth of 8 m, were discovered. These had all been destroyed, and the Byzantine church built with stones from these Roman buildings. These remnants were found over-lying older structures from the Maccabean period. There may also have been a Roman temple, which stretched further south, under the present church of St. Anne. Two vaulted underground chambers were found south of the church and are open to the public. A complex system of water conduits throughout the area was also found. Finds were made providing evidence of a cult of baths dedicated to the god of healing – these included part of a stele bearing a sinuous serpent, a marble fragment in the form of a reclining nude, the clay figurine of a woman disrobing, two model ships, and other items. The god of healing was the Egyptian god Serapis, identified in Greece and Asia

Roman inscription dedicated to the god Serapis

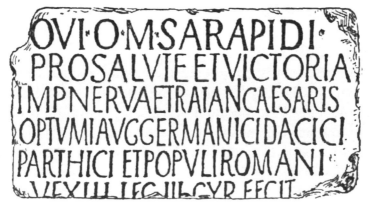

Minor with Aesculapius. No coins bearing the image of Serapis were found at the site, but they have been found in Jerusalem and elsewhere. This was the most important of the foreign cults in Aelia Capitolina after Hadrian's reign. Serapis was the sailors' patron, and offerings of ships were therefore found here. He was also revered by soldiers, and the baths were in fact close to the Antonia Fortress.

Below is the translation of the Roman inscription dedicated to the god Serapis by the soldiers of the Sixth Legion who passed by there in the days of Emperor Trianos:

> *To Jupiter, the Supreme God, who is Serapis*
> *To peace and victory*
> *The imperial Caesar Nerva Trianos*
> *Augustus Germanicus Decicus*
> *Parthia and to the Roman people*
> *Presented by the Third Company of the Sixth Cyrini Legion*

The Basins of the Pool of Bethesda

Two large basins were discovered in the pool, running north to south lengthwise, and separated by a wide wall. The southern basin is filled with silt and rubbish, and therefore the exact plan of the two basins could not be determined. Their estimated length was 120 m, their width 50–60 m and their depth 10–15 m. Archaeologists believe they were dug during the Maccabean period. Surplus water, from Birket el-Hajj, at the head of the valley (outside the present wall) probably flowed to the Bethesda Pool basins after purification, where it was used for washing the sheep to be sacrificed; this was probably the source of the name "Sheep Pool." The purer water flowed into the Birket Israil to be used for washing in the Temple.

The Byzantine Basilica

The Byzantine basilica was well-known in literature, and for a long time was identified with the Church of St. Anne, south-east of the pool. Père Vincent was the first to show that the Byzantine basilica was built over the main basins; its central hall adjoined the wall separating them, and the two aisles were partly based on the foundations of the basins. The central hall with its mosaic floor was revealed in the excavations, as well as sections of seven piers and arches that reached a depth of 13 m, to the bottom of the pool, and supported the southern aisle. The northern aisle was built, together with a middle story, which was apparently used for baptism, over a smaller, older basin, in the south-east corner of the northern basin. The smaller basin was probably used by pilgrims, and was always full of water; it would seem that this was the miraculous pool mentioned in the New Testament. Remains of the three apses of the hall and aisles were found 25 m away from the basins.

The Byzantine basilica was apparently constructed by the Empress Eudocia in the fifth century and dedicated to Mary, mother of Jesus, whose birthplace it is traditionally thought to be. The Empress came to Jerusalem in 438 C.E. with the intention and the means of putting up churches, monasteries and hospices. It is believed that the church was destroyed in 1005 C.E. by the Fatimid ruler el-Hakim b'Amr Illa, although another opinion is that the church was razed to the ground during the Persian conquest of the city in 614 at which time over two thousand Christians were killed.

Crusader Church

The conquering Crusaders erected a church in the early twelfth century, southeast of the Byzantine church and the Pool of Bethesda, and dedicated it to St. Anne, the mother of Mary, whose dwelling place this was according to tradi-

Church of Saint Anne

tion. The church, perfectly preserved, is Romanesque, and one of the finest examples of Crusader art in the country. Its plan is basilical; it is divided into a main hall and two aisles and transepts, each terminating in an apse, as in other Crusader churches. The church is 34 m long and 19.5 m wide; its façade leans slightly to the left, symbolizing the leftward leaning of Jesus' head on the Cross (*St. John* XIX, 30).

Saladin, who conquered Jerusalem in 1187, turned the church into a Moslem theological seminary in 1192, and it was named Salahiyeh, after him. An inscription above the main entrance of the building calls upon God to help all believers and reward them. The church and monastery were abandoned before the early nineteenth century. The Turks began building a minaret in 1841, but this project, too, was given up. After the Crimean War, in 1856, the Sultan 'Abd-el-Majid gave the site to the French Catholic Church, and the church was restored in 1863–77. Since then it has been in the care of the White Fathers, who also founded a theological seminary and a museum of the antiquities found in the course of work on the site. The church suffered damage during the Six Day War, and the Israeli Government carried out repairs.

The Golden Gate

At the end of the First Temple period the eastern gate was closed (see *Ezekiel* XLIV, 1: "Then he brought me back the way of the outer gate of the sanctuary which looketh toward the east; and it was shut"). During the Second Temple period there was an eastern gate named Shushan Gate, mentioned in the *Mishnah* (*Middot* I, 3), or the Eastern Gate (*Nehemiah* III, 29). A causeway supported by arches ran from the gate across the Kidron Valley, and was known as the Causeway of the Heifer, since the High Priest used this way to reach the Mount of Olives where the ritual burning of the Red Heifer took place, to purify the pilgrims with its ashes (*Parah* III, 6; *Shekalim* IV, 2).

The Golden Gate, 257 m north of the southeastern corner of the Temple Mount, is the most beautiful of all the gates of Jerusalem. It is approached from within the Temple Mount by twenty-two stairs; these lead into a magnificent entrance, decorated with unusually intricate carvings of acanthus leaves, which appear to be moving. The gate room is a hall with six domes supported by huge marble pillars. On the east side of the hall are two gateways, now blocked up, beautifully decorated on the outside.

The New Testament (*Acts* III, 2) calls this the "Beautiful Gate"; there is mention of a gate which was later identified with the Golden Gate. However,

Mercy Gate in the eastern part of the Temple Mount wall

its present beauty was not attained at least until the reign of Justinian, in honor of the Christian tradition, which fixes this as the site of Jesus' entry to the Temple courtyard. The gate was probably built during the Byzantine period by the Emperor Heraclius who entered through it after taking Jerusalem in 629. After the Moslem Conquest, when the Dome of the Rock and the El-Aqsa Mosque were built, it was locked to prevent unsupervised access to the mosque area.

Al-Muqaddasi (985) mentions the gate for the first time with its two openings, the southern one called Bab e-Rahma (Gate of Mercy) and the northern one Bab e-Tauba (Gate of Repentance); both were closed. The double gate is also mentioned by Nasir i-Khosrau (1047) and Mujir e-Din (1496). Shams e-Din e-Suyuti, who visited Jerusalem in 1470, ascribes a reference in the *Koran* (LVII, 13) to this gate: "Then there will separate them a wall wherein is a gate, the inner side whereof containeth mercy, while the outer side thereof is toward the doom." According to this verse the inner gate, containing mercy, is Bab e-Rahma, while the outer one is Bab e-Tauba, indicating the punishment in Gehenna. The Kidron Valley is known in Arabic, among other names, as Wadi Jehennum (Valley of Gehenna) implying punishment and torture. The gate is also mentioned in Arabic, although rarely, as Bab el-Dahariyah (Gate of Eternity), recalling the visions of *Joel* (IV, 2 and 12), or the Twin Gate, because of its shape, which can be seen quite clearly from the Mount of Olives. In the time of the Crusaders it was opened twice a year for Christian festivals: once in the spring, on Palm Sunday, recalling Jesus' triumphal entry to the city through this gate (*St. Matthew* XXI, 1–8); and once in the autumn, to commemorate the entry of the Emperor Heraclius. The gate was finally closed under Ayyubid rule in the thirteenth century.

Charles Warren examined the gate in 1867–69 and found a wall descending 13 m below the level of the gate; the wall of the Temple Mount at this point is thus 20 m high; 80 m further north Warren found the base of the wall at a depth of 40 m. Schick cleaned the gate in 1891. It is to be hoped that this magnificent gate will again serve its original purpose, making possible pilgrimages to the Temple Mount from the Mount of Olives.

The Temple Mount Courtyard and The Southern Wall

The wall from the southeastern corner to the southwestern (at Mount Zion) is 1,100 m long. The recent excavations at the southern wall, carried out by B. Mazar, disclosed signs of five periods of construction. The lower courses are Herodian, with the characteristic fine dressing, double margin and slightly prominent smooth boss. Next are the large blocks, smoothly dressed, apparently dating to Aelia Capitolina. These are surmounted by smaller, smooth stones, alternating with discs (cross-sections of columns inserted in the wall), which are probably Mameluke. This section is interspersed with small blocks having very prominent bosses and margins, apparently Crusader. The final courses are of small stones of later periods. The wall at the south-western corner was 37 m high, and the height of the south-eastern wall was 52 m. As it is written: "And the wall itself was the greatest achievement of which humans beings had heard" (*Antiquities*, 15:11, 3).

Three groups of gates are visible in the southern wall of the Temple Mount. The Single Gate, probably dating to the Crusaders and repaired by the Mamelukes, is 37 m from the southeast corner of the wall. The Triple Gate is 183 m from the southwest corner and 90 m from the south-east corner. This was the site of one of the two pairs of the Southern Gates of the Second Temple. The Double Gate is south of the El-Aqsa Mosque and was the other pair of the Southern Gates mentioned in the *Mishnah* (*Middot* 1, 3). During the Second Temple period these two gates divided the Temple Mount wall into three almost equal sections. The courses of the southern wall of the Temple Mount range from 0.75 m to 1.40 m in height. The twenty-eighth course from the foundation

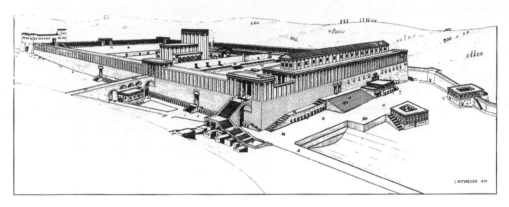

The Temple Mount and reconstruction of Herodian buildings

is known as the "Master Course"; it is 1.85 m high, and runs from the south-eastern corner to the Double Gate, on the same level as the gate thresholds. The stone size of the "Master Course" is almost twice the average. It is a kind of belt that connects and stabilizes the wall on its high spots. The weight of one of the biggest stones south-east of the Temple Mount is 100 tons.

The Double Gate

The Double Gate can be approached from within the Temple Mount courtyard, at the north-east corner of the El-Aqsa Mosque. Sixteen stairs and a double gallery lead down to a hall whose ceiling is supported by a row of gigantic pillars. From here one can see the front of the Double Gate in the southern wall of the Temple Mount. This underground structure, known as Al-Aqsa el-Qadima, or the Double Gate, now walled up, is said to be one of the two pairs of the Southern Gates of the Second Temple period. During festivals (before Herod), pilgrims entered the Temple area from the Ophel square by the Huldah Gates. The gate is 12.8 m wide, and is divided in two by a large pillar. El-Muqaddasi calls it Buab e-Nabi (Gates of the Prophet) and the Persian traveler Nasir i-Khosrau refers to it as Bab e-Nabi (Gate of the Prophet), both meaning the Prophet Mohammed. Mujir e-Din calls it Bab El-Aqsa el-Qadima. Ibn Batuta, the Tangiers traveler who visited the city in 1355, wrote that on three sides of the Temple Mount were many gates, but on the south it had only one gate which the Imam entered through (according to G. Le Strange, *Palestine under the Muslems*, p. 182). El-Muqaddasi calls another gate in the southern wall the Fountain Gate, since the water brought to the Temple Mount from the Gihon and Rogel springs flowed through at this point. Nasir i-Khosrau noted that this was the gate leading to Silwan (Siloam). The southern gates of the Temple Mount were walled up after Saladin's conquest of Jerusalem in 1187 or by his nephew.

The Triple Gate

This was originally a double gate, one of the southern gates built by Herod for the use of pilgrims. Part of the west doorpost remains from the original Second Temple structure. The thresholds of both the Double and the Triple Gates lie some 12 m below the present level of the courtyard. The Triple Gate received its present form during the Crusader period, or just before their arrival.

Triple Gate in the southern wall of the Temple Mount

The Cradle of Jesus

The Cradle of Jesus, known to the Arabs as Mahd 'Issa, is part of the so called "Stables of Solomon." It is reached by way of a staircase near the south-east corner of the Temple Mount courtyard, east of the El-Aqsa Mosque. The chamber measures 21 m from north to south and 17 m from east to west, and the ceiling is supported by columns. In the west wall is an opening decorated in secondary use with Byzantine arts probably dating to Justinian, or earlier. This is now represented by a dais supported on four small marble columns. Nasir i-Khosrau notes that there was a subterranean mosque at the south-east corner of the Temple Mount, where the cradle of Jesus was, and that he (Nasir) prayed at that place. He writes that Jesus' childhood was spent there, and this was where he spoke with the people. In the mosque were many lamps of silver and brass, which were lit every night (Le Strange, pp. 166–67). The Church of St. Simeon stood here in Crusader times.

"The Stables of Solomon" – dating 1034–1064

When Herod built the Temple Mount courtyard he made it 485 m long and 315 m wide. The courtyard sloped southwards, and the southern part of the platform therefore had to be raised to keep the surface level. Herod filled in only the lower part of the space between the retaining wall and the natural slope, and he built the remaining space, to the top of the platform, in the form of vaults, with their ceilings supported by pillars. The south-east corner of the Temple Mount, which had a retaining wall 48 m high, was filled with rubble and soil to a height of 32 m; over this filling was a hall, its roof forming the pavement of the courtyard, and above this rose the upper wall. The walls of the Temple Mount were five meters thick and consisted of enormous ashlar blocks weighing up to 150 tons. This formidable structure made the Temple into a mighty fortress, unequalled in the architecture of antiquity. Josephus writes (*Antiquities* xv, 11): "…which wall was itself the most prodigious work that was ever heard of by man." The southern wall had a height equal to that of a modern eighteen-story building. The stables are comprised of two halls with an area of 5000 sq m, the ceilings supported by eighty-eight pillars in twelve parallel rows with thirteen aisles between them, thus raising the level of the courtyard by 12 m. The arches were 9–10 m high, the length of the halls from east to west was 83 m and the width, from north to south, 60 m. There were additional structures, which changed the shape of the halls somewhat. The pillars consisted of large, square blocks, over 1 m high, and each pillar

Southeastern wall of the Temple Mount. At its left, a Byzantine wall of Jerusalem.

was 1.2 m thick. At the bases of the pillars were holes for tethering horses. The Single Gate, now walled up, can be seen at the southern end of the sixth row of pillars, from the east, and the Triple Gate is at the south end of the twelfth row; it is clearly visible from outside the wall. Tunnels and aqueducts were found underneath the Double and Triple Gates, and a drain ran under the halls.

During the Second Temple period these halls were entered by the Southern Gates, and stairs led to the upper level of the Temple courtyard. When the Crusaders took Jerusalem, they identified the halls of pillars as the "stables of King Solomon," as did Nasir i-Khosrau and other Moslems. The Crusaders used the halls to stable the horses of the Knights Templar, whose headquarters were in the El-Aqsa Mosque. The Crusaders entered their stables through the Triple and Single Gates (both now walled up).

Excavations at The Southern Wall

During the Second Temple period the area south of the Southern Wall, which led into the Temple Mount, was a paved square where the pilgrims gathered, and trade in sacrifices took place, for the site was close to the Judean Desert, where sheep and goats were reared, as well as to the Gihon and Rogel water sources, where the livestock was watered and washed. The square was also used by the populace of Aelia Capitolina and of the Byzantine city, since the subterranean conduits of Herod's water system, supplied from Ein 'Arrub north of Hebron and leading to the Temple Mount by way of Wilson's Bridge,

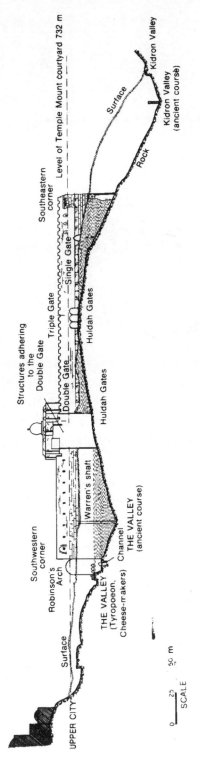

Southern wall of the Temple Mount

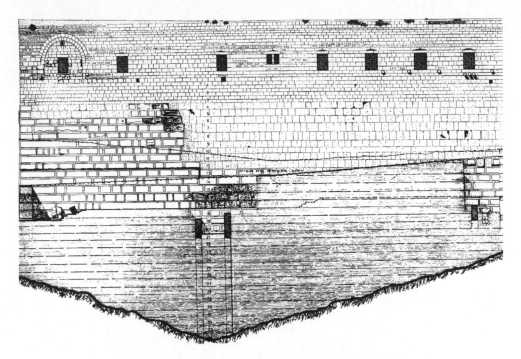

The excavations at the southwestern wall of the Temple

opened out to the Lower City and the Kidron Valley, as did the drainage of the city. During the Crusader period public activity was concentrated further east, to the Single and Triple Gates, through which the Crusader knights rode to the stables ("Stables of Solomon").

The southwest wall of the Temple Mount was probed in a trial dig by K. Kenyon and Père de Vaux in 1961. They uncovered a fragment of pavement and the wall of a structure south of the Temple wall. A more thorough, methodical excavation was conducted by B. Mazar beginning in 1968. First results, which have served as the basis for this chapter, were published by Mazar, in *Sefer Eretz Israel, Mehkarim be-Yedi'at haAretz ve-'Atikotehah,* Vol. IX, *Hafirot Arkheologiyot bi-Yerushalayim ha-'Atikah,* pp. 161–74, 1968, and Vol. X, pp. 1–40, 1971.

The excavations were carried out along the southern wall, from the southwest corner of the Temple Mount to the Crusader-Mameluke structure south of the El-Aqsa Mosque and the eastern wall adjoining it. Capt. C. Warren, who carried out pioneering excavations from 1867 to 1870 (*The Recovery of Jerusalem,* Capt. Wilson and Capt. Warren, Appleton Co. New York, 1872, pp. 58–86), dug many deep shafts down to the bedrock around the walls of the Temple Mount. He provided details of the structure of the walls below the surface and of their immensity, as well as of the water and drainage systems of the ancient city. Two shafts were sunk at the southwest corner of the wall, one at the corner itself and another some 30 m further east along the original course of the Tyropoeon Valley. Warren found twenty-three courses of the Herodian wall intact at the south-west corner, below the surface, and twenty-six courses at the Western Wall. The six lowest courses, which were underground during Herodian times, consisted of roughly dressed blocks, with very prominent bosses – these were the foundation courses. The overlying courses, visible in Herodian times, were more finely worked, with slightly prominent bosses and smooth surfaces.

The ground level at the southwest corner at the start of Mazar's excavations was at the height of the eighth course, some 20 m above bedrock; further east the surface dipped to the eleventh course. A roughly paved street was uncovered along the southern wall, from the western corner to the Double Gate, gradually rising towards the east. This was found to be of the Umayyad period, from the time of 'Abd el-Malek (685–705 C.E.) or his son al-Walid (705–715). The eastern section of the street is visible near the wall. The southern wall reaches its greatest depth, 23 m, under the Umayyad street, near the natural valley, with 21 courses. Byzantine remains were discovered under the Umayyad street, and a Byzantine clay pipe was found along the southern wall, from the Double Gate.

Another street was discovered lower down, 15 m beneath the Umayyad Street. This street, dating to the Herodian dynasty, is paved with large smooth slabs and ascends eastward by means of steps towards the Double Gate. A Roman-Byzantine drain was found at the seventeenth course. The maximum depth of the wall beneath the street down to the Valley bedrock is 18 m, and consists of seventeen courses. Pottery from the end of the First Temple period (seventh to sixth centuries B.C.E.) was found under the Herodian pavement.

Warren reached a depth of 26 m in the shaft, which he dug in the Valley down to the lowest, the thirty-fourth, course. Here he found drainage conduits from the Temple area leading south along the Valley. Two courses above the Umayyad street, in courses eight, 12 and 16 of the southern and western walls, there are in the wall three channels that held clay pipes during the Byzantine and Umayyad periods.

Six successive strata were uncovered in the latest excavations at the southern wall. The two lowest are Roman, from the time of Hadrian to the end of the third century (Diocletian); this is evident from the coin and bricks bearing the stamp of the Tenth Legion. The four upper strata are Byzantine, identified by characteristic coins and pottery.

Square of The Southern Wall

The "Street of the Town" was paved along the southern wall of the Temple Mount, leading to the main gates of the Temple, the pair of Southern Gates, the western (Double) and the eastern (Triple). Pilgrims arriving from the west ascended the steps on this street to the vicinity of the western gate, and the street then led from the eastern gate to the Kidron Valley, first as a level street and then by stairs.

Just south of the gates the street widened into a great square, 80 m wide as far as the eastern gate, with two great staircases for the convenience of the pilgrims. The thirty steps were made of different widths, with two to four narrow ones to one wide one, to make the way easier for pilgrims.

Plan of the Umayyad palace

LAYOUT OF THE
UMAYYAD PALACE:
A. Outhouses
B. Concourse from
   the Second Temple
   Period.
C. Staircase connecting
   the palace floors.
14. Display of the devices
    used to elevate and
    transport large
    building stones.
15. Staircase leading
    to the medieval
    area building and
    facing towards the
    excavation area.
16. Spiral staircase made
    of metal which leads
    to the Byzantine era
    building.

Between the Double Gate and the Triple Gate two complete rows of small rooms of equal size were found; these were probably ritual baths for worshippers. Coins from the time of Herod and from the First Revolt were found in these buildings.

The Temple and the Holy of Holies were located on the mount between the two gates, and pilgrims generally entered through the eastern (Triple) gate, circled the Temple, and left through the western gate. Mourners and outcasts entered through the western gate and left by way of the eastern gate, so that the public could comfort and support them. This is explained in the *Mishnah* (*Middot* I, 2). "All who entered the Temple Mount entered by the right and went round [to the right] and went out by the left, save for one to whom something untoward had happened, who entered and went round to the left. [If he was asked] Why do you go round to the left? [If he answered] Because I am a mourner [they said to him] He who dwells in this house comfort thee. [If he said] Because l am excommunicated [they said] May he who dwells in this house inspire them to befriend thee again."

Remnants of dwellings of the Herodian, Roman, Byzantine and Umayyad periods were found along the Street of the Towns and the remains of a large, many-chambered Byzantine building were found south of the Triple Gate.

The District of the Rule of the Umayyads

According to M. Ben Dov (*The New Encyclopedia of Archeological Excavations in Eretz Israel*, Jerusalem, 1992 (Hebrew), p. 719), six edifices were constructed in the Umayyad district, two of which were large structures – palaces – each of which measured 95 × 85 m. In Ben Dov's opinion, the palaces were not completed in the Umayyad period. In the Abassid period, their Umayyad enemies conquered Jerualem and took it from the Jebusites. The palaces were destroyed and from their stones the Abassid produced lime; 15 lime furnaces were discovered amongst the palaces' ruins.

The Byzantine Quarter South of The Temple Mount

South of the Temple Mount, next to the southern wall, Mazar's expedition discovered building remnants from the Second Temple period. One of the impressive buildings is from Herod's time, which was built dovetailing with the walls of the building from the First Temple period. In this house, from the Second Temple period, ten rooms were uncovered, as well as waterholes and graded reservoirs.

*At the top: the southwestern corner of the Temple Mount containing an excavated
water channel; at left: Robinsons' Arch; at the bottom: corner of Umayyad palace;
at its left: dye-shop uncovered during the excavations of Professor Mazar*

In the excavations south of the Temple Mount, a Byzantine living quarter
from the fourth to sixth centuries was discovered (*New Encyclopedia, op. cit.*,
pp. 696–697). The quarter was built south of the Temple Mount, surrounded
by buildings with open courtyards as well as two-story rooms and cellars
hewn in the rock. The walls of the houses were plastered with fresco paintings
and stucco. In many of the houses, mosaics were found, within which there
were Greek writings quoting verses of Holy Scripture. The roofs of the houses
were of wood, and the rooms had stone arches holding up the ceilings. In the
courtyards and rooms, industrial equipment for painting clothes and ovens
for melting metals were discovered.

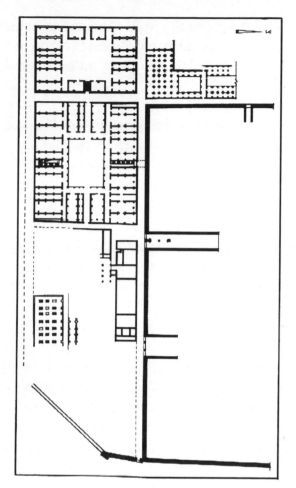

The Umayyad buildings on the south-western Temple Mount

South of the Triple Gate, in the southern part of the Temple Mount, a Byzantine structure, impressive in size and shape (two stories), was found above the cellar level. The structure was probably built in the days of the Empress Eudocia, in the middle of the fifth century B.C.E., and was originally used as a lodge or monastery. Most of the structures were destroyed during the Persian conquest in 614.

In the Byzantine Quarter, in the portion southwest of the Temple Mount, a plastered stone lintel was uncovered, and upon it was drawn in red plaster a seven-branched candelabra. Under this was a palm branch and perhaps even a *shofar* and an *etrog*. Additional paintings of the seven-branched candelabra, and notches for placing *mezuzahs* in the open doorways were also found. These artifacts indicate that Jews resided here, in the days of the Persian conquest in 614 or in the era of the Arab conquest of Jerusalem in 638 C.E. The Byzantine structures were inhabited also in the days of the Arab rule in Jerusalem, which was destroyed in 748 C.E. by an earthquake.

The Umayyad Capital City

Six buildings, mentioned above, were erected in the Umayyad period, among them two large ones, palaces, each of which was 95 m long and 85 m wide.

The large building found south of the south-west wall of the Temple Mount and of the paved Umayyad street is also Umayyad, with an area of 90 × 100 m. Its walls are 2–2.5 m thick, constructed with the blocks and columns scattered after the ruin of the Second Temple and the Roman-Byzantine city. The edifice resembles the square palaces of the Umayyad rulers, such as Khirbet Mafjar, north of Jericho, and el-Miniya, west of Lake Kinneret (= the Lake of Gallilee). The building consists of a large, two-story structure, centered on an open courtyard, and surrounded by a portico and a series of rooms, with a magnificent gate in the center of the eastern wall. At a later period the gate was transferred to the northern wall, facing the paved street. A series of rooms was discovered west of the building, decorated inside with frescos in the Umayyad style of geometric patterns, B. Mazar assumes it was a bathhouse. West of the building, near its north-west corner, a vat was found, hewn from a single piece of rock. It consisted of two basins, with a connecting pipe near the base. In the pavement east of the vat there was a plastered water channel. The installation was most likely part of a dyeing plant.

The Cufic (early Arabic) inscription on an ashlar from a later building in the area gives the date as 82 A.H. (701 C.E.), and the large building is therefore assumed to have been built in the time of 'Abd el-Malik, builder of the Dome of the Rock (685–705 C.E.). Opinions differ as to its purpose and use. According to one theory it was the ruler's house and a guest house for noble pilgrims. M. Rosen-Ayalon thinks the building was a palace from the time of al-Walid I; M. Ben Dov suggests that it was used by the servants of the Haram.

The building was badly damaged in the earthquake of 747–48, but restoration work was carried out on the building and its system of channels during the Abbasid period. A new gate was opened in the northern wall, on to the paved street, in place of the eastern gate. Large-scale construction work on the city walls and the Temple Mount area began during the time of the Caliph e-Dhahir (1033 C.E.) and the city wall at this point may well date from this period. Gold coins from the days of el-Mu'iz to the time of el-Mustansir, son

Remains of Umayyad palace south of the Temple Mount (A. Erev)

Elevated concourse at the Temple Mount steps and the El Aqsa Mosque (A. Erev)

*Ceiling of a room in the Byzantine quarter in the southern
part of the Temple Mount (A. Erev)*

The Cardo at the Dung Gate (A. Erev)

Sheep in the Judean desert, with the Horkenos Citadel in the background (M. Har-El)

Ritual bath from the Second Temple period at the southern wall of the Old City (A. Erev)

Ritual bath, as above. Photo: (A. Erev)

*Aruv aqueduct penetrates below the southern wall of the
Old City towards the Temple Mount (A. Erev)*

*Pilgrims' path, with original flooring from the Second Temple period,
in the Cheesemakers' Valley. Section of Robinson's Arch (to the left
of the wall) and shops on the left side of the path (A. Erev)*

Ancient channel near the Dung Gate. Photo: (A. Erev)

Corner of the Nea Church jutting out from the southern wall of the Old City (A. Erev)

of e-Dhahir, were found in the Fatimid building. Settlement in this area ceased at the time of the Seljuk Conquest (1071). A hoard of 77 silver coins minted at Chartres in France in 1200 C.E. was found from the Crusader period. Some remnants of the Mameluke period were also found. The southern and western walls of the city apparently also date from this time. In the days of Suleiman the Magnificent the eastern gate of the building was blocked up, thus closing up the eastern side of the building, which fell into disuse from that time and using the Ummayyad walls as foundation to the present eastern wall. A Byzantine mosaic floor was found under the Umayyad palace, and beneath this a paved square dating to Herodian times.

Part of the palace was restored in the year 1997. North of the western entrance to the palace a toilet cubicle was preserved, and below it a drainage channel ("A" on the map, see page 236). Under the northern section an open space was revealed, the floor of which was tiled with large stones from the Second Temple period ("B" on the map). East of it a staircase was discovered leading to the upper floors ("C" on the map). The palace in the south and the El-Aqsa mosque in the north were connected by a bridge.

A good view of all the excavations south of the Temple Mount can be had from the tall building remaining from the Middle Ages (15 on the map).

Finds in the Excavations at the Southern Part of Temple Mount

Among the finds were pottery, stoneware, coins and inscriptions. The sherds include a handle bearing a *Lamelekh* למלך stamp of the First Temple period, as well as cookware and a decanter, a small jug, a pot, and other Herodian artifacts. Singles and pottery vessels bearing the symbol of the Tenth Roman Legion were found, and a pottery oil lamp of the the fourth century C.E., decorated with a nine-branched candelabrum with a *shofar* on its right and a censer on its left. Among the Herodian stoneware were a stone altar and a vessel for offerings, with the Hebrew word *Korban* (sacrifice) and two bird figures carved on it. There were fragments of two sundials and a Corinthian stone capital, which ornamented the Temple wall and the Royal Portico. Up to 15,000 coins were found, some dating to Alexander Jannaeus and others to Herod. There were coins from the four years of the Revolt, coins of the Roman Emperor Vespasian (73 C.E.) and of the Byzantine Emperors Constantine, Theodosius I and II, Eudocia and Justinian (527–566 C.E.), gold coins from the Fatimid period (985–1056 C.E.) and silver Crusader coins. The earliest inscription is engraved on a limestone slab and is a dedication to Septimius

Severus and his family (202–205 C.E.) on the occasion of the completion of a public building (or possibly of a water system). Byzantine inscriptions were also found on sherds, and there were three fragments of Arabic inscriptions of the Umayyad or Fatimid periods. The most interesting find was discovered in the south-west corner of the Temple Mount wall, a stone bearing a carved inscription in Hebrew: *le-veit ha-teqi'ah*. This stone must have come from a building at the south-west tip of the Temple Mount courtyard, where the *shofar* was sounded to notify the townspeople of the onset of the Sabbath.

The Western Wall

After the destruction of the Second Temple, the Western Wall symbolized the Temple to the Jewish pilgrims who came to express their yearning for Jerusalem. When Jews were forbidden to live in Jerusalem they used to pray at several sites: on the Temple Mount, as long as they were allowed entry; on the Mount of Olives, from which the Temple Mount could be seen (the High Priest burned the Red Heifer on the Mount of Olives, and it was therefore a sacred spot, devoted to prayer and worship; at the end of the *Sukkoth* festival the pilgrims would circle it seven times; at the eastern wall, near the Mercy Gate, because of their faith that the Messiah would enter Jerusalem at that point; in front of all the gates to the Temple Mount, including the southern wall, where Professor Mazar found a clay lamp brought by Jewish pilgrims in the time of Julian; and near the Western Wall, of which it is said: "The Holy *Shekhinah* Presence never moves away from the Western Wall' " (*Midrash Song of Songs Rabbah*). The reference is to the Temple itself and not the Temple Mount.

About the Western Wall it was said that "the Divine Presence will never leave the Western Wall, as it is said that 'He stands behind our Wall.'" According to the author, the Western Wall was the most sacred place, because those engaged in prayer in the Holy Temple would turn west towards the Mediterranean, the source of rain.

B. Mazar's expedition found a Hebrew inscription on a block of the sixth course under Robinson's Arch. It is believed to date from the fourth century C.E., and is a quotation from *Isaiah* (XLVI, 14): "And when ye see this, your heart shall rejoice, and your bones shall flourish like young grass." This is part of the prophecy of verses 13–14: "As one whom his mother comforteth, so will I comfort you, and ye shall be comforted in Jerusalem and the hand of the Lord shall be known toward His servants, and He will have indignation against His enemies."

The Pilgrim of Bordeaux (333 C.E.) wrote that (on the Temple Mount) there were two statues of Hadrian, and not far from the statues was a perforated stone which the Jews used to visit every year, to make libations of oil, mourn and lament and sigh, rend their clothes, and sit there. Hieronymus, the Church Father who lived in Bethlehem and Jerusalem during the fourth and early fifth centuries, noted that the Jews were allowed to enter Jerusalem only on the Ninth of Av, to lament the destruction of Jerusalem. Of the pilgrims it was said: "In silence they go up, in silence they come down, in weeping they go up, in weeping they come down, in the dark of night they go up, in the dark of night they come down" (*Lamentations Rabbah*, 17–19). The wall is therefore known to non-Jews as "the wall of weeping", "the wall of tears" or "the wailing wall." Yehezkel Judah noted that the Western Wall of the Temple was mentioned as a holy site as early as the time of Rabbi Yohanan Ben Zakkai, and that the *Shekhinah* had never left it. It was mentioned as a place of Jewish prayer from the time of the Caliph Omar. Rabbis, as well as Karaites and Christians, reported the presence of a synagogue there.

The Wall has always been a place of prayer and meditation for the Jews of Jerusalem, as well as for pilgrims from all over the country and from abroad.

Benjamin of Tudela, who visited Jerusalem from 1168 to 1170, wrote of the *Templum Domini*, on the site of the Temple, over which Omar ibn al-Khattab had built a great, very beautiful, dome. The gentiles did not bring there a statue or picture, but only came to pray. The Western Wall, one of the walls of the Temple, of the Holy of Holies, was in front of it and was called the Gate of Mercy, and all the Jews used to come there to pray at the Wall.

Rabbi Ishtori HaPharhi, who immigrated to the Land of Israel in 1322 and was the first to explore it thoroughly, noted that the walls still standing were those of the Temple Mount. The Shushan Gate in the east and Ciponos Gate in the west could still be seen. Although Israel, because of its sins, could not enter the Temple, it was possible to approach the walls to pray.

Throughout the sixteenth and seventeenth centuries visitors to the Holy Land wrote of going to pray at the Western Wall of the Temple.

The Wall was sanctified in the twentieth century by the Moslems and called el-Burak, after the horse ridden by Mohammed, according to the legend, on his ascent to Heaven and his journey to the furthest mosque (the location of which, at the seventh heaven of Mecca or Jerusalem, is a matter for argument): "Praised be He who brought His servant by night from the Holy Mosque (Mecca) to the furthest mosque" (*The Koran, The Night Journey*, 17).

The Western Wall of the Temple Mount is 485 m long. The southern section, 57 m long, from the Moslem Court and Wilson's Arch to the Gate of the Moors (Barclay's), was of great importance, since it included the bridges connecting the Upper and Lower Cities, as well as the royal portico at the southern end of the Temple area and the gate linking the Upper City with the portico and the Temple. Warren discovered, by means of a shaft at the Western Wall, 26 courses of great stones, seven of which were originally visible and beautifully dressed in the Herodian style, with margins and bosses (two of these were uncovered by Prof. B. Mazar after the Six Day War), and 15 which were below the surface originally. Four courses of smooth blocks (apparently from the time of Aelia Capitolina) are visible above the Herodian courses and the wall is surmounted by seventeen courses of small stones of a much later date. The tumbledown shacks near the Wall were cleared after the Six Day War, and the Western Wall from Wilson's Arch to the south-west corner is now 175 m long.

Various nineteenth century travelers wrote of Jews having to pay the government for the privilege of praying at the Wall. One Englishman, J. Finn, writing of the period 1853–56, reported that, in addition to paying 300 pounds sterling annually for the right to pray at the Wall, the Jews also had to pay 100 pounds to the villagers of Silwan to prevent the destruction of the graves on the Mount of Olives, 30 pounds to the tribe of Arab e-Ta'amreh to prevent damage to Rachel's Tomb, and a further sum to safeguard the passage of travelers through Abu Ghosh.

Moses Montefiore, in his impressions of his seventh journey to the country, in 1875, wrote of his great efforts to make the Western Wall into a place of awe. An agreement was made to carry this out, but a certain unforeseen and insurmountable obstacle arose, and the entire plan was canceled. One of the elders had tried unsuccessfully to place benches there for the numerous visitors who came to pray every day. He was then allowed to place several marble blocks to provide seats, but these did not remain there for long; they were stolen one by one (*Forty Days Sojourn in the Holy Land*, London 1875, p. 134).

Baron de Rothschild tried in 1887, under Turkish rule, to purchase the plaza at the Wall, but without success.

In 1912 the management of the Anglo-Palestine Bank took the initiative in trying to reclaim the area of the Wall, but the outbreak of war in 1914 put a stop to the negotiations.

In 1912 the Qadi (Moslem judge) of Jerusalem forbade the Jews to light candles at the Wall, or place benches in the square. At this period, the Moslems made efforts to deprive the Jews of their rights at the Wall. During the British Mandate period, an international inquiry commission decided in 1930 that ownership of the Western Wall was legally Arab, but the historical right of the Jews to pray at the Wall was also recognized. The decision did not allow *Torah* scrolls at the Wall, or benches or seats, nor the sounding of the *shofar* at the close of *Yom Kippur*. The British adhered to the decision, but the Jews thronged to pray at the Wall. A special group of the Betar youth movement was detailed to sound the *shofar*, aided by members of the *Irgun Tzvai Leumi* and the Stern Group; during the latter period of the Mandate the *shofar* was sounded every year at the close of *Yom Kippur*. The Old City, the Temple Mount and the Western Wall reverted to Jewish jurisdiction in the Six Day War.

The Western Wall, in its limited sense, was found to have included a gate, an arch and a bridge, which connected the Upper City and the Temple Mount, built in Herod's reign; remains of these structures have been found since 1865. In the 1850s, J.T. Barclay (*City of the Great King*, p. 281) discovered the remains of an ancient gate (which bears his name) at the foundations of the Gate of the Moors, 82 m north of the south-west corner of the Temple Mount wall. The height of the gate was 8.76 m and the length of the lintel 7.5 m. It was located in the twenty-second course of the Western Wall, in the same course as the water channel hewn out of the stones. N. Avigad assumes that flights of stairs led from the Tyropoeon Valley to Barclay's Gate ("The Architecture of Jerusalem in the Second Temple Period," *Kadmoniot, Quarterly for the Antiquities of Eretz Israel and Biblical Lands*, Nos. 1–2, 1968, p. 31). The alluvium which covered the Western Wall and filled the valley collected here after the city's southern wall, in the vicinity of the Dung Gate, had been built, damming the southward flow of the alluvium.

Robinson's Stairway

About 12 m north of the south-west corner of the Temple Mount there was a massive arch, under which the road ran along the western wall. The stairway was identified by the American explorer, Edward Robinson, in 1838. At present the Western Wall of the Temple Mount bears only part of the eastern spring of the arch, based on three courses with a total length of 15.25 m. The arch was 13.4 m wide. Judging by the distance from the Western Wall of the pier in Wilson's Bridge, which remained intact, B. Mazar found the base of the pier supporting the arch. The maximum height of the arch, near the valley, was 20 m.

The excavations of B. Mazar in 1971 revealed southwest of Robinson's Arch, the remains of the wide staircase, supported by arched structures of increasing height, rising from south to north. The stairs made a right-angled turn opposite the arch, joined the top of the arch and led to an opening in the wall. This was the gate used by Herod and the royal entourage to reach the Royal Portico at the south of the Temple Mount. This portico is mentioned by Josephus (*Antiquities* xv, 11): "...and this cloister deserved to be mentioned better than any other under the sun; for while the valley was very deep, and its bottom could not be seen if you looked from above into the depth, this farther vastly high elevation of the cloister stood upon that height."

A paved street ran the entire length of the Western Wall, underneath Robinson's Arch, northward to Wilson's Bridge and beyond; Mazar calls it the "main street." The street was 12.5 m wide. Pilgrims who entered the city by way of the Damascus or Jaffa Gates passed along this main street, and at the southwest corner of the Temple Mount turned eastwards along the foot of the wall; remains of this section have also survived. The street eventually reached the Huldah Gates, through which the pilgrims entered the Temple Mount.

The excavations conducted by B. Mazar during 1968–1978 and by R. Reich and Y. Billig during 1995–1996, revealed a 70 m paved street at the south-western part of the Temple Mount. From the collapse of the Temple wall after the destruction of the Second Temple, as revealed by the archeologists, we recognize the intensity of the mutiny and the ravages under Robinsons' stairway.

The road is 10 m wide with raised curbstone. The stones that pave the road are 2–4 m. In Reich's opinion these enormous stones date from the time of Agripas II who ruled during the mid first century and conducted massive construction works on the Temple Mount (*Kadmoniot*, xx, 9, 7). On both sides of the street, beneath the arch, 20 booths were revealed with gates to the street and covered with stone arches, probably functioning as shops. In the shops were some scale stones illustrating the commercial manner of the street. Underneath the pavement, draining systems for rain water were discovered.

Among the findings was also a Roman milestone bearing a Latin script with the names of the Emperors Vespasian and Titus, as well as that of the Tenth Legion. Also found were living quarters dating from Second Temple days and the Roman and Byzantine periods. At the corner of the Temple Mount, stairs made of hewn stone and leading to the shops' rooftops were revealed, together with coins dating from the second, third and fourth years of the great revolt.

Jewish tradition obligates every visitor to the Temple Mount to purify his body: "The Temple Mount is holier than it... The Temple is holier than that, no one can enter it without having washed his hands and feet" (*Kelim*, 1:8–9). And indeed, west of Robinsons' Arch public ritual baths were discovered, used by pilgrims during the Second Temple period, as well as a ritual bath that had been dug out from rock and plastered. Down the middle of the flight of stairs leading to it there was a bannister separating between those entering and those leaving the bath.

A large structure, north of Robinson's stairway, was believed by B. Mazar to be Jerusalem's archive which is mentioned by Josephus (*Wars*, vi, 6, 3).

Warren found a vaulted water conduit running from north to south about 22 m under Robinson's Arch, at the foundation of the wall. The lower part of the conduit was cut out of the bedrock, and the upper part roofed by blocks.

Inscription on the Western Wall reads: "And when you will see this, your heart will rejoice and your bones will flourish like an herb." (Isaiah 66:14). The inscription was made by a Jewish pilgrim in the Talmudic era.

The conduit was 3.6 m from the wall, 3.6 m high and 1.2 m wide. The water was conveyed to a rock-cut cistern, 4.8 m in diameter and 4.3 m high, with a roof 0.6–0.9 m thick. Warren reported that a paved street ran along the foot of the Western Wall to the Dung Gate, with houses on either side and drainage running beneath it. Mazar rediscovered this covered channel under the pier of Robinson's Arch, and it is being prepared for public viewing.

Wilson's Arch and the Bridge Above It

This bridge was first discovered by Tobler in 1835, and studied and published in 1865 by Ch. Wilson, after whom it is named. The bridge apparently had two main functions: connecting the Chamber of Hewn Stone, in the Upper City, with the Temple, a distance of 90 m (the Gate of the Chain in our days is the heir of a Second Temple Gate here) and serving also to carry the two aqueducts, which brought water from the Hebron Mountains and reached the Temple Mount at this point.

Wilson's Arch adjoins the Western Wall and forms the ceiling of an underground hall. It was cleaned by the Israel Ministry of Religion. The arch can be reached from two entrances, one at the northern end of the Western Wall square and the other in a building some 50 m due west of the former entrance today the western wall tunnels entrance – today the Western Wall tunnels entrance.

The hall of the arch includes two illuminated shafts, originally sunk by Warren. The eastern shaft, adjoining the Western Wall, is 18.5 m deep, and gives a view of 17 courses of Herodian masonry. The western shaft is 8 m deep and leads to a built-up entrance.

A road along the Western Wall, from the Antonia fortress along the entire length of the Tyropoeon Valley to the Siloam Pool was found 8 m below Wilson's Bridge. The pavement of this street was broken through by Warren in his efforts to reach bedrock at the foundation of the Wall. The road, which was paved with slabs at least 1 m × 1 m in size, was overhung by the arches supporting the road into the Temple Mount.

The eastern side of Wilson's Bridge is scarred by square depressions. These also existed in the western wall of the bridge, but were later plastered over. Such depressions are known in many vaulted structures such as "Solomon's Stables." They were made for the purpose of building scaffolding for the construction of the vaults. Later they were covered (e.g. by plaster) but not always.

The structure immediately adjoining the bridge to its west consists of

Wilson's Arch

many vaults and arches; it has a central corridor, barrel-vaulted, running from east to west. On each side of the corridor is a series of vaulted chambers arranged in one or more rows. The corridor, which is 2.8 m wide, leads from the square of the Western Wall to a wicket gate which gives access to Wilson's Bridge. Underneath the rows of chambers is another vaulted series, connected at some points with the upper series. The repairs carried out in the lower series, as well as the entire upper complex, are from the eighth century C.E., from the Umayyad, Crusader and Mameluke periods. This is demonstrated by the character of the masonry and the arch in the corridor, which resemble the Umayyad stonework found in the palace of that period south of the Temple Mount wall. The smaller stones in Wilson's Arch are also apparently Umayyad or later. Evidence of Crusader activity is found in the arches in some of the side rooms.

During the Mameluke period the corridor served as a passageway from the west, from the upper part of the city to the Temple Mounts. However, the corridor and its flanking rooms were used as storerooms from the Mameluke period onwards, since the level of the street had risen to that of the Street of the Chain leading to the Gate of the Chain. The storehouses of the Old City of today were all chambers in antiquity. The Street of the Chain lies at present 5.5 m above the arch.

This bridge probably led to a gate through which the people entered the Temple. The bridge is mentioned by Josephus, and according to him it connected the Upper City and the Chamber of Hewn Stone (Xystos) with the Temple Mount (*Wars* II, 16,3; VI, 6,1). The western gates of the Temple are mentioned in *Antiquities* XV, 11.

The Tunnels of the Western Wall (Kotel)

Southwest of Wilson's Arch, a magnificent hall from the Second Temple period was discovered, called "the Herodian Hall." Built of hewn limestone, the hall features art depicting Corinthian headings in its corners and along its walls. It is thought that here was the hewn limestone bureau or council building mentioned in the *Wars of the Jews* V, 4, 2.

Near the Western Wall was uncovered a large stone that weighs about 550 tons and is part of the *Nidbakh Rabba* ("Master Course"). This course is triple (3.3 m) the average size and is a kind of belt tying and stabilizing the wall in its high places.

About 40 meters north of Wilson's Arch on the Temple Mount wall, Charles Warren discovered remnants of a gate (Warren's Gate), which originated from underground steps that ascended into the Temple Mount. Today it is covered by a later arch and closed up. Continuing down the tunnel, south of the northwestern corner of the Temple Mount, a quarry of large stones was discovered for building the Western Wall. This stood out in the Western Wall about 40 m long by 3 m wide.

An aqueduct in the north–south direction was discovered here by Konder and Warren in 1867, and rediscovered by the archaeologist D. Bahat. According to Bahat, the aqueduct that passes high up the tunnel is from the Hasmonean period and the aqueduct waters lead to the Baris – the early Second Temple Period fortress that protected the Temple Mount from the north, to be replaced by Herod when he constructed the Antonia.

To the best of my knowledge, this tunnel shows that the aqueduct was in use even in Solomon's and Hezekiah's days. Following is the evidence:

1. The natural tunnel, 10–12 m high and very narrow, has a covered ceiling built from large, rectangular stones. This ceiling and its stones are similar to the water tunnel ceiling of Givon in Benjamin, also built in the days of the First Temple.

2. This tunnel is natural, mostly karstic, as asserted by the geologist D. Niv,

who states that even during previous geological periods, the water flowed down, smoothing the walls to a high gloss.

3. I assume that with the building of the Solomon's Temple, there was a need for fresh water in the Temple, to purify the sacrifices and prevent sickness and disease from the blood, excrement and waste of the sacrifices, as in the days of the Second Temple (M. Har-El, "The Water for Purification, Hygiene and Ritual in the Temple in Jerusalem," *The Land of Israel, The Company for Excavations in the Land of Israel and Its Ancient Ruins*, 1987, pp. 310–313).

Indeed, on the altar Solomon built in the Temple, at the dedication of the Temple, 142,000 animals were sacrificed (*I Kings* VIII, 63; IX, 25); and in Hezekiah's day, at Passover, 607 oxen and 3,000 sheep (*II Chronicles* XXIX, 32–33).

From this derives the name of the Jewish tunnel, "the Tunnel of King Solomon and of the Judean and Hasmonean kings." In the last days of the Second Temple, the Hasmoneans drew the aqueduct water from the spring to the Temple Mount, to the tune of 60 cu m per hour.

The Dung Gate

The Dung Gate, in the southern wall of the Old City, is the lowest one, lying 725 m above sea level. The present gate is in the central part of the Tyropoeon Valley. We believe that the original Dung Gate was at the southern tip of the Valley, near the Ben-Hinnom Valley (see Chapter on the Walls and Gates of the City in the First Temple period).

The gate may have existed in the Roman city of Aelia Capitolina, since it is represented on the Madaba map. It is alluded to by the Pilgrim of Bordeaux when describing his journey from the Temple Mount to the Pool of Siloam, and Antoninus also mentioned an arch which was part of an ancient gate on the way down to Siloam. It is possible that the present gate may have been built originally by the Mamelukes, as the pillow arch of the gate resembles certain archways on the Temple Mount which date from the Mameluke period. To this day Mameluke buildings exist around the Temple Mount, mainly at the Lions' Gate, the Single Gate, the Dark Gate, the Cotton Gate and the Dung Gate, which was originally the smallest gate of Jerusalem.

Muqaddasi called this gate Bab Silwan, after the Gihon spring, which is also known as Ein Silwan. Shams e-Din e-Suyuti, who visited Jerusalem in 1470, called it the Moors' Gate, explaining that the Bab el-Maghariba (Gate of the Moghrabis, or north-western Africans) is so-called because it is in the neighborhood of the Gate of the Mosque of the Moghrabis. The quarter named from this gate is in the south-east corner of the city. The gate is also known as Bab e-Nabi, the Gate of the Prophet. Mujir e-Din called it Bab Harat (quarter) al-Maghariba, Gate of the Western African Quarter, after the Moslems who emigrated from Algiers and Morocco. The Crusaders knew it as the Tanners' Gate, since the water needed by the tannery trade was supplied from the Pool of Siloam through the gate.

The Dung Gate was closed under Turkish rule except in the late summer periods, when because of a lack of water, skinfuls were brought to the city from the Gihon and Ein Rogel. Barclay reported that on October 26, 1852, one thousand donkeys hauled skins of water from Ein Rogel to the city. On September 12, 1853, 2,000 donkeys carried 4,000 skinfuls to Jerusalem every day, reaching a total amount of 25,000 gallons (113 cu m).

The Dung Gate may be reached by three roads: along the Kidron Valley in the east by the road which branches off the Jericho road near Gethsemane, south-east of the Lions' Gate; in the west from the Jaffa Gate, along the road branching off from the Hebron Road toward the south-east, at the foot of the southern wall; and in the south from Mount Zion, along the one-way road passing the Church of St. Peter in Gallicantu.

The Upper City

During the Six Day War, on June 7, 1967, a force of the Jerusalem Division swept down "Mount Zion" and entered the Old City through the Dung Gate, taking and clearing the Jewish and Armenian quarters. This seems to have been the only time in history that the Old City was breached in the south through the Dung Gate. The Jerusalem Division met up with the paratroopers, who had come through the Lions' Gate, at the Citadel, the last stronghold of the Zealots in their Revolt against the Romans in 70 C.E., and thus completed the conquest of the Old City of Jerusalem.

The Remnants of the Secondary Cardo Next To the Dung Gate

The secondary Cardo, which appears on the Madaba map, went the length of the Valley of Tyropoeon, past the Dung Gate. C.N. Jones and R.W. Hamilton discovered it in the beginning of the 1930s. In the 1970s, M. Ben Dov uncovered part of the route from the west to the Dung Gate of today and beyond the walls. This portion is 12 m wide and is paved with large, broad slabs of stone, underneath it was a drainage ditch. To the west, a column of pillars was discovered, with several of its bases hewn out of the rock. West of these pillars, is a paved stair 3 m wide, with a number of hewed spaces used as shops. On the southern tip of the open street portion forks a side street that rises westward to "Mount Zion" (M. Ben Dov, *The New Encyclopedia, ibid.*, p. 703).

The Ayyubid Tower

About 33 m west of the present-day Dung Gate, Bielig and Reich in 1995 discovered the Ayyubid Gate, built by the Ayyubid Sultan, Malik al Mu'attam 'Issa (1180–1227). This gate opened both outward and inward (A on the map). From the south and the north to the gate, the secondary Cardo was exposed, which apparently dates from Roman and Byzantine times (B on the map).

The gate was discovered in the tower (under the later Turkish wall) that al Malek al-Mu'attam 'Issa built in 1202–1212, when he fortified the tower walls of Jerusalem against the Crusades. The Sultan destroyed the walls he built in 1219, for fear that the Crusaders, who then invaded Egypt, might conquer the land and the fortified city and build new fortifications. With the building of the Turkish wall, the Turks plugged the Ayyubid Gate and built the present-day Dung Gate. North of this gate, the remnants of an Umayyad palace – one of the six which were uncovered – is visible.

About 50 meters southwest of the Ayyubid Gate, near the Ma'aleh Hashalom Way, a ritual bath (*mikveh*) from the Second Temple period was discovered, along with cisterns hewn into the rock and plastered.

Tower from The Middle Ages

About 20 m southwest of the *mikveh* and cisterns, a tower was discovered attached to the corner of the Turkish Wall, which is a part of the Ayyubid fortifications of the city (D on the map). Under this and under the Turkish Wall lies an aqueduct from the Second Temple period, conducting water from the Solomon's Pools to the Temple Mount by means of an Ottoman clay pipe (C on the map). South of the tower, a purifying *mikveh* from the Second Temple period was discovered, and about 10 m westward another *mikveh*, which had a double opening and stairs (E on the map).

In the other corner of the Turkish Wall, remnants of an obtruding corner that crosses the wall were found. This is the southern continuance of the tremendously large Byzantine Nea Church, that was built at the southern edge of the Byzantine Cardo in the Upper City.

A. Street in the secondary Cardo paved with stones from the Herodian or Byzantine era

B. Cistern from the Second Temple Period

C. Building from the Byzanatine or ancient Arabic era

D. Tower, part of medieval fortification, and pipe from the acqueduct "Solomon's Pools" from the Ottoman period

E. Ritual bath with two openings and stairs from the Second Temple Period

F. Byzantine water well

G. Ritual bath with double opening

H. Lower acqueduct from "Solomon's Pools" from Second Temple Period

I. Southeastern corner of the Nea Church protruding outside the later city wall

J. Public Byzantine building

K. Ottoman Sulphur Tower built on the remains of an Ayyubi tower

L. Another section of the lower acqueduct from the Second Temple Period, in which a pipe was laid in the 16th century

M. Gate tower from the Ayyubi period

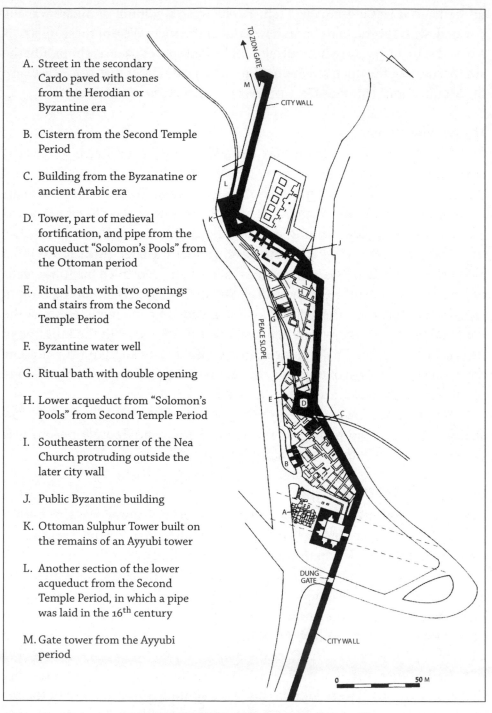

Remains of buildings of the city's southern wall between the Dung and Zion Gates in the Beth Shalom Garden

The Zion Gate

This is the southwestern gate of the City, located between the Armenian Quarter in the west and the Jewish Quarter in the east, at a height of 770 m. A gate of the Roman Aelia Capitolina was nearby. This gate is probably represented on the sixth-century Madeba map. El-Muqaddasi called it Bab Sahiyun, i.e., Zion Gate. The Crusaders knew it as the Zion Gate since, following El-Muqaddasi, they identified Mount Zion nearby. However, it is not clear whether this was the gate stormed by the Crusaders under Raymond St. Gilles, or whether there was another gate west of this.

Mujir e-Din wrote of Bab Sahiyun, known as the Bab Hart al Yahud, or Gate of the Jews' Quarter, founded by Nachmanides in 1267. A fragment from the Cairo Genizah (tenth or eleventh century C.E.) notes that, under the patronage of Omar, the Jews settled near the Temple Mount and the Dung Gate.

According to the inscription of Suleiman the Magnificent, found on the gate-tower, the gate was erected in 1540–41 C.E. (927 A.H.). It had a low, pointed arch, with firing-slits on both sides of the gate, 2 m above the floor; these are surmounted by a Mameluke pillow-pattern arch (similar to the arch of the Lions' Gate), topped by flower-carved discs in the Turkish style. It can thus be assumed that the lower part of the gate is Ayyubid, as proved by the excavations at the gate, and the upper sections Turkish. The Arabs know it as Bab a-Nabi Daud, the Gate of the Prophet David, because the traditional tomb of David is nearby. During Turkish rule the key to this gate was held by Jews. In the War of Independence twenty-two *Palmah* fighters broke through this gate and reached the besieged Jewish Quarter with its 1,600 inhabitants, who were at that time concentrated in the Hurvah Synagogue. Because of the acute shortage of arms, ammunition and manpower, the relieving force had to retreat, and the Quarter then surrendered. Following the evacuation, the Jordanians destroyed the synagogues of the Quarter, most of which have today been restored.

The Tomb of David on "Mount Zion" (The Upper City)

In the chapter dealing with Jerusalem in the First Temple period, and particularly the section on "Mount Zion" and the City of David, we noted that the true "Mount Zion" was in the Lower City. A part of the First Temple City wall was found during Professor Avigad's excavations in the present-day Jewish Quarter. The Hasmonean masonry found on the western slope of the hill known today

as Mount Zion, in the courtyard of Bishop Gobat's School and in the Citadel
("David's Tower"), make it quite clear that the city expanded west to Mount
Zion at the end of the First Temple period or under the Hasmoneans. Thus
we see that the site of David's tomb was also in the Lower City.

At the end of the Roman period a Jewish synagogue was built in the
entrance hall of the structure known traditionally as "David's Tomb." The architect J. Pinkerfeld discovered and identified the remains of this synagogue
on "Mount Zion" in 1949–51 (*Bi-Shevilei Omanut Yehudit*, Merhavia, 1957,
pp. 28–30; according to Professor H.Z. Hirschberg, *"Serideihem Shel Battei
Kenesset Kedumim beYerushalaim Kadmoniot"* *Quarterly for the Antiquities
of Eretz Israel and Biblical Lands*, Vol. 1, Nos., 1–2, 1968, pp. 56–59). The recess for the Ark of the *Torah* faced north toward the Temple Mount, and this
has been maintained in the restoration of the synagogue. In the courtyard
of David's Tomb and its southern wall there are large stone blocks from the
Roman period, probably from the synagogue structure, topped by smaller
Crusader stones in the wall of the Coenaculum (place of the Last Supper).
The synagogue was built on this site because of the belief that David brought
the Ark of the Covenant to this spot from Beth Shemesh and Kiryat-Yearim

Plan of "David's Tomb"

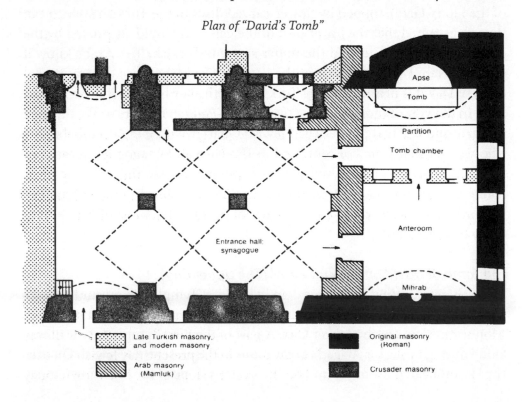

before the Temple was built. This was probably the source of the tradition identifying the site as David's Tomb and Mount Zion, as during the Byzantine period Jews were forbidden to settle in Jerusalem, and the true site of the royal tombs was forgotten. Mass pilgrimages to "David's Tomb" were carried out on the *Shavuot* festival, traditionally linked with the memory of King David. The rooms surrounding the courtyard were used by Franciscan monks.

The Christian tradition regarding the site of David's Tomb on "Mount Zion" is referred to in the *Acts of the Apostles*, II, 29: "…the patriarch David, that he is both dead and buried, and his sepulcher is with us unto this day."

Al-Tabari (838–923), who accepted the Christian tradition, noted that the Tomb of David is on "Mount Zion," and al-Muqaddasi (985) wrote that "the people of the Bible" located David's Tomb on "Mount Zion." Raymond of St. Gilles, the Crusader, who attacked Jerusalem from the direction of "Mount Zion" in 1099, notes holy places on the hill, among them the tombs of David and Solomon, the tomb of St. Stephen, and others. The Arab geographer Idrisi (1154) mentioned the Zion Gate and the Church of Zion, and the traveler Benjamin of Tudela (1070) mentioned the Tomb of David at this site. Mu'thir al-Ghiram (1351) also reported visiting the Church of Zion and the Mosque of David, near the Tomb of David. Hieronymus, however, who settled in Bethlehem in the fourth century C.E., instituted a tradition that the tomb of David was in that city; this belief persisted to the seventh century but eventually disappeared.

Parts of the structure known today as the "Tomb of David" were built by the Franciscans in the fourteenth century as part of the monastery and the room of the Last Supper. The Jews made repeated efforts to acquire the site of the Tomb and erect a synagogue, but without success. An anonymous pilgrim wrote in 1427 that the graves of David, Solomon and other kings lay beneath the Chapel of the Holy Spirit and were much venerated by the Jews, who made great efforts to purchase them from the Franciscan Brothers in order to establish a synagogue (J. Prawer, *"Minzar ha-Franciscanim be-Har Zion vi-Yehudei Yerushalayim ba-Meah ha-15," Bulletin of the Society for the Exploration of Israel and its Antiquities*, Vol. 14, 1–2, 1948). The Moslems, who later took over the hall and the Tomb, denied access to the Jews and forbade Christians to visit the room of the Last Supper. Only after the War of Independence, when the hill of Mount Zion became part of the Jewish section of Jerusalem, was a synagogue reestablished in the hall, as in the Roman period, and free access provided to the "Tomb of David" and to the room of the Last

Supper. The Tomb itself is wrapped in embroidered cloths, and surmounted by a Torah scroll inscribed on "Mount Zion" to commemorate the six million Jews killed during the Second World War. Some years ago, the south-eastern part of the building was turned by the Israel Ministry of Religion into the Cellar of the Holocaust. It holds remnants and displays of the Nazi extermination camps in Europe.

On the festival of *Shavuot*, which, according to tradition, is the date of death of King David, many Jews visit the Tomb of David.

CHAPTER VII

JEWISH QUARTER IN THE OLD CITY

The Jewish Quarter Through the Centuries

The Jewish Quarter of the Old City has not always been in its present location. Jews occupied different parts of the city at different times, trying always to get as close as possible to the Temple Mount and its walls. After the destruction of the Second Temple, the Jews wanted to erect a synagogue on the Temple Mount, in place of the ruined Sanctuary. The Pilgrim of Bordeaux wrote that there was a perforated stone on the Temple Mount where the Jews used to gather for prayers (B.Z. Dinaburg, *Zion* 3, 1929, p. 78). Although Jews were forbidden to settle in Jerusalem during the Roman and Byzantine periods, the existence at that time of a Jewish community was proved by the Hebrew inscription found in the course of B. Mazar's excavations at the south-west corner of the Temple Mount. The hermit Cyril of Scythopolis (Beth Shean) recounted that Mar Saba traveled to Constantinople in 512 C.E. to beg the emperor to ease the taxes of the poor people of Jerusalem, and Merinus appeared before the emperor to argue against freeing the Jews of taxes.

The synagogue on the Temple Mount is mentioned by Sibaos (661 C.E.) who reports that the Jews enjoyed freedom and aid under the Arabs, and eventually decided to rebuild the Temple of Solomon on the place known as the Holy of Holies. They used the foundations and remains of the ancient building and turned them into a synagogue. However, the Arabs would not tolerate this and banished the Jews from the spot (Dinaburg, *ibid.,*p. 73). According to E.L. Sukenik, there was, in the burial chamber within the Is'ardiyah *madrasa*

259

north of the Temple Mount, a Hebrew inscription describing Jewish pilgrims visiting the Holy Palace, which existed somewhere around the Temple Mount under the Arabs (Dinaburg, *ibid.,* p. 141). Dinaburg (Dinur) noted that the *piyyutim* (fragments of liturgical literature) from the Cairo *Genizah* mention a synagogue on the Temple Mount where a *sukkah* was built during the festival. A synagogue existed on the Temple Mount during the ninth and tenth centuries, up to the time of the Crusader Conquest of Jerusalem. Ben Meir, head of the Eretz Israel Yeshivah, noted that the courtyard of the Temple Mount was a place of assembly for the Jews in the time of Rabbi Mosi, in the first half of the ninth century C.E. (Dinaburg, *ibid.,* pp. 69–70). In the middle of the tenth century, Salmon ben Yeroham the Karaite lists three periods in the existence of synagogues on the Temple Mount:

1. Immediately after the Arab Conquest, the Jews were allowed inside the city to settle, and the courtyard of the Temple Mount was permitted as a place of prayer.
2. In the course of time the Jews were allowed only on to a small part of the Temple Mount.
3. The Jews were expelled from the Temple Mount (Dinaburg, *ibid.,* p. 72), but allowed to pray at one of the Gates.

According to Rabbi Bar Hiya, there was a synagogue on the Temple Mount until the Crusader Conquest of Jerusalem. In his words: "Therefore, the kings of Ishmael treated us well and permitted the Israelites to enter the Temple Mount and to build there houses of prayer and study, and all the Jewish exiles close to the Temple went up to it on feasts and holy days in lieu of the *Tamid* and *Mussaf* sacrifices."

The first Jewish Quarter was apparently in the vicinity of the Gate of the Moors and the Ciponos Gate in the southwest section of the Western Wall. After conquering the city, Omar asked the Jews where they preferred to live, and they asked to be allowed to settle in the south of the city, close to the site of the Temple and its gates, and near the waters of Siloam, which they could use for ritual bathing. Their wish was granted (*Sefer ha-Yishuv* II, p. 18). According to B.Z. Dinaburg, the Jewish Quarter was located near the Wall, which was sacred to the Jews (*Yisrael ba-Golah*, p. 54). There was thus a revival of the Jewish community under the Arabs.

The Jewish Quarter eventually expanded north of the Western Wall, and included the area between the Dung Gate in the south and the Damascus Gate in the north. After the quake of 1033, the Jews left their old neighborhood in the south and moved to the northeast. Supplementary evidence on this point was given by the Crusader assault on Jerusalem; after they had breached the city in the north, there was heavy fighting in the Jewish Quarter to defend the northern wall of the city. The Crusaders massacred the Jews of the northern quarter and burned their homes and synagogues (J. Prawer, *Toledot Mamlekhet ha-Tzalbanim be-Eretz Yisrael*, pp. 136, 141, 419, 426, 553).

After 1267, beginning with the arrival of the Ramban [Nahmanides], considered to be the father of the modern Jewish community of Jerusalem, the Jewish Quarter was established southwest of the Temple Mount, at first on "Mount Zion," and in the fourteenth or early fifteenth century they moved to the present Jewish Quarter.

The Jewish Quarter in More Recent Times

Jews from Spain settled in the country and in Jerusalem after their expulsion [from Spain], and especially in the sixteenth century, joining the Arab-speaking Jews of the land and acquiring the name of Musta'arabs. This Spanish immigration included rabbis and Jews of wealth, with considerable influence among the Turkish ruling classes. The magnificent synagogues of the Sephardi community were built during this period: the Rabbi Yohanan ben-Zakkai synagogue, the Eliyahu ha-Navi, the Central and the Istambuli. Ashkenazi Jews from Europe, who arrived in the country under the leadership of Rabbi Judah the Hassid in 1699, lived in poverty; they were unfamiliar with the language and customs of the city and suffered greatly from diseases, which were then widespread. The foundations of the Hurvah synagogue were laid at this time. The Moghrabi Jews from Morocco began arriving after the Spanish Jews; their numbers started to increase after the immigration of 1854. These communities were followed by Jews from other oriental countries, Georgia, Bukhara, Yemen, etc.

The cultural and economic standards of the Arab inhabitants of Jerusalem and its environs were low and their needs few. In consequence only 25–30% of the Jews of Jerusalem were able to make a living through commerce or craftsmanship; the rest were supported by the Jews of the Diaspora, who sent funds for the Jews of Jerusalem (*halukkah*). The Jews suffered considerably from the attitude of the government as well as from their neighbors. This situation existed until Mohammed 'Ali rebelled against the Turks and assumed power over the country in 1831. Under Ibrahim Pasha the Egyptian rulers established a new order in the country, made efforts towards its development, recognized the civil rights of the Jews and Christians, and restored property which had been wrested from these minorities. Montefiore proposed to Mohammed 'Ali that he should lease from him a hundred or more villages in order to settle Jews on the land; this would have been totally unthinkable under Turkish rule. The development of the country began to accelerate at this time. After the Egyptians left the country in 1840 (due to the intervention of Great Britain, Russia, Austria and Prussia, who backed the Turks), and with the investment of European capital which was aided by the capitulations, the European powers established consulates in Jerusalem to look after the interests of those of their citizens who had gone to live in Jerusalem. These included Christians as well as Jews.

There was a great surge of Jewish immigration from the 1850s onwards. This flow of people was primarily directed to Jerusalem. The increasing numbers of immigrants and tourists, with the attendant change in economic and cultural requirements, stimulated the economy of the city. New hotels were built at this time, and a brisk trade was carried on in religious articles, souvenirs and citrus fruit; construction work also increased. After permission was given to aliens to purchase land, Jews began owning plots beyond the city walls and erecting new living quarters, first around Jerusalem and eventually throughout the country. Jewish artisans built the Beth Ya'akov Synagogue in the courtyard of the Hurvah (1866), and the complex of Battei Mahaseh (beginning in 1862), as well as other buildings both within the walls and beyond them, such as Nahalat Shiv'ah.

Before the rule of the Egyptian Ibrahim Pasha the city had nine synagogues: the complex of the four Sephardi synagogues, four Ashkenazi synagogues, and the one of the Moghrabi community. After the Egyptian rule and the establishment of foreign consulates, there were sixty synagogues, divided about equally between the Sephardi and Ashkenazi communities. The magnificent synagogues of Jerusalem were built after the Crimean War: the Hurvah synagogue of the *Perushim* (disciples of the great Rabbi Eliyahu of Vilna, the *Gaon*), was built in 1866, and the Tifereth Yisrael (also known as Nissan Bek) synagogue of the *Hassidim* in 1872. The following schools were established alongside the synagogues: the Sha'arei Tzion, Ahavat Tzion, Beth Meir, Beth Ya'akov, Ohel Moshe, Hayyei Olam. The revived activity of the Jewish community under the stimulation of Montefiore and Rothschild led to the establishment of hospitals in Jerusalem to deal with the frequent epidemics, which swept the Jewish, Arab and Christian communities alike. The Rothschild Hospital was opened in 1854, Bikkur Holim in 1857, and Misgav Ladakh in 1879.

The traditionally-minded members of the community opposed the establishment of schools that offered a general education, for fear that the non-religious sections of the curriculum would estrange the pupils from their religious studies; the supporters of the general schools were ostracized by the leaders of the religious community. Nonetheless, the Vocational School for Girls was established by Montefiore in 1855, and the Laemel School in the same year. The Doresh Tzion School was founded later, and in 1868 the Alliance Israélite Universelle School and the Evelina de Rothschild School for Girls were opened.

There was also social and cultural activity. In 1863 the first Hebrew newspaper appeared in Jerusalem, *Ha-Levanon*. Later periodicals were *Ha-Havatselet, Ha-Ariel, Sha'arei Tzion* and *Yehudah vi-Yerushalaim*, which appeared once or twice a month.

The chief factor underlying the lack of economic development in the country was the poor road network. There were no carriages in the country until the 1870s, let alone paved roads or railways. Highwaymen ruled the rough tracks and cast their fear over the horse- and donkey-caravans of pilgrims and merchants. The ride from Jaffa to Jerusalem took sixteen hours. It was reported in *Ha-Levanon* that an Ark of the *Torah* brought from Kherson in Russia was carried from Jaffa to Jerusalem on the backs of 12 camels. The first carriage road from Jaffa to Jerusalem was opened in 1869, at the same time as the grand opening of the Suez Canal, to afford access to Franz Joseph, Emperor of Austria, who wished to visit the Holy City. The road shortened the route by six hours. Way stations were established at Ramleh, Sha'ar Hagai and Motza, west of Jerusalem. A Jewish hotel, stable and coffee-house were opened in Motza for the convenience of travelers. The carriage road facilitated postal services by Jewish drivers (P.Z. Grayevsky, *Zikkaron le-Hovevim Rishonim*, VII, p. 44). The first telegraph was installed in the country in 1866, and the railway from Jaffa to Jerusalem through Nahal Sorek was completed in 1892. The economic development of Jerusalem was greatly stimulated by these factors, which signaled the beginning of similar processes throughout the country and in Transjordan.

The elders of the ultra-religious immigrants who arrived in the middle of the nineteenth century did not encourage their sons to learn crafts; however, the generation born in the country was conscious of the need to master a trade, in order to be free of the dependence on donations. Certain of these youths went to Europe in order to study useful subjects. Sir Moses Montefiore, who visited the country seven times between 1825 and 1875, financed weaving shops, as well as the Israel Bek printing shop, which produced work in several European languages and in Hebrew.

Until the 1870s the Jews were wary of agricultural ventures in the vicinity of Jerusalem, for fear of robbers. However, the colony of Motza was founded by farmers in 1868, and after the establishment of the Mikveh Israel Agricultural School by Carl Netter in 1870, young Jews began to farm the land and to establish new colonies.

Synagogues in the Old City

After the surrender of the Jewish Quarter in the War of Independence, the Arabs wrought destruction on the synagogues; since the Six Day War the Jerusalem municipality has restored the most magnificent of these, and below I describe the main ones (see J. Pinkerfeld, *Battei ha-Kenesiyot be-Eretz Yisrael*, Mossad ha-Rav Kook, Jerusalem 1946).

Ramban Synagogue

Nahmanides (the *Ramban*), who was an exegete of the *Torah* and the *Talmud*, a poet and a physician, emigrated from Spain to Jerusalem in 1267, when he was 73 years old. During the last three years of his life he established the synagogue bearing his name, and revived the Jewish community after the Crusader massacre. The community then began to concentrate in its present quarter, opposite the Temple Mount.

In the Street of the Jews, in the western part of the Jewish Quarter, stands the building, which, according to tradition, was the synagogue of the Ramban at the end of the thirteenth century, although it is agreed by all the scholars who deal with the problem that this is not the case – that Nachmanides' synagogue was near the city wall, either inside or outside of it. A long, narrow corridor leads into the hall of the synagogue, which was divided by four great pillars into two porticos roofed over with circular vaults. According to Pinkerfeld, these pillars were from older buildings, as the capitals of three of them were Roman and the fourth Byzantine. They probably came from the Cardo.

Before the Six Day War, only the upper thirds of the columns supporting the roof were visible, as the remaining two-thirds were underground. After the war, in 1970, the four marble pillars were excavated, as were the floor and the two recesses for the Ark of the *Torah*. Rabbi Ovadiah of Bartenura, a Talmudic exegete, in describing the Ramban Synagogue in a letter in 1488, said that "the synagogue of Jerusalem was built over columns; it was long, narrow and dark, with no light except from the entrance, and it had a water cistern." Rabbi Moses Basola wrote in 1522 that "there was only one synagogue in Jerusalem. It was handsome, with four columns in a row. Its length was 63 *piedi* (feet) and its width 28. Inside the hall was a room with over sixty scrolls of the *Torah*. They prayed toward the east opposite the Temple, and the synagogue was lit only by the western doorway and the little window above it; even in the daytime lamps were used. The congregation was varied, with fifteen Ashkenazi householders and many Sephardim." (I. Ben Zvi, *Mas'ot Eretz Yisrael le-Rabi Moshe Basola*, Jerusalem, 1939, pp. 60–61). The synagogue was first seized from the Jews by Moslems in the early 15th century, and by the end of the sixteenth century had been taken over permanently. It became first a workshop for grinding raisins and then for producing honey, then a storehouse, and finally, up to the Six Day War, a cheese factory.

The Sephardi Synagogues

From 1516 onwards the Jewish community of Jerusalem was augmented by considerable numbers of immigrants from Spain, who arrived via Turkey. The Sephardi community built the Eliyahu ha-Navi synagogue in the center of the Jewish Quarter, at the southern end of the Jewish Quarter Road. The Yohanan ben Zakkai Synagogue was built several years later, and the Istambuly and Central Synagogues during the following decades. The four synagogues form a complex connected by a small courtyard, and constituted the center of the life of the Sephardi community. The interiors of all four were destroyed by the Jordanians but have now been restored in their traditional form.

Yohanan Ben Zakkai Synagogue

This synagogue has three entrances, one external, and the other two opening from the inner courtyard of the complex. The hall is elongated, facing east towards a double Ark of the *Torah*. The hall measures 20 m × 8.2 m and is 7.5 m high. The arched roof is divided into three: the central section is in the shape of an elongated cross, while the eastern and western sections have short, rounded arches. The three sections of the ceiling are separated by narrow arches. The walls contain wide recesses serving as cupboards or, in the southern wall, as windows. The windows, arranged in stories along the wall of the building, are Turkish in style, and provide maximum light and ventilation. In the center of the hall stood the *bimah*, the platform from which the service was conducted. This was octagonal, and approached by three small flights of stairs. The base was of stone, with a decorative iron grill, and over the lectern was an arch of iron.

Eliyahu Ha-Navi Synagogue

The hall has a dome in Turkish style with a diameter of 6.5 m, supported on a drum. This is placed over four barrel vaults separated by pendentives. In the center of the hall is a large stone *bimah*, the upper part made of wood, approached by steps. The Ark of the *Torah* is not on the centerline of the hall, but at its side. South of the Ark is the doorway leading to the inner courtyard connecting with the Yohanan ben Zakkai and Central Synagogues. In the west, a thin partition separates the hall from a small room used as a depository for worn-out religious articles and for tools. There were three women's galleries in the north and west. A niche in the north-west corner leads down by way of stairs to the Cave of the Prophet Elijah, a small cavern 3 m × 1.6 m wide, and 3 m high, where candles were lit there for good fortune. It seems to have been the remnant of an older structure.

The Central Synagogue

The hall of this synagogue resembles that of the Yohanan ben Zakkai Synagogue. Its dimensions are 12.8 m × 3.7 m. At the center of the wall is a tall double door, terminating in an arch slightly higher than the two symmetrical windows on either side. The hall has three cruciform vaults, supported by flat corbels. The Ark of the *Torah* covers the entire eastern wall; it is in an arched recess, with the women's gallery above it. The *bimah* was long and narrow, resembling that of the Yohanan ben Zakkai Synagogue. There were also benches along the walls.

The Istambuli Synagogue

This is the largest of the four synagogues. Its dimensions are 14.4 m × 15.5 m. Its height to the rim of the drum is 5.5 m, and to the summit of the dome 10 m. The walls are 1.2 m thick. The main door of the hall is near the Ark of the *Torah*. The gate was decorated in 17ᵗʰ-century Turkish style, and there are large windows in the same architectural style. The windows are in recesses, each recess containing three elongated symmetrical windows, topped by one wide window. The hall is surmounted by a drum and dome, supported by four pendentives above the piers and pointed arches. The sections of the hall, which flank the central domed square section, are cross-vaulted. The arrangement of the Ark resembles that in the Yohanan ben Zakkai Synagogue, and next to it are two Corinthian pillars carrying cornices with arabesque engravings. The high *bimah* is like those in the other synagogues. Benches were fixed along the walls and there were women's galleries.

The Synagogue of Rabbi Judah the Hassid

This synagogue and the nearby Tiferet Israel Synagogue were located in the center and at the highest point of the Jewish Quarter. The two buildings were contemporary and similar in their basic plan and appearance. Before their destruction by the Jordanians the buildings commanded a view of the entire Jewish Quarter, since their domes were the highest in the area and were visible beyond the walls.

Rabbi Judah the *Hassid* came to the country with his followers in 1699. On his arrival in Jerusalem he acquired the courtyard adjoining the Ramban Synagogue and began to build the synagogue in 1700. However, his death soon afterwards stopped the building work, which was only resumed some 150 years later. The foundations were laid anew in 1857, and the magnificent building was known among the Jews as the *Hurvah* (ruin) of Rabbi Judah the *Hassid*. The hall was almost square, measuring 15.3 m × 13.7 m. The drum was 16 m high, and the dome was 24 m above the floor. Inside the dome was a circular balcony. The *bimah* was in the center of the hall, paved with marble and open on all sides. The hall was lighted by the 12 windows of the drum and by two rows of large windows in the walls. Now (2002–2003) it will be entirely restored to its original shape.

Tiferet Israel (Nissan Bek) Synagogue

This synagogue was built by the *Hassidim* at the same time as the *Perushim* were building the Hurvah, and was dedicated in 1865. The façade of the building was divided into three stories by the rows of entrances, and was surmounted by a drum and dome. A gallery ran around the dome as in the Hurvah. The ground floor contained the rooms of the synagogue, and the

Tiferet Israel Synagogue (Rabbi Nissan Bek), in the Jewish Quarter
(destroyed at the end of the War of Independence)

great hall occupied the second and third floors. The cellar contained a ritual bath, 10.3 m square, which was later divided into separate sections for men and women. It was entirely destroyed in 1948, and only some scant parts were preserved to the present.

Karaite Synagogue

The Karaite community of Jerusalem traditionally goes back to the days of 'Anan, who founded the sect in the ninth century C.E. It flourished in the succeeding centuries. The synagogue, opposite the Tiferet Israel Synagogue, was founded in the tenth to twelfth centuries, although one inscription inside the building links its foundation with 'Anan. According to Pinkerfeld, the cruciform vaulting with its high vertices points to a later date. The governors of Jerusalem traditionally forbade the building of synagogues with windows. The building was therefore subterranean, and only a faint light penetrated through the panes in the skylights of the vaults. All the rooms adjoining the synagogue are windowless and dark. Over the centuries the synagogue buildings diminished; they included, in addition to the hall, a courtyard, ritual bath, water cistern (the two latter were interconnected) and a small prayer room used only on the Holy Days by a small number of worshippers. The present building dates from the end of the eighteenth century or the beginning of the nineteenth, and it was devastated by the Jordanians after the War of Independence.

Planning of the Jewish Quarter

One hundred and twenty dunams of the Old City have been allocated to the Jewish Quarter. One third of this consists of alleyways, squares and the courtyard of the Wall. Two thirds are being restored, with slight alterations to the original plan that existed before the destruction, so that there will be buildings with arches and domes.

Among institutions which have been or are in process of being built here are: Yeshivat ha-Kotel, Yeshivat Porat Joseph, which is a branch of Bar Ilan University, an Institute for Research on Spanish Jewry, the Rabbinical Court, the Institute for Biblical Research, Beth ha-Sofer, Bazaar of the House of the Arches, souvenir shops, hotels and a theater. The following synagogues, destroyed under Jordanian rule, are being restored: the Ramban, Hurvah, Tiferet Israel, Karaite, Ari, Torat Hayim, Habad, Sha'arei Shamayim, Beth-EI, Sha'arei Hessed, Etz Hayim, Hayei Olam and Moghrabi.

In 1895 there were 15,000 inhabitants in the Jewish Quarter and in 1947 2,500; after the restoration has been completed there will be 5,000. In 1996 the Old City was inhabited by 3,100 Jews, 22,200 Muslims and 6,300 Christians.

Archaeological Excavations in the Jewish Quarter

Excavations were carried out in 1969–79, headed by Professor N. Avigad.

The Excavations of the Upper City in the First Temple Period

In light of the excavations of N. Avigad in the Upper City in the course of ten years (1969–1979), several unknown and important details became evident (*The Upper City of Jerusalem*, Jerusalem, 1980):

The Upper City in general was not inhabited before the First Temple period in the eighth to seventh centuries B.C.E., and its main colonization was in the Second Temple period.

1. The remnants of a permanent town from the First Temple period were discovered within a high, fortified wall. Within it there was a tower 8 m high, the only one in Jerusalem from the days of Hezekiah, king of

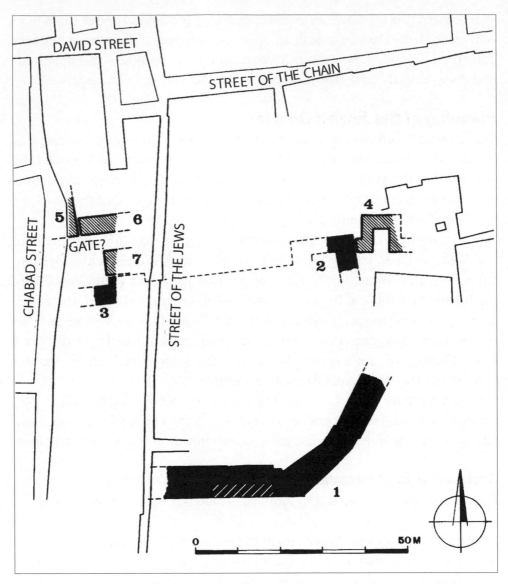

Remains of the fortifications in the Upper City: Israelite 1–3; Hasmonean 4–7

Judah (698–727) (map of the remnants of the Israelite and Hasmonean wall in the Upper City, nos. 1 and 2 on the map). The wall from the days of Hezekiah, which was up to 3.30 m in height, was excavated 65 m in length and 7 m in width. It is possible to visit most of it today northwest of the Jewish Quarter, east of the Byzantine Cardo. Close by remnants of the wall and a Hasmonean tower were also discovered, linking the

Israelite tower and wall (numbers 2 and 4 on the map) that seem to be in shafts under the Byzantine Cardo. About 50 m west of the tower, from north of the Street of the Jews and south of David's Street in the Jewish Quarter, a portion of an additional Israelite tower was found. This was, it seems, a continuation of the wall to the north and to the west of the city (number 3 on the map).

During the excavation of the wall, signs of a large fire were discovered. In the ruins archaeologists found iron arrowheads and typical Babylonian bronze arrowheads that testify to the fact that here Nebuchadnezzar, king of Babylon, fought when conquering Jerusalem in 586 B.C.E. as stated in *II Kings* XXV, 9–10: "And he burnt the house of the Lord, and the king's house, and all the houses of Jerusalem, and every great man's house burnt he with fire. And he broke down the *walls of Jerusalem* round about." It seems that Hezekiah's wall was widened westward in the Upper City, because the kings of Judea received the refugees from Judea and Samaria that were banished by the Assyrian kings in 721 B.C.E.

The Places of the Mishneh (Secondary Quarter) and the Makhtesh (Crater) in Jerusalem

In the Bible, the *Mishneh* and the *Makhtesh* are mentioned in the city of Jerusalem. N. Avigad recognizes them as suburbs of the city or neighborhoods outside of the City of David, because there is a geographical meaning to these words. Regarding the *Mishneh*, Avigad was of the opinion that this respectable neighborhood of the city was mentioned by the prophetess Huldah: "And she dwelt in Jerusalem in the *Mishneh*" (*II Kings* XXII, 14), and of her respected husband, Shalum Ben Tikva, it is said that he was "keeper of the wardrobe." Also, regarding the overseer of the *Mishneh* it is said: "and Judah the son of Senuah was second over the city," who was one of the sons of Benjamin (*Nehemiah* XI, 9). From here it can be concluded that the *Mishneh* was apparently a special suburb outside of the City of David and westward, which was second in its settlement in Jerusalem, and leaning, as it were, on the eastern slope of the Upper City (see the excavation map of Jerusalem of N. Avigad after the Six Day War).

The *Makhtesh* was apparently in the main valley of Jerusalem (*Nehemiah* XXII, 13, 15). Its hollowed-out shape resembled a *Makhtesh* (= "crater," "morter"etc.). This main and central valley (= Tyropoeon) of the city originated north of the city and spilt into the Ben-Hinnom Valley, which ran off into the Kidron River in the south. The *Makhtesh* was surrounded by triangular hillsides: in its east the City of David, in its west the hill of the Upper City, and in its north the Temple Mount – Mount Zion. In this *Makhtesh*, whose shape was like a giant amphitheater, Zephaniah prophesied the great judgment day of the nations, amongst whom were Judah and Jerusalem. In this *Makhtesh* flowed a larger portion of the city's water and thus here was the center of crafts and industry, and the commerce of Jerusalem. Because of the gorge's depth and lack of exit, Zephaniah foretold the tribulations of the evil people, who traded in the city's big market, such as the Canaanites, saying: "Howl, ye inhabitants of Makhtesh, for all the merchant people are cut down: all they that bear silver are cut off" (*Zephaniah*, I, 11).

The Upper City in the Second Temple Period

During the archaeological excavations of N. Avigad's team and previous excavations by R. Amiran and A. Eitan, no settlement remnants were found in the Upper City from the Return to Zion period. However, many magnificent remnants from the Hasmonean and Herodian periods were found.

West of the Upper City, in the fortress's courtyard ("David's" Citadel) in the north, through the Armenian Quarter and up to southwest of the Upper City, alongside the Turkish wall, remnants of the Hasmonean city wall were possibly discovered. This wall was built in several places that were excavated upon remnants of the Israelite wall in the Upper City. For testimony to the building of this wall, we read of the fortifications of Jonathan, Simeon and Johanan, saying: "And Jonathan resided in Jerusalem and began to build and renew the city. And the craftsmen were ordered to build the walls…" (152–143 B.C.E.), (*I Maccabees* X, 10–11). Of Simeon (142–135 B.C.E.) it was said: "and he hurried to consume the walls of Jerusalem and fortify them round about" (*I Maccabees* XIII, 10). And regarding Johanan Hyrcanos, the son of Simeon (134–104 B.C.E.), it was said: "and the remaining articles of Johanan and his wars and his bravery and building the walls that he built and his work" (*I Maccabees* XXVI, 23).

In the days of the House of Herod (37 B.C.E.–70 C.E.), Jerusalem and its walls were built in splendor and power, such as the city had never known in all the history of the Land of Israel, according to written and archaeological evidence. The living quarters uncovered in the Upper City were magnificent and belonged to the upper class of the Jewish community, headed by the

Frontal view of the El Aqsa's seven arches (A. Erev)

Dormition Abbey and the southern wall of Jerusalem (A. Erev)

Mameluke iron gate in the Temple Mount courtyard (A. Erev)

Byzantine Cardo in the Upper City (A. Erev)

Crusader Cardo in the Old City (M. Har-El)

Ruins of the Old City after the 1948 War of Independence (M. Har-El)

Path to Upper Beit Horon heights with steps for use by camels (M. Har-El).

Hezekiah's wall in the Upper City (A. Erev)

Third wall in Jerusalem in the Second Temple period,
some distance north of the gate (M. Har-El)

Mercy Gate as seen from the courtyard of the Temple Mount – Byzantine and western remains, below which are Second Temple remains (A. Erev)

Tomb of Beni Hezir and Tomb of Zecheraiah at the Gihon Spring (A. Erev)

Remains of Robinson's Arch and southwestern wall of the Temple Mount (A. Erev)

Dome of the Rock, from the west (A. Erev)

Dome of the Rock and arches on the Temple Mount, eastern view (A. Erev)

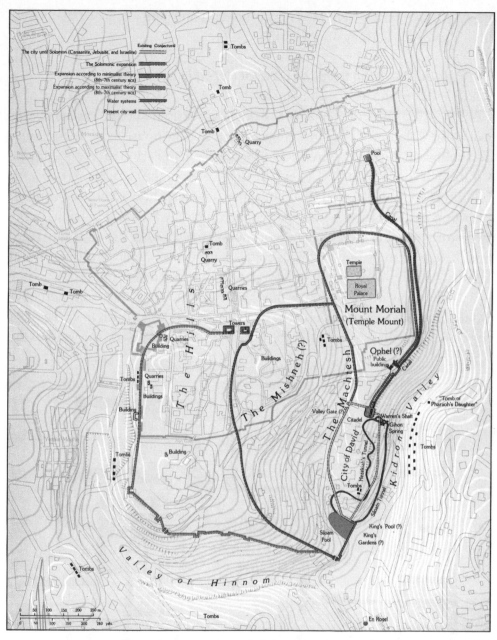

Jerusalem from the end of the Monarchy Period

great priests (*Kohanim*). In these buildings there were one or two purifying *mikvehs*, because during the Second Temple period, purification was strictly observed. The *mikveh* was a sloping pool hewn in the rock, with a ceiling built of limestone. Its waters were supplied from the many water sources in

the city. The *mikvehs* were used for immersion only and alongside them were
built rooms for bathing and washing.

The Palatial Mansion from the Days of Herod in the Upper City

On the edge of the northeast point of the Jewish Quarter in the old city of Jerusalem at the east end of Misgav Ladakh Street, a grand house was uncovered
called the "Mansion" by archaeologists. The elegant house went up in flames
and collapsed during the Great Revolt in the Roman Period in 70 C.E., during
the Roman conquest of the Upper City in the east. In the excavations two large
buildings were discovered, including the northern house, which occupied
over 600 m. It was uncovered and reconstructed by N. Avigad's team. In the
two-story building there are suites of rooms surrounding a central courtyard
and, below them, basement living quarters for the servants, plus water installations – pools, *mikvehs* and wells – as well as storehouses and rooms.

The courtyard (no. 1 on the map) is tiled with stone, and from here they
would enter the living rooms of the building. Water was drawn from a collecting well under the courtyard for the inhabitants of the rooms. The walls of the

Plan of the House of Measurements

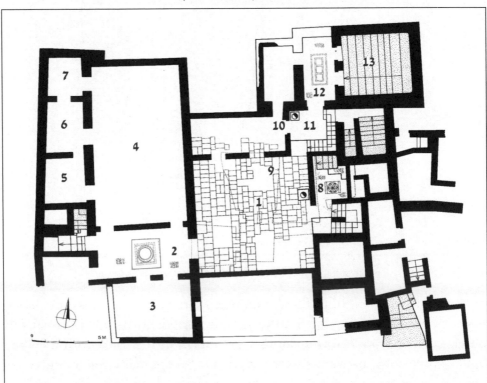

rooms are built of limestone up to 3 m in height. Room two is the vestibule to the remaining living rooms where a floor of handsome, colored mosaics, with a square frame decorated with a design of intertwined mandarins, was uncovered. The corners of the frame were decorated with pomegranates. In room 3 from the south, is a colorful fresco (a painting on damp plaster). This is the largest, measuring 2.5 meters painted in red and yellow panels resembling windows. Room four is 11 meters in length and was used to receive guests. Its walls were plastered stucco (a mixture of glue and plaster) with wide panels resembling granite stone with margins, that were three meters in height. In the western wing of the courtyard (room eight) a small bathhouse was uncovered, tiled in colorful mosaics in the design of the rose of two-toned leaves. At the edge of the room is a sunken bath.

To reach the cellar, one goes down the southern stairs to a long corridor, the walls of which are hewn in rock and the roofs made of large stone slabs. The corridor leads to three pools hewn in rock, which are the sources

Seven-branched candelabra, Table for the Shewbread, and Altar,
carved in the plaster of the House of Measurements

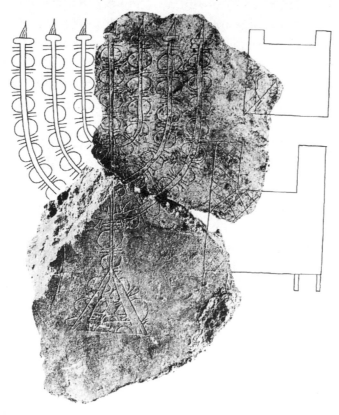

of the building's vaults, built of limestone. The pool at the end of the corridor (no. 9) has two openings, one alongside the other, measuring 3.5 × 4 m. It has a vaulted ceiling built of limestone. (During the Arab period it became a water well with a hole in the ceiling.) The two openings to the pool show that there was a purifying *mikveh*, with one opening serving as an entrance, for the purpose of immersion, and the other as the exit.

North of the central courtyard, there is a slope descending to a small and lower courtyard (room 10) tiled with white mosaic, and in its corner a well of water. East of the courtyard is a large, vaulted room (room 11), apparently a storage place that was mostly destroyed. From the east side one comes to two *mikveh*s. In the north, there is a mosaic-tiled corridor in the design of a chessboard (room 12). Room 13 is an additional *mikveh,* which has two openings and an impressive vault of limestone. N. Avigad explains the number of *mikvehs* and the splendor of the "Palatial Mansion" with the assumption that this was the house of one of the great priests.

Special findings and exhibits: In the "Palatial Mansion" were found rectangular, stone tables with one leg, and round, stone tables with three legs. Also, stone cups and glass dishes were found, showing that the house owner used dishes that cannot become impure. (A workshop from the Second Temple Period for the production of stone dishes was discovered in a big cave on a hill east of Givat-Shaul.) In the "Palatial Mansion" there is also a sundial called the "stone of hours" in the *Mishnah* (*Keilim* 10a; *Parah* 3b). It is made of soft stone and measures 11 × 12 cm in width and 11.5 cm in height.

The Burnt House of Priests and Chemists of Incense and Perfume

This house was burnt in the Great Revolt in 70 C.E. and discovered at Misgav Ladakh Street near the "Palatial Mansion." The whole house was burnt and its clay pottery is from the first century C.E. Coins were found here from the days of the Great Revolt against the Romans: "Year Two / Freedom of Zion"; "Year Three / Freedom of Zion"; "Year Four / Redemption of Zion." The house is built on the remains of a building from the First Temple period, and its rooms were found in the cellar. The layout of the house is composed of the courtyard (no. 1) tiled in stone; three built rooms (no.'s 2 to 4), a small room (no. 5), which isn't burnt and in which nothing was found; a small kitchen (no. 6) and a small *mikveh* (no. 7) that was reached by stairs. The walls of the rooms were usually preserved up to one meter in height. They were plastered in white paint and the floors were of clay. In several of the rooms, there were

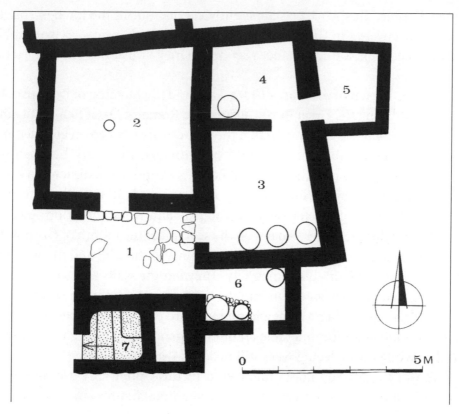

Plan of the Burnt House in the Upper City

sunken ovens in the floors, and in the rooms were found stone vessels, stone tables and clay pottery, attesting that they were not used as living quarters.

In the Burnt House there were: tables, cooking pots, basins and small bowls, cups made of soft stone and prepared by carving; perfume flasks of clay and glass, mortar, door frames, stone weights and stone moldings for minting coins, confirming the archaeological team's opinion, that this was a crafts or industrial shop. If so, what craft or industry was carried out here?

The team members found here an Aramaic inscription: דבר קתרס, Hebrew for: "belongs to the son of Katros." The House of Katros (*Pesahim* 57, p. 1; *Tosefta Menachot* 13, 21) was a priestly family, and because of the discovery of certain manufacturing of pharmaceutical items, it is believed that the family cultivated incense and perfumes in Jerusalem, and produced pharmaceutical products such as incense and perfumes for the Temple. Thus, the sons of Katros needed an abundance of pure water, which was collected in large stone pots and other stone utensils for the production of incense and perfume for the Temple. This work was apparently carried out in the kitchen (no. 6) and was discovered in the Burnt House, together with a stove, a work table, a round clay oven, a round table, a set of square grindstones and a portable stone oven.

On the breach of the Upper City's walls and the burning of its houses by Titus' army during the Great Revolt against the Romans, Yosef Ben Matityahu wrote: "and when the Caesar saw that the Upper City is steep on all sides and cannot be conquered without ramparts, he divided this work between his soldiers on the 20th day of the month of Lo'os (Av), and it was difficult to bring all the required trees, because they exposed, as I said, all the places around the city, a distance of 100 for the first troops... and when the troop reserves were totally exhausted after 18 days, on the seventh of the month of Gorphious (Elul) the Romans brought closer their weapons to the wall and many of the rebels gave up hope in saving their city. They left the walls and went up into the fortress and they went down into the tunnels... After this they (Romans) burst into the streets like a river and hit by sword everyone who fell into their hands and killed an innumerable amount of people and burned the houses with fire while those fleeing were still inside" (*Wars* VI, 8–10).

Ten of the mosaic floors uncovered in the Upper City are mostly in geometric and plant patterns; the absence of animal figures amongst them is of note, and complies with the Jewish Law.

Stone jugs and cups from the House of Measurements

CHAPTER VIII

THE CHRISTIANS IN JERUSALEM AND THEIR HOLY SITES

The Main Christian Sects

Many of the Christians in the country are the descendants of Byzantine Christians who were in the country before the Moslem Conquest, and who speak Arabic. There are about 100,000 Christians west of the Jordan.

The Christians in the country are divided into four main sects: Orthodox, Catholics, Monophysites and Protestants.

Eastern Orthodox Church

This division of Christianity consists primarily of Greek Orthodox and is the oldest of the Christian denominations in the country, with about 45,000 members. The Eastern Orthodox are the spiritual descendants of the Byzantine tradition, with its center at Constantinople, and constitute the majority of Arab Christians in the country. This denomination includes Christians from Cappadocia and Greece, as well as Russians and Balkan Christians. The financial situation of the Orthodox Church has worsened in the last century, since Russia and the Balkan States ceased to support it after the Bolshevik Revolution. All the hermit sects in the Judean Desert and the Sinai Peninsula belong to the Orthodox Church. The community in the country is headed by an "autonomous" Patriarch whose seat is in Jerusalem; by a long-established tradition he is always Greek.

Western Catholic Church

This church, centered in Rome, includes the majority of Christians in the country, with 30,000 members. The sect developed after the Crusader Conquest, and friction was caused between the Byzantine Orthodox and the newly-arrived Catholics. About half of the sect consists of Roman Catholics concentrated in Nazareth and the vicinity, as well as in Haifa, Acre, Shefar'am, Jaffa, Ramleh and Jerusalem. The other members of the sect are Greek Catholics who accepted the creed after the Crusader Conquest and are also centered in Nazareth. The Catholics also include the Franciscans, who established their order in the thirteenth century and are to be found in Jerusalem, Ein Kerem, Jaffa, Ramleh, Haifa, Acre, Nazareth, Zippori, Mount Tabor, Tiberias and Capernaum. The Catholics also include some 3,000 Maronites and several hundred Catholic Armenians, Syrians and Assyrians who split off from their churches and established "united" congregations with the Catholics.

There are 45 Catholic monasteries and convents in the country belonging to various orders. The Catholic Church is headed by the Latin Patriarch of Jerusalem, subject to the Pope in Rome.

Monophysite Coptic-Syrian Church

This sect was founded in the fifth century C.E., with the belief that Jesus was of a single divine nature, and not of a double human-divine nature as other Christian sects believe. This Church developed in Egypt and Syria, and the contention and discord between it and other Christian churches helped the Arabs to overcome their Byzantine enemy. The sect includes the Armenian and Monophysite Church, with its centers in Jerusalem, Ramleh, Jaffa and Haifa; the Copts, in Jerusalem, Jaffa and Nazareth; and the Syrians and the Ethiopians in Jerusalem. The rituals and traditions of this sect are ancient and resemble those of the earliest Christians. The Armenian Orthodox comprise about 3,500 members, the Copts some 1,500, the Syrians about 1,200 and the Ethiopians about 100.

Anglican and European Protestant Churches

The Anglican Church, with its support for reform in religion and its non-recognition of papal authority, has its roots in the Reformation. It is the newest denomination to appear in the country, and has 2,300 members. Its activity is mainly of a missionary nature, and began in the Old City in 1833, after the conquest of the country by Mohammed 'Ali, the first ruler to show tolerance towards Jews and Christians. The Anglicans built a church near the Jaffa

Gate, and one of their leaders, Bishop Gobat, founded a missionary school on "Mount Zion." The German Lutherans erected a church near the Church of the Holy Sepulcher in 1898.

There are several other Protestant Churches in the country, such as the Scottish Church, with chapels in Jerusalem, Jaffa and Tiberias; the Baptists, who arrived in 1923 and are concentrated in Nazareth; the Adventists, who believe in a second coming of Jesus; and the Mennonites, who oppose baptism and army service. Altogether these sects comprise 3,500 members.

Jerusalem has 16,000 Christians of all sects, and there are 38,000 in Judea, Samaria and the Gaza Strip. Israel has some 200 churches and chapels, concentrated mostly in the places holy to Christianity, and used by pilgrims as well as by their church members.

Christian Churches and Chapels in Jerusalem

Three of the most important centers of Christianity in the country are in Jerusalem. These are, the Church of the Holy Sepulcher, the site of the Last Supper on "Mount Zion," and the place where Jesus dwelt and walked with the Apostles on the Mount of Olives.

After the Hadrianic Conquest of the city, the rulers and most of the inhabitants of Jerusalem were pagans for about 200 years. Under the rule of Constantine (who accepted Christianity as a tolerable religion, though there is no proof that he converted, except possibly on his deathbed), church-building began all over the city. Three of the most important churches in Jerusalem are: the Church of the Holy Sepulcher in the Old City, the Chapel of Ascension, and the Tomb of the Virgin near the the Mount of Olives.

Pilgrims and the Status Quo of the Holy Places

Christians have made pilgrimages since the earliest days of the Church to visit the holy places of the country. The stream of pilgrims swelled with the dissemination of Christianity throughout the world. Christians regarded it as a duty to visit the Holy Land at least once in their lifetime. The obstruction of pilgrimages was one of the chief reasons for the Crusades of the 11th century C.E. The same reason later served to justify the gradual penetration of various European powers into the Ottoman Empire. The pilgrimages reach a peak during Easter, when thousands of Christians from all over the world come to Jerusalem and Bethlehem. The greatest number of Christian pilgrims arrived in Jerusalem and at the Jordan (scene of the activities of John the Baptist) during

Easter 1913, when tens of thousands came, among them 30,000 from Russia alone. Evidence of these particular pilgrimages (which ceased after the Russian Revolution) is provided by the large hostels in the Russian Compound in Jerusalem and elsewhere: Jaffa, Ein Karem, Jericho. To counterbalance these large-scale pilgrimages of Christians, the Turkish authorities began to organize mass marches of Moslems to the site traditionally identified in Islam as the tomb of Moses (Nebi Musa) on the Jericho Road, timing it to coincide with Easter.

The supreme importance of the Christian Holy Places, and the division of the Church into rival sects at an early stage, led to bitter strife over the ownership of the sites. This rivalry was intensified during the Turkish period, when the various European Christian powers supported particular Christian sects in order to effect political penetration into the empire. During the sixteenth and seventeenth centuries, Catholic influence over the Holy Places increased as a result of the intervention of France. Beginning in the eighteenth century, Czarist Russia was active in ensuring the rights of the Greek Orthodox Church. As a result of this struggle a long-lasting international conflict arose, known as the "problem of the Holy Places." In order to stop the political pressures and diplomatic machinations, the Turkish Government promulgated two *firmans* (proclamations of the Sultan), in 1852 and 1853, determining for all time the rights of ownership, maintenance and prayer in the places holy to Christians in Jerusalem and Bethlehem. A bizarre partitioning of the holy places was thus perpetuated, with the Greek Orthodox, Catholics and Armenians each owning certain objects and sections in the same church. This principle was accepted at the Paris Conference of 1856, after the Crimean War, and ratified by the Berlin Treaty (1878); by the League of Nations, along with its approval of the Mandate for Palestine; and by the United Nations with the Partition Resolution of November 1947. It is thus part of international law. The regulations of this arrangement are still strictly observed, although certain irregularities in the rituals determined over 100 years ago cause the old quarrels to flare up anew at times. This arrangement has delayed the restoration of the Church of the Holy Sepulcher, despite its poor condition, bordering on collapse, since any repairs would have meant an infraction of the status quo. The most recent agreement between the three sects has enabled repairs to begin, under the authority of Israel.

Via Dolorosa and the Church of the Holy Sepulcher

Via Dolorosa is the name of the route between the residence of the Roman governor, believed to be at the Antonia Fortress, and the Hill of Golgotha within the Church of the Holy Sepulcher. There are 14 stations on the road, which Jesus trod with the cross. The stations are clearly marked by numbers and inscriptions, and the churches situated there display paintings of the agony of Jesus along the way, as described in the New Testament. Jesus carried the cross the whole route after his judgment, to the place of the Crucifixion. The distance, from the Church of the Flagellation in the east to Golgotha in the west is 700 m.

The Church of the Holy Sepulcher lies at the end of the Via Dolorosa. The following important churches were established along the way: the Church of the Flagellation, near the Lions' Gate, the Chapel of the Condemnation, and the Basilica of the Ecce Homo, where following Christian belief the judgment of Pilate took place. These three churches are built near the site of the Antonia Fortress, which guarded and defended the Temple Mount during the Second Temple period. The Church of the Flagellation is attached to a Franciscan Bible School and includes an archaeological museum. These were the first two stations of the Via Dolorosa. Golgotha, within the Church of the Holy Sepulcher, marks the final station and is the most sacred of sites to Christianity. Every Friday afternoon at three o' clock the Franciscans retrace the steps of Jesus and pray at each of the stations.

First Station: Jesus Is Condemned to Death

This station is known as the Praetorium (headquarters of the Roman procurator). It has been identified in the courtyard of the 'Omariyeh Boys' School, the structures of which were built by the Mamelukes and named Zawiyah in 1315–1320, with later restorations by the Turks. This courtyard formed part of the Antonia Fortress, and the inscription on the Temple partition prohibiting the entry of strangers was found near King Feisal's Gate. The inscription is now in the Istanbul Museum. According to Christian tradition, Jesus was handed over to Pontius Pilate, Governor of Jerusalem, for judgment, and was scourged and crowned with thorns (*St. John* XIX, 2, 5). By tradition the judgment took place in the Lithostrotos (paved floor), sections of which are shown in the Basilica of the Ecce Homo (opposite the 'Omariyeh courtyard) north of the Via Dolorosa. The place has been known by this name since the sixteenth century, when it was identified as "a place that is called the Pavement," in *St. John* XIX, 13. The first station is sometimes shown in the Church of the Flagellation, near the courtyard of the Convent of the Sisters of Zion. The Church of the Flagellation and its dome are decorated with a painting of

Jesus crowned with thorns. The church is Franciscan. The Franciscan monks have been in Jerusalem since the thirteenth century, and bear the name of St. Francis, who founded the Order in 1212, and cared for the indigent sick; it is the largest of the Catholic orders and is the custodian of the holy places. The Flagellation is recorded in *St. Mark* xv, 15: "And so Pilate, willing to content the people, released Barabbas unto them, and delivered Jesus, when he had scourged him, to be crucified."

Second Station: Jesus Receives the Cross

The station is located on the site of the eastern gate of the Hadrianic Aelia Capitolina. The gate was triple-arched, like the remains of that found at the Damascus Gate. The central arch is visible above the present street; the northern one has been incorporated into the apse of the church, while the southern one has disappeared. At the back of the hospice of the Ecce Homo, part of the rock-cut wall of the moat which protected the Antonia fortress is visible and is in use today as one of the church walls. The second station was outside the Chapel of the Condemnation, within which was the "Lithostrotos" (*John* xix:13) The pavement where, according to tradition, the trial and arrest of Jesus took place is shown in the courtyard of the church. Marked on the paving stones is the outline of a game played by the Roman soldiers. Along the sides of the courtyard run gutters, which carried the rainwater to the Struthion Pool, a double pool below the level of what is believed to be the "Lithostrotos," which can be approached by a stairway. The name of the church, Ecce Homo, means "Behold the man," the words by which Pontius Pilate presented Jesus to the people (*St. John* xix, 15): "Then came Jesus forth, wearing the crown of thorns and the purple robe. And Pilate saith unto them, Behold the man."

Near the Convent of the Sisters of Zion there is a Greek Orthodox monastery built in 1906, with the inscription "Prison of Christ" over the door. There are underground tunnels in the monastery, with holes carved out of the rock for tethering horses, probably those of the soldiers in the Antonia Fortress. Some of these tunnels appear to have been used as prisons.

Third Station: Jesus Falls For the First Time

The road passes under the ancient Hadrianic arch in a westerly direction to the corner of Ha-Gai Street (*El-Wad*, or the Valley Street), which leads north to the Damascus Gate. Turning south (left), we face the Armenian-Catholic church, which is just east of the street, on the site of a former Turkish

Greek-Catholic chapel at the Third Station

bathhouse. The third and fourth stations are shown at this corner, and the Armenian Catholics purchased the site in 1856. A column, near which Jesus stumbled with the cross, can be seen.

Fourth Station: Jesus Meets His Sorrowing Mother
There is a Catholic Armenian church, Our Lady of the Spasm, built on the site in 1881. In the crypt is a section of mosaic from the sixth or seventh century, with a representation of a pair of sandals belonging to Mary, the mother of Jesus. The church is built on the site traditionally identified as that where Mary stood when she exchanged a look with her son.

Fifth Station: Simon of Cyrene Helps Jesus to Carry the Cross
This is near the third and fourth stations, at the junction of El-Wad Street and Via Dolorosa, on the western corner. The building belongs to the Franciscans, who built it in 1895. The Roman soldiers forced Simon, a Jew from a Roman province in North Africa, to carry the cross the rest of the way to Golgotha (*St. Luke* XXIII, 26): "And as they led him away, they laid hold upon one Simon, a Cyrenian, coming out of the country and on him they laid the cross, that

he might bear it after Jesus." On a wall of the building, there is a stone slab on which two arms are engraved, and on them a cross. The bare arm is that of Jesus and the clothed one belongs to St. Francis.

Sixth Station: Veronica Wipes the Face of Jesus With a Cloth Dipped in Cold Water

The station is up the street on the left, under several arches. A probably Greek Catholic chapel is on the site. The oldest section of the building is probably part of the sixth-century monastery of St. Cosmas, which was bought by the Greek Catholics in 1883. A church of St. Veronica was built in 1895, and renovated in 1953. According to the Christian tradition, the handkerchief has been in the Cathedral of St. Peter since 1297.

Seventh Station: Jesus Falls for the Second Time

This station is in the street of the oil press, where today there is a Franciscan chapel. Close by, according to Christian tradition, there was an ancient gate, called "Gate of the Trial," through which Jesus entered the place of the crucifixion.

Eighth Station: Jesus Speaks to the Daughters of Jerusalem

At the junction of the street of the Damascus Gate (*Bab el-'Ammud*) with St. Francis Street, the route leads west. On the left is the German Lutheran Hospice of St. John, and adjoining it is the Greek Orthodox Convent of St. Charalambos, the former residence of the Greek canons of the Holy Sepulcher. The station is marked by a stone inserted in the wall of the Greek church, bearing a Latin cross and the Greek word *Nike-Le xo Nika,* which means, Jesus will always triumph. An altar inside the church marks the eighth station, where Jesus begged the women of Jerusalem to weep for themselves and for their sons, but not for him (*St. Luke* XXIII, 28).

At this point the Via Dolorosa ceases to follow the streets and runs between some buildings and the Coptic Convent.

Ninth Station: Jesus Falls For the Third Time

We ascend the winding street and come to a staircase of twenty-eight steps, leading to a lane, which leads to the entrance of the Coptic church. The shaft of a column in the doorpost marks the ninth station, close to Golgotha. A door leads to the crypt of the Holy Sepulcher and the Church of St. Helena, where the True Cross was said to have been found. The canons of the Holy

Sepulcher had their refectory and living quarters here in the Crusader period. The rooms in the courtyard are now inhabited by Ethiopian monks.

The last five stations are within the confines of the Church of the Holy Sepulcher.

Tenth Station: Jesus Is Stripped of His Garments

Turning by the Russian Hospice and the Alexander Church (1860), we enter the courtyard of the Church of the Holy Sepulcher (= Parvis). Inside the church we turn right at the foot of Golgotha and ascend 14 steps to the top of the hill. The hill is known as 'Golgotha' in Greek and 'Calvary' in Latin. "And he bearing his cross went forth to a place called the place of the skull, which is called in the Hebrew Golgotha" (*St. John* XIX, 17). Golgotha, where, according to the Christian tradition, the skull of Adam, the first man, was buried, is divided into two naves. In the right-hand one, in which is a Latin chapel, is the Tenth Station. The hill was given its name because of the Christian tradition that it was the grave of Adam, and a drop of Jesus' blood fell on Adam's skull.

Eleventh Station: Jesus Is Nailed to the Cross

Jesus was crucified on a cross near the present Latin altar. The silver-plated bronze altar was made in 1558. There is a Crusader mosaic depicting the Ascension. The scenes of the Passion are represented on six panels; on the altar two crosses are depicted, one on each side of Jesus, bearing the two thieves condemned with him (*St. John* XIX, 19, 20; *St. Mark* XV, 26). The mosaic of the chapel was restored in 1937.

Twelfth Station: Jesus Dies on the Cross

Crossing from the Latin chapel on the right, we come to the Greek one on the left. An altar in this chapel marks the spot where the cross of Jesus was installed. A chapel underneath is known as the Chapel of Adam, the first sinner, and Golgotha above it offers salvation to the human race. The representation of a skull at the foot of Jesus symbolizes this comparison.

Thirteenth Station: The Body of Jesus Is Taken Down From the Cross

Between the eleventh and twelfth stations stands the Latin altar, which marks the place of the thirteenth station. Over the altar is a wooden statue (16th to 17th century) of the Mater Dolorosa, covered in gold and diamonds, sent from Lisbon in 1778.

Fourteenth Station: Jesus Is Laid in the Sepulcher

We descend from Golgotha to the Stone of the Anointing. Formerly the Chapel of St. Mary stood here; the present slab dates from 1810. We come into the circular Rotunda, with its round dome supported on 12 columns, and enter the Tomb through a vestibule, the Chapel of the Angel who announced the Resurrection. A decorated doorway leads into the Tomb, and a marble slab on the right marks the burial place of Jesus.

History of the Church of the Holy Sepulcher

A temple to the goddess Venus, or to the god Jupiter, was built on this site by Hadrian; it was still in existence during the time of the Empress Helena, mother of Constantine. In the year 326 C.E., Helena erected churches in Jerusalem to commemorate the scenes of Jesus' activities. The Church of the Holy Sepulcher was destroyed and rebuilt on several occasions, the first time by the Persians during their invasion in 614 C.E.

The remnants of the Herodian wall, discovered in the Russian Alexander Convent nearby, are evidence that the site of the Church of the Holy Sepulcher was originally outside the Herodian city, but was incorporated within the walls during the reign of Agrippa (44 C.E.) when the third wall was built. The precise location of the Tomb of Jesus was first debated by Christian scholars in 1738,

Christian Quarter and the Church of the Holy Sepulcher

in particular by the German, Jonas Kurt, and the controversy has not yet been resolved. The chief argument is between the Protestants and the Catholics, since the site identified as the Tomb lies within the present walls. As no burials took place inside the walls because of the sanctity of the Temple, certain Protestants have, since 1842, identified the Tomb at a site outside the present walls, 250 m north of the Damascus Gate, called the Garden Tomb. ("Now in the place where he was crusaded there was a garden, and in the garden a new Sepulcher, wherein was never man yet laid. There laid then Jesus therefore because of the Jews' preparation day; for the Sepulcher was nigh at hand" (*St. John* XIX, 41, 42). The Garden Tomb is west of the Moslem cemetery, and is entered through Nablus Street. It was bought by the Protestants in 1895.

Bishop Macarius showed Empress Helena the site of Golgotha inside the Temple of Venus in the Roman city of Aelia Capitolina. The Madeba map shows two walled, domed buildings in the area depicting the Church of the Holy Sepulcher. The church built by Constantine in 326–335 stood for three hundred years, till it was robbed by the Persians. The Patriarch Modestus refurbished it in a less ornate mode, using the materials of the previous structure. This second church suffered an earthquake in 747. (About fifty earthquakes have shaken the church over the centuries, the most recent in 1927, and 15 of them were highly destructive.) In 967 the Moslems burned down the church and killed the Patriarch. In 1009 Al-Hakem, the Fatimid ruler of Egypt, ordered the destruction of all the Christian churches, including the Church of the Holy Sepulcher. In 1048 the Byzantine Constantine Monomachus rebuilt the church, and this was the structure found by the Crusaders. The latter restored the dome of the Byzantine church and the crypt of St. Helena, and in 1144 built the basilica and dome between the Church of St. Helena and the Rotunda, the structure of columns supporting the Byzantine dome over the Tomb of Jesus. From that time the Church of the Holy Sepulcher has had two domes.

Since the Crusader period all five of the most sacred sites of Christianity have been under one roof: Golgotha, the Tomb, the corridor between the Basilica and the Tomb, and the Crypt of the Cross. No major changes have occurred in the structure of the church since Crusader times, except for the renovation of the marble slabs covering the Tomb in 1555. The dome was repaired and restored in 1648, but was again in danger of collapse in 1719. The dome was strengthened, and the mosaic decorating it was cut up and sold as souvenirs. In 1808 the building was damaged by fire and was repaired the following year. The present dome was built with the aid of the governments of France, Russia and Turkey in 1863–1868, and was recently refurbished.

A Visit to the Church of the Holy Sepulcher

The church is divided into five main sections: Golgotha, the Tomb, the Basilica, the corridor, and the Crypt of the Cross.

The Byzantine church built by Constantine was the greatest in Jerusalem, extending to a length of 115 m. The church was entered through three gates on the east. The apse of the church faced west, towards the Tomb of Jesus, which is the most sacred site in Christendom.

The southern façade, originally built in the eleventh century by the Byzantines and re-erected by the Crusaders, is divided into several parts: the main gates, adorned with arches carved with acanthus and medallions, dating to the Crusaders; the dome of Golgotha, to the right of the gates, rising above the two stories of the building; and the bell tower, left of the gates, six stories high during the Crusader period but with only fewer than four stories today.

On the ground just inside the door of the church there is a marble slab, the Stone of the Anointing, where Joseph of Arimathea and Nicodemus anointed the body of Jesus after the Crucifixion (*St. John* XIX, 39, "…and brought a mixture of myrrh and aloes, about a hundred pound weight").

To the right of the entrance is a staircase leading up to Golgotha, which is covered in slabs of marble to prevent pieces being broken off for souvenirs.

To the left is the entry to the Rotunda, which supports a large dome, borne on 18 round, marble, Byzantine pillars. In order to give protection against earthquakes, the pillars were enclosed in square blocks. The inner diameter of the Rotunda is 20.9 m and the cupola is 21.5 m above the ground. The Tomb of Jesus in the Rotunda includes the Chapel of the Angel, after the Angel who announced the Resurrection, and the Rotunda is consequently known in Greek as the Anastasis.

The arch connecting the Rotunda and the Crusader church on its east is Byzantine, and constitutes a passageway between the sixth-century building in the west and the twelfth-century one in the east.

The Crusader church was built between the Church of St. Helena and the Rotunda. The apse of the Crusader church, facing east, was restored in 1850, and has recently undergone repairs, along with other parts of the church. The center of the church is marked by a stone ball, representing the center of the world (*Omphalos Mundi*) for Christianity, in the same way as the Rock of the Foundation on the Temple Mount is the center of the Jewish

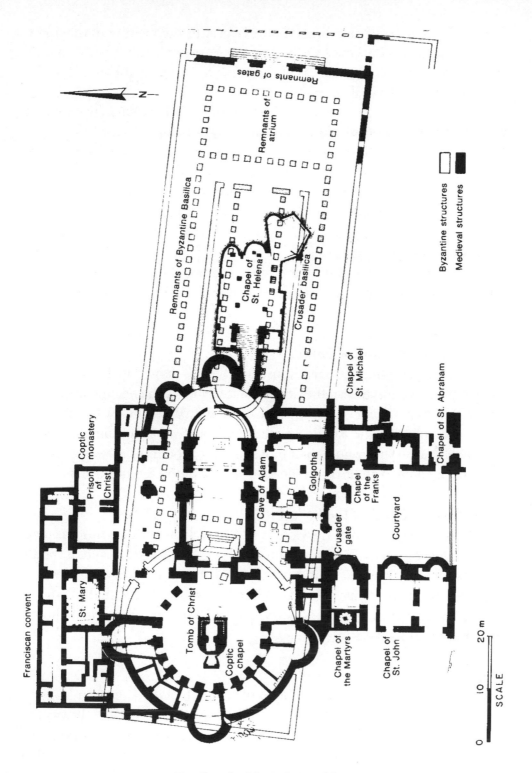

The Church of the Holy Sepulcher

world. The church surrounding it is the largest in the vicinity of the Tomb, the Katholikon, and is Greek Orthodox. It is surrounded by several chapels, commemorating the final scenes of the Passion. The Katholikon is thus the central church in Jerusalem.

From there we go eastward to the Church of St. Helena. The Crusaders restored the cupola of this church, and it now belongs to the Armenians. This was the scene of the torments of Jesus. The pillars carrying the dome are Byzantine, from the seventh century. East of the church there are approximately 13 steps leading to a Crusader chapel, the Chapel of the Finding of the Cross. This was the cave in which the crosses of Jesus and the two thieves were found; it was originally under Georgian supervision and today belongs to the Orthodox and the Latins.

The canons of the Church are today members of the following sects: Greek Orthodox, Roman Catholic, Armenian Catholic, Coptic, Syrian and Ethiopian.

Minaret of the Mosque of Omar

When the Caliph Omar entered Jerusalem, he was invited by the Byzantine Patriarch Sophronius to visit the Church of the Holy Sepulcher and pray there. Omar, however, did not want to give the church further fame by praying in it, and chose a place further south. The site of his prayer was commemorated in 1216 by Shihab e-Din, who built a mosque there. The minaret was added in 1417, although the true site is on the eastern side of the Byzantine Church.

The Lutheran Church of the Redeemer

The church is south-east of the Church of the Holy Sepulcher, and was dedicated in 1898 by Kaiser Wilhelm II during his visit to the Holy Land. It stands on the site of the Crusader church of St. Mary Latin. The medieval doorway is preserved on the northern side of the church, and is carved with the zodiacal figures traditional in Europe. This was the first Lutheran Protestant church to be built in Jerusalem.

Muristan

The Muristan Quarter extends south of the Church of the Holy Sepulcher, as far as the Street of David. Its name means "hospital" in Persian. It was the site of hospices and hospitals for pilgrims in Crusader times, and probably even in the Byzantine period. In 1901 a bazaar was built on the site, called the Greek bazaar. In its center stands a fountain, but it has never worked. In Roman days this was the Forum.

Arab Orthodox Church of St. James

North-west of the Church of the Holy Sepulcher is an Orthodox church of Arab-speaking Christians, named after St. James. The Eastern Orthodox Church includes the four Patriarchs, of Constantinople, Alexandria, Antioch and Jerusalem (and also the Russian, Greek, Yugoslav, Bulgarian and Rumanian Churches). The Greek Orthodox follow the rite in Greek, the Arabs in Arabic, and so on.

The Greek Orthodox Patriarchate nearby was the seat of the Crusader king of Jerusalem, and the northern wall of the building includes Crusader masonry. The western and north-western sections were rebuilt before the First World War. The complex includes a convent and a large library containing fragments of the Judean Desert scrolls, as well as Georgian manuscripts from the Monastery of the Cross in Jerusalem. There is a press, which publishes a periodical, *New Zion*, dealing with subjects connected with the sect and with the exploration of the country. There are 19 other convents, monasteries and chapels of the Greek Orthodox Church in the Old City.

The Anglican Christ Church

This church is south-east of the Citadel, in the area close to where Herod's palace stood during the Second Temple period, near the site of the Hippicus Tower. It was consecrated in 1849, and was the first Anglican church in the Ottoman Empire. It was established with the help of Britain and Austria, after the retreat of the Egyptian rulers from the country. The church, English-Gothic in style, was built near the former British Consulate and the English missionaries center, and was also close to the Austrian Post Office, which can still be seen on the side of the road east of the Citadel. Two granite columns were found in the course of the construction; they were probably part of Herod's palace, and came from Aswan, in Egypt.

The Roman and Byzantine Jerusalem and the Cardo

Upon Titus' conquest of Jerusalem in 70 C.E., the city became smaller, especially after its reconstruction by Hadrian (135 C.E.), when he razed the city to its foundation. He built a new city and called it "Colonia Aelia Capitolina," in honor of himself – Aelius Publius Hadrianus – and Jupiter Capitoline, the

Reconstruction of the Cardo in the Upper City of Jerusalem

chief god of the city. The Romans built the forum along with the municipal basilica. The Temple of Venus – Aphrodite, spread from an area between the Holy Sepulcher in the north to the Muristan in the south. Jerusalem was built according to a Roman city plan, with intersecting streets.

The main street, called Cardo, crosses through the city like a main street from north to south, from the Damascus Gate southward to near the Zion Gate. The *dekumanus* crosses the main street from west to east, from Jaffa Gate eastward through David Street and the Street of the Chain to the Temple Mount at Wilson's Arch.

The Tenth Roman Legion was stationed at a fortified camp in the Upper City, in the place where Herod's palace once stood. During the archaeological excavations of the Avigad team, no Roman remnants were found in the south-western part of the Upper City, the Jewish Quarter of our times, which would testify to 250 years of their rule, but only reminders of the destruction of the Second Temple were revealed. Upon this was found a layer a settlement from the Byzantine period – a neighborhood called Mount Zion Quarter.

Byzantine Jerusalem

In Byzantine times the Holy Land was a Byzantine Empire. The Christian Byzantines built churches, monasteries and hospices in Jerusalem; in particular, Emperor Constantinus did so in the Upper City of Jerusalem. He erected in the Upper City the Church of the Holy Sepulcher, as well as the Church of the Holy Zion in the south-west part of the Upper City.

The Empress Eudocia, the wife of Theodosious the Second, took up residence in Jerusalem (443–460 C.E.) and developed the city. She built the Church of Shiloah Pool and rebuilt the city's walls around the Upper City and the Holy Zion Church. In the days of Emperor Justinian (527–565 C.E.),

Jerusalem reached a record level of Christian growth. He built the new St. Mary's Church known as the "Nea" (the new) that was excavated by N. Avigad's team. In 614, the Sassanid Persians conquered Jerusalem from the Byzantines and destroyed it. In 628, the Sassanids returned the city into the hands of Emperor Heraclius, who was the last Byzantine ruler of Jerusalem. In 638, Jerusalem was conquered by the Moslem Arabs, ending the Byzantine Christian rule over the city and the country. But the Christians and the Jews remained the majority in Jerusalem and in the land at the beginning of the Arab and Moslem rule until the end of the tenth century C.E.

The Madaba Map

The depiction of Jerusalem was enlarged (compared to other sites) in the mosaic Madaba Map dating from the sixth century C.E., and Jerusalem there measures 54 cm by 93 cm. The Madaba Map and Jerusalem within it point toward the east, and thus also to the prayer places in the Christian churches, towards the

Jerusalem on the Madaba Map

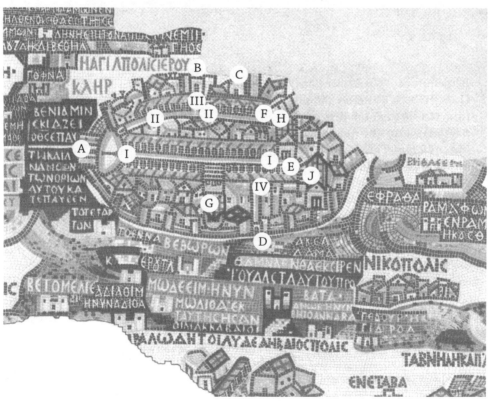

rising sun, in the direction of Apollo – the god of light and the sun in classic mythology; when left represents the north, right is Yemin (Hebrew for "right") and the south, Kedem (Hebrew for "front") the east, and the west is in back. The Byzantine city on the map is surrounded by the principal buildings: walls and towers, gates, churches and main highways. However, the Temple Mount, which existed in the time of the Moslems and was destroyed by the Byzantines, was shown in a very modest way, having a church and the Golden Gate only, in the hope of wiping out any reminder of Jewish existence.

The gates were set out to the four winds of the heavens: the northern gate – Shechem (Damascus) Gate – is the main gate in the wall (from the left) and in front of it the monumental column or statues of the ruler (number 1 on map). The eastern gate – *Lions' Gate* of our times in the east, from which a road leads to the Jordan Valley (B), and in our times the *Golden Gate* – the gate of mercy of the Temple Mount and the Temple (C). The *Southern Gate*, the Dung Gate in our times, apparently existed in Hadrian's day (F) and at its end is the Hadrianic Cardo. Another southern gate existed in Hadrian's day at the edge of the Roman-Byzantine Cardo, called the *Nea Gate* (E). The *Western Gate* is the Jaffa Gate of our times (D), and the extending street eastward is apparently the Street of David.

The Streets: The Cardo II (that was, in my estimation, apparently built for the first time in Herod's day), issued from the Damascus Gate through the Biblical "gorge," or the Tyropoeon Valley, in the Second Temple period. It is the central and most convenient traffic route. Evidence of its having been built in the early days of Herod's reign is:

1. Because Herod built Jerusalem in great splendor in the style of Greco-Roman classical architecture. Thus, it is most likely that he built the intersecting main streets.
2. Because of the giant stones with which a section was built, from the Cardo at the Damascus Gate in the north to a section seen next to the present-day Dung Gate which look Herodian, i.e., much larger than the stones of the Roman-Byzantine Cardo that was discovered in the present-day Jewish Quarter.

The Roman-Byzantine Cardo (I) also started at the Damascus Gate, passed by the Aphrodite Temple (near the Tomb of Jesus) and reached to the Tenth Legion Camp, which was in the southwest of the Upper City in Hadrian's day.

The Byzantine churches were built along the Roman-Byzantine Cardo, the western and northern wall of the city, and upon the ruins of the Jewish Upper City from the days of the Second Temple. Along the Cardo was built: the Tomb of Jesus Church (G) in the center of the thoroughfare, Zion Church (J), and the Neo Church (H) at the southern edge of the Cardo. The Church of the Forgiving Holy Mary was built close to the eastern gate of the city, and the Church of Mary of Magdalene northwest of it.

In the Jewish Quarter near the present-day Street of the Jews, N. Avigad's team uncovered 150 m of the Cardo. Why was the Cardo built here and who built it? The excavators reached this site after perusal of the Madaba Map which depicts the Cardo continuing south of the Tomb of Jesus. When pottery and coins were discovered, it became apparent to the team that this section was built where the Roman Legion had an encampment, and because no earlier Roman structures were found. The Cardo was built by Emperor Justinian in the middle of the sixth century C.E. for the purpose of connecting the Church of the Holy Sepulcher with the entrance to the Nea Church, which also was built in his time. This section was used mainly for processions and religious celebrations. During Crusader times, the gate in the wall south of the Cardo was called "Zion Gate," for the Zion Church and the Christian "Mount Zion," erected 120 m east of present-day Zion Gate.

The excavators dug down 2.5 m to the Street of the Jews, where their initial discovery was the boulevard of destroyed columns of the Cardo. Each column is composed of three parts: its *base*, *trunk* and *heading*, at a height of 5 m. The headings are in Byzantine-Corinthian style. The width of the Cardo Street, with colonnades and sidewalks on both sides, measured 22.5 m, equivalent to 70 Byzantine feet (one Roman foot equals 29.6 cm; one Byzantine foot is 32 cm). The sidewalks were covered with wooden roofs that were anchored in holes of the sidewalk's walls. At both ends of the street and underneath it, alongside the columns, were drainage channels for rainwater.

According to N. Avigad, the narrowing of Jerusalem's streets to today's measurements began after the Moslem conquest of the land. During the Moslem period, the columns of the eastern colonnades were replaced, and, instead of the spreading, tile roof, intersecting vaults were built, the remnants of which can be seen in the eastern part of the Cardo. During the Middle Ages, the days of the Crusaders, the Mamelukes and the Ottomans, stores and workshops were built along the Cardo, using some of the Cardo's structures, until the bazaars were established – the narrow markets of our day – from the Damascus Gate in the north up to the Street of the Jews in the south.

The Nea (New) Church of Saint Mary the Mother of God

The Nea Church, built by Justinian, was one of the biggest and grandest in Jerusalem, but only its ruins, down to one foundation, remain. The church is known in historic literature due to Justinian's historian, Procopius, who lived in Caesarea. He related how the emperor established this church in 543 C.E.

Plan of Byzantine and Crusader remains in the southern section of the Jewish Quarter

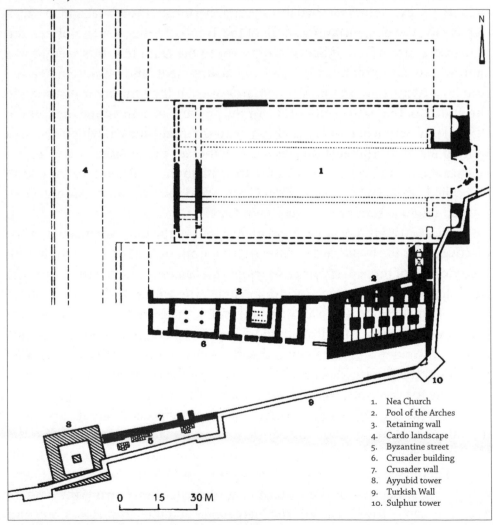

1. Nea Church
2. Pool of the Arches
3. Retaining wall
4. Cardo landscape
5. Byzantine street
6. Crusader building
7. Crusader wall
8. Ayyubid tower
9. Turkish Wall
10. Sulphur tower

0 15 30 M

and wrote: "and in Jerusalem he (Justinian) consecrated a tabernacle to the Mother of God, such that no other dwelling place would equal it; the local people call it the New Church." (In regard to the buildings, see v, 6 N. Avigad translation). According to Procopius, the church also included a monastery, hospice, hospital and library.

During the excavations by Avigad's team in 1973–1977, in the courtyard of the *Batei Machaseh* near the Rothschild House, south of the present-day Jewish Quarter, a segment of a Nea Church wall was uncovered, in a north–south direction, 13 m long and 6.5 m thick, the foundations of which go down 8 m. The wall is built of large, chiseled stones. Within the wall there is a crescent-shaped prayer niche, 5 m in diameter and facing east. The thickness of the wall testifies to the church's huge size – 115 m long and 57 m wide. Four columns of pillars supported its roof, but only the south-eastern corner was discovered – about 5 m in height – near the south-eastern corner of the sulfur tower in the Turkish wall. In 1977, the team found the supporting southern wall of the Nea Church near the Turkish wall. It was in an east–west direction, 66 m long and 7.6 m high (no. 3 on the map), and within a row of vault openings and pressure-relieving arches. A building from the Crusader period was placed against the wall. What we are talking about here is a system of vaults whose internal area comprises 33 m × 9.5–17 m, composed of six vaulted rooms, placed next to one another (no. 2 on the map). The arches were supported by four square-shaped bases, 5 m × 3.5 m, built of plastered parchment stone. These vaults supported the Nea church above them, and later were turned into a large, plastered waterhole, as described by Procopius in his book: "…the church is partially based on the rock, while the other section is hung in the air by means of a large, artificial cantilever, which was added to the hill at the behest of the emperor." The surprising find was a Greek inscription of five lines, 158 cm in length, as follows: "and this is the project carried out through the generosity of our most pious emperor, Flavius Justinian, under the supervision and guidance of Constantine, the most holy priest and monastery abbot (in the year) 13 of Indication."

From the above, the archaeological team concluded that the Byzantine Cardo and the New Church were built in the same period, under the rule of Emperor Justinian. The church was destroyed by the Arabs in 638.

Crusader Structures

According to the archaeological team, it is important to point out that no Moslem remnants were found in the Jewish Quarter from the Umayyad, Jebusite, or Fatimid periods. Alterations were made during the rule of the Crusaders in Jerusalem (1099–1187) to church and fortress structures. In the city they rebuilt the St. Anne Church next to Jehosophat's Gate, (today's Lions' Gate), and added a front and dome to the Tomb of Jesus; the Church of St. Mary at the southern edge of the Misgav Ladakh Street in the Jewish Quarter; refortified "David's Citadel" next to present-day Jaffa Gate; reconstructed the Byzantine Cardo from the Damascus Gate up to the Street of the Jews, in a narrower layout; and built shops in the markets, the roofs of which are now arched and reconstructed; a Crusader building 62 m long (no. 6 on the map) in which there is a large public hall 11.4 m × 16.3 m in area, with four thick columns, next to the underground structure of the Nea, where, in the opinion of the excavators, there may have been a Crusader church. South of this structure, a Crusader wall of the city was discovered, 45 m long and 2.5 m thick (no. 7 on the map) at the Turkish wall.

Close to the Crusader wall, a large Ayyubid tower was found in a wall, measuring 23 m × 23 m. It is partly outside of the city wall excavated by M. Broshi, who discovered a building inscription of the tower from the year 1212, in the days of the ruler al Malek al-Muattem 'Issa (no. 8 on the map). Seven years later, Muattem 'Issa destroyed the wall that had been built, in order to prevent the Crusaders from fortifying the city, should they conquer it. The wall of Jerusalem remained breached from 1219 until 1538, i.e., for 320 years.

Crusader Church

North-east of the ruins of the Tiferet Israel Synagogue, in the direction of an alley leading down to the Western Wall, a Crusader Church was found, the Church of St. Mary of the Germans. It was built in the twelfth century, and its inner dimensions are 20 m × 12 m. It is built on the basilica plan, with a long, rectangular building divided into a central nave and two porticos by means of two rows of square columns, which support the ceiling. Only the north-east column was found *in situ*. Three internal recesses face east, each containing a window, and under the recesses was a water cistern. The western wall of the building has three entrances, the central one wide and tall, and the others small. Four entrances in the northern wall lead to a complex of buildings north of the church. A wide door in the southern wall leads to the buildings south of the church. The roof was not preserved, and the roofing one can see today is modern. South of the church the remains of a two-storied Crusader monastery were found. The lower story had three halls, and the upper story had five square columns, which supported arches.

Armenian Quarter
The Armenian Community

Christianity has been the chief religion in Armenia, on the border between Russia, Turkey and Persia, since the fourth century C.E. It was founded there by St. George (the Giver of Light), who received his religious education at Caesarea, and baptized the Armenian king Tiaridates. The Armenians were thus the first Christian nation in the world. Eusebius, court historian and personal friend of the Emperor Constantine, who lived in Caesarea early in the fourth century, is the first to mention the Christianity of the Armenians. In 404 C.E. the Armenian alphabet was invented, with its thirty-six letters, and the Bible was then translated into this language from the Syrian and Greek sources. The main church in Armenia, founded by St. Gregory, was established at Etchmiadzin, and since that time the vicinity, along with Mount Ararat, has been sacred to Armenians.

At present some 70% of the Armenian people live in the former Soviet Armenia. Their centers in the Middle East are Syria, Lebanon, Antioch and Cyprus, in addition to Jerusalem. The theological center for these countries is in Beirut, in Lebanon.

According to tradition, after the Crucifixion of Jesus, his disciples chose St. James (Jacob), the brother of Jesus, to be their religious leader and the first bishop of Jerusalem. His home, on Mount Zion, became a spiritual and religious center.

In 62 C.E., St. James was killed, and his body flung into the Kidron Valley, where, according to Armenian tradition, it was buried. He was re-interred in the fourth century in the church bearing his name in the Armenian Quarter. The church also contains the head of St. James, the brother of St. John the Apostle, who was beheaded by Agrippa I in 44 C.E.

From the information found on two mosaics, and from Armenian inscriptions discovered in the Russian Convent on the Mount of Olives and at a site north-west of the Damascus Gate, it is clear that Armenians have been in Jerusalem since the sixth century C.E. An Armenian pilgrim of the seventh century noted that about 70 monasteries existed in Jerusalem. Until the seventh century, the Greek Orthodox Patriarch was head of the Armenian Church; since that time the Armenian Church has had its own Patriarch. The Armenian Patriarch of Jerusalem is regarded as the successor to St. James, the brother of Jesus, after whom the Patriarchal Convent and Order are named. 'Omar ibn-al-Khattab provided the Armenians with a written permit (kept in the Library of the Armenian Patriarchate) recognizing the rights of the Armenian Patriarch over the places holy to Christianity in Jerusalem, Bethlehem, Nablus and Samaria.

The Armenian Catholic Church, a faction that arose during the Crusades, recognizes the authority of Rome.

Under Crusader rule the status of the Armenian Patriarch rose, since the Crusaders included Armenians from Cilicia. The Armenians were the Crusaders' only allies in the Middle East. According to Armenian tradition, Saladin granted the Armenians a *firman* (permit) concerning their Holy Places, and after the Turkish Conquest of 1517, Sultan Selim I gave them a *firman* stating their rights and setting them over the Syrian, Coptic and Ethiopian communities in the city.

During the time of the Patriarch Kerikor Baronder (1613–45), there was large-scale construction in the Armenian Quarter, and at this time many of the existing buildings were put up. The ownership of St. James' Church was contested for a long time by the Armenians and the Greek Orthodox, until the final judgment of Sultan Mahmud II (1813) in favor of the Armenians. From that date the Armenian community in Jerusalem developed rapidly. In 1843 the theological seminary was founded, and assumed an importance second only to that of Etchmiadzin. In 1866 the Armenian Press, which prints religious works for Armenians all over the world, was established. After 1918, when a million and a half Armenians were massacred by the Turks (according to Armenian estimate, although the international committees believe the number to be about 800,000), some 10,000 Armenians arrived in Palestine, of whom about 4,000 found shelter in the Armenian Convent of Jerusalem. The present Patriarch, Turkus Manujian, was enthroned in 1990.

The Armenian Patriarch, together with the Greek Orthodox and Latin Patriarchs, is responsible for the Holy Places. Each sect conducts its prayers in its own language, as at the Church of the Holy Sepulcher and the Church of the Nativity in Bethlehem. The Church of the Tomb of the Virgin, in Gethsemane (in the Kidron Valley) belongs to the Armenians and the Greek Orthodox only. There are Armenian convents in Jaffa, Ramleh and Bethlehem, and an Armenian school and church have recently been established in Amman. Jerusalem has about 3,500 Armenians.

The Armenian Quarter

The Armenian Convent was established on the highest spot on Mount Zion, at a height of 780 m, on the site of Herod's palace. The Armenian Quarter is self-contained, since it is surrounded by walls and iron gates, and is thus separated from the other sections of the Old City. Within the complex there are several important ancient buildings, such as the Church of St. James, the Church of St. Theodorus (at present housing a library of ancient Armenian manuscripts), the residence of the Armenian Patriarch, the theological seminary, the Armenian Press, the monastery and the Church of St. Archangels, now known as Deir e-Zeituneh.

Armenian architecture is unique in that each monastery is a complex including several churches, bell towers, tombs of saints, public buildings and dwellings, surrounded by a wall. The apse of the Church of St. James is not visible externally, as is the case with the Byzantine churches; the church has a tall narrow Romanesque arch and a high cupola. The dome of an Armenian church is unusual in that it is placed at the center of the church rather than at one end, and is supported on a square or angled base instead of on a circular one. The dome does not rest directly on the roof, as in the early Byzantine churches, but on a high drum, as in the later Byzantine style; this seems to have been an Armenian innovation. The external dome is not rounded in the Byzantine style, but is conical or pyramidal.

Church of St. James (Jacob)

The iron gate at the main entrance to the Armenian Quarter, in the west, dates from the time of the Patriarch Kerikor (1646), as is recorded in the inscription over the gate. There is also an inscription in Arabic, put there by the Sultan Jakmak (1452), telling of the cancellation of the special tax on the church and warning away potential intruders. In the wall of the entrance on the left side of the courtyard of the Church of St. James there are tombstones engraved in Armenian; one of these goes back to 1192, to the days of the Patriarch Abraham II.

Armenian tradition dates the church to the fourth century, when it was named after James (Jacob) the brother of Jesus; it is known in Arabic as Deir Mar Ya'acub. The church is located at the place where James, the brother of St. John, the Disciple, was beheaded by Agrippa; the head is interred under the paving of the small chamber north of the church nave: "Now about that time Herod the king stretched forth his hands to vex certain of the church. And he killed James the brother of John with the sword." (*Acts of the Apostles XII*,

1–2). The body of Jesus' brother is interred, according to Armenian tradition, under the main altar of the church. If so, who was Jacob? In Christian tradition there were three figures of that name:

1. Jacob the son of Zebedee, one of the 12 Apostles, the elder brother of John. He was a fisherman on Lake of Galilee (*Kinneret*), and he and his brother were among the first disciples (*Matthew* IV, 21). This St. James is the patron saint of Spain, since according to tradition he was active in Spain, where he was given the name of Santiago.
2. James the son of Alphas, another of the Twelve Disciples (*Mark* III, 18 ff.)
3. St. James the brother of Jesus who, according to Catholic tradition was the stepbrother or cousin of Jesus. After the death of Jesus and the departure of Peter from Jerusalem, James was one of the first leaders of the Christian community in the city (*Acts* XV, 13–21; XXI, 18–25; *Galatians* I, 19; II, 9–12; etc). He was the representative of Jewish Christianity. In the year 62 C.E. he was executed on the initiative of the Zadokite priest Ananus (*Antiquities of the Jews* XX, 9), since his title as the brother of Jesus who was called the Messiah caused much irritation among the Pharisees. Eusebius also mentions the sect of poor Christian Jews.

The original Church of St. James was very large; it was partly destroyed during the Persian Invasion, was restored in the eighth century, and resumed its original form, with certain changes, in the twelfth century, after the Crusader occupation of the city.

Today the church has an area of 17.5 m × 24 m, and is divided by four square, broad columns covered in blue tiles, into a central nave and porticos. The columns support a cupola with eight arches, through which the light penetrates. The walls are covered in blue tiles – some of the best in the country – to a height of two meters above the floor. They are decorated with seventeenth century icons. In the front part of the church there are three altars: the central one is named after St. James the brother of Jesus, the right-hand one after John the Baptist, and the left-hand one after St. Mary. The gilded wooden decorations of the altars date from 1731. Two thrones stand opposite the central altar: the one on the left, surmounted by a cupola, marks the tomb of St. James, built in 1661 and restored in 1812, and the one on the right is the throne of the Patriarch, which was restored in 1812. In the southern wall, near the altar, is the Chapel of St. Peter and St. Paul, with its door ornamented with pearls. Just west of this chapel is the Chapel of Etchmiadzin. The altar here was put up in 1733, but on the right there is an additional altar named after Mount Sinai, with three stones underneath it from Mount Sinai, Mount Tabor and the Jordan, for the benefit of pilgrims unable to visit these places. The throne is used by the Armenian Patriarch when he visits Jerusalem. The walls of the church bear painted tiles from 1760, depicting the life of Jesus, and other historic events. 16 stairs lead up to a room built in 1835, containing fragments of a cross and ancient tombstones.

Church of Theodorus

This church was built in 1266, and has an area of 9 m × 18 m. The walls are decorated with blue tiles, and the altar has an eighteenth century painting of St. Mary. The library houses 3,500 ancient Armenian manuscripts and translations, dating from the thirteenth and fourteenth centuries.

The residence of the Armenian Patriarch is in the south-western part of the church courtyard and surmounted by a dome. The elementary school was founded in 1929, and the Armenian secondary school in 1953; the staff and students are all Armenian.

Convent of the Archangels
(House of Annas, Father-in-Law of the High Priest)

The convent called in Arabic 'Deir e-Zeituneh', is south-west of the school. The Arabic name means "Convent of the Olive Tree," after the olive tree to which Jesus was tied on the night of his arrest, near the house of Annas, father-in-law of the High Priest Caiaphas, during the reign of Agrippa: "Then the regiment and the captain and the officers of the Jews took Jesus, and bound him. And led him away to Annas first: for he was father-in-law to Caiaphas, who was the high priest that same year. Now Caiaphas was he, who gave counsel to the Jews, that it was expedient that one man should die for the people." (*St. John* XVIII, 12–14).

Tradition claims that a commemorative chapel was built on the spot in the fourth century, but the present church was erected, according to the Armenians, in the 12th century, on the site where Jesus was first arrested. To the right of the church there is an arched passageway leading to the Chapel of St. Hripsime, which has a wooden door decorated in Oriental style with an inscription dated 1649. An olive tree in the courtyard is believed to be the one to which Jesus was tied.

The iron gate of the quarter leads to Mount Zion, on the eastern part of which is located the Armenian cemetery, next to the Church of the Dormition.

"Mount Zion" and Its Churches

The Upper City, mistakenly called by Josephus Flavius "Mount Zion" (and later the name Mount Zion was allotted to the part of Zion which is outside the city wall), like the Mount of Olives in the east, is one of the highest points near the walls of the Old City, and the only position that commands a view of a considerable part of the city and its surroundings. It has therefore been the scene of decisive battles for Jerusalem throughout history. "Mount Zion" is one of the few places in the city holy to Jews, Christians and Moslems. To Jews, the hill is important as the site of David's Tomb and as the traditional location (marked by an ancient synagogue) of the Ark of the Covenant prior to the building of the First Temple.

"Mount Zion" has been hallowed by Christians since it was identified as the scene of the Last Supper, and also as the site of the tomb of St. Stephen (*The Acts of the Apostles*, VII, 58). The Last Supper of Jesus and the Disciples took place on the Feast of Passover in the upper story of Caiaphas' palace, according to *St. Luke* XXII, VIII–13: "And he sent Peter and John, saying, Go and prepare us the Passover, that we may eat. And they said unto him: Where wilt thou that we prepare? And he said unto them, Behold, when ye are entered into the city, there shall a man meet you, bearing a pitcher of water, follow him into the house where he entereth in. And ye shall say unto the good man of the house, The Master saith unto thee, Where is the guest chamber, where I shall eat the Passover with my disciples? And he shall shew you a large upper room furnished: there make ready. And they went, and found as he had said unto them: and they made ready the Passover." After Jesus was taken, he was brought to the house of the High Priest (*St. Matthew* XXVI, 57; *St. Mark* XIV, 53; *St. Luke* XXII, 54; *St. John* XVIII, 24). Christian tradition deduced from this that the house of Caiaphas was on "Mount Zion," the Upper City, south of the palace of Herod and south of the present wall. Professor Avi Yonah identifies the house of Caiaphas from the Madaba Map as being south of the Zion Gate. South of Caiaphas' house he identifies the Church of Mount Zion and south of that the Church of St. Stephen. Bishop Epiphanius, who lived in the country in the fourth century, noted that there was a small church on Mount Zion. From the fourth century onwards the Christians called the hill

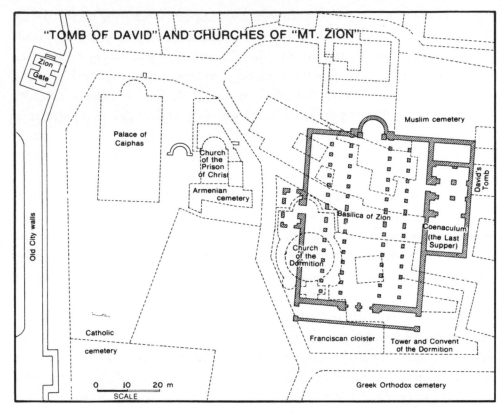

"Tomb of David" and Churches of Mt. Zion

of the Upper City Mount Zion, and since that time the site of the Last Supper has been identified.

The Church of Mount Zion was built by Maximus, Jerusalem's bishop, in 340 C.E. and its significance is evident from its appellation "Mother of the Churches."

The House of Caiaphas

The site of the house of Caiaphas on which later was built, first, a Byzantine church, and then a Crusader chapel, is now in the Armenian cemetery. The actual position of the house of Caiaphas and of the church, of which no trace remains, is shown in a courtyard south of the Zion Gate. A gate in the southeast of this courtyard leads into the Armenian cemetery, where Armenian patriarchs are buried in vaults near the walls and priests under the paving. The two cisterns in the courtyard were used for purification. A small church in the south-west part of the courtyard is identified by the Armenians as the place where Jesus was arrested after the Last Supper. Under the altar is a fragment of the stone, which, according to Armenian tradition, sealed the Tomb of Jesus. Due to its sanctity, "Mount Zion" became an area for the cemeteries of other Christian sects, which are found along the slope of the hill from the Church of St. Peter's in Gallicantu to David's Tomb. The Protestant cemetery is the resting place of the great archaeologist Sir Flinders Petrie, a pioneer in the study of the Holy Land; and in the Catholic cemetery lies Christopher Costigan, who died in 1835 during one of the first explorations of the northern part of the Dead Sea.

Archaeological excavations at the House of Caiaphas were carried out in 1971 by M. Broshi, some 30 m south-west of the Zion Gate. A section of Israelite masonry was discovered, with pottery vessels and figurines, and two stone weights, one with the inscription *shenei shekalim* (two shekels) and the other *arba gerah* (four geras). This find provides evidence of the westward expansion of the city during the First Temple period, in the seventh century B.C.E.

Three rooms with arched roofs, from the late Second Temple period, were found. They appear to have been part of the dwelling of a wealthy family, since they were finished in colored plaster, and were decorated with a great variety of geometric patterns, plants and birds; fragments of the plaster were found in a large pile. Broken roof tiles and bricks from the late Roman period, bearing the stamp of the Tenth Legion, were also found.

Three mosaic pavements from Byzantine churches were discovered, and there were fragments of Arab pottery in the cisterns.

Armenian Garden

During D. Bahat's and M. Broshi's excavations (in 1971 and 1972, respectively), the retaining walls of the foundations of Herod's palace were uncovered. These walls were 2.25 m thick; no remains of the superstructure were found.

The excavations under the Ottoman city wall at the same site revealed the foundations of the Second Temple wall, which was thicker than the present wall.

Remains of the palace of the Crusader kings of Jerusalem were also uncovered. The lower story contained two vaulted halls, of an area of about 17 m × 6.5 m, with cisterns underneath them. The eastern cistern, which was the larger of the two, bore the relief of a Crusader cross, the symbol of Anjou at that period. The building appears to have been erected in the year 1131, in the reign of Fulk of Anjou, husband of Queen Melisande and grandfather of

Richard the Lion Heart. The building was also used by the Mameluke rulers of the city.

Church of the Last Supper

According to Christian tradition, the bones of St. Stephen were discovered and re-interred in the early fifth century on Mount Zion, in the Church of the Last Supper. The Church of Mount Zion, or Holy Sion, named for the Holy Mary, is depicted on the Madaba map, with a distinctive red roof. The church was second in importance in ninth-century Jerusalem, after the Church of the Holy Sepulcher, and was walled. The structures around the Church of Sancta Sion are also depicted with red roofs, and according to Avi Yonah, these were hospices and a convent. The church was probably destroyed in the Persian invasion of 614, and restored by Modestus, the Patriarch of Jerusalem, in 634.

J.T. Barclay, in his book *City of the Great King* (pp. 337, 340), noted that Bishop Arculf, who visited Jerusalem in the seventh century, reported six gates and 84 towers in the city. On "Mount Zion" Arculf saw the square Church of the Last Supper, the marble pillar to which Jesus was tied during his arrest, the place where the Virgin Mary died, and the scene of St. Stephen's tortures. Barclay also noted (p. 343) that Bernard the Wise, who visited the city in 867, found another church on "Mount Zion," named after St. Simon, or Sion-Zion, where Jesus washed the feet of the Disciples.

The present Church of the Dormition is located over Byzantine and Crusader remains, as recounted by the Pilgrim of Bordeaux, who saw a chapel on the site. (The Pilgrim also mentioned that "Mount Zion" once had seven synagogues, only one of which existed in his time.) The Crusaders discovered the ruins of buildings, which comprised the two sections of the Church of "Holy Zion," in the north, and a chapel commemorating the Last Supper, in the south. The Church of the Last Supper was a two-storied building with four chapels. When Saladin took Jerusalem in 1187 the Church of the Holy Mary was destroyed. Later, in 1192, the Crusaders fenced in the church, but the Sultan of Damascus, Al-Malek al-Mu'attam 'Issa, destroyed it in 1219. In 1244 the Khwarizmians, from the valley of the Oxus in central Asia, invaded the country, massacred the Christians of Jerusalem and devastated the Church of Mount Zion for the third time. The Franciscans acquired the site (including "David's Tomb") from the Mamelukes during the years 1335 to 1337, and restored the present Church of the Last Supper in 1438, using material from the ruined Byzantine and Crusader churches. In 1468 the Moslems destroyed the Franciscan buildings, and the Christians rebuilt it in 1489. The building then changed hands several times until it finally came under Moslem authority and no Christians were permitted to enter.

The traditional hall of the Last Supper is on the second story of "David's Tomb," on the north side. The area of the hall is 15.3 m × 9.4 m, and is divided by three rows of limestone pillars, of Byzantine and Crusader origin, which support a ceiling with early Gothic arches. In the sixteenth century the Moslems built a prayer niche (*mihrab*) in the southern wall and a pulpit (*minbar*) in the southwestern corner, in order to emphasize their hold on the building. To the right of the *mihrab* there is inscribed a quotation about King David from the *Koran*. "O David! Lo! We have set thee as a viceroy in the earth, therefore judge aright between mankind, and follow not desire" (xxxviii, 27).

Suleiman the Magnificent did not include Mount Zion within the walls, and the area has been outside the walled city ever since. In works of art "Mount Zion" appears within the city as well as outside it. During the Ottoman period the Dajani family was in charge of "Mount Zion" and "David's Tomb," and neither Jew nor Christian was permitted to pray there.

Church of the Dormition

The church was built and consecrated in memory of the last sleep of the Virgin Mary, since Christian tradition identifies this spot as the dwelling place of Mary after the Crucifixion. It is probably built over the ruins of an ancient church. In 1898 the Turks presented the garden to the German emperor, Wilhelm ii.

Between 1906 and 1910 German Benedictine monks built the church, in the style of a medieval German Church – more precisely – the cathedral of Aachen. It has two stories of chapels. In the eastern part of the hall, in the apse of the lower story, is a mosaic of Mary and Jesus, with representations of the prophets of Israel, surrounded by an inscription from *Isaiah* (vii, 14). Another mosaic with inscriptions is to be found within the hall, and niches in the walls are decorated with mosaics of saints: St. Benedict, founder of the Order, Mary, John the Baptist, Michael, Joseph, and the city of Cologne, whose archbishop was given the site by Emperor Wilhelm.

In the basement there is a dome, resting on six piers, each decorated in a different style. Beneath the center of the dome is a statue of the recumbent Virgin. The dome itself is decorated with a mosaic showing Jesus in the center and Biblical women at his feet: Ruth with the sheaves, Yael with a hammer, Miriam and her timbrel, Judith and the head of Holofernes, Esther wearing a

The Church of the Dormition (left) and the Benedictine monastery (right)

royal headdress, and Eve with the apple and the serpent. Seven niches in the walls of the hall are ornamented with frescoes.

The building was damaged during the War of Independence and the Six Day War, and was restored by the Israeli Government.

Church of St. Peter in Gallicantu

The present church was built in 1931 over ancient caves, with crosses engraved in the walls. According to one Christian tradition, the House of Caiaphas, where Jesus was detained (*St. John* xviii, 12–14) was on this site. (Archaeological investigation has established the site of the palace on "Mount Zion," south of the Zion Gate, while Armenian tradition places it in the Armenian Quarter.) The church appears to be built over the ruins of a Byzantine and Crusader church. During the Crusader period the church was called St. Peter in Gallicantu (at cock-crow). Under the church, there are caves where is shown the place to which the Apostle Peter fled and cried, because he had given in to his impulse and had strayed from Jesus; here the monks indicate the place of Jesus' incarceration: "And Jesus saith unto him, Verily I say unto thee, That this day, even in the night before the cock crow, thou shalt deny me thrice" (*St. Mark* xiv, 30). "Peter then denied again; and immediately the cock crowed" (*St.*

John, XVIII, 27). The caves under the church are shown as the place where the apostle Peter fled to weep for his denial of Jesus, and the actual prison of Jesus is also shown. The church was destroyed in 1320. Archaeological investigations were carried out in 1887, and a Hebrew inscription, *le-asham hu korban* (it is a sacrifice for a guilt-offering) was found on a door lintel, as well as a stone weight from the Temple millstones, a detention room with crosses on the walls, and store-rooms. An ancient terraced street was uncovered, leading up from the Pool of Siloam in the Tyropoeon Valley to "Mount Zion" and onwards to the Mount of Olives. In addition there were Byzantine coins of the sixth and seventh centuries, fragments of statues, a bronze ring with a seal and figure of a cock, another seal with a cock, Byzantine pottery and oil lamps, and a mosaic with a Greek inscription including verse 8 from *Psalms* CXXI: "The Lord shall guard thy going out and thy coming in from this time forth and for ever."

Syrian Orthodox Church of St. Mark

This building lies east of the Armenian Quarter within the Old City. It is one of the oldest churches in the Old City, founded by the Syrian Christians, who are considered to have been the earliest Christians there. They recite their prayers in the ancient Syriac language, which closely resembles the Aramaic commonly spoken during the Second Temple period. By Syrian tradition, this was the site of St. Mark's home, and thus also the site of the Last Supper. He was the first bishop of the Syrian sect, at the beginning of the second century C.E. after the founding of Aelia Capitolina.

During restoration work carried out in 1940, an ancient Syriac inscription was found in the internal wall of the church, to the right of the entrance gate. The inscription was covered in white cloth and plaster, and was carved in hard limestone. The translation reads as follows: "This is the house of Miriam, the mother of Yohanan, also called Mark. The building was consecrated as a church by the Apostles, in the name of the Virgin Mary, after the ascension of our Lord Jesus to Heaven, and was rebuilt in the year 73, after King Titus had destroyed Jerusalem." On the basis of the Aramaic lettering of the inscription, the building may be dated to the fifth or sixth century.

The Syrians are one of the Monophysite sects.

Sites in the church: The main gate was erected in the 12th century. The altar and prayer niche were built in 1733, as was the throne, and *Kubbet el-Ma'mudiyeh*. The closet for religious articles dates from 1733, and that for ritual books from 1783. Among the important manuscripts are the *Letters of*

St. Bullis (seventh century), Characlete's translation of the New Testament (728) and the *Ritual of Consecrating the Church, of the Great Fast, and of the Saints*, written in the ninth century according to the ritual of Antioch. The great silver cross was made in 1891, and the goblets for the ritual blessing are from the eighteenth to the twentieth centuries.

Chapels and Churches on the Mount of Olives

A third group of holy places, located on the Mount of Olives and its slopes, is that through which Jesus passed on his way to Jerusalem, as he was accustomed to spending the nights on the hillside rather than in the city: "And in the day time he was teaching in the temple; and at night he went out, and abode in the mount that is called the Mount of Olives" (*St. Luke* XXI, 37). Sometimes Jesus spent the night in Bethany: "And he left them, and went out of the city into Bethany; and he lodged there" (*St. Matthew* XXI, 17). Most of the churches on the Mount of Olives are in commemoration of the ascent of Jesus to Heaven, and are linked to various events in the lives of Jesus and his disciples along the way from the hill to the Temple and Jerusalem.

Church and Dome of the Ascension

The early Christians consecrated the peak of the Mount of Olives, at the site of the village of a-Tur, because of the tradition of the "inscrutable mysteries" which Jesus taught his disciples here, and because it was from here that he disappeared on his ascent to Heaven. The place was so sacred to Christians that Constantine erected a basilica second in importance only to the Churches of the Nativity, in Bethlehem, and the Holy Sepulcher, ascending to the Mount of Olives and continuing on to "Mount Zion."

The church lies 818 m above sea level. In the fifth century there was a Church of the Ascension on the spot. The present Crusader building is octagonal, enclosed by a circular wall, within which a concentric row of columns supports the cupola. In the center of the court there is a rock on which, according to legend, is the footprint left by Jesus on his ascension. In 1187 Saladin turned the church into a mosque. Various Christian sects celebrate the Feast of the Ascension here, putting up tents in which to spend the night.

Viri Galilaei

Also at the top of the Mount of Olives, there is another church connected with Jesus' ascent to Heaven. This the Viri Galilaei, so named because of the verse in *Acts* (I, 11): "Which also said, Ye men of Galilee, why stand ye gazing up into heaven? this same Jesus, which is taken up from you into heaven shall so come in like manner as ye have seen him go into heaven."

In 1881 the Greek Orthodox Church erected a church here and enclosed it by a wall. There are the remains of a Byzantine chapel in the south-west corner of the closure. There was also a vineyard, known as *Karm e-Sayad* (the Hunter's vineyard), and the altar could be identified as the Mount of the Anointing of the Old Testament.

Church of Pater Noster (Our Father)

This is the site of a Carmelite church and convent. The Byzantine Church of the Eleona was originally built by Constantine, who also erected the Church of the Holy Sepulcher in Jerusalem and the Church of the Nativity in Bethlehem. The Church of Pater Noster is still unfinished. In its foundation are two grottoes whose immense rocks bear the names of those who donated funds for the church. According to Christian tradition, this was the place where Jesus prophesied concerning the end of Jerusalem and of the world (*St. Matthew* XIII 1–8; XXI, 5–9). The Church of the Eleona was destroyed in 614, and rebuilt when the Byzantines resumed power over the city. El-Hakem, ruler of Egypt, destroyed it again in the eleventh century (1009), and the Crusaders rebuilt it; after their departure it was again ruined. Excavations carried out in 1868 by Ch. Clermont-Ganneau uncovered tombs and a cistern under the foundations of the church. A French convent was established in 1874, and given to the Carmelite Order. In 1910 the "White Fathers" took it over. The Lord's Prayer the "Pater Noster" (*St. Luke*, XI, 2) appears on the walls of the church and cloisters in 44 different languages.

Russian Church at A-Tur

The Russian church and hospice for pilgrims were built on one of the peaks of the Mount of Olives between 1870 and 1880. The belfry is six stories high, with 214 steps, and is on the site claimed by the Russians to be the scene of the Ascension. In 1907 it was given to the Russian nuns, who are in charge of the church and its unusual rites to this day. The frescoes and paintings within the church were executed by the nuns. From the belfry there is a magnificent view of the Judean Desert, the Jordan Valley, the Dead Sea, and the mountains of Moab and Gilead.

Church of Dominus Flevit (The Lord Wept)

The church stands on the western slope of the Mount of Olives, facing the Kidron Valley and Gethsemane. The Crusaders identified the site as the scene of Jesus' weeping over the future destruction of Jerusalem (*St. Luke* xix, 37–44), and built a church, which was later destroyed. In 1518 the Turks built a mosque, which was used as a religious school; its ruins are still visible. The Franciscans acquired a plot of land near the ruins of the mosque, and built a small chapel in 1891. The present church was built in 1953, and the chapel became a monastery. The church was designed by the Italian architect Berlucci in the shape of a cross, with a dome resembling a teardrop. The interior of the dome is decorated with reliefs depicting events in the life of Jesus. In the center of the church can be seen sections of ancient mosaic flooring, decorated with plant and geometric patterns. A Greek inscription was found on the subject of Simeon, a follower of Jesus, who built the prayer hall, decorated it and dedicated it to the Lord Jesus and the monks Georgius and Demisio. Stone ossuaries were discovered in caves hewn from rock, as well as many inscriptions in Aramaic and Greek. Excavations have revealed graves of the late Canaanite period, the late Second Temple, late Roman, and early Byzantine periods.

Russian Church of St. Mary Magdalene

This church, near the Kidron Valley, was built between 1885 and 1888 by Czar Alexander iii, and bears the name of his mother, Maria. For this reason it was dedicated to Mary Magdalene. It is in the style of sixteenth and seventeenth century Russian churches, and its characteristic onion domes are a landmark. The pictures inside were painted by Russian artists in the nineteenth century. Behind the apse stands out the rock of the Apostles who, according to a fourteenth century Christian tradition, fell asleep at the feet of St. Peter, St. James and St. John, while their Lord Jesus was undergoing his tribulations (*Matthew* xxvi, 36–38). The church was used as a hospice by elderly or infirm Russian pilgrims who were unable to go down to the site of John's baptism at the Jordan. Able-bodied pilgrims went down to the river and immersed themselves wrapped in sheets, which they took home with them kept to be used as shrouds. In the courtyard of the church graves were found, probably from the Second Temple period, as well as an ancient staircase going up to the Mount of Olives.

Basilica of the Agony or Church of All Nations

This church, near the Kidron Valley road, was originally built by Theodosius I (379–393), to commemorate the arrest of Jesus. The Crusaders built a modest church which was later destroyed, and the present building was erected in the early 1920s. It has windows of alabaster. Sections of the Byzantine mosaic are visible, but there are no Crusader remains, except outside the church. The church was built with the donations of the churches of many Catholic nations, and was therefore called the Church of All Nations. The paintings bear the names of the sixteen states which took part in the building; each of the domes of the church is named after a nation. The façade of the church is decorated with colorful frescoes, depicting the suffering Jesus with his four disciples, and underneath them a verse from the *Epistle to the Hebrews*, 5:7.

Basillica of the Agony, also called the Church of All Nations

Tomb of the Virgin Mary (Church of the Assumption)

The Tomb of the Virgin can be seen in Gethsemane, in a crypt resembling the Grotto of the Cross in the Church of the Holy Sepulcher, at some depth underground. The church adjoining it is called the Church of the Assumption, because of the Christian belief that Mary was taken to Heaven. The present edifice was probably on the site of a Byzantine church, over which was built a Crusader church, destroyed by Saladin in 1187, and of which only the richly-carved gates remain. The church was restored by the Franciscans in the fourteenth century. The Greek Orthodox Church decided to rebuild it in 1757, and they share it today with the Armenians. The Syrians, Copts and Ethiopians have minor rights, including that of praying.

The church, which was built by Emperor Theodosius I in 385 C.E. (although the present one dates from the Crusader period), is reached via 45 steps

Tomb of the Virgin Mary, Gethsemane

TOMB OF THE VIRGIN, GETHSEMANE

leading down from the road. Halfway down, on the right, there is a chapel to Joachim and Anna, parents of the Virgin Mary. A chapel of St. Joseph is on the left, and his tomb is opposite. South of it there is a *mihrab* (prayer niche) where Moslems pray. The altar in the west, opposite the grave, belongs to the Armenians. In 1946, a cistern with a roof supported on 143 columns, was found west of the grave, directly opposite it. The Grotto of Gethsemane has an area of 17 m × 9 m, and a maximum height of 3.5 m. The walls were painted in the twelfth century, and the floor covered in a mosaic, which has been almost completely obliterated. According to Christian tradition, Jesus was teaching his disciples in the grotto at the time the messengers of Caiaphas came to arrest him (*St. John* xviii, 1–7). Since 1392 the cave has belonged to the Franciscans. It was restored in 1959, when its entrance was rebuilt and verses (*St. John* xviii, 2–6) were engraved on it. It was also enclosed by a wall.

CHAPTER IX

THE TEMPLE MOUNT AND JERUSALEM UNDER THE MOSLEMS

The Temple Mount is known in Arabic as *Al-Haram e-Sherif* (the Noble Sanctuary), even though *Haram*, which means shrine or temple, is applied only to the *Ka'abah* in Mecca, and not even to el-Medina. Its center is occupied by a platform (*mastaba*) surrounded by a courtyard. The platform has an area of 23 dunams, and the Dome of the Rock rises at its center. The courtyard (*sahn*) is 4–6 m lower than the platform, and includes the entire area of the Temple Mount (113 dunams). The *El Aqsa* (distant) Mosque stands at the southern end of the courtyard, adjoining the southern wall. A third of the courtyard is planted with trees, mostly olive trees.

At present there are ten gates open in the Temple Mount wall. The seven western ones are, from south to north: the Gate of the Maghrebis (Moors, of northern Africa), the Gate of the Chain, the Gate of the Cotton Market, the Gate of Ablutions, the Iron Gate, the Prison Gate and the Ghawanmeh Gate. The three northern gates are the Dark Gate, the Gate of Hutta (Penance), and the Gate of the Tribes. The 'Atm (= darkness) Gate also bears the name of King Feisal of Iraq, who entered the Temple Mount through it in 1930.

During the period of Moslem rule the Temple Mount was divided into four main parts:

1. The upper platform bearing the Dome of the Rock, and additional small domes used for private prayer.

2. The El-Aqsa Mosque and original Mosque of Omar, adjoining the southern wall of the Temple Mount.
3. The courtyard, including additional secondary domes, praying platforms, niches and fountains.
4. The arched colonnades at the western and northern sides of the enclosure, where religious schools (*madares*) and additional mosques and minarets were built.

Dates In the History of Jerusalem Under the Moslems

The Moslem Conquest occurred in 638 C.E.

The tenth caliph, 'Abd el-Malek, built the Dome of the Rock, 692–697, basing the plan on that of the Rotunda in the Church of the Holy Sepulcher.

From 969 the Fatimid Caliphs ruled Jerusalem from Egypt; in 1009 one of them, El-Hakem, ordered the destruction of all the churches and synagogues in Jerusalem.

The Turkish Seljuks seized power over the mountainous regions of the country in 1071. The Crusades began in this period, and in 1099 the country was taken by the Crusaders from the Seljuks, and the Fatimids, who still ruled the coastal area.

The Egyptian-Syrian sultan, Saladin (Salah e-Din) defeated the Crusaders in 1187. In 1250 the Egyptian Mamelukes invaded the country, took power from the hands of Saladin's successors, and maintained their rule for 270 years, until the Ottoman Turks took over in 1517.

Ibrahim Pasha, ruler of Egypt, conquered the country in 1831. A great wave of Jewish immigration to the country and to Jerusalem began, and Jews and Christians started to establish Houses of Prayer in the city.

In 1840 the Turks, with the help of England and Austria, took the country from the Egyptians.

In 1855 Europeans entered the Temple Mount for the first time.

During 1,120 years of Moslem regimes in Palestine, the Arabs ruled only 114 years.

The Dome of the Rock

The *Koran* describes the Night Journey of Mohammed in his dream, on his miraculous steed el-Burak, from Mecca to El-Aqsa ("a remote place" in Arabic), where, with the angel Gabriel, he prayed to all the prophets of old,

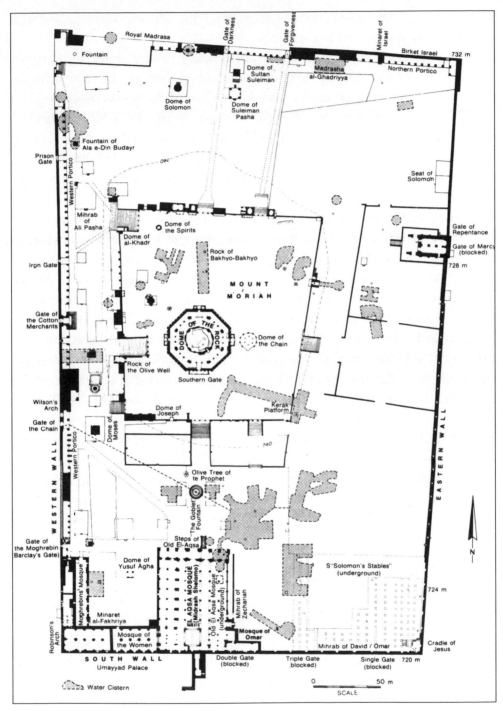

Plan of the Temple Mount

passed through the seven heavens, met Abraham, Moses, Aaron and all the holy men, then returned to earth.

Mohammed rose from Mecca to heavenward and reached the seventh heaven. There he saw the El-Aqsa. For political reasons, the El-Aqsa mosque in Jerusalem was built about 60 years later when El-Aqsa was described.

The early Moslems identified the El-Aqsa, from which Mohammed ascended to Heaven, not as the Temple Mount in Jerusalem, but as the seventh heaven of a celestial shrine; that is to say, Mohammed ascended directly from Mecca, since in fact there was no temple in Jerusalem during Mohammed's lifetime.

The pilgrimage to Mecca confers a special status on those making it, and they receive the title *hajj*. In contrast, a pilgrimage to Jerusalem is considered as a *ziyarah*, a visit to a holy place which does not confer a special status.

In 622 the Moslems and pagans of Medina faced the *Ka'abah* at Mecca during prayers, and the Jews faced towards Jerusalem. For 18 months Mohammed also turned to Jerusalem, but then Mohammed forced the Jews to turn towards Mecca as well. One can assume from this that Jerusalem was not sacred to Islam in earlier days. Indeed, the insignificance of Jerusalem for the Moslems at this time may be deduced from the fact that it was one of the last cities to be taken by the Syrian Moslems after the death of Mohammed. It was conquered by a mediocre commander, and not by 'Omar, whom legend only later identified as the conqueror. It was known at first to the Arabs as Ilya (Aelia Capitolina) rather than as Beit el-Maqdas (the Holy House).

Jerusalem ranks third in Moslem tradition, after Mecca and Medina. A proverb says: "One prayer in Mecca is valued at ten thousand prayers; a prayer in Medina is valued at one thousand prayers; and a prayer in Jerusalem is valued at five hundred prayers."

Structure of the Dome of the Rock

The octagonal Dome of the Rock is one of the most beautiful edifices in the Middle East. It contains two concentric rows of pillars. The inner row of pillars supports the dome, while the outer row supports the structure of the building itself. Faithful Moslems used to circle the rock under the center of the Dome, as was the custom at the *Ka'abah* in Mecca. This custom was continued during the Umayyad period to divert the pilgrimage from Mecca. According to El-Muqaddasi the Moslems of Jerusalem wanted a House of Prayer, which would rival the Christian churches in magnificence. The building inscription also indicates rivalry to Christianity, as it confronts and challeges the Holy Trinity. This view is based on the fact that in building the Dome of the Rock the Moslems imitated the Church of the Holy Sepulcher in form and dimension: the internal diameter of the Holy Sepulcher is 20.9 m, and its dome is 21.5 m high; the corresponding dimensions of the Dome of the Rock are 20.3 m and 20.48 m respectively. The form of the Dome of the Rock is that of an octagon within a circle, symbolizing the ancient concept of the center of the world.

The Dome of the Rock was erected by 'Abd el-Malek, the Umayyad ruler in the years 692 to 697, on the highest level of the Temple Mount, some four to six meters above the surrounding area. Succeeding rulers, caliphs, kings and sultans, left inscriptions on the gates, thresholds, doorposts and walls of the Dome, and made known the repairs they had instituted in the various structures. Some scholars hold the view that 'Abd el-Malek intended to draw the Faithful away from the *Ka'abah*, where his enemy, the counter-caliph, 'Abdullah Eben Zubayer, ruled, until the conquest of Arabia could be effected; the aim was political as well as religious.

The dome rises above 12 round pillars of marble and four of granite. The 16 windows of the cupola are made of colored glass against a background of gold; the light they shed on the Rock and through the building is enchanting. Some of the windows go back to the fifteenth century, but most of them are from the eighteenth and nineteenth centuries. The octagonal walls of the building have 56 windows, seven in each wall. The ceiling of the building surrounding the dome is supported by eight pillars of marble and 16 of colored granite and limestone. The pillars, coloured by various stones coating them, are surmounted by capitals which are Moslem, but the columns may come from older strata.

The first Moslems identified the place from which Mohammed ascended to heaven not on the Temple Mount in Jerusalem, but in Mecca from where he rose to the seventh celestial heaven where El-Aqsa was. He rose to the celestial heaven directly from the sacred mosque in Mecca, since El-Aqsa in Jerusalem did not exist in Mohammed's time.

The pillars under the dome and its lower mosaic are from the seventh century. The southern entrance is both the most ornate and the most important, since it faces Mecca. A Cufic inscription surrounds the base of the dome. At the beginning of the ninth century the cupola was of brass, sheathed in gold, but the brass disappeared and then the sheathing was changed to lead. Two earthquakes in the eleventh century shook the dome, and the upper mosaic was replaced. Over the centuries the Dome was affected by fire and earthquake, which changed its structure to a certain extent.

The Holy Rock (Even Ha-Shethiyah, Rock of the Foundation)

This is identified, by tradition and by history, as the place where Abraham offered Isaac on Mount Moriah (*Genesis* XXII, 2, 4) as well as being the threshing floor of Araunah the Jebusite, which King David bought and made into an altar to the Lord (*II Samuel* XXIV, 18–19; *I Chronicles* XXI, 18–19). Mount Moriah was also the site of Solomon's Temple (*II Chronicles* III, 1). Was the Rock indeed the site of the Holy of Holies in the Temple? A problem arises in connection with this.

The High Priest used to place the pan of incense on the Rock of the Foundation, as stated in the *Mishnah* (*Yoma* 5, 2): "…there was a stone from the time of the earlier Prophets, called the *shethiyah*, three fingers above the ground, on which he would place (the pan of burning coals)." The Rock, therefore, was three fingers high, but the Rock within the present Dome is one to one and a half meters high.

The significance of the Rock of the Foundation is noted in *Tanhuma Kedoshim* 10, where it is described as being the absolute center of the world, and Jerusalem the center of Eretz Israel, the Holy Temple the center of Jerusalem, the *Heichal* the center of the Holy Temple, the Ark the center of the *Heichal* and from the Rock of the Foundation the world was founded. This tradition was taken over by Christianity, and the stone denoting the center of the world (*Omphalos Mundi*) is shown in the Church of the Holy Sepulcher. According to Moslem tradition, the Dome of the Rock is built over the Rock of the Foundation, and there is a cave hollowed within the Rock. Moslems show the spot on the Rock from which Mohammed ascended to Heaven, and they identify a depression on the surface as the footprint of the Prophet. The Crusaders chipped off fragments of the Rock and sold them as souvenirs to devout pilgrims, who paid their weight in gold. To put a stop to this trade, the Crusader kings surrounded the Rock with an iron screen, sections of which exist to this day in the Islamic Museum on the Temple Mount.

The Dome During the Umayyad Period

The Dome of the Rock was built by 'Abd el-Malek in 72 A.H. (to the *Hejira*); this is shown by an inscription in Cufic (ancient Arabic script) on a blue-green metal plaque on the south-eastern arch of the columns below the dome. Originally it read: "The servant of Allah 'Abd el-Malek ibn Marwan, Commander of the Faithful, built this dome in the year 72. May Allah receive his prayer and favor him. Amen."

The Dome During the Abbasid Period

When the Abbasid Caliph Al-Mamun visited Jerusalem in 831 C.E., he ordered restoration work to be carried out in the Dome of the Rock. In the course of the work the name of 'Abd el-Malek was removed and replaced with the name of Al-Mamun. However, the date was not changed, so the falsification was obvious.

The Dome During the Crusader Period

After the Crusader conquest of the city, the crescent at the top of the Dome was exchanged for a cross, and an altar was erected of stone quarried from beyond the enclosure. The Dome of the Rock became a church, *Templum Domini*, and was given over to the Augustinian Canons. The Crusaders surrounded the Rock by an iron screen, parts of which may be seen in the Islamic Museum on the Temple Mount; similar screens were sent to churches in Europe. The Knights Templar were established in the El-Aqsa Mosque as a military order in 1128, in order to defend the Holy Places and the pilgrims' routes. The architecture of the Dome of the Rock was copied in churches all over Europe.

The Dome in the Ayyubid Period

Saladin, who took Jerusalem in 1187, removed the icons and other Crusader additions from the Dome of the Rock and the El-Aqsa Mosque, with the exception of the iron screen around the Rock. The structure became a place of Moslem worship again, and a gilded inscription describing the works of Saladin was placed under the dome.

In 1190 the arches supporting the dome were gilded, as they appear today, and the walls overlaid with marble slabs, while the dome was decorated in mosaic patterns. The following inscription was put up to commemorate the work: "In the name of Allah, the Compassionate, the Merciful, our Master the Sultan, the victorious King, the Sage, the just Salah-ad-Din Yusuf ibn Ayyub, may Allah encompass him in his mercy, hath commanded the renewal of the gilding of this noble Dome, in the year 586 A.H."

The Dome During the Mameluke Period

The Mameluke rulers, and foremost among them Sultan Baybars, repaired the Dome structure, in particular the mosaic of the upper sections of the external walls. It was renovated in 1270 under the Baybars and again in 1290 by Sultan el-Ashraf Khalil. Next to carry out restoration was Nasser Muhammad ibn-Qalaoun in 1318, who repaired the gilding and mosaic of the drum as well as the external lead sheathing. An inscription to that effect was placed above a window. The King A-Taher Barquq erected a pulpit and platform of marble slabs, supported by 10 marble pillars at the south entrance of the building. In 1448 there was a fire, started by children playing with candles on the roof. Additional repairs were made in 1467 by Qait Bay, who installed the four brass doors with their carvings. A fountain west of the Dome bears the name of this ruler.

The Dome Under Turkish Rule

Suleiman the Magnificent added Persian tiles to the external walls of the building, as well as in the Dome of the Chain, east of the Dome of the Rock. He restored the gilded colored windows as well as the northern, southern and western doors. In 1735 the Turkish Sultan Mahmud I ordered repairs to the Dome of the Rock and to the El-Aqsa Mosque, using some twelve tons of lead to sheath the dome. The marble of the western entrance was put there by Sultan 'Abd el-Hamid in 1780. In 1835 the dome was buttressed and the mosaic renewed. Sultan 'Abd el-'Aziz mended the wooden ceilings in the wings of the building in 1874, and also repaired the mosaic, the marble slabs on the walls, and the broken windows. The successor of 'Abd el-Hamid II supplied carpets, and Persian crystal lamps (transferred to the El-Aqsa Mosque in 1951), and had verses from the *Koran* inscribed on the external walls of the building.

The Dome Under Jordanian Rule

The Jordanian government strengthened the foundations of the pillars and walls, as well as the wooden ceiling, repaired the damaged windows and the tiles of the outer walls, and installed electric light. This work took ten years and was completed in 1965.

Present Day Sites on the Temple Mount

There are some one hundred structures on the Temple Mount, in seven major categories:

1. Domes (*qubbeh*). These are small edifices for praying, surmounted by a dome, with a *mi'hrab*, or prayer niche, in the southern side. They were built mainly during the Ayyubid, Mameluke and Turkish periods.
2. Arcades (*mawwazin*). These consist of several pillars supporting three to five arches. They stand at the top of the stairs connecting the courtyard and the platform. The arcades date from the Ayyubid and Mameluke periods.
3. Religious schools (*madares*) for Moslems. These were also erected in the Ayyubid and Mameluke periods.
4. Praying platforms (*mutasalla*), not enclosed by walls, paved and slightly raised. The southern side incorporates a *mi'hrab* facing Mecca.
5. Porticos (*riwwaq*) running along the western and northern walls of the Temple Mount. The porticos consist of pillars supporting arches, and were built during the Mameluke period.
6. Minarets (*manara* or *maazneh*), towers from which the *muezzin* summons the Faithful to prayer five times a day. These were built in the Mameluke period.
7. Fountains (*sabil*), troughs for drinking and washing, used by the Faithful in preparation for prayer in the mosque. These were erected during Mameluke and Turkish times, as water was conveyed to the city from distant sources by aqueduct in those days. They were erected near the mosques and arcades, as well as along the streets leading to the gates of the Temple Mount.

Structures of the Upper Platform Arcades (*Mawwazin*)

The word *mawwazin* means "scales," and according to Moslem legend, at the Last Judgment, scales for weighing souls will be hung there. The platform is reached by flights of stairs, each terminating in an arcade. The dates of some of the arcades is uncertain, but the south-eastern ones were built in 1211, during the reign of Al-Malek al 'Aadel, brother and successor of Saladin. The south-western arcades were restored in 1893 by Abdul Hamid II. The two northern arcades were built in the reign of the Mameluke Nasser Muhammad ibn-Qalaoun (1321–25), when the area was paved.

Summer Pulpit (Minbar E-Saif)

This stands near the south-western arcade. It was apparently built by Saladin (1190) but was restored by a judge, Burhan e-Din (1325–88) and bears his name. It was next repaired by the Turkish emir, Mohammed Rashid, in 1483. The pulpit is made of marble, and is a combination of re-used materials and elements from Crusader, Mameluke and Turkish times. At the foot of the stairs is a pair of columns on onion-shaped bases, topped by woven-basket capitals. The pulpit seat at the top of the stairs is hexagonal, covered by a polygonal dome supported by four columns joined in horseshoe arches. A *mi'hrab* decorated with marble mosaic stands nearby. The pulpit is used for open-air prayers during the summer.

Grammar Dome (Qubbet E-Nahawwiyah)

This stands at the south-west corner of the platform. It was built during the reign of Sultan al-Malek al-Mu'attam 'Issa in 1217, of marble slabs probably taken from a Crusader building. It was originally used as a place for studying Arab literature and grammar. During the British Mandate it housed the library of the Arab Higher Committee.

Dome of the Chain (Qubbet E-Silsileh)

This building, east of the Dome of the Rock, is ascribed to 'Abd el-Malek, the builder of the Dome of the Rock. The two domes are essentially different in shape, despite their obvious similarities. The Dome of the Chain served, according to tradition, as the treasury for the Moslems of the city. The eleven outer and six inner columns supported a round room, which housed the actual treasure. Treasure houses were erected near temples by the Romans in various countries, and similar structures were found near the mosque in Damascus and other big cities in Syria. It was impossible to enter the building without being seen from the inside, and the treasure could only be reached by way of a ladder. The treasure was later moved into the mosque. The building was sanctified by the Crusaders and dedicated to St. James, the brother of Jesus and first bishop of Jerusalem. The *mi'hrab* of the Dome of the Chain was added by Baybars, the Mameluke who ruled the country from 1260 to 1277. Suleiman the Magnificent sheathed the dome in tiles in 1561.

Dome of The Ascension (Qubbet El-Mi'araj)

This octagonal structure is north-west of the Dome of the Rock. Moslem tradition identifies it as the place where Mohammed prayed before his ascension to Heaven. The building, supported on 12 marble columns, was erected, according the inscription, in 1220, but it is believed by many scholars to be the Crusader Baptistry of the Church which existed in the Dome of the Rock, converted into a dome.

Mi'hrab of the Prophet (E-Nabi)

A small dome with a handsome *mi'hrab* stands west of the Dome of the Rock, built by the Turkish governor of Jerusalem, Muhammed Bey, in 1538.

Qubbet El-Khadr

An open dome at the northwest corner of the platform is dedicated to el-Khadr, the legendary figure identified in popular Moslem tradition as the prophet Elijah. The dome is supported by six marble columns, and there is a small place for prayer under it.

El-Aqsa Mosque

The Dome of the Rock was erected for the use of those wishing to pray alone, while the purpose of the el-Aqsa Mosque was for public prayers. Historians disagree about the date of the erection of the building, but all the scholars believe the builder was El-Walid, the son of Abd el-Malek, who also erected the great Umayyad Mosque in Damascus. The builder sheathed the dome in brass plate and brought a mosaic from Constantinople to decorate the interior of the mosque, as El-Walid also did for the mosques at Mecca and Medina.

El Aqsa mosque – "Solomon's Temple" of the Crusaders – eastern and northern view

The Dome of the Rock has its foundations in the bedrock, while the el-Aqsa Mosque is built on the substructure of the Double Gate and earth-fill of Herodian times. Traces of the original Mosque of Omar, which was decorated with double rows of columns, are visible in the south-east corner of the el-Aqsa.

The mosque is divided into a central nave and two transepts. The nave, running from north to south, is supported by seven arches, resting on marble and stone columns with stylized capitals and windows above them. There are 114 columns and 135 windows in the mosque. Its length is 80 m and its width 55 m. To the north of the building is a decorated portico built in 1217 by Mu'attam 'Issa. The northern facade above the seven Ayyubid arches and seven great entrances, was built during the Fatimid period. There are four other doors to the mosque, two in the west, one in the south, and one in the east.

During the Umayyad period the mosque was wider and shorter. Its floor was of marble and its gates were gilded. The sole remnants of that period are the columns east of the *mi'hrab* in the mosque. Wars and earthquakes caused the repeated destruction and restoration of the mosque. According to el-Muqaddasi, the earthquake of 774 brought down the east and west walls of the mosque. The 'Abbasid Caliph Abu Ja'afar el-Mansur carried out repairs, but only three years later another earthquake caused additional destruction. In 780, Caliph el-Mahdi commanded the new mosque to be made shorter and wider than the earlier structure. This too was destroyed, in the earthquake of 1033, and rebuilt a year later by the Fatimid Caliph e-Tahir. He erected the dome and mosaic, the central nave and the seven gates in the northern wall of the façade. This is Ayyubid, built with re-used Crusader architectural pieces. In the *mi'hrab* with its gilded mosaic he placed a Cufic inscription, which reads as follows: "In the name of Allah the Compassionate, the Merciful. Praise be to Him who brought His servant (Mohammed) by night from the *Masjid el-Haram* (at Mecca) to the *Masjid el-Aqsa*, the outermost mosque (in the seventh heaven), on the Precincts of which we invoke a blessing; this mosque was restored by our lord 'Ali abu Hasan el-Iman e-Zahir, to increase the faith of Allah, Lord of the Faithful, the son of 'el'Hakem, God bless his soul and the souls of his father and his sons, through Abu Mohammed el-Hasan ibn 'Ali ibn 'Abd e-Rahman, in the year 427 of the *Hijra*."

The dome is 17.7 m high. As in the Dome of the Rock, the interior is of wood and the exterior of lead. The dome is supported by four arches and eight pillars, restored in 1927. The *mihrah* in the south and the pulpit next to it (burned down in 1968 by a mentally disturbed [Christian] Australian) were built by Nur e-Din, ruler of Syria, in 1170, and placed in Jerusalem after the expulsion of the Crusaders by his successor, Saladin. The same was done with the mosaic of the *mi'hrab* and the dome. A gilded inscription above the *mi'hrab* recounts the construction.

At the south-east corner of the mosque is a small mosque known as the Mosque of Omar. It is 8 m × 30 m. North of it is a hall, 9 m × 9 m, called the Mosque of the Forty Martyrs. Next to this, northwards, is the *Mi'hrab* of Zakariya (Zechariah) who, according to *St. Matthew* XXIII, 35, was slain between the altar and the Temple. The *Mi'hrab* of Zakariya was built on the site of a Crusader chapel. The Mosque of the Women, to the west, was built during the Fatimid period, and Christian tradition identifies it as the Oratory of the Knights Templar.

The Crusader Conquest of Jerusalem and of the mosque in 1099 led to major changes in the dome and in the entire building. Part of the mosque became a church, and part became a temple used by the Knights Templar (as did the Dome of the Rock); it was called at this time Templum Solomonis. A large structure was built along the southern wall to serve as an armory, and the basements were used to stable the horses. After Saladin took the city, he repaired the mosque, covered the walls with light and dark colored marble slabs, restored the *mi'hrab* which had been blocked up by the Crusaders, and covered the interior of the Dome with a mosaic of colored glass, resembling that in the Dome of the Rock. He brought cedar beams from Lebanon for the pulpit, and placed this inscription recording his work in the golden mosaic: "In the name of Allah the Compassionate, the Merciful! The servant of Allah and His regent, Yusuf ibn Ayyub 'Abd el-Muz'affar, the victorious king Saladin, hath ordered the repair of this holy mi'hrab, and the restoration of the Aqsa Mosque, which was founded in piety, after Allah had conquered (the city), in the name of God in the year 583; he thanks God for this victory, and prays that Allah will have mercy upon him."

The interior and the mosaics of the mosque were redecorated by Saladin, except for the pink and blue glass windows in the west, the *Mi'hrab* of Zakariya, and the arched rooms in the west of the mosque, in the Women's Mosque, which are from the Crusader period. The mosaic inscriptions on the dome are evidence of further repairs carried out by the Mameluke king Qalaun in 1327.

Several glass windows were added by the Turkish Sultan, 'Abd el-'Aziz, in 1874, and the Persian carpets were donated by the Sultan 'Abdul Hamid in 1816. The dome and columns were strengthened in the years 1922 to 1927, as well as after the earthquakes of 1928 and 1937. In 1943 King Farouk of Egypt restored the mosque and its windows, and inscribed the following on a marble slab: "His Majesty the good and admired king Farouq 1, King of Egypt, may Allah preserve him and his reign."

The fire in 1968 caused the destruction of the preacher's pulpit and the *mi'hrab* built in the time of Nur e-Din and his successor Saladin. The mosque can accommodate as many as 5,000 worshippers.

The ancient El-Aqsa el-Qadimah is at the south-east corner of the Mosque, and is approached by a descent of 18 steps. It is actually a gate dating from Herod's time forming one of the two Southern Gates to the Temple Mount.

In addition to the El-Aqsa Mosque, Jerusalem has 34 mosques, 28 of them within the city wall and six in the Temple Mount enclosure.

Major Structures in the Courtyard
Water Devices on the Temple Mount
The fourteenth-century historian Ibn Fadel el-'Umari notes that the Temple Mount had 22 water cisterns, and three others which were unfit for use. The historian and Qadi (judge), Mujir e-Din, writing in the fifteenth century, mentions 34 cisterns on the Temple Mount. (From the British survey of the Temple Mount (1864, 1867–1870), we know about 37 cisterns; the 38th was added recently to the list.) In 1947 'Aref el-'Aref counted 27 cisterns two of them unfit for use: eight were in the upper platform, seven in the El-Aqsa area, and the remainder in the courtyard – six in the west, three in the east and one in the north. The largest cistern is 42 m × 45 m. Their estimated capacity is 45,000 cu m, and some of them were built during the Second Temple period.

The Goblet (El Kas)
The Goblet fountain north of the El-Aqsa Mosque was built by the Mameluke Emir Tankiz e-Nasri in 1327. It was supplied by the aqueduct from "Solomon's Pools," and restored by the Mameluke rulers in 1328. The fountain is used for ablution by the worshippers of El-Aqsa, and is supplied by the city waterworks.

The Fountains (Sabil)

The fountains, supplied by the aqueduct and the pipe from "Solomon's Pools," were used by the worshippers at the mosques on the Temple Mount. The major ones are located near the main gates of the Temple Mount and the arcades.

Sabil e-Sha'alan, near the north-western arcade, was built by el-Malek el Mu'atham 'Issa in 1216. Sabil Qait Bey, near the western arcade, was erected in 1455 and restored by Qait Bey in 1482. Further repairs were made by 'Abdul Hamid II in 1882. Sabil Kasem Pasha, near the south-western arcade, was built in 1527 by Kasem, ruler of Egypt and vizier of Suleiman the Magnificent. The latter had four fountains built: near the Gate of the Chain, near the Cotton Merchants' Gate, near the Inspector Gate, and at the Lions' Gate, past the Gate of the Tribes.

Paving of the Temple Mount Courtyard

The courtyard, paved with stone slabs, was restored under the reign of the 'Abbasid Caliph el-Muqtadar (908–932). An inscription to that effect not *in situ* and with its three lines in the wrong order, is found near the stairs leading down to the Cradle of Jesus, in "Solomon's Stables."

Dome of Suleiman (Qubbet Suleiman)

This dome was built near the center of the northern portico, south of the Dark Gate. The walled structure is octagonal, supported by 24 marble columns, and is covered by a dome 5.5 m across. Its southern wall has a *mi'hrab*. Moslem tradition has it that Solomon sat there while the angels built the Temple. The dome was, however, actually built during the Umayyad period (the present structure is post-Crusader) and is named after the seventh Umayyad Caliph, Suleiman (715–717). A low rock protrudes from the floor of the dome, and is called *Qubbet el-Sakhra e-Saghira* (the small Dome of the Rock). According to Moslem tradition the small rock is a fragment of the Rock of the Foundation, which the Jews carried into exile in Babylon.

Dome of Suleiman Pasha (Qubbet Suleiman Pasha)

East of *Qubbet Suleiman* is a square structure, supported by four piers terminating in pointed arches. The inscription on the northern wall is evidence of its period, the reign of the Turkish Sultan Mahmud Khan (1817).

The Porticos (Riwwaq)

Most of the arches of the porticos, especially on the west, are Mameluke, and were mostly built in the time of Nasir ibn Qalaoun (1307–1313) and his successors, el-Malek el-Awwhad, el-Malek el-Ashraf and Sha'aban. The northern portico is more ancient, dating from the time of al-Malek Mu'attam 'Issa, after whom the Mu'attamiya *madrasa* is named. When the porticos were built by the Ayyubids and Mamelukes, they served as religious schools and offices. During the Turkish period they became dwellings for the poor, after the entrances were blocked up. The porticos were restored to their original form in 1922.

The western portico adjoins the Temple Mount wall; it is 340 m long and about six m wide. It is covered by 60 arches, and ends about 60 m from the north-west corner, near the Gate of the Chain.

The northern portico runs the length of the northern wall of the Temple Mount, and is 240 m long. In this portico there are 30 pointed arches surmounting square piers. It ends near the Dark Gate and past the Repentance Gate (= bab Huta).

The Minarets (Manara)

There are four minarets in the Temple Mount enclosure from which the *muezzin* summons the people to prayer five times a day. The minarets are located near the residential areas of the Old City and the gates of the enclosure.

1. The al-Fakhariya minaret is at the south-western corner of the Temple Mount, and was built in 1278 by Sharaf e-Din 'Abdul Rahman, the son of Fakhr e-Din el-Khalili. It was restored in 1922.

2. A minaret was built above the Gate of the Chain in 1392 by the Prince Seif e-Din Tankiz e-Nasseri. He also built the adjoining *madrasa*.

3. At the north-western corner, above the Ghawanimeh Gate, a minaret was built in 1297 by order of the Mameluke Sultan El-Mansur Husam e-Din Lajin, and restored in 1329 by Qalaoun. The material for constructing this minaret was found in the ruins of Byzantine buildings destroyed by the Persians and was re-used from the Crusader period onwards. Its facade is decorated by small columns from a Christian structure. On one of the capitals is a picture of Jesus' baptism. On the steps of a tower on this spot, according to belief, St. Paul was saved by the Romans from the anger of the people (*Acts* XXI). The minaret was restored in 1927.

4. A minaret called the Minaret of Israel was built at the north wall west

of the Gate of the Tribes, under the rule of Nasir ibn Qalaoun, in 1347. The upper section of the minaret was damaged in the earthquake of 1927 and restored.

The Mameluke Buildings Beyond the Iron Gate and the Gate of the Chain

The following edifices lie along the Street of the Chain, from east to west. Just past the Gate, on the right, is the tomb of the Princess Turkan (1352). Across the street is the Tomb of Barakat Khan, head of the Tatar Kingdom in the Crimea, whose daughter married Baybars in 1244; the tomb has a small Persian dome, and also contains the graves of his two sons. At present it houses the library founded by the Khalidi family. On the right again, on the north side of the street, is a magnificent building called the Tai'ziyeh, built in 1361, and opposite, at the corner of the street leading to the Western Wall, is the Tashmuriyeh, built in the same year.

Near the Iron Gate, on 'Aqabat e-Sitt Street, is the palace of the Lady (*Sitt*) Tunbug el-Muzaffari; the lady's tomb is opposite. These two edifices are among the most striking in Jerusalem, and were built by her in the fifteenth century.

Five features of Mameluke architectural art appear in these magnificent buildings:

1. The gateway recess is a high, elongated arch, while the actual gate is relatively small.
2. The top of the arch is built in the stalactite style.
3. The ashlar blocks are smoothly dressed and laid in rows, in alternating colors of white, black and brown.
4. The blocks forming the metope (lintel) of doors and windows are interlocked in a square or rounded pattern.
5. The gateway is flanked by stone benches for the convenience of the guard or for those living there.